'This book should be essential reading for all of those who are interested in working with offenders, young and old. Written by a group of leading practitioners and researchers, the book provides a detailed account of how to work in community settings in ways which not only address the psychological and social needs of offenders, but also effectively manage the risk of further offending occurring.'

Professor Andrew Day, Clinical and Forensic Psychologist,
Deakin University, Australia

'This book provides a wide-ranging overview of theory and practice in a previously neglected area. This neglect is all the more remarkable because of the area's crucial importance at so many levels. The area – that of forensic practice in the community – now has a major new text to support and stimulate its growth.'

Adrian Needs, Principal Lecturer, Department of Psychology,
University of Portsmouth, UK

'This book is a joy: clearly and straight-forwardly written, it addresses subjects which remain under-explored in the academic and professional literature. "Forensic" practice can mean many things, but the focus of this book is on helping criminal justice practitioners working in the community to assess their clients and, indeed, to assess whether they, the practitioners, are doing a good job. Community-based services are often the "poor relation" of custodial services, and not only in funding terms. Yet the job of practitioners working in the community is vitally important, hugely complex, and brings with it equally daunting moral responsibilities. This wise, honest, thoughtful and thought-provoking book will contribute hugely not only to the decision-making of those who have to make these decisions, but also to those academics and students who are thinking about the subject "from the outside".'

Nicola Padfield, Master, Fitzwilliam College, Cambridge and
Reader in Criminal and Penal Justice, University of Cambridge, UK

FORENSIC PRACTICE IN THE COMMUNITY

Forensic practice in the community is a neglected subject. There are many books looking at forensic work in secure settings, such as prisons or hospitals, but very little has been written about forensic practice in the community. This book describes the current and exciting developments in this area, for both young people and adults, by leaders in their field. It is in the community where interventions with those who have offended are all ultimately tested. Bringing together a range of experts from both the practitioner and academic community, this book covers:

- Multisystemic Therapy for families
- sexual and violent offending
- learning disabilities
- substance misuse
- risk assessment, prediction and management
- personality disordered offenders
- resettlement following custody
- desistance from criminal behaviour
- community interventions.

Beginning with an overview of forensic practice in the community, the book addresses policy, practice and ethical issues, focusing on the specific dilemmas facing practitioners and providing an analysis of international perspectives. It describes how to meet the challenge of significantly diverting and reducing the prison population through more effective community intervention with adults and young people and also makes suggestions for the future.

This book offers a range of recent case studies, has descriptions of new areas of community practice by those working or studying in that area and covers cutting-edge developments in practice and policy. It will be of interest to academics, practitioners and students in forensic psychology, as well as social workers, probation officers, youth offending officers, police officers, criminal justice agencies and mental health professionals.

Zoë Ashmore is a Consultant Forensic Psychologist and Multisystemic Therapy (MST) Expert employed by Cambridgeshire and Peterborough NHS Foundation Trust and seconded to South London and Maudsley NHS Foundation Trust.

Richard Shuker is a Chartered Forensic Psychologist, and Head of Psychology and Research at HMP Grendon, a therapeutic community prison for personality disordered offenders.

ISSUES IN FORENSIC PSYCHOLOGY

Edited by Richard Shuker, HMP Grendon

Issues in Forensic Psychology is a book series which aims to promote forensic psychology to a broad range of forensic practitioners. It aims to provide analysis and debate on current issues and to publish and promote the work of forensic psychologists and other associated professionals.

The views expressed by the authors/editors may not necessarily be those held by the Series Editor or NOMS.

FORENSIC PRACTICE IN THE COMMUNITY

Edited by
Zoë Ashmore and
Richard Shuker

LONDON AND NEW YORK

First published 2014
by Routledge
2 Park Square, Milton Park, Abingdon, Oxon, OX14 4RN

and by Routledge
711 Third Avenue, New York, NY 10017

Routledge is an imprint of the Taylor & Francis Group, an informa business

British Library Cataloguing in Publication Data
A catalogue record for this book is available from the British Library

Library of Congress Cataloging-in-Publication Data
  Forensic practice in the community / edited by Zoë Ashmore and
  Richard Shuker.
  pages cm. — (Issues in forensic psychology ; 5)
  1. Forensic psychology. 2. Forensic psychiatry. 3. Community mental
  health services—Planning. I. Ashmore, Zoë, editor of compilation.
  II. Shuker, Richard, editor of compilation.
  RA1148.F5557 2014
  614'.15—dc23
  2013050499

ISBN13: 978-0-415-50031-9 (hbk)
ISBN13: 978-0-415-50032-6 (pbk)
ISBN13: 978-0-203-48580-4 (ebk)

Typeset in Bembo and Stone Sans
by Florence Production Ltd, Stoodleigh, Devon, UK

Printed and bound by CPI Group (UK) Ltd, Croydon, CR0 4YY

To Paul, Ben and Grant Nolan – this book, my first and last, is for you, with love (ZA)

To Heather and Josie (RS)

CONTENTS

ILLUSTRATIONS

Figures

Tables

CONTRIBUTORS

Zoë Ashmore is a Consultant Forensic Psychologist and Multisystemic Therapy (MST) Expert employed by Cambridgeshire and Peterborough NHS Foundation Trust and seconded to South London and Maudsley NHS Foundation Trust. She was the first MST Expert appointed in the UK to train and advise teams in the effective clinical delivery of MST, now being introduced across the UK. She has specialised in intervention programmes for adolescents and their families both in the community and in custody for over 30 years working in the Prison Service, the Home Office, the National Health Service and the Youth Offending Service. In 2011 she was awarded the Senior Practitioner Award by the British Psychological Society for her distinguished lifetime contribution to Forensic Psychology.

Andrew Bates has worked as a Forensic Psychologist since 1987 in custodial, community and voluntary sector settings. He has provided training, consultancy and professional supervision of other psychologists for many agencies including the National Health Service, NSPCC, Social Services and the private sector. He teaches Forensic Psychology at the University of Reading and is on the editorial board of the *British Journal of Forensic Practice* and is currently Research Associate at the University of Oxford, Centre for Criminology.

Anthony Bottoms is Emeritus Wolfson Professor of Criminology at the University of Cambridge and Honorary Professor of Criminology at the University of Sheffield. With Professor Joanna Shapland of Sheffield University, he co-directs the Sheffield Desistance Study, a prospective study of desistance from crime among male young adult recidivists.

The Rt Hon. the Lord Bradley of Withington is Honorary Special Adviser at the University of Manchester. He is Chair of MaST LIFT Co, Chair of the BTG Lift Company, a Council Member of the Medical Protection Society and a Trustee of the Centre for Mental Health and the Prison Reform Trust. Formerly

Member of Parliament for Manchester Withington from 1987 to 2005, he was Parliamentary Under Secretary of State for Social Security (1997–98), Deputy Chief Whip (1998–2001), Minister of State at the Home Office (2001–02) and a member of the Health Select Committee (2002–05). He was appointed a Privy Councillor in 2001 and ennobled in 2006. The Bradley Report on people with mental health problems or learning disabilities in the criminal justice system was published on 30 April 2009.

Andrew Bridges worked in and around the Probation Service for nearly 40 years from 1973, both in England and in Wales, sometimes inside prisons but mostly in mainstream settings. From being a practitioner Probation Officer for eight years he progressed through other posts to become Chief Probation Officer for Berkshire in 1998. He completed nine months as a part-time Research Fellow at the University of Oxford Probation Studies Unit in 1996, his research being published in 1998 as 'Increasing the Employability of Offenders: An Inquiry into Probation Service Effectiveness'. He moved in 2001 to the Inspectorate, from which he retired in 2011 after seven years as HM Chief Inspector of Probation.

Matt Bruce is a Senior Clinical Psychologist in the Forensic Intensive Psychological Treatment Service (FIPTS), South London, and Maudsley NHS Foundation Trust. He holds an honorary contract with the Department of Forensic and Neurodevelopmental Sciences, Institute of Psychiatry, and also works privately as an expert witness on civil, criminal and family cases. In 2005, Dr Bruce graduated from University College London as a Clinical Psychologist and has since acquired specialist knowledge and experience in dangerousness and severe personality disorder across various security settings and service providers. He has a research interest in ethnic differences in clinical needs, offending profiles and personality disorder etiology in men with severe mental illness.

Sara Casado is a Forensic Psychologist who has worked for Sussex Partnership NHS Foundation Trust since 2005 and currently oversees the therapeutic services provided at the Service's Low Secure Unit. In addition part of her role is to support the Forensic Community Outreach Team with assessment and treatment. Both areas of her work incorporate reflective practice support structures for staff.

Gerard Drennan is a Consultant Clinical Psychologist and Lead for Forensic Clinical Psychology and Psychological Therapies in Sussex Partnership NHS Foundation Trust. He edited, with Deborah Alred, *Secure Recovery: Approaches to Recovery in Forensic Mental Health Settings* (2012). He has trained in psychoanalytic psychotherapy and leads a project to introduce restorative justice practices into forensic mental health settings.

Simone Fox is a Consultant Clinical and Forensic Psychologist, and Multisystemic Therapy (MST) Supervisor. She is employed by South West London and St George's Mental Health NHS Trust to work with adolescents who are at risk of entering care or custody due to antisocial behaviour. She is also Deputy Clinical Director and a Senior Lecturer on the Doctorate in Clinical Psychology Programme, Royal Holloway, University of London.

Matthew Gaskell is a Consultant Addictions Psychologist with the Leeds and York Primary Foundation NHS Trust. He is also the Programme Manager for the BHSc in Addiction Studies at the University of Leeds. He has spent the last seven years working with community addiction patients with a variety of forensic, psychological and social needs. He specialises in psychological therapy for addictions and co-occurring psychological disorders. Prior to this he spent eight years working as a Forensic Psychologist in the high security prisons directorate, specialising in the psychological assessment and treatment of offenders with addiction problems.

Joel Harvey is Lecturer in Clinical Psychology and Programme Lead for the MSc in Clinical Forensic Psychology at the Institute of Psychiatry, King's College London. He has worked clinically in various secure and community forensic settings. He is author of *Young Men in Prison: Surviving and Adapting to Life Inside* (Willan) and co-editor of *Psychological Therapy in Prisons and Other Secure Settings* (Willan).

Richard Latham is a Consultant Forensic Psychiatrist with clinical experience in inpatient and community forensic psychiatry. He also provides expert opinions in cases involving serious crime including pro bono work in capital cases in East Africa and the Caribbean. He has an interest in the interface between law and mental health as well as medical education, teaching doctors, psychologists and other professionals in the UK and internationally. His affiliation is East London NHS Foundation Trust.

Louise Minchin is a Consultant Clinical and Forensic Psychologist employed by Sussex Partnership NHS Foundation Trust and is Lead Psychologist for the Community Forensic Mental Health Services that span East and West Sussex. Louise has over 15 years experience of facilitating team and individual reflective practice forums within probation hostels, prisons, secure hospitals and community mental health teams.

Phil Minoudis is a Consultant Clinical Psychologist and Lead Psychologist at Millfields Personality Disorder Unit, a forensic medium secure unit based at the John Howard Centre, East London NHS Foundation Trust. The unit runs a therapeutic community programme for high risk personality disordered offenders. He is also a Clinical Lead for a consortium of four London NHS Trusts, called the London Pathways Partnership, delivering the community pathways consultation service to London Probation Trust – an initiative of the Offender Personality Disorder Strategy.

Rebecca Morland (Consultant Counselling Psychologist) works at Peterborough Youth Offending Service. Rebecca has a particular interest in the early assessment of and intervention in the complex health, social and learning needs of children and young people in the criminal justice system. She manages the Peterborough Youth Justice Liaison and Diversion Service, which was one of the original pilot sites developed from Lord Bradley's recommendations.

Dave Nash has worked as a Clinical Psychologist working with clients with a learning disability for over 30 years in all settings, with a primary motivation to pursue therapeutic outcomes especially through collaborative cognitive behavioral therapy (CBT)-based approaches. Over the last 15 years his work has had a strong emphasis on developing and delivering effective therapeutic services in community and secure settings for offenders with violent and sexually abusive histories. Since retiring from the National Health Service he has worked in the private sector and is currently Clinical Director of a secure hospital in Yorkshire.

Derek Perkins is a Consultant Clinical and Forensic Psychologist based at Broadmoor High Secure Hospital and Visiting Professor of Forensic Psychology at the University of Surrey. He has published a number of papers and book chapters on forensic psychology, sexual offending and personality disorder. For 25 years he was the Head of Psychological Services at Broadmoor Hospital, having previously worked as a Clinical Psychologist in the Prison Service and forensic psychiatric outpatient services. He was involved in setting up and evaluating sex offender treatment programmes in prison, community and forensic mental health settings, in the establishment of the UK dangerous and severe personality disorder services and in the international forum on sexual homicide and paraphilias, published by the Correctional Service of Canada.

John Shine is a Consultant Forensic Psychologist working on a specialist ward for patients with autistic spectrum disorders at St Andrew's – a charity leading innovation in mental health. John has worked for 30 years in forensic settings including placements at HM Prisons, the Probation Inspectorate, the National Probation Directorate, the National Health Service and private sector health care. John has edited two books and written numerous research papers during his career in areas such as personality disorder, psychopathy, prison therapeutic communities and offence paralleling behaviour. His current interests are in the assessment of forensic risk and the development of psychological treatment approaches for patients with autistic spectrum disorders.

Richard Shuker is a Chartered Forensic Psychologist and Head of Psychology and Research at HMP Grendon, a therapeutic community prison for personality disordered offenders. He has managed cognitive behavioural treatment programmes within adult and young offender prisons and is currently Lead Clinician on the assessment unit at Grendon. His special interests include the assessment and treatment of offenders with personality disorders and other complex needs. He is series editor for the book series Issues in Forensic Psychology. He has published in areas including risk assessment, treatment readiness, therapeutic outcome and clinical intervention. He co-edited a book in 2010 on Grendon's work, research and outcomes.

Kasturi Torchia completed her BSc in Psychology at Goldsmiths, University of London, in 2010. Her interest in applied psychology with adolescents within the forensic setting led her to completing an MSc in Forensic Psychology. She worked in various settings while studying, with a range of different populations with diverse presentations, from borderline personality to autism. She went on to work on the UK-wide randomised control study of Multisystemic Therapy, the START Trial at University College London and the Anna Freud Centre, and is currently a Counselling Psychologist in Training on the Doctorate of Counselling at London Metropolitan University.

Natalie Woodier, after completing a degree in Criminology and Sociology from Cardiff University and an MSc in Criminal Justice Policy from the London School of Economics, began her career with the International Team at the National Offender Management Service (NOMS). During this time Natalie also took up a secondment to the European Prison organisation 'Europris' based in Brussels and now has a role within the UK Ministry of Justice. Natalie's experience has been focused around international criminal justice, specifically project management of European projects on advancing criminal justice systems and reducing reoffending.

ACKNOWLEDGEMENTS

Many thanks to the contributors to this book. The practitioners, researchers and academics who are involved in forensic work in the community are, in our view, best placed to write about it. They have an interesting story to tell about their work which others are keen to hear. Thank you to all for finding the time for this. We would also like to thank Heidi Lee, Editorial Assistant, for her support and patience.

Richard would like to thank Zoë for agreeing to work together on this book and her relentless drive, the authors for generously contributing their creativity, ideas, and energy, and Jamie, Peter and Michael for their ongoing support.

Zoë would also like to thank her support team of whom there are many, thank you to all of them. Special mention to Ben and Grant Nolan, Sara Wills and Yvonne Webster. Thanks to Josephine Mustone for her encouragement and feedback on the book cover. To my coach Lori Moore and my managers Cathy James and Dr Niel McLachlan, thank you and it's done. Just two more to mention, firstly Richard Shuker, with whom I had the pleasure to work many years ago and who suggested this book. Happily he also agreed to co-edit it. As always, it is a pleasure to work with Richard and one I did not expect to have again – thank you. Finally thanks to Paul Nolan for trying to talk me out of doing this in the first place and then supporting me both practically and emotionally throughout the whole journey.

Thank you to Guilford Publications for permission to reproduce Figure 10.1 and also to Routledge, who gave permission to reproduce Figure 13.1.

PART 1

Introduction and assessment

1

OVERVIEW OF FORENSIC SERVICES IN THE COMMUNITY

Andrew Bridges and Kasturi Torchia

In the literature of Probation and Youth Offending work the actual word 'forensic' is a term that rarely appears. Yet in England and Wales, with individuals who have offended, the core forensic role in community settings has been undertaken by Probation or Youth Offending staff, and they have been doing so for many years. In fact, at the time of writing, in England and Wales well over 200,000 sentenced offenders aged 18 or over are being managed by one of 35 Probation Trusts at any one time, while around 100,000 sentenced offenders aged under 18 are managed by one of 158 Youth Offending Teams or Services, the precise numbers vary depending on which cases are being counted (www.justice.gov.uk/statistics/youth-justice). In Scotland in 1968 the Probation function was taken into the local authority and the then generic Social Work Departments, although in more recent years each local Head of Criminal Justice Social Work has become increasingly subject to central (Scottish) government direction. In Northern Ireland the Probation Board provides Probation services for both young people and adults. In the United States probation is the most common form of sentencing for offenders and two-thirds of offenders are serving community sentences supervised by Probation on any one day (Petersilia, 1997).

But although the word 'forensic' has not been part of the traditional language of either Probation or Youth Offending work it is still very much a legitimate way of describing what its practitioners do with around a third of a million individuals at any one time in England and Wales, including the preparation of over a quarter of a million reports for the Courts and related bodies per year.[1] In essence they assess individuals who have offended, engage with them, provide forensic practice-based interventions, and review progress and outcomes achieved.

This chapter will provide an introductory overview of these processes as well as an analysis of recent applications, developments and challenges. It is also written not only with the two main statutory community forensic services (Probation and

Youth Offending) in mind, but also it recognises the non-statutory, forensic mental health, specialist forensic and substance misuse services that also carry out forensic practice in the community. Important specialist work is done to divert some cases at the arrest stage (i.e. before ever going to court) as well as at the court stage itself – very important for the cases affected, but these are only a tiny proportion of all the cases appearing in court for sentence.

Assessment and review

Throughout this chapter, assessment is defined as both an analysis of 'what the problem is' and a statement of what the practitioner proposes to do about it. The formal assessment of each case is made by the practitioner in charge of the case, frequently presented in a formal report prepared for a court appearance (pre-sentence report, formerly social enquiry report) and also on regular occasions for internal purposes. Such an assessment should consist of a reasoned analysis of why this particular individual committed the current offences, and also a plan of what could be done in future that would make further offending less likely.

Assessment takes place in principle when the case 'starts', but in practice the reality is often less clear-cut, especially with individuals who may make frequent appearances in court, and in more than one location, resulting in several quick successive 'starts' to a case. The initial assessment might therefore take the form of several reports issued to court(s) as well as documents within the organisation's formal internal record system. Probation and Youth Offending cases should also be formally reviewed by the practitioner in charge of the case at specified intervals – an integral part of the process of 'assessment' for the purposes of this chapter.

Probation officers have been preparing 'probation reports', later known as 'Social Enquiry' or 'Social Inquiry' Reports (SIRs), for courts since soon after the Probation of Offenders Act 1907, the role and purpose of the reports ever deepening, and their content widening. Although fairly limited in scope initially, they evolved into the much stronger and more influential role of making 'recommendations' of sentences to courts from the 1960s onwards. However, following the Criminal Justice Act 1991 the reports were rebadged Pre-Sentence Reports (PSRs), their format standardised so that they now concluded with 'proposals' rather than 'recommendations' (Cavadino, 1997).

To promote the more focused role for such reports after 1991, shorter formats were developed, such as 'Specific Sentence Reports'. To this end the Criminal Justice Act (CJA) 2003 formally declared the purpose of a pre-sentence report to be 'with a view to assisting the Courts in determining the most suitable method of dealing with an offender' (s.158 Pre-Sentencing Reports, Criminal Justice Act 2003). Later, PSRs evolved into three separate formats – 'Standard Delivery', 'Fast Delivery' and 'Oral' – for reasons we outline further below.

Alongside these developments, the evolution of the use of structured assessment tools as an integral element in preparing court reports and initial assessments is also evident. For adults the Offender Group Reconviction Scale (OGRS) (Copas and Marshall, 1998), for example, was established in the mid-1990s. It consisted of certain static factors – fixed items of information about each case and not subject to change such as previous convictions and age at first conviction – which enabled a score to be calculated that gave a 'likelihood of reconviction'.

Although potentially useful for managers, offering a benchmarked profile of the range of seriousness of all the cases being handled, it was of limited value to each individual practitioner. This is in large part due to it being emphatically a 'Group' reconviction scale and not a prediction about the particular individual – instead it is an actuarial statement of the percentage of cases in a *group of individuals with the same static factors* that would be reconvicted in the next two years.

Potentially more useful to the practitioner was OASys (for Probation) and Asset (for Youth cases). These were much more complex to apply, with many more items of information or judgement to record about each case, but they included dynamic as well as static factors and therefore offered the possibility of future 'improvement' in the score. Although some practitioners continued to resist the use of these tools, seeing them as a time-consuming bureaucratic burden of limited benefit, the majority now recognise that the benefits both to practitioners and managers outweigh the costs. Most practitioners can complete the structured assessments fairly efficiently, and if they use them wisely, they find that they are aided by OASys's benchmarking function.

The added benefit of a tool such as OASys is that it can provide a 'Likelihood of Reoffending' score at the start of supervision, and then another score later on or at the end of supervision – thereby providing a quantitative measure of progress achieved (or not achieved) during the course of the supervision. This is the advantage for a practitioner of a dynamic scale such as OASys over a wholly static scale such as OGRS – albeit that both scales have different valuable uses overall.

We can highlight two particular issues concerning the assessment aspect of Probation and Youth Offending work: planning as well as analysing and the Assessment conundrum.

Planning as well as analysing

An assessment needs to include both an analysis and a plan, that is both 'what I think the problem is' and 'what I propose to do about it'. However, historically practitioners have generally been much better at doing the analysis than the plan (Bridges, 2011). Practice always varies of course, but a high proportion of reports for Courts in the past have concluded with a brief and vague statement that a period of supervision will 'enable the causes of the offending behaviour to be addressed' or words to that effect. This syndrome is clearly evidenced in the findings of inspections of cases by HM Inspectorate of Probation over the last decade (Adult, Youth, and others), in which assessments were seen as fairly strong on analysing the problem and weak on setting out the proposed solution.

However, in very recent years there has been some improvement, with more attention being given to devising much more explicit, coherent, specific supervision plans, a development that needs to continue.

The Assessment conundrum

The 'Assessment conundrum' takes a little more explaining. Practitioners face managing the reality that, at a time when efficient use of resources is becoming increasingly topical, some cases require considerably more 'assessment work' than others.

Historically, when there was less pressure on resource efficiency, every case was in effect weighted equally, and by implication the time devoted to each case was at each practitioner's disposal. Standards initially stressed the quantity and quality of work that ought to be undertaken in every case without taking into account at all that the time and resources available to do the work might be finite. Practitioner time was treated as a demand-led 'free good'.

Once managers formally started giving attention to the amount of work that each case required this highlighted the variety of cases that came the way of Probation staff in particular. Complex cases, for example defendants with long records of violent or sexual harm to others, could require third-party inquiries and analysis of numerous records in addition to the interviews themselves (while in custody or not) and such cases might take over 15 hours of work each.

They are however, a small proportion of the total number of court reports prepared in a year as nearly a fifth of all reports (Adult and Youth) are on cases where there are no previous convictions, and in these cases the Court may have a particular sentence or disposal in mind. An assessment that is 'fit for purpose' requires considerably less work in such cases. Therefore different case types require varying quantities of 'assessment work' in order to prepare assessments that are 'sufficient for each case', focusing specifically on what the Court needs to know (and no more) in order to make a sentencing decision.

As such, one option is that managers could instruct their practitioners to 'sufficiently assess', 'sufficiently analyse' and 'sufficiently plan' to ensure that enough work is done to allow the Court to formulate a record and a sentence (Bridges, 2011). In this way time and resources would be sufficient and proportionate to the type of case being managed. For various reasons, however, this approach is rarely adopted. It is unattractive to many managers because it puts power in the hands of the practitioner and gives very little control to the manager, and it is especially problematic if there are staff with different formal qualifications and skill levels within a local team.

One of the other approaches to tackling this hurdle is a 'triage approach' (Holt, 2000; Bonta et al., 2004). It attempts to place control directly with managers and policymakers. Although the term 'triage' is borrowed from the world of medicine, where resources are distributed on a need-specific basis to maximise the number of survivors, it is sometimes used in the Probation context to allow managers

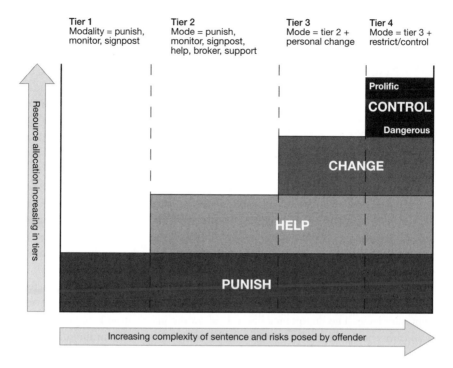

FIGURE 1.1 Tiering system introduced to Case Management in the Probation Service, 2007

to put cases into set classifications or categories at an early stage in the assessment process.

One major symptom of this approach was the evolution of the various new forms of court report we outlined earlier: Specific Sentence Reports, Oral, Standard Delivery and Fast Delivery.

In addition to these report formats there have been other innovations that seek to put cases into different categories of 'work demand'. Figure 1.1 shows the 'Tiering' system, introduced to Probation in 2007, in a series of presentations made at the time by senior managers. This was a credible attempt to allocate each case into a resource tier of which a comparable system, called the 'Scaled Approach', was introduced for Youth Offending Teams by the Youth Justice Board from 2009.

However, sometimes it is not possible to know how complicated or demanding a case is going to be until you have completed the assessment. In theory one needs to know the outcome of the assessment before knowing which level of assessment to undertake – this is the 'Assessment conundrum'. It is for this reason that many practitioners have sought to resist the shorter report formats, arguing that every case put back by a court for a report should have a 'full' PSR prepared to avoid missing important information. This is a resource-hungry way of managing the potential problem of exceptional cases – instead a much smarter approach is needed. The effectiveness of an organisation is tested by how well it manages such exceptional cases – it also illustrates how the members of that organisation think about their work.

To illustrate, a young male adult with no previous convictions who has committed an offence of driving with excess alcohol might be put back for a report because the Court is minded to impose an unpaid work requirement (formerly community service, now branded as Community Payback) in addition to any financial penalty or costs. On the face of it the case 'only' requires an FDR ('Fast Delivery Report') and accordingly the same day the defendant might well be duly sentenced to Community Payback.

It could transpire, however, that the man regularly abuses his female partner, and the local Police Domestic Violence Unit has been called to the home on several occasions. Though this information would probably not change the original sentence by the Court, his current conviction being solely for driving with excess alcohol, it should undoubtedly be taken into account in the way that the case is subsequently supervised after sentence.

It could be argued that this additional information should become available before sentence but in practice the timing of the additional information is not the important issue. The importance lies instead on the information being discovered at an early enough stage of supervision to be taken into account in the subsequent management of the case.

Reports for courts need to be done in a timely fashion – to minimise delays to justice – but caseworkers need to be alert to new information and be prepared to undertake a fuller assessment accordingly, to ensure they are managing the case effectively.

This is not easy in those instances where what had initially looked a 'straightforward' case like this example at the start has been allocated to a relatively junior, new or less qualified member of staff. It is essential that the practitioner does 'know enough to know' that there is more to the case than was at first apparent, so that a fuller assessment can be done – after court if necessary. A competent Probation or Youth Offending team will be able and willing to adapt to this development; a less competent one will be locked into a 'process mentality' which says that 'This was a Tier One case when we first allocated it, so it will continue to be worked as a Tier One case', with potentially adverse consequences.

Probation and Youth Offending teams will need to try to adopt an approach similar to the one outlined above. Managers will need to ask their practitioners to exercise careful skill and judgement with each individual case so that they do just enough work (and no more) to undertake an assessment that is 'sufficient' for the purpose of the case.

Prerequisite to effective practice – 'engagement'

'Engagement' is vital when working with individuals who have offended. It is a prerequisite to effective assessment and intervention whereby practitioners establish a constructive working relationship with the offender (Beech and Mann, 2002). Engagement is also thought by some to be the gateway for establishing the level of motivation that an adult or young person has, which has shown to be useful in predicting the success of interventions (Prochaska and DiClemente, 1983, 1986). Some call this 'treatment readiness' (see, for example, Howells and Day, 2003).

This readiness can be enhanced through work to increase offenders' motivation, self-efficacy and performance levels rendering them more receptive to it (Miller and Rollnick, 2002), commonly referred to as 'motivational interviewing'. Good engagement and developing high levels of motivation enable the practitioner to intervene more effectively with the individual under supervision (Polaschek and Ross, 2010).

'Engagement' is therefore a theme currently inherent in most forensic settings. It is encouraged by Probation, the Youth Offending Service, Mental Health Services and Social Services to help improve case management from assessment, through interventions, to outcomes achieved and case closure. The National Offender Management Service's (NOMS's) 'Offender Engagement Project' is an example of such developments and a strong indicator of how engagement fits into today's practice. However, engagement is not a direct indicator of success in its own right; 'Engagement' is a skill that is 'necessary but not sufficient', a key 'Enabler', but not in itself a 'Result', in the language of the widely used European Excellence Model (EEM) advocated by the European Foundation for Quality Management (EFQM).

Interventions

Where 'assessment' was about analysing what has happened before and then planning the actions to be taken from now on, 'interventions' are about carrying out those actions. If one were to use medical language, assessment would be 'diagnosis' and interventions would be 'treatment', but for good reasons the worlds of Probation and Youth Offending tend to avoid such medical language. It implies adherence to a medical model, which limits practice to a 'test, diagnose and treat' process that in effect is not holistic enough to take into account the individual 'desistance journey' that the offender may be undergoing. For the purpose of this chapter 'interventions' captures all the work done by Probation, Youth Offending, Social and Mental Health Services and others that aims to achieve the purposes of statutory or non-statutory supervision of offenders in the community.

Historically, Probation practice was rather idiosyncratic. Highly creative and imaginative examples of projects and approaches to practice were sometimes carried out. However, too often probationers/offenders received a service that was very inconsistent and unaccountable, and it was very rarely evaluated in an evidence-based way.

Then in the mid-1970s the results analysis of the IMPACT Project (Folkard et al., 1976) and of Martinson (1974) in America were both published. IMPACT was an experiment in London in which a sample of cases received much more intensive contact than was normally the case. The research concluded that with the more serious cases the more intensive contact made no difference to reoffending, while with the less serious cases it actually made it worse – a very disappointing finding for Probation staff. This followed closely behind the conclusion mistakenly drawn from Martinson's (1974) American analysis, and the 15 or so years immediately after this is now often described as the period of 'nothing works'.

The negative conclusion arose that no particular practice was any more effective than any other. Without any other guiding policy, practitioners continued to work according to their own individual/ideological beliefs. Thus during the 1980s Probation became for some the avenue to divert offenders from custody, giving them space to 'grow up and grow out of crime'. It was seen positively as benefiting society as it was cheaper than prison, but others felt negatively about taking on a 'do as little harm as possible' approach (Bottoms and McWilliams's 'Non-treatment paradigm', 1979).

A much more optimistic approach to forensic practice developed from 1990 to the turn of the century. With the arrival of the 'What works?' movement (McGuire, 2001), 'evidence-based practice' began to gain currency; certain interventions did 'work' if and when applied with the right individuals at the right time and in the right way. Reasoning and Rehabilitation (Robinson and Porporino, 2001) programmes along with Enhanced Thinking Skills devised by, for example, HM Prison Service, were introduced to cater for community as well as institutional interventions, with the flexibility to be adapted for young offenders.

While maintaining programme integrity through proper training and adherence to the provision of the interventions (Hollin, 1995), further types of programmes were developed in both prison and community settings, many centring on personal effectiveness and combining individual as well as group interventions to focus on pro-social adaptations, moral reasoning (Palmer, 2003) and cognitive thinking (cognitive behavioural therapy (CBT), Lipsey and Landenberger, 2006) and development.

Policy by the Home Office was increasingly centralised, with notably the creation of a single National Probation Service in 2001, and then the merging with the Prison Service following the creation of the National Offender Management Service (NOMS) in 2004. In relation to Probation interventions specifically, there was a strong national steer towards developing formally accredited groupwork programmes like the ones just mentioned in both the prison and probation services at the turn of the century (see also www.justice.gov.uk/offenders/before-after-release/obp) – followed by a gradual decline during the next decade due to a policy implementation failure.

Partly there were distractions from subsequent policy drives, first on enforcement and then on responding to notorious cases of serious further offences. Partly too, accredited programmes started to seem expensive, and this led to them being unwisely implemented in some instances. For example, when the range of accredited programmes was being developed, it was projected (correctly) that the programmes that would be of most benefit to the majority of individuals under supervision would be those that sought to develop cognitive skills – cognitive behavioural therapy (CBT). Accordingly two of the first programmes to be accredited were, reasonably, CBT programmes. But because they were expensive to devise and start up, there was a strong central drive to put as many offenders as possible through such programmes in order to make the unit costs look less expensive.

In the resulting drive to fill as many programme places as possible unsuitable cases were increasingly referred, and this was of course followed by a decline in the reported effectiveness of those programmes. This in turn led to reduced confidence and interest of policymakers in the 'What works' movement in the first decade of the twenty-first century.

Nonetheless, groupwork programmes still run, both in Probation and Youth Offending, though the evidence-based nature of much Youth Offending groupwork has sometimes been less apparent (see Youth Offending (YO) inspections by HM Inspectorate of Probation). In contrast most Probation groups have been accredited by an independent Accreditation panel. Although much harder to organise in the community than in custodial settings, for logistical reasons, groupwork remains one of the key interventions available for practitioners in the community. In reality, however, only a small proportion of the total contact received by individuals under supervision takes place in groups. Most contact consists of 'routine' weekly or other regular individual bilateral interviews, in an interview room, office or reporting centre. Though there are some (often forgotten) accredited 'one-to-one' programmes (Davis, 2005; Burnett, 2004) that are being implemented with a range of cases, this still only constitutes a relatively small proportion of total contact with individuals who have offended. Practitioners have to spend a large proportion of contact time on ensuring compliance with various requirements of the Court, and checking and updating the current circumstances of each individual. Accredited programmes themselves, groupwork or one-to-one, still only occupy a finite period within the overall length of each community order and most post-sentence licences.

Nevertheless the evidence from the HM Inspectorate of Probation in the long term is that in recent years most current cases are now experiencing at some point in their supervision coherent individual plans of interventions, many of which originated as evidence-based practice – this represents a marked step forward from the idiosyncratic practice prior to 1990.

Intervention issues

The notable continuing issues with interventions for practitioners, however, mainly revolve around the modern distinction drawn by many between 'offender management' and 'interventions'. The idea that case officers are not expected to do everything pertaining to their cases, as no one person is an expert in all aspects of a case, began in the 1990s. 'Offender managers' (in current parlance) were required to 'let go' and to allow other colleagues to undertake certain aspects of 'their' cases. The rather possessive attitude/ethos of some case managers meant that this took some getting used to.

Nevertheless, by the turn of the century most practitioners had become accustomed to case referral, facilitating the provision of groupwork programmes or employment training or other services by other colleagues, both from within and outside their own organisation.

When NOMS was established in 2004, it was proposed that offender management and delivery of interventions should become completely separate. The debate continued as NOMS went on to draft a suite of service specifications to enable each aspect of Probation practice to be put out for competitive tender. These reinforced the separation of intervention delivery and offender management.

The underlying issue was that although there were some sound reasons for separating out certain aspects of Probation practice as mentioned previously, there also continued to be the need for joining the work back up again. As with all personal services there is a need for the practitioner in charge of the case to have the means and ability to manage the case as a whole. In this sense the work has to be both 'broken up' and 'joined back up again' – both are necessary, but the latter has received much less attention from NOMS than the former in recent years.

Outcomes

Synonyms for outcomes could include 'results', 'measures of effectiveness', 'purposes achieved', 'benefit to the community' or 'measurable improvement'. For the purposes of this chapter these other terms may usefully appear, but they all come under the group heading of Outcomes.

The main point to grasp for the reader new to the Probation or Youth Offending worlds is that the precise definition of desired outcomes is extremely problematic in a number of ways. Indeed this is a symptom of the ambiguities within the wider Criminal Justice system itself – the sentence passed on each offender may have one or several of the following purposes: retribution, deterrence of the individual, deterrence of others, help or 'rehabilitative treatment' for the individual (Norrie, 1993), or, in certain cases, act to announce a special mark of society's disapproval, as with some of the sentences handed down following the summer riots of 2011. Given that community supervision formally became a sentence of the Court in the 1990s (and no longer a case of 'advise, assist and befriend' *instead of a sentence*) the ambiguity of its purpose should not be that surprising.

Thus on the one hand we are critical of those managing Probation and Youth Offending work for failing to focus effectively on evaluating the outcomes of their practice, but on the other hand we readily acknowledge that attempts to do so are always fraught with difficulties. People new to the subject tend to assume that the aim is simply to reduce reoffending, and that there must be straightforward ways of doing that, but in reality the picture is very complicated.

Today it might seem strange to anyone who has received any basic training in 'Management by Objectives' that a key service was once managed without any defined success criteria, as was broadly the case historically in Probation. Until the 1970s it was believed by many that Probation supervision or 'social casework' reduced reoffending although, as discussed earlier, what one actually did during these 'social casework' interviews was largely down to each practitioner.

As previously outlined the IMPACT research in England, and the mistaken interpretation given to Martinson's (1974) American analysis, eroded this belief. Hence from the late 1970s came the rather modest aspirations arising from Bottoms and McWilliams's 'Non-treatment paradigm' (1979), the 'Sentenced to social work?' of Bryant et al. (1978) and the Home Office's *Statement of National Objectives and Priorities* for Probation, circulated in 1984. By the late 1980s the most frequently cited definition of success for Probation was 'diversion from custody' – practitioners were told that if they obtained a community sentence from court for an offender who was of 'High Risk of custody' this was a success because community sentences were cheaper and no less ineffective than custodial sentences. However, the 1990s saw the arrival of the 'What works' movement (McGuire, 2001), that, to distance themselves from the so-called 'Nothing works' hypothesis, stressed that certain things did 'work' if undertaken with the right individuals.

There was also a particular emphasis on the value of cognitive behaviour therapy (CBT) in groups, which focuses on the process of learning in maintaining behaviour (Rachman, 1997). The individual under supervision is encouraged to identify connections between thoughts, feelings and offending behaviours. Although the research supported CBT use with a high proportion of offenders for community-based interventions (Goldstein et al., 1989), probation (Golden, 2003) and in custody cases (Friendship et al., 2003), it was often subsequently misrepresented and was then advocated as the answer to everything in all cases. One consequence of this was that it lost some political credibility when the effect of CBT on reoffending reduced following the somewhat indiscriminate big rollout of these programmes in the early 2000s, as outlined earlier.

At the same time for political reasons there were other policy distractions such as an increasing emphasis on the importance of 'Enforcement' – requiring offenders under supervision to attend frequent appointments and for them to be taken back to court promptly if they failed to attend. This was part of the wider development of a detailed list of National Standards, which went through a number of editions at the turn of the century. Defining the 'Enforcement' objective clearly enough proved elusive at first, but during this period the centrally driven target in Probation was that in those cases where there had been a 'second unacceptable failure to attend' (itself not easy to define clearly) then court action must be initiated within ten days in at least 90 per cent of such cases. This, alongside a number of the other key National Standards, became in effect the key measures of success for Probation – and to a lesser extent for Youth Offending (which had a looser formal standard) – at this time.

However, the picture changed again in the middle of the decade because of growing public attention to the fact that a (small) number of current Probation or Youth Offending cases were committing notorious serious crimes during their period of supervision. Greatly increased attention was given to 'managing risk' in the community, although defining the precise measure of success again proved (and stayed) elusive. Policymakers were attracted by the idea of setting target minimum reoffending rates for these 'Serious Further Offences' (SFOs), and only reluctantly accepted that since only about one in 200 'MAPPA' cases – cases managed through Multi-Agency Public Protection Arrangements – committed an SFO this was not a realistic approach. (Furthermore, over three-quarters of SFOs were committed by current cases who were not as yet assessed as being High or Very High risk of harm to others.)

Managers tried to deal with this by setting standards for the content of assessments, as well as for the speed of their completion, but this too proved unsatisfactory. Ticking off the items contained in a document is not the same as assessing whether or not it is of satisfactory quality – a quality test requires a qualitative judgement. Meanwhile practitioners could be forgiven for questioning whether their managers were clear about whether they wanted reduced reoffending, or increased 'Enforcement' (actually Compliance and Enforcement), or better quality of assessment and management of risk of harm to others.

The truth, of course, is that all three are required, but this has rarely been stated in any formal documentation for Probation or Youth Offending work (except by HM Inspectorate of Probation – see Figure 1.2), so they are often portrayed as competing fashions rather than as necessary complements to each other. This sense of rotating flavour of the month was renewed in 2009, as a renewed focus on reconviction rates (or 'proven reoffending') came to the fore again.

Hence our first point here is that we are critical of those managing Probation and Youth Offending work for failing to focus effectively on evaluating the outcomes of their practice – one consequence of failing to set your own success criteria clearly enough is that someone else (media, politicians, etc.) will set some for you instead. However, our second point is that setting them satisfactorily is genuinely difficult.

For the sake of this introduction we will curtail most of the further discussion about outcomes to asserting that success criteria are needed for all three of the key purposes of Probation or Youth Offending work. Moreover, all of them require a greater or lesser degree of human judgement to 'measure' whether they are being achieved in practice (see Figure 1.2).

Nevertheless it is worth commenting here on why the second purpose – reduced reoffending – is so hard to measure in practice, and apply as a performance measure. First is the often-cited problem that reconvictions are often recorded only after a long time delay (and only if the offender is caught), that each conviction can encapsulate between one and a hundred or more offences that may be more or less serious than the earlier offending, or that they can sometimes refer to offences actually committed prior to previously recorded convictions. Next is the problem of comparing like with like – either a control group approach, or a proxy for one, is therefore needed. Next is the obvious dilemma that you need to trade off accuracy against immediateness – the longer you wait the more accurate the finding (as to whether or not someone is reoffending), but the more you lose the immediateness of any 'feedback on performance' (essential for effective management). And that all raises the question of whether you want to measure incidences of further offending, or total quantity of further offences, or seriousness of new crimes.

At the time of writing the Ministry of Justice has tackled these problems by taking a 'twin track' approach. On one track it is becoming increasingly committed to commissioning some prison services (e.g. Peterborough) and potentially most Probation services too using a Payment by Results (PbR) formula based simply on what is now known as the 'binary measure' – whether or not there is a reconviction within a 12-month period. But on another track is a version of an 'Actual v Predicted' approach. They measure incidences of 'proven reoffending' by current cases during a period of a few months within the first year of supervision.[2] Since every case can now be located within a cohort in which reoffending can reasonably be predicted, they can in principle compare like with like between different Probation Trust areas using this Actual v Predicted approach.

However, there continue to be problems. On a technical point, the formula for 'Predicted' includes a calculation for previous reoffending within that geographical area, meaning that areas with a previous 'good' record are disadvantaged compared with areas with a previous 'poor' record. On a more fundamental point the early quarterly reports showed scores bouncing around between very narrow margins, with only a few even technically statistically significant (and yet still bouncing from quarter to quarter). This approach has been a worthy attempt to solve the dilemma of accuracy v immediateness, but in the end it is neither sufficiently accurate nor sufficiently immediate. This means that it is not going to work as a measure of local short-term performance. However in our view it will certainly continue to be necessary to measure reoffending, ideally Actual v Predicted after a two-year period, as a measure of national long-term performance.

For local short-term performance purposes it will be necessary instead to use a proxy measure, assessing whether or not 'Likelihood of reoffending' has decreased during the course of, say, the first six or twelve months of supervision. This can be done either by measuring each individual on a dynamic scale (such as OASys) at the start of supervision, then later, and measuring the difference, or by recording whether certain 'outcomes' have been achieved during the course of supervision; those outcomes being ones that wider research suggest promote desistance from offending.

To summarise concerning outcomes, defining success criteria is extremely problematic and there is not yet widespread agreement – indeed for Youth Offending work there is the additional complication of an additional 'welfare of the child' purpose to be achieved. But in our view it will be a useful step forward if (in addition to the child welfare purpose for Youth Offending) there were a wider acceptance that Probation and Youth Offending work has three separate but

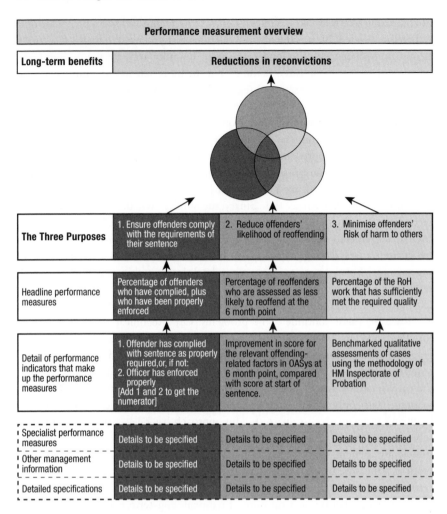

FIGURE 1.2 The Three Purposes of Probation and Youth Offending work and how to measure them. Andrew Bridges (2011).

overlapping complementary purposes to fulfil. Furthermore, it is an awkward but inevitable fact of life that the way of measuring each of these three purposes will need to include an element of human qualitative judgement.

Desistance

We cannot conclude this opening chapter without briefly mentioning the theme of 'Desistance', which will be discussed by Anthony Bottoms in greater detail in Chapter 13. As previously stated we prefer to avoid where possible terms such as 'treatment' that may imply a medical model, and instead we look at social dimensions, the onset of the offending behaviour and how it comes to an end. In examining how offending behaviour ceases we find it more useful to employ the concept of 'desistance' from offending, as set out by Maruna and Farrall (2004), which emphasises how desistance is a process rather than a sudden result, and how it is largely a personal journey experienced by each individual.

Structured groupwork and other 'What works' programmes retain their value and importance under this approach, as they certainly have a part to play in assisting the process of each individual's journey of desistance. Accordingly, practitioners should think about their role in a less instrumental or medically modelled manner. It needs to be less a case of 'this behaviour should be treated with this programme' and more a case of 'this individual is likely to find this programme a timely and effective intervention in helping him/her change his/her behaviour over time'.

As such, most Probation and Youth Offending practitioners use the individual's whole social context in order to explain the *onset* and *persistence* of offending and accordingly to plan how to help the individual's future *desistance* – consistent with, if not knowingly sourced from, the ideas of Bronfenbrenner (1979). They carry out their forensic role with whomever the Courts or other authorities send their way, with no formal power to reject such referrals.

Conclusions

What, then, are the implications for forensic practice in community settings? When discussing cases with Probation or Youth Offending practitioners, remember that even if they do not use the word 'forensic' to describe their work it is still a fair way of describing most of what they do with offenders in the community. The term may be more frequently employed by psychologists but the cases that are seen by psychologists will only be a tiny proportion of the total number that the mainstream services supervise.

Probation and Youth Offending services have to take on every case sent to them by the Courts, and with every case that goes beyond the court report stage they need to assess, engage, intervene, review, and aim to achieve outcomes. As we have seen, each of these functions has complications and issues. Assessments have to be 'fit for purpose within available resources' rather than 'comprehensive', and the practitioner must be alert to the need to review each case both at regular intervals and in the light of new information. Engagement must be a means to an end and not an end in itself. Interventions, now often separated from 'offender management', should aid the individual's own personal desistance journey by doing 'the right thing with the right individual in the right way at the right time'. This, however, begs the question of 'the right thing' – in order to achieve what precisely?

A common assumption is that the purpose of all this supervision of about a quarter of a million individuals (adults and youths) in the community at any one time is 'simply' to stop or at least reduce reoffending. It is certainly one key purpose, although we have seen that it is much more complicated to 'measure' precisely than most people at first realise. The greater complication is that in practice, whether it is made explicit or not (as we have done in this chapter), there are two additional separate but overlapping purposes to be achieved. Even if the person under supervision does not reoffend, the Probation or Youth Offending practitioner will not be seen as having done their job properly if they have not required the individual to maintain a reasonable frequency of appointments, or if they have failed to take all reasonable action to manage any potential risk of harm to others.

As we have seen, there have been many uncertainties and several changes over the last 40 years in any attempts to define what these practitioners have been required to achieve. At the time of writing (2011/12) the intention of government policy is to focus more strongly than ever before on achieving outcomes, with its strong emphasis on 'Payment by Results' (PbR). Although this principle has much merit in it in theory, it remains very problematic in practice. We have outlined the difficulties involved in measuring reoffending, in the dilemma between 'accuracy' and 'immediateness', while the unwillingness to make explicit the other two purposes belies the fact that it is the perceived failure to protect individual victims that can cause staff to lose their jobs, as in the Baby Peter and the Sonnex cases. Nevertheless we have to acknowledge the genuine difficulties in measuring the achievement of the Three (plus one) Purposes, as set out in this chapter, because all require an element of qualitative judgement by the person doing the measuring.

However, there is also a danger in getting lost in the difficulties. Just because it is hard to define a 'precise' way of measuring a result, that not does prevent a practitioner from being able to assess for herself or himself whether she or he is doing a good job with each individual case. The Probation or Youth Offending practitioner can ask herself or himself the following three questions:

1: Am I holding this individual to the terms of the court sentence or licence? (Compliance)
2: Am I helping this person to become less likely to reoffend in future, and how will I evidence that? (Likelihood of Reoffending)
3: Am I taking all reasonable action to protect others from harm from this individual? (Risk of Harm to others), and
    with individuals under the age of 18, there is also a *fourth* ('plus one') purpose: Am I taking all reasonable action to protect this young person from coming to harm, either from self or others? (Risk of harm to self).

The specialist practitioner, whether a forensic psychologist or another specialist provider, needs to understand this. It should be noted that, although it is true that there are numerous complications and difficulties in this work as we previously outlined, it is also true that there is a simplicity to what mainstream staff are being asked to achieve. 'Simple' is not the same thing as 'easy', and with most probation officers having at least 35 cases each (Youth Offending practitioners typically fewer than 20) it is never an 'easy' job for the conscientious worker. On her or his own part, when working with a Probation or Youth Offending colleague, the forensic psychologist has to be able to demonstrate that her or his own work has contributed appropriately, when needed, to the achievement of these Three (plus one) Purposes.

Notes

1   http://www.justice.gov.uk/publications/corporate-reports
2   http://www.justice.gov.uk/downloads/statistics/reoffending/proven-reoffending-definition-measurement-260112.pdf

Bibliography

Andrews, D.A., Zinger, I., Hoge, R.D., Bonta, J., Gendreau, P. and Cullen, F.T. (1990) Does correctional treatment work? A clinically relevant and psychologically informed meta-analysis. *Criminology*, 28, 369–404.

Andrews, D.A., Bonta, J. and Wormith, S.J. (2006) The recent past and near future of risk and/or need assessment. *Crime and Delinquency*, 52, 7–27.

Aye-Maung, N. and Hammond, N. (2000) *Risk of Re-offending and Needs-Assessments: The Users' Perspective* (Home Office Research Study No. 216). London: Home Office.

Baker, K., Jones, S., Roberts, C. and Merrington, S. (2003) *Validity and Reliability of Asset*. London: Youth Justice Board.

Beech, A. and Mann, R. (2002) Recent developments in the assessment and treatment of sexual offenders, in J. McGuire (ed.) *Offender Rehabilitation and Treatment: Effective Programmes and Policies to Reduce Re-offending*. Chichester: Wiley.

Bonta, J., Rugge, T., Sedo, B. and Coles, R. (2004) *Case Management in Manitoba Probation* (Users Report 2004–01). Ottawa: Public Safety Canada.

Bottoms, A.E. and McWilliams, W. (1979) A non-treatment paradigm for probation practice. *British Journal of Social Work*, 9(2), 159–202.

Bridges, A. (2011) Probation and Youth Offending work: a tribute to those who do it well. Lecture given by HM Chief Inspector of Probation 2004–11, University of Oxford, May.

Bronfenbrenner, U. (1979) *The Ecology of Human Development*. Cambridge, MA: Harvard University Press.

Bryant, M., Coker, J., Estlea, B., Himmel, S. and Knapp, T. (1978) Sentenced to social work. *Probation Journal*, 25, 110–14.

Burnett, R. (2004) One-to-one ways of promoting desistance: in search of an evidence base, in R. Burnett and C. Roberts, *What Works in Probation and Youth Justice: Developing Evidence-based Practice*. Cullompton: Willan Publishing.

Cavadino, M. (1997) Pre-Sentence Reports: the effects of legislation and national standards. *British Journal of Criminology*, 37(4), 529–48.

Chapman, T. and Hough, M. (1998) *Evidence-based Practice*. London: HMIP.

Clarke, R.V. and Felson, M. (eds) (1993) *Routine Activity and Rational Choice. Advances in Criminological Theory, Vol. 5*. New Brunswick, NJ: Transaction Books.

Copas, J. and Marshall, P. (1998) The offender group reconviction scale: a statistical reconviction score for use by probation officers. *Applied Statistics*, 47(1), 159–71.

Copsey, M. and Spurden, S. (1998) 'Say what you mean – mean what you say': Addressing the effectiveness agenda. *Vista*, 4(2), 143–54.

Davis, E. (2005) Appendix D: The One-to-One Programme: Guidance for Use with Racially Motivated Offenders. Probation Circular PC 67/2005. London: Home Office.

Folkard, M.S., Smith, D.E. and Smith, D.D. (1976) *IMPACT: Intensive Matched Probation and After-Care Treatment. Vol. 2.* Home Office Research Study No. 36. London: HMSO.

Friendship, C., Blud, L., Erikson, M., Travers, R. and Thornton, D. (2003) Cognitive-behavioral treatment for imprisoned offenders: an evaluation of HM Prison Service's cognitive skills programmes. *Legal and Criminological Psychology*, 8(1), 103–14.

Gendreau, P., Goggin, C. and Smith, P. (1999) The forgotten issue in effective correctional treatment: program implementation. *International Journal of Offender Therapy*, 43(2), 180–7.

Golden, L.S. (2003) Evaluation of the efficacy of a cognitive behavioral program for offenders on probation: thinking for a change. Doctoral dissertation, University of Texas Southwestern Medical Center at Dallas. Dissertation Abstracts International, 63(10), 4902.

Goldstein, A.P., Glick, B., Irwin, M.J., Pask-McCartney, C. and Rubama, I. (1989) *Reducing Delinquency: Intervention in the Community.* New York: Pergamon Press.

Hollin, C. (1995) The meaning and implications of 'programme integrity', in J. McGuire (ed.) *What Works: Reducing Reoffending.* Chichester: John Wiley.

Hollin, C.R. (2006) Offending behaviour programmes and contentions: evidence-based practice, manuals, and programme evaluation, in C.R. Hollin and E.P. Palmer (eds) *Offending Behaviour Programmes: Development Application and Controversies.* Chichester: John Wiley.

Holt, P. (2000) *Case Management: Context for Supervision.* Community and Criminal Justice Monograph 2, Leicester: De Montfort University, 13–18.

Home Office (1984) *Probation Service in England and Wales: Statement of National Objectives and Priorities.* London: Home Office.

Howells, K. and Day, A. (2003) Readiness for anger management: clinical and theoretical issues. *Clinical Psychology Review*, 23, 319–37.

Lane, D.A. (2006) What does it mean to be a science-practitioner? Working towards a new vision, in D.A. Lane, *The Modern Science-Practioner: A Guide to Practice in Psychology.* London: Routledge.

Lipsey, M.W. (2003) Those confounded moderators in meta-analysis: good, bad, and ugly. *Annals of the American Academy of Political and Social Science*, 587, 69–81.

Lipsey, M. and Landenberger, N. (2006) Cognitive-behavioral interventions, in B. Welsh and D. Farrington (eds) *Preventing Crime: What Works for Children, Offender, Victims, and Places.* Dordrecht: Springer.

Lipton, D.S., Thornton, D., McGuire, J., Porporino, F.J. and Hollin, C.R. (2000) Program accreditation and correctional treatment. *Substance Use & Misuse*, 35(12–14), 1705–34.

McGuire, J. (2001) What works in correctional intervention? Evidence and practical implications, in G. Bernfeld, D.P. Farrington and A. Lescheid (eds) *Offender Rehabilitation in Practice: Implementing and Evaluating Effective Programs.* Chichester: John Wiley.

Martinson, R. (1974) What works? Questions and answers about prison reform. *The Public Interest*, 35, 22–54.

Maruna, S. and Farrall, S. (2004) Desistance from crime: a theoretical reformulation. *Kölner Zeitschrift für Soziologie und Sozialpsychologie,* 43, 171–94.

Melton, G.B., Petrila, J., Poythress, N.G. and Slobogin, C. (1997) *Psychological Evaluations for the Courts,* 2nd edn. New York: Guilford Press.

Miller, W.R. and Rollnick, S. (2002) *Motivational Interviewing: Preparing People to Change,* 2nd edn. New York: Guilford Press.

Norrie, A. (1993) *Crime, Reason and History: A Critical Introduction to Criminal Law.* London: Weidenfeld and Nicolson.

OASys Development Team (2001) *The Offender Assessment System: User Manual.* London: Home Office.

Palmer, E.J. (2003) *Offending Behaviour: Moral Reasoning, Criminal Conduct and the Rehabilitation of Offenders*. Cullompton: Willan Publishing.

Petersila, J. (1997) Diverting nonviolent prisoners to intermediate sanctions: the impact on California prison admissions and corrections costs. *Corrections Management Quarterly*, 1(1), 1–15.

Polaschek, D.L.L. and Ross, E.C. (2010) Do early therapeutic alliance, motivation, and stages of change predict therapy change for high-risk, psychopathic violent prisoners? *Criminal Behaviour and Mental Health*, 20(2), 100–11.

Prochaska, J.O. and DiClemente, C.C. (1983) Stages and processes of self-change of smoking: toward an integrative model of change. *Journal of Consulting and Clinical Psychology*, 51(3), 390–5.

Prochaska, J.O. and DiClemente, C.C. (1986) Toward a comprehensive model of change, in W.R. Miller and N. Heather (eds) *Treating Addictive Behaviors: Processes of Change*. New York: Plenum Press.

Rachman, S. (1997) The evolution of cognitive behaviour therapy, in D. Clark, C.G. Fairburn and M.G. Gelder (eds) *Science and Practice of Cognitive Behaviour Therapy*. Oxford: Oxford University Press.

Robinson, G. (2002) Exploring risk management in the probation service: contemporary developments in England and Wales. *Punishment and Society*, 4, 5–25.

Robinson, G. (2003) Risk and risk assessment, in W.H. Chui and M. Nellis (eds) *Moving Probation Forward: Evidence, Arguments and Practice*. Harlow: Pearson Longman.

Robinson, D. and Porporino, F.J. (2001) Programming in cognitive skills: the Reasoning and Rehabilitation program, in C.R. Hollin (ed.) *Handbook of Offender Assessment and Treatment*. Chichester: Wiley.

2

ASSESSMENT IN COMMUNITY SETTINGS

Joel Harvey

Introduction

It is a dynamic, diverse and complex process to carry out assessments in community forensic settings. Adults and young people who have offended need to be thought about and worked with carefully. They bring with them a complex set of difficulties and there is a complex set of systems around them. As a group, they have generally experienced social exclusion and have a range of social and psychological needs (Bradley 2009; Singelton et al. 1998; Social Exclusion Unit 2002). The offence histories of people presenting, or being presented, to forensic community teams are varied and include sexual violence, physical violence, arson, and a range of acquisitive and other offences. These people who have offended come into contact with forensic services at different stages in their movement through the criminal justice system (CJS), from the point of arrest, through community sentences, to release from prison back into the community (Williamson 2006). Some are in contact with statutory services such as the National Probation Service or Youth Offending Services (YOS); others may be referred on to a National Health Service (NHS) forensic team. Timely assessment can ensure that people are identified early, diverted as necessary and thereby have their needs met (Bradley 2009).

Psychologists carry out forensic assessments in varied contexts, including adult forensic mental health services, adult forensic learning disabilities services, and adolescent forensic services. Psychologists, for example, may work in a service as part of the criminal justice system (such as probation or YOS) or in an NHS forensic team. Services vary in the extent to which they are multidisciplinary, but there is often the potential for psychologists to work alongside people from different professional backgrounds, such as speech and language therapists, occupational therapists, forensic nurses, social workers, forensic psychiatrists, probation officers, and youth offending service officers. Some collaborative work with other services (i.e. the police, housing, education, social care, the voluntary sector) is an essential part of an assessment. But achieving effective collaboration can be a complex and demanding process which as a minimum requirement calls for the development of joint-working protocols between different agencies.

Within adult community forensic mental health services, there are generally two different service models: an integrated model, working within the associated community mental health team (CMHT), and a parallel model, where the forensic team is separate from the CMHT but works alongside it instead (Thomson 2008; Mohan et al. 2004). Judge et al. (2004), in their survey of community forensic mental health teams (CFMHTs), found that 80 per cent used a parallel model. All the teams offered risk assessment and management, and half offered anger management and cognitive-behavioural therapy (CBT). Adults who have a learning disability may be referred to specialist adult forensic learning disabilities services. Since the closure of asylums there has been a development of community forensic learning disabilities teams (Benton and Roy 2008). People with learning disabilities who have offended also have complex needs. For example, people with learning disabilities who have committed offences are seven times more likely to have mental health problems than people with learning disabilities who have not offended (Robertson and Barnes 2010). Psychologists may also carry out assessments within adolescent forensic services and youth offending teams. (For details of adolescent services see Hoare and Wilson 2010; Khan and Wilson 2010.) Again, the key to working across these services is to work alongside other disciplines and agencies.

This chapter will explore the general considerations required when carrying out forensic assessments in these community settings. It will focus on criminal rather than civil assessments. But rather than focusing on assessments that are carried out to answer specific legal questions (for example, fitness to plead), the chapter will be more general in its approach and will examine the key areas that need to be considered when carrying out forensic assessments in the community. Developing a collaborative understanding *with* the person who has offended, and often with key people in their system, is necessary in order to assess and manage their risk and vulnerability. It is the role of the psychologist, and of any team with which he or she might work, to acknowledge and understand the complexities of the person and of the systems around him or her. It is also the psychologist's responsibility to communicate this understanding with that person and with other appropriate people in the systems. Assessment reports need to be communicated in a safe, contained, and understandable manner. With the help of this effective communication recommendations for monitoring, supervision and interventions have the potential to be implemented in a meaningful manner and to be sustained, or adapted where needed, over time.

Of course, alongside these responsibilities to the client, psychologists working in forensic settings also have legal and ethical duties to the public. These duties include protecting the public from violence, which can also involve helping the service user 'avoid the self-harmful consequences of perpetuating violence' (Hart and Logan 2011, p. 84). Over the years, risk assessment tools have developed for specific groups (e.g. adults and young people) and for different forms of violence (e.g. arson, sexual violence and physical violence) (see Hart and Logan 2011). But protecting the public and protecting the service user are not always mutually exclusive. Assessments carried out in forensic settings, and the formulations developed subsequently from them, need to include more than a list of static and dynamic risk factors. As Vess and Ward (2011) point out, 'what is required is a more comprehensive understanding of [a person's] developmental history and current functioning on a variety of domains, so that an integrated etiological, explanatory framework for his offending can be provided' (p. 183). Although there has been a predominant focus on 'criminogenic' factors, in order to attempt to understand another person's presenting difficulties, it is important to focus on both criminogenic and non-criminogenic needs (Harvey and Smedley 2010).

Assessment and its relationship to formulation

Psychological formulation is the ultimate goal of a forensic assessment; assessment forms the basis for developing psychological formulations and interventions. Assessment in forensic settings involves 'the systematic collection of relevant information in order to detect clinically relevant phenomena or problems in functioning, in order to provide clear treatment targets and risk management strategies' (Vess and Ward 2011, p. 175). When carrying out assessment with forensic clients, providing a formulation of their presenting difficulties goes hand in hand with assessing their associated risks and vulnerabilities. A forensic formulation has been defined as 'a conceptual model representing an offender's various problems, the hypothesized underlying mechanisms, and their interrelationships' (Vess and Ward 2011, p. 179). It is necessary to develop an aetiological understanding of the person's difficulties and to ascertain which individual and systemic factors continue to maintain a person's problems. A contextual understanding is essential; although often socially isolated, people who have offended do not exist in a social vacuum.

In recent years the important role of formulation has been increasingly emphasised within forensic practice (Eells and Lombart 2011; Sturmey and McMurran 2011; Harvey 2011). However, whilst the importance of formulation has been recognised within forensic practice, there is a lack of empirical evidence on formulation in forensic contexts; more research is needed in this area (Sturmey and McMurran 2011). Many of the functions of formulation in forensic practice have been highlighted (Eells and Lombart 2011). They include providing a structure to organise the information about a person; providing a 'blueprint' to guide treatment; providing a way to measure change; and 'help[ing] the therapist understand the patient and thereby exhibit greater empathy for the patient's intrapsychic, interpersonal, cultural and behavioural world' (p. 4). By keeping formulation at the heart of assessment the psychologist is able to synthesise existing theoretical knowledge (for example, a particular pathway model of sexual offending) to the specific individual being assessed. Indeed, 'formulation provides a structure to apply nomothetic knowledge to an idiographic context' (Eells and Lomart 2011, p. 5). Formulation also demonstrates to an individual that there is another person who is at least *attempting* to hold them in mind and through this is communicating to the person that they are worthy of being understood (Harvey 2011). When carrying out assessments within forensic community settings it is important for the psychologist to always hold formulation in mind and to assess in order to formulate. The resulting formulation, which should be adapted to accommodate new information as it comes to light, will then guide interventions and help inform the level of supervision required. Just as assessment is a continuous process throughout treatment, likewise, formulations should be reviewed and updated to help inform interventions.

When carrying out an assessment within any community forensic team, whether working with adults or young people, there are a number of key areas to take into consideration. It is important to consider what to assess and, associated with this, why an assessment is being carried out in the first place. It is necessary to think about how to assess, in other words, to consider what method of assessment to use, and to think about where to physically carry out the assessment. Furthermore, it is important to think about the ethical issues when carrying out any assessment and it is crucial to reflect on how to work collaboratively with the person being assessed and how to work with other systems around that person. It is to these considerations that we now turn.

Topics of assessment

People are referred, often by statutory services, to community forensic services with a number of interrelated needs; there is also usually concern about the level of risk that the person poses to others in society and to themselves. It is often the referrer who has aspirations to have the client's forensic needs met rather than the client himself. This is particularly the case when the referrer has concerns about the client's risk to others but the client himself does not hold such concerns. It is possible that the referrer's perception of the client's needs may differ from the client's own perceptions. It is therefore important to consider these possibilities at the time of referral. Does the client know he has been referred in the first place? What needs does the referrer think the client might want to meet? Is there any indication of the extent to which the client has an insight into his difficulties? How well has the client engaged with services in the past? Some preliminary thinking about these questions will help the psychologist to work out how to start the assessment, how to structure the questions and how to construct the narrative during the assessment sessions.

There are a number of set topic areas that the psychologist needs to address during an assessment, in order to develop an understanding of the individual; but how these questions are asked, and in which order, should be considered in relation to the particular client. For example, if the referrer and the client seem to have 'competing' perceptions of needs (e.g. the referrer is concerned about risk of future violence but the client about low mood and about the future) then it is important that the psychologist listens actively to the concerns of the client first and only then moves on to the risk assessment. Moreover, it is essential that the psychologist is aware of whether clients have had actual or perceived negative experiences of professionals, or are mistrustful of others; then the psychologist can reflect on how they, as a psychologist, appear to the client – as a figure of oppression or a rescuer and carer? Neither, or both? It is essential that the psychologist is able to communicate to the client that they are interested in the client's perception of their problems and to construct the assessment process accordingly. It is essential that the psychologist ensures that the client feels heard and that the psychologist tries actively to understand the client's perspective; the attempt to understand is the psychologist's core business. Of course, this does not prevent the psychologist from asking questions to help inform an assessment about risk of future violence. On the contrary, through demonstrating *an attempt* to understand, through thinking carefully about when and about the manner in which these questions are asked, and then through explaining why the questions are being asked, there may be a more thorough assessment. Table 2.1 presents a number of areas that can be considered within a forensic assessment in the community. The priority of assessment areas to be covered within a clinical interview will be dependent upon the referral and the information available to the psychologist. However, it is essential that imminent risk of harm to others, and from others, is covered early in the assessment. Indeed, it is the psychologist's responsibility if assessing a person to ensure they have responded appropriately to any safeguarding concerns, regardless of the reason for the initial referral.

By covering these areas the psychologist can develop a formulation of the onset, development, and maintenance of the client's presenting problems. An aetiological model can be developed that includes both individual and systemic factors. Including systemic factors, too, moves the practitioner away from a pathological individualistic model and allows for recommendations to also include interventions working with the systems around the person (Harvey and Smedley 2010).

As already mentioned, in forensic community services people are often referred to the psychologist for a risk assessment of the possibility of future violence (see Chapter 6, this volume). There is an extensive literature on risk assessment in forensic practice (see BPS 2006; Doyle and Dolan 2008; Kemshall and Wilkinson 2011; Craig et al. 2008). Tools include both actuarial assessments (such as the STATIC-99, Hanson and Thornton 2000) and structured clinical judgement (SCJ) assessment tools (such as the HCR-20, Webster et al. 1997; the Risk of Sexual Violence Protocol (RSVP), Hart et al. 2003) Sexual Violence Risk-20 (SVR-20), Boer et al. 1997). Both the HCR-20 and the SVR-20 have been adapted for use with people with learning disabilities (Boer et al. 2010a, 2010b). Moreover, the Assessment of Risk Manageability for Individuals with Developmental and Intellectual Limitations who Offend (ARMIDILLO-S, Boer et al. 2004) has been devised as a risk assessment tool for sexual offenders who have learning disabilities.

TABLE 2.1 Key areas to assess

– capacity to consent
– the person's perceived difficulties
– the person's goals, aspirations and strengths
– sources of social support and other protective factors
– neurocognitive abilities and difficulties
– social functioning and daily activities
– speech and communication
– physical health concerns
– developmental history
– family background (including developing a genogram) and family functioning
– social care history
– accommodation history
– trauma history
– education and employment
– finance and income
– psychosexual background
– relationship (romantic and peers) history
– attachment style
– mental health and substance misuse history
– personality
– history of hospital admissions and time spent in prison
– offending history
– attitudes towards offending
– attitudes towards treatment and motivation
– treatment history (both mental health and offending behaviour)
– current mental state (including assessment of self-harm/suicidality)
– medication and attitude towards taking medication
– legal restrictions
– safeguarding issues

Risk assessment tools have also been developed for adolescent offenders. For example, the Structured Assessment of Violence Risk in Youth (SAVRY) (Borum et al. 2005) has been devised to assess risk of future violence, and the Assessment Intervention Moving on (AIM) assessment (Print et al. 2007) has been devised to assess risk of future sexually harmful behaviour. Even if they work with adults, it is important that psychologists also know and understand the risk assessment tools for adolescents, in order to help make sense of any assessments that have been carried out during their clients' adolescent years. It is also important for psychologists to have an understanding of developmental issues in adolescence in order for them to be aware of the context in which an adult's problems may have emerged during childhood and adolescent years (Smedley 2010).

When carrying out a forensic assessment in any community setting, it is necessary to include a generic risk screening tool (e.g. Morgan 2000). It is important to consider the risk a person might pose to vulnerable adults or to children and to be aware of any immediate victims. Psychologists must be prepared for disclosures during any sessions and be aware of their local agency's safeguarding procedures, as immediate action may be required when assessing forensic clients. Also, it is important to consider whether the person being assessed is vulnerable to harm and exploitation by others and to assess risk of self-harm and suicide. Immediate referrals to other services may be required if the person presents in crisis; for that, the psychologist needs a local knowledge of services and accident and emergency departments. When carrying out assessments, the psychologist must be prepared to develop a safety plan in the here-and-now so that any immediate risks are appropriately managed. Moreover, it is important for psychologists to know about mental health law, as it relates to offenders with mental health difficulties (Fennell 2008a, 2008b), and to know how to contact relevant services if a Mental Health Act assessment is needed.

Methods of assessment

In order to carry out a comprehensive assessment it is necessary to gather inform-ation from a number of sources using a number of different methods. These different methods will be considered in this section.

Reviewing previous reports and notes to develop an integrated chronology

An essential part of the assessment process is to develop an integrated chronology (integrating information from different sources) of significant events in a person's life. Many people who have offended have a vast amount of information available about them from a number of different agencies including the police, health services, probation, housing, youth offending services, education and social care, and it is important that key reports are accessed and documented. For example, a wealth of information may already be available from nationally established assessment tools, such as OASys in probation and ASSET in YOS, and information from these assessment tools should be carefully analysed.

If there are any gaps in the chronology, it is important to highlight them and to ensure that all sources have been exhausted. Sturmey and McMurran (2011) state that those with the most serious offence histories are those with a long contact with mental health services, the criminal justice system and social services; therefore, 'the challenge is how to organise the large quantity of material, and how to make sense of developmental and forensic histories' (p. 292). It is therefore important that the information is gathered systemically and is recorded along with the source of the information. It is also useful to record when the information was reported and whether or not the client is aware of the information. So, for example, a psychiatry report might state that the client's father reported that the client's mother physically assaulted the client as a young baby. It is important to highlight that it was detailed in the psychiatrist's report, that the source was his father, and whether or not this information is known by the client. Moreover, it is also the responsibility of the psychologist to detect any inaccuracies in information that may have occurred over the years (e.g. misreporting of an event that is then carried through reports for several years). The development of a chronology also ensures that the psychologist reflects on the person's earlier life experiences and that the psychologist takes into account systemic factors. These considerations can then be included within the psychological formulation.

Clinical interviews

When carrying out a forensic assessment, the clinical interview is the primary means of developing a relationship with the client and gathering assessment information. Psychologists may decide to develop a semi-structured interview schedule, in order to cover, for example, the topics presented in Table 2.1. For offenders with mental health difficulties the psychologist may also decide to use a structured interview such as the Structured Clinical Interview for DSM 1 Disorders (SCID I, First et al. 1996). The clinical interview is an essential part of conducting risk assessments and it is particularly useful as a way of looking at dynamic risk factors. The clinical interview can help the psychologist to understand the client's own perceptions of his or her risk, and then to develop contextual risk scenarios. It is also valuable, if possible, and with consent, to interview family members, carers, and other professionals who work with the client. Psychological assessment in the community lends itself to include family members and carers. This breadth again allows the psychologist to gather important systemic information, to inform the formulation. In the community, many people who have offended may live in residential settings, such as a children's home or a probation hostel; if so, an interview with key network members is vitally important as it can provide valuable insights into a person's presentation and behaviour in different contexts. Interviews with family members are especially useful when developing chronologies, in order to obtain useful developmental background information.

Life-mapping

A useful method for assessing and formulating in this way is 'life-mapping' or developing a 'time-line'. This involves working collaboratively and creatively with the client and looking at different times in his or her life. One can use flipchart paper, coloured pens, and 'Post-it' notes to 'map out' an individual's life. The psychologist might develop the map in chronological order or might ask the client to talk about the different houses that they have lived in, and then ask questions about their life at those different times. This assessment method can aid the process of engagement. But it can do more than that: it can also reveal any problems, for example, in memory or concentration; it can elucidate basic constructs such as thoughts and feelings in a non-threatening manner; and it can reveal the person's willingness to discuss, or avoid, certain aspects of their life or certain topics. Furthermore, by focusing extensively on the client's life, the psychologist demonstrates a willingness to understand and learn about that person. Once one has developed a basic life map, then one can ask specifically forensic questions, for example, about police involvement or 'difficult times or situations when you got into trouble'. That can enable the person to start thinking about offending across their life cycle. This strategy is particularly useful for clients who are not willing to discuss their offence at first; it may serve as a less hostile way of approaching their specific offence cycles and other offence-focused interventions.

Psychometric measures and neurocognitive assessments

Psychometric testing is common in forensic settings, and in the forensic literature there is an array of psychometric measures available which pertain to different offences (Gudjonsson 2000; Ubrina 2004; Heiburn 1992; Browne et al. 2013). For example, there is a large number of psychometric measures which measure dynamic risk factors for sexual offending (Thornton 2002; SARN (Structured Assessment of Risk and Need)). A total of 16 psychometric tests measure four domains: sexual interests, cognitive distortions, socio-affective functioning, and problems with self-management. The SARN uses a structured risk approach that is supported by evidence from the psychometric assessments (Craig et al. 2008). Moreover, in recent years there has been an increased interest in the assessment and treatment of sex offenders who have learning disabilities; the various measures for use with this group have been reviewed by Craig et al. (2010). For example, the Questionnaire on Attitudes Consistent with Sexual Offenders (QACSO, Broxholme and Lindsay 2003) was designed specifically for offenders with learning disabilities. It measures cognitive distortions across eight different domains: rape and attitudes towards women, voyeurism, exhibitionism, dating abuse, homosexual assault, offences against children, stalking and sexual harassment, and social desirability.

As well as psychometric measures such as these, which are offence-specific, it is important to think also about psychometric assessments relevant to mental health. For example, it may be useful to assess depression and anxiety using the Beck Depression and Anxiety Inventories (Beck et al. 1996; Beck and Steer 1993). With adolescents, the Strengths and Difficulties Questionnaire (SDQ, Goodman et al. 1998) provides information across five domains (emotional symptoms, conduct problems, hyperactivity/inattention, peer relationship problems, and pro-social behaviour), and the Resiliency Scales provide valuable information on constructs such as relatedness, mastery, and emotional reactivity (Price-Embury 2005) and the Beck Youth Inventories (Beck et al. 2005) are also useful. Because the information gleaned from psychometric tests is useful to develop formulations (Eells and Lombart 2011), it is necessary to reflect on when and how to obtain this information to maximum effect.

It might also be necessary to carry out an assessment of personality, using a standardised measure such as the Millon Clinical Multiaxial Inventory-III (MCMI-III, Millon et al. 2009), which would help to identify personality difficulties. This information could not only inform risk assessments and possible interventions but could also help the psychologist to structure the assessment sessions themselves, in the first place. The Psychopathy Checklist-Revised (PCL-R, Hare 2003) is also used within forensic community services to inform risk assessment and management or identify personality characteristics which may have an adverse impact on treatment engagement.

It may also be necessary to carry out neurocognitive assessments before any offence-focused assessments are completed or recommendations for intervention are delineated. Many people in the criminal justice system have neurocognitive difficulties (Young et al. 2009). If the psychologist, or others, identifies potential cognitive problems, he or she should consider which neurocognitive assessments to use; they may include assessments of general intelligence, memory, language, and executive functioning. The results of neurocognitive assessments can then be included within psychological formulations to ensure that any recommendations take any cognitive difficulties into account.

Observation schedules and monitoring tools

Another useful method of assessment might be observation schedules and monitoring tools and there is considerable scope for working with family members, carers, or other professionals in the community. Observations can be carried out by other staff, if the person is living in a residential setting such as a local authority children's home, or, if a young person is living at home, by a parent, carer or teacher. An example of the sort of observation that might be used is an antecedent-behaviour-consequence chart for a clearly defined specific behaviour such as aggressive episodes. An additional important source of observation is the client's own monitoring of their thoughts, feelings and behaviour. For example, if a client reports distressing intrusive thoughts of violence, difficulties controlling feelings of anger, or thoughts about setting fires, it would be useful to ask the client to record them in a process of self-monitoring, in order to aid the assessment process. Monitoring can also take place within sessions in order to capture the dynamic nature of presenting difficulties and to assess fluctuations over time. Careful thought is needed when asking clients to self-monitor. The impact self-monitoring has on the client also needs to be monitored by others.

Places of assessment

The place where assessment occurs is another important consideration with forensic assessment in the community. Assessments can take place in various settings, including the office-base (or 'clinic'), the client's home, a public area in the local community or in a secure setting prior to discharge. Of course, when deciding whether to conduct assessment outside the clinic, the first consideration must be safety; the psychologist must consider whether there are any known risks for the professionals or for particular demographic groups (such as women, if a client is known to be hostile towards women) and must consider the particular triggers to aggression by the particular client. It is essential to follow guidance on lone working, and it is often beneficial to carry out joint visits. Assertive outreach teams are designed for such work in situations where other teams might find the logistics difficult.

There is a growing literature that traces the value of assertive outreach in meeting the needs of people with mental health difficulties (Williams et al. 2011), and there are also several forensic services that offer such an approach, such as Birmingham's Forensic Service for People with Learning Disabilities or Multi-systemic Therapy (MST), now available for young people aged 11 to 17 across the UK. Rather than asking the client to come to the clinic, the psychologist conducts the assessment in a place that is more convenient for the client. Even if some assessments take place in a traditional 'clinic' setting, it might be beneficial for other assessments to take place elsewhere. Given the socially or geographically isolated position of many clients, it is often necessary to carry out assessments away from the clinic. There are distinct advantages as well: home visits can prove useful for encouraging engagement; and they can prove useful for gathering further contextual information about the person's home environment and ability to cope there, which will help inform the overall assessment. For example, meeting clients elsewhere in the community, as in a café, might feel safer for the client but might also provide useful information about how the person interacts and behaves with other members of the public. It is therefore important in service development to consider one's client group and to design a service to meet the needs of a diverse population in its particular social and geographical setting – obviously within the limits of a finite budget.

Ethics of assessment

Forensic assessments require many complex ethical considerations (Adams and Lusher 2003; Eastman et al. 2010; Towl 2010), too many to consider more than briefly in this chapter. It is important for the psychologist to have time to reflect on ethical issues during the course of the assessment. Indeed, Adshead (2010) reminds us that 'best-quality ethical decision-making takes time; time to reflect on the nature of the issues and where the main tensions lie' (p. 301). Prior to completing assessments, psychologists need to be aware of their organisations' protocols and procedures. Indeed, 'organisations must have clear protocols and procedures, which are understood by both staff and service users, indicating when and how the police should be called. Those procedures need to be owned and applied consistently' (Jaydeokar and Barnes 2010, p. 42).

One of the major ethical considerations, highlighted by Eastman et al. (2010), is the tension between protecting the rights of the client and protecting the public.

Adshead (2010) points out that ethical dilemmas occur because there are 'collisions' between 'the interests and values of different groups or individuals' (p. 301). The psychologist has a dual role: he or she must ensure that s/he identifies the needs of the client but, at the same time, must ensure that the public is kept safe from future harm. These two demands are not mutually exclusive, though, because harm to the public is also likely to result in harm to the client, when the client endures the consequences for his or her actions.

The two demands are most evident in information-sharing. It must be made clear to the client that information will be shared with other agencies, such as the police or MAPPA (Multi-agency Public Protection Arrangements), should there be imminent concerns of them causing serious harm. It is also necessary, when working as part of a multidisciplinary team (MDT), to inform the client about the limits to confidentiality and that information will be shared within the team, as well as with other agencies (DH 2003; HM Government 2008). As Robertson and Barnes (2010) state 'appropriate information sharing is vital if multidisciplinary and inter-agency working is to function effectively' (p. 64). This must be made explicit to the client prior to the assessment. It is good practice, wherever possible, to empower a person to share that information themselves. For example, if a client had a history of arson, it would be good to encourage them to take the opportunity themselves to inform the housing authorities. Such empowerment, though, would also require monitoring to ensure that this has taken place.

It is also important to consider the dilemma faced by clients in relation to sharing information with the psychologist during risk assessments. It is possible that the more the client engages with the psychologist, and places trust in them, the more likely it is that the psychologist will make decisions that seem unwelcome to the client, for example, informing another agency of their presenting risk. On the other hand, if the client does not engage in the process, less will be known about their perception of their risk, and the lack of disclosure in itself might be interpreted as a risk factor, for example, as a lack of compliance with the process of assessment. This might then heighten the psychologist's anxiety and prompt them to take more restrictive decisions. Such dilemmas reflect the fact that there is a power imbalance between the practitioner and the client. Therefore, it is important for psychologists to reflect on their position of power: such reflection is not only ethical, it might also make for better engagement and assessment. Clinical supervision may be valuable for such reflections.

Collaborating with the individual

At the point of referral it is important for the psychologist to begin to think about ways of engaging with the client – to think about ways of developing a therapeutic relationship. The importance of the therapeutic relationship has increasingly been seen as important when working with people who have offended (Ward et al. 2007). Chadwick (2006) prefers using the term 'relationship building' rather than 'engaging', in his case in person-based cognitive therapy for clients with psychosis, because 'relationship building' refers to more of an interpersonal process. He stresses the importance of 'meeting the person, not the problem' (p. 25); describing the value of a 'good enough' understanding of a person, he stresses the need to 'convey a wish to understand, not necessarily understanding itself' (p. 28). The same can be said for work with forensic clients: it is important that the assessor shows an interest in the person. Working collaboratively is especially crucial with people who have offended: warmth and empathy can facilitate change and encourage engagement (Ward et al. 2007). One model that is particularly useful for collaborative work with forensic clients is the Good Lives Model (Ward et al. 2007). This approach 'involves a genuine commitment from the therapist to working transparently and respectfully and to emphasising that the client's best interests are to be served by the assessment process' (Ward et al. 2007, p. 95).

The psychologist's interest must be evident from the initial session, or even prior to this, as when making a telephone call to arrange an appointment. Indeed, as Davidson (2008) states, at the initial contact, 'the therapist has to convey a professional attitude while being warm and understanding of the patient's difficulties from the outset' (p. 66). When assessment begins, negotiating a common language is important (Chadwick 2006) and has relevance to work with forensic clients. Chadwick (2006) states that the therapist attempts to understand the client in the client's own language, and that the therapist should use the client's language to summarise back and reflect on what they are saying. Then, the therapist should introduce such elements of their own language or concepts that the client is likely to find acceptable. The final stage involves the therapist and client negotiating 'a mutually acceptable dialogue and framework'. This has relevance when developing an understanding of a client's problems and also working on developing risk-based scenarios.

When working with clients it is also important to be aware of potential difficulties. Davidson (2008) points out 'those with personality disorders will have complex and longstanding problems whose assessment requires structure as well as thoroughness, and it is not possible to hurry the process' (p. 66). It is important, then, to take time, when working with people who have personality difficulties, in order to ensure that the response of the psychologist does not become uncaring, overly detached or overly involved. It is also important, too, for the psychologist to reflect on the boundaries of the therapeutic relationship in an open manner during supervision with another professional, in order to conduct the assessment in a contained manner.

Working with systems around the person

There is, to conclude, a final area to consider when working in the forensic community setting: working with systems around the person. One advantage of assessing clients in the community is the opportunity to develop an understanding of the systems around clients and to work closely with those systems. These systems include the person's family, friends, school or college placement, and the other agencies involved in the person's life. This type of work is standard in approaches such as multisystemic therapy (MST) (Henggeler et al. 2009) but they should be integral to any forensic assessment.

By working alongside family members, carers, and other services, the psychologist can assess the level of support available for the client and the extent to which the client can access that support. Indeed, Thomson (2008) states that 'access to appropriate accommodation and social services is essential for successful management of forensic patients within the community' (p. 39). Furthermore, it is important to assess the support and supervision that the person is currently receiving in order to decide whether a particular assessment can be carried out safely and to gauge the depth of the assessment that might be safely carried out in the community. For example, if an assessment involves asking a person about their sexual fantasies, it is important that there is adequate monitoring and supervision in place, to ensure that the behaviour of the client is observed; as the assessment progresses, there is an opportunity to observe any behavioural changes. With risky and vulnerable people, it is essential to share information in a timely manner, as the assessment unfolds, so that other agencies will respond appropriately. Also, understanding the level of support that is available in the community can help to inform the recommendations for intervention. All this requires good working relationships and trust between agencies, to know that colleagues will communicate important information and act upon it, to meet the client's needs.

Good relationships with other agencies are also needed if the psychologist wants to understand systemic factors and to include them in a formulation. Other agencies can help to produce an accurate and up-to-date integrated chronology of the person's experiences, in order to provide useful information for the assessment and formulation. Moreover, within a multidisciplinary team, an assessment will benefit from different theoretical and professional skills and perspectives. For example, assessments of the risk of violence will benefit from an MDT approach which incorporates contributions from psychology, psychiatry, nursing, speech and language therapy, social work, and occupational therapy. The different professional backgrounds, and training in carrying out risk assessments, can be beneficial for collaborative work, if one respects the professional judgement and insights of other professional groups. Joint assessments allow for this shared expertise and allow for reflection between professionals; they can also be a safer way to work. Wherever possible, a psychological assessment should be carried out as part of the MDT and as part of the Care Programme Approach (CPA) process within the NHS (DH 2008) or as part of the MDT case management approaches within probation or YOS.

Indeed, integrated forensic assessments would be a useful way of consolidating information and drawing upon a range of professional backgrounds. Producing a single professionally integrated report would allow for the developing of one formulation and one set of recommendations. Rather than having assessment reports organised by professional groups, so that separate psychology reports, psychiatry reports and speech and language reports, for example, are structured around the different disciplines, it would be beneficial for psychologists to work in an integrated manner with their peers and to produce reports jointly which are structured around the life of the client. At the heart of any assessment report is the importance of thinking carefully about this person: an integrated approach creates a space to reflect with other professionals on that person, so that the assessment takes into account not only individual but also systemic factors.

Yet whether the assessment is completed as part of such an integrated team, or still singly by a psychologist, the process of completing a forensic assessment report involves creating a narrative about that person's life. This narrative will be carried with that person and could eventually become an influential representation of their past which will have an influence on his or her future. It is important that the psychologist keeps in mind the responsibility that goes hand in hand with this construction of a narrative during assessment. One important way to create that narrative responsibly is to do so by collaborating not only with other agencies but with the client him/herself. It is hoped that the process of assessment can then lead to a collaborative formulation and clear recommendations and will not just be a process applied to a person without their active engagement. It is then hoped that, through collaboration with the client, the *process* of assessment itself will be an opportunity for the client to have a conversation with another person who has valued them, who has attempted to understand them, and who has thought carefully about how to keep them, and relatedly how to keep others, safe.

References

Adams, H.E. and Lusher, K.A. (2003) Ethical Considerations in Psychological Assessment. In W. O'Donohue (ed.) *Handbook of Ethics for Professional Psychologists*. London: Sage.

Adshead, G. (2010) Principles of Ethical Reasoning in Forensic Psychiatry. In A. Bartlett and G. McGauley (eds) *Forensic Mental Health: Concepts, Systems and Practice*. Oxford: Oxford University Press, pp. 295–302.

Beck, A.T. and Steer, R.A. (1993) *Beck Anxiety Inventory Manual*. San Antonio, TX: Harcourt Brace.

Beck, A.T., Steer, R.A. and Brown, G.K. (1996) *Manual for the Beck Depression Inventory-II*. San Antonio, TX: Psychological Corporation.

Beck, J.S., Beck, A.T. and Jolly, J.B. (2005) *Beck Youth Inventories*, 2nd edn. San Antonio, TX: Harcourt Assessments.

Benton, C. and Roy, A. (2008) The First Three Years of a Community Service for People with a Learning Disability. *British Journal of Forensic Practice*, 10(2), 4–12.

Boer, D.P., Hart, S.D., Kropp, P.R. and Webster, C.D. (1997) *Manual for the Sexual Violence Risk-20. Professional Guidelines for Assessing Risk of Sexual Violence*. Vancouver, Canada: Mental Health, Law, and Policy Institute, Simon Fraser University.

Boer, D.P., Tough, S. and Haaven, J. (2004) Assessment of Risk Manageability of Intellectually Disabled Sex Offenders. *Journal of Applied Research in Intellectual Disabilities*, 17, 275–83.

Boer, D.P., Frize, M., Pappas, R., Morrissey, C. and Lindsay, W.R. (2010a) Suggested Adaptations to the HCR-20 for Offenders with Intellectual Disabilities. In L. Craig, W. Lindsay and K. Browne (eds) *Assessment and Treatment of Sexual Offenders with Intellectual Disabilities: A Handbook*. Wiley: Chichester, pp. 177–192.

Boer, D.P., Frize, M., Pappas, R., Morrissey, C. and Lindsay, W.R. (2010b) Suggested Adaptations to the SVR-20 for Offenders with Intellectual Disabilities. In L. Craig, W. Lindsay, and K. Browne (eds) *Assessment and Treatment of Sexual Offenders with Intellectual Disabilities: A Handbook.* Wiley: Chichester, pp. 193–210.

Borum, R., Bartel, P. and Forth, A. (2005) Structured Assessment of Violence Risk in Youth (SAVRY). In T. Grisso, G. Vincent, and D. Seagrave (eds) *Mental Health Screening and Assessment in Juvenile Justice.* New York: Guilford, pp. 311–23.

BPS (2006) *Risk Assessment and Management.* Occasional Briefing Paper No. 4. Leicester: British Psychological Society.

Bradley, Lord K. (2009) *The Bradley Report: Lord Bradley's Review of People with Mental Health Problems or Learning Disabilities in the Criminal Justice System.* London: Department of Health.

Browne, K.D., Beech, A.R. and Craig, L.A. (eds) (2013) *Assessments in Forensic Practice: A Handbook.* Chichester: Wiley.

Broxholme, S.L. and Lindsay, W.R. (2003) Development and Preliminary Evaluation of a Questionnaire on Cognitions Related to Sex Offending for Use with Individuals Who Have Mild Intellectual Disabilities. *Journal of Intellectual Disability Research,* 47(6), 472–82.

Chadwick, P. (2006) *Person-Centred Cognitive Therapy for Distressing Psychosis.* Chichester: John Wiley.

Craig, L.A., Browne, K.D. and Beech, A.R. (eds) (2008) *Assessing Risk in Sex Offenders: A Practitioner's Guide.* Chichester: John Wiley.

Craig, L., Lindsay, W. and Browne, K. (eds) (2010) *Assessment and Treatment of Sexual Offenders with Intellectual Disabilities: A Handbook.* Chichester: Wiley.

Davidson, K. (2008) *Cognitive Therapy for Personality Disorders: A Guide for Practitioners.* London: Routledge.

DH (2003) *Confidentiality.* NHS Code of Practice. Leeds: Department of Health.

DH (2008) *Refocusing the Care Programme Approach: Police and Positive Practice Guidance.* London: Department of Health.

Doyle, M. and Dolan, M. (2008) Understanding and Managing Risk. In K. Soothill, P. Rogers and M. Dolan (eds) *Handbook of Forensic Mental Health.* Cullompton: Willan, pp. 244–66.

Eastman, N., Riordan, D. and Adshead, G. (2010) Ethical Roles, Relationships, and Duties of Forensic Mental Health Clinicians. In A. Bartlett and G. McGauley (eds) *Forensic Mental Health: Concepts, Systems and Practice.* Oxford: Oxford University Press, pp. 313–21.

Eells, T.D. and Lombart, K.G. (2011) Theoretical and Evidence-Based Approaches to Case Formulation. In P. Sturmey and M. McMurran (eds) *Forensic Case Formulation.* Chichester: Wiley, pp. 3–32.

Fennell, P. (2008a) Mental Health Law and Risk Management. In K. Soothill, P. Rogers and M. Dolan (eds) *Handbook of Forensic Mental Health,* Cullompton: Willan, pp. 267–90.

Fennell, P. (2008b) The Law Relating to Mentally Disordered Persons in the Criminal Justice System. In K. Soothill, P. Rogers and M. Dolan (eds) *Handbook of Forensic Mental Health,* Cullompton: Willan, pp. 291–327.

First, M.B., Spitzer, R.L., Gibbon, M. and Williams, J.B.W. (1996) *Structured Clinical Interview for DSM-IV Axis I Disorders, Clinician Version (SCID-CV).* Washington, DC: American Psychiatric Press.

Goodman, R., Meltzer, H. and Bailey, V. (1998) The Strengths and Difficulties Questionnaire: A Pilot Study on the Validity of the Self-Report Version. *European Child and Adolescent Psychiatry,* 7, 125–30.

Gudjonsson, G. (2000) Psychometric Testing. In C.R. Hollin (ed.) *Handbook of Offender Assessment and Treatment.* Chichester: Wiley.

Hanson, R.K. and Thornton, D. (2000) Improving Risk Assessment for Sex Offenders: A Comparison of Three Actuarial Scales. *Law and Human Behavior,* 24(1), 119–36.

Hare, R.D. (2003) *Manual for the Revised Psychopathy Checklist*, 2nd edn. Toronto, ON: Multi-Health Systems.

Hart, S.D. and Logan, C. (2011) Formulation of Violence Risk Using Evidence-Based Assessments: The Structured Professional Judgment Approach. In P. Sturmey and M. McMurran (eds) *Forensic Case Formulation*. Oxford: Wiley, pp. 83–106.

Hart, S.D., Kropp, P.R., Laws, D.R., Klaver, J., Logan, C. and Watt, K.A. (2003) *The Risk for Sexual Violence Protocol (RSVP)*. Burnaby, BC, Canada: Mental Health, Law, and Policy Institute of Simon Fraser University.

Harvey, J. (2011) *Young Prisoners and Their Mental Health: Reflections on Providing Therapy. Special Edition: Young People in Custody*, 26–31, HMP Leyhill: Crown Copyright.

Harvey, J. and Smedley, K. (eds) (2010) *Psychological Therapy in Prisons and Other Secure Settings*. Abingdon: Willan.

Henggeler, S.W., Schoenwald, S.K., Borduin, C.M., Rowland, M.D. and Cunningham, P.B. (2009) *Multisystemic Therapy for Antisocial Behavior in Children and Adolescents*, 2nd edn. New York: Guilford Press.

Hieburn, K. (1992) The Role of Psychological Testing in Forensic Settings. *Law and Human Behavior*, 16, 257–72.

HM Government (2008) *Information Sharing: Guidance for Practitioners and Managers*. Nottingham: Department of Children, Schools and Families Publications.

Hoare, T. and Wilson, J. (2010) *Directory of Services for High Risk Young People*. London: Centre for Mental Health.

Jaydeokar, S. and Barnes, J. (2010) Criminal Justice System. In E. Chaplin, J. Henry and S. Hardy (eds) *Working with People with Learning Disabilities and Offending Behaviour*. Brighton: Pavilion, pp. 41–8.

Judge, J., Harty, M. and Fahy, T. (2004) Survey of Community Forensic Psychiatry Services in England and Wales. *Journal of Forensic Psychiatry and Psychology*, 15, 244–53.

Kemshall, H. and Wilkinson, B. (eds) (2011) *Good Practice in Assessing Risk: Current Knowledge, Issues and Approaches*. London: Jessica Kingsley Publishers.

Khan, L. and Wilson, J. (2010) *You Just Get On and Do It. Healthcare Provision in Youth Offending Teams*. London: Centre for Mental Health.

Millon, T., Millon, C., Davis, R. and Grossman, S. (2009) *MCMI-III Manual*, 4th edn. Minneapolis, MN: Pearson Education.

Mohan, R., Slade, M. and Fahy, T.A. (2004) Clinical Characteristics of Community Forensic Mental Health Services. *Psychiatric Services*, 55, 1294–8.

Morgan, S. (2000) *Clinical Risk Management: A Clinical Tool and Practitioner Manual*. London: Sainsbury Centre for Mental Health.

Price-Embury, S. (2005) *Resiliency Scales for Children and Adolescents*. San Antonio, TX: Harcourt Assessments.

Print, B., Griffin, H., Beech, A.R., Quayle, J., Bradshaw, H., et al. (2007) *AIM2: An Initial Assessment Model for Young People Who Display Sexually Harmful Behaviour*. Manchester: AIM Project.

Robertson, D. and Barnes. J. (2010) Mental Health Act (2007). In E. Chaplin, J. Henry and S. Hardy (eds) *Working with People with Learning Disabilities and Offending Behaviour*. Brighton: Pavilion, pp. 49–57.

Singleton, N., Meltzer, H. and Gatward, R. (1998) *Psychiatric Morbidity among Prisoners in England and Wales*. London: The Stationery Office.

Smedley, K. (2010) Cognitive Behaviour Therapy with Adolescents in Secure Settings. In J. Harvey and K. Smedley (eds) *Psychological Therapy in Prisons and Other Secure Settings*. Abingdon: Willan, pp. 71–101.

Social Exclusion Unit (2002) *Reducing Re-Offending by Ex-Prisoners*. London: Social Exclusion Unit.

Sturmey, P. and McMurran, M. (2011) Forensic Case Formulation: Emerging Issues. In P. Sturmey and M. McMurran (eds) *Forensic Case Formulation*. Chichester: Wiley, pp 283–304.

Thomson. L. (2008) The Forensic Mental Health System in the United Kingdom. In K. Soothill, P. Rogers and M. Dolan (eds) *Handbook of Forensic Mental Health*. Cullompton: Willan, pp. 19–63.

Thornton, D. (2002) Constructing and Testing a Framework for Dynamic Risk Assessment. *Sexual Abuse: A Journal of Research and Treatment*, 14, 139–53.

Towl, G. (2010) Ethical Issues in Forensic Psychological Policy and Practice. In G. Towl and D. Crighton (eds) *Forensic Psychology*. Oxford: BPS-Blackwell.

Ubrina, S. (2004) *Essentials of Psychometric Testing*. Chichester: Wiley.

Vess, J. and Ward, T. (2011) Sexual Offenses against Children. In P. Sturmey and M. McMurran (eds) *Forensic Case Formulation*. Chichester: Wiley, pp 175–94.

Ward, T., Mann, R.E. and Gammon, T.A. (2007) The Good Lives Model of Offender Rehabilitation: Clinical Implications. *Aggression and Violent Behavior*, 12, 87–107.

Webster, C.D., Douglas, K.S., Eaves, D. and Hart, S.D. (1997) *HCR-20: Assessing Risk for Violence (version 2)*. Burnaby, BC, Canada: Mental Health, Law, and Policy Institute of Simon Fraser University.

Williams, C., Firn, M., Wharne, S. and MacPherson, R. (eds) (2011) *Assertive Outreach in Mental Healthcare: Current Perspectives*. Chichester: Wiley-Blackwell.

Williamson, M. (2006) *Improving the Health and Social Outcomes of People Recently Released from Prisons in the UK. A Perspective from Primary Care*. London: Sainsbury Centre for Mental Health.

Young, S., Kopelman, M. and Gudjonsson, G. (eds) (2009) *Forensic Neuropsychology in Practice: A Guide to Assessment and Legal Processes*. Oxford: Oxford University Press.

3

DILEMMAS AND ETHICAL DECISION-MAKING

Reflective practice in community settings

Gerard Drennan, Sara Casado and Louise Minchin

Alice: This is impossible.
The Mad Hatter: Only if you believe it is.

Lewis Carroll, Alice in Wonderland

Experience without theory is blind,
but theory without experience is mere intellectual play.

Immanuel Kant

It is often said that community practice is the most risky of all forms of forensic mental health practice. The offender patient is at large in the community and there is not the security of a locked door and a perimeter fence when the practitioner goes home at night. And yet community forensic mental health teams are typically small and sparsely resourced. Many in-patient forensic mental health services have no or little community arm to their service and, when they do, practitioners cover large geographical areas or have substantial caseloads of high risk individuals, not as large numerically as Assertive Out-reach Teams, but the risk profile of the client group typically necessitates close statutory supervision and monitoring. Community teams are frequently made up of the minimum staffing required to provide statutory supervision of patients conditionally discharged from criminal and civil sections of the Mental Health Act (MHA). Child and adolescent services working with young people with offending histories often do not have dedicated specialist forensic staff. Community forensic services, where they exist, are often comprised of Consultant Forensic Psychiatrists and Forensic Social Work Practitioners (FSWP), backed up by Forensic Community Psychiatric Nurses (or FCPNs). Admittedly, only the most experienced Social Workers and Community Psychiatric Nurses are appointed to these roles; however, they often work without the wider multidisciplinary support of occupational therapists and chartered psychologists, or any other roles that go towards an enriched in-patient provision, such as arts therapists, technical instructors and social therapists. Some forensic services offer 'assessment only' as a means of managing complexity. Exemplary services, such as the Forensic Intensive Psychological Treatment Service (FIPTS; part of the South London and Maudsley NHS Foundation Trust) are the exceptions that prove the rule; risk management can occur in a psychosocial treatment vacuum.

However, it is imperative that the challenges of community forensic practice are tackled. In an age of austerity and payment by results (PbR), the so-called 'down-sizing' of high, medium and low secure in-patient services, 'accelerated pathways' and 'reduced length of stay', it is of critical importance that community forensic work is better understood. And yet it is all too often the disavowed stepchild of in-patient services. Commissioners do not commission. The Quality, Innovation, Productivity and Prevention (QIPP) Programme, a large-scale transformational programme for the National Health Service (NHS) (http://www.dh.gov.uk/health/category/policy-areas/nhs/quality/qipp/), has not targeted a single quality improvement directly implemented in community settings. Commissioning for Quality and Innovation (CQUIN), a system introduced in 2009 to make a proportion of healthcare providers' income conditional on demonstrating improvements in quality and innovation in specified areas of care, have not required a community-specific innovation in forensic services, and yet in 2012/13 a key national CQUIN was reduction of length of stay in in-patient services. Some community services are made up of unfunded posts, established on the monies borrowed from in-patient services. The currency of mental health services has been 'beds' and, while this is changing in mainstream mental health services, the clinical and risk profile of offender patients and public perception weigh heavily in favour of detention in conditions of security. The Royal College of Psychiatrists' Forensic Quality Network's recently published Standards for Community Forensic Mental Health Services (Kenney-Herbert et al., 2013) is to be welcomed.

It is hardly surprising that this set of circumstances throws up a whole range of dilemmas for the community-based practitioner. Risky clients bring with them hazards to their professional workers. In this chapter we will set out a number of dilemmas encountered in our work in community forensic mental health teams. To orient the reader we provide an overview of the literature on ethics in mental health practice and include a brief overview of the checklist guidance to ethical decision-making while remaining grounded in the cut and thrust of everyday practice. Before considering a selection of dilemmas we describe the growing importance of reflective practice forums to good governance in forensic practice. The selection of dilemmas and ethical challenges we describe here are those encountered in our experiences of facilitating peer reflective practice sessions in forensic community mental health teams. The first issue we illustrate is that of simply recognising practical challenges as ethical dilemmas. We go on to consider the issues involved in balancing risk management imperatives with promoting recovery in clients. This manifests itself in a range of ways depending on the progress of the client on a recovery pathway and leads on to considering dilemmas underlying questions of thresholds to access services. Issues of disclosure are ubiquitous and considered next. Finally, we conclude with a set of dilemmas encountered as reflective practice facilitators that are in some ways oblique to direct client work but which nevertheless hold many pitfalls for the unwary practitioner.

Conceptual tools for ethical decision-making: the place of theory in practice

The theoretical literature on ethics stretches back at least as far as the philosophers of Ancient Greece and there have been a great many contributions to that body of thinking through the ages. It is beyond the scope of this chapter to review that history of thought and there are many excellent overviews available to the reader who wants to deepen their understanding of the development of moral and ethical philosophical theory (see Barker & Baldwin, 1991; Barker, 2011; LaFollette, 2000). At least one reason for not embarking on a detailed review of the literature is that it very quickly becomes an intellectually highly challenging discussion. Even accessible texts such as Barker's (2011) require the reader to tackle technical terms and philosophical jargon.

However, the cornerstone text for any discussion of ethics in health care is Beauchamp and Childress (2001). The principles that they set out have been developed in an equally magisterial text specifically for use in psychiatric practice by Bloch et al. (1999), in which Gutheil sets out issues for forensic psychiatry and Szmukler sets out ethical issues for community practice. We highlight both because texts that address ethical issues for forensic practice typically focus on the interface with the legal system or in-patient treatment. However, it is the issues for general mental health practice in the community that interface most with community forensic practice, with a number of additional twists and turns due to the nature of the client group. (See box on facing page.)

Professional ethics are the standards governing the conduct of members of a profession (Grounds et al., 2010). And of course each of the professions involved in forensic practice in the community – nursing, social work, psychiatry, probation, psychology and so forth – will have its own professional ethical code. These codes are broadly similar, and likely to be founded on similar principles. Where there are minor differences they are unlikely to resolve ethical questions or dilemmas. Almost by definition, there are rarely situations that constitute an ethical dilemma where the question of how to act is governed by a single imperative. Grounds et al. (2010) make the case for the simplicity and intellectual weight of the American Academy of Psychiatry and the Law (AAPL) Guidelines for the Practice of Forensic Psychiatry and explore how relatively easily they could be adapted for use in the UK. Part of the appeal of the guidelines is their brevity: 650 words under six headings: Preamble; Confidentiality; Consent; Honesty and Striving for Objectivity; Qualifications; and Procedures for Handling Complaints of Unethical Conduct. However, for the forensic practitioner brevity may not be a virtue in an ethical

Beauchamp & Childress (2001) named the principles that provide a framework:

Autonomy: respect for the decision-making capacity of autonomous people
Non-maleficence: to avoid causing harm
Beneficence: providing benefits and balancing benefits against risks
Justice: fairness in how benefits and risks are weighed.

Beauchamp & Childress (2001) augmented these principles with four rules:

Veracity: be truthful and honest
Privacy: respect for the individual's right to keep information about them private
Confidentiality: ensure all records of a person's circumstances are managed consistently with the rule of privacy
Fidelity: strive to maintain a duty of care to the individual under all circumstances.

guideline as the interpretation of pithy statements in a particular set of complex circumstances may be exactly what is bewildering.

There are gaps in everyday practice between ethical codes and what would constitute ethical behaviour. In philosophical terms: there is no 'categorical imperative' or 'should' in an 'ought'. This highlights what Knapp and VandeCreek point out when they wrote that 'Ethical codes are incomplete moral codes' (Knapp & VandeCreek, 2003, p. 7, quoted in Bush et al., 2006). Ethical codes in professional practice set down a minimum set of parameters within which a practitioner should operate, but they do not provide a moral foundation for action. One way of looking at this is that ethical codes provide a moral compass but not the actual route across rough terrain. And yet, in practice, ethical conduct is also moral conduct or, as Gwen Adshead (2010) described it: 'ethics in health care is putting morality into practice' (p. 293). Other writers, such as Bush et al. (2006), have encouraged the adoption of a 'positive ethics', which implies not only a focus on best defensive practice within the narrow purview of an ethical code, but rather a practice that is pervasively values-based. Thus, ethical reasoning inevitably involves reference to values, professional and personal. The rise of values-based practice and the link between this frame of reference and the recovery paradigm (MacDuff et al., 2010; Walker & Langdon, 2012) provide further support for the development of our ethical sensibility in the field of practice. However, Pouncey and Lukens (2010) have highlighted the need for the gap between mainstream mental health recovery practice and forensic contexts to have far greater articulation. Writing from the field of bioethics they outline the need for a programme of work to consider the implications of recovery values, such as self-determination, accountability and moral agency in forensic settings where culpability and stakeholder rights are also at issue.

The phrase 'ethical dilemma' will be one that is nevertheless easily recognisable – so much so that the terms can be seen as an almost indivisible entity. However, when confronted with a situation, or a set of circumstances, in which the practitioner is uncertain about what to do, and hence 'in a dilemma', it does not follow that this will be seen as having ethical implications. This requires the practitioner to be 'ethically vigilant' to the 'subtle conflicts encountered in practice' (Barker, 2011, p. 7). All too often, practitioners will be separated from a recognition that ethics and ethical questions could be relevant to the everyday clinical decision-making questions they face. As Barker (2011) argues, 'the sheer complexity of much ethical terminology often obscures the ethical decision-making that goes on in everyday life' (p. 5). In other words, practitioners can be forgiven for not keeping an eye on 'the theoretical high ground' when trying to get by in 'the swamp of action' (Rhodes, 1991). Barker (2011) addresses this issue well, from two points of view. The point about philosophical language and concepts and their accessibility, of course, but also just as importantly for our focus here, he highlights that the 'big' ethical questions can obscure the dilemmas of everyday life:

> Ethics are an everyday concept. Ethics are not, or should not, be some form of navel-gazing, or observation of the care setting from a remote vantage point. Raising questions about 'ethical issues' can, too often, be interpreted negatively as 'trouble-making'. In many situations the 'trouble' already exists, in the form of inadequate or inappropriate service. The emphasis of traditional ethical debates upon 'major' issues, such as abortion, euthanasia and sterilisation, may have misled many workers into thinking that ethics are not the stuff of everyday life. For mental health workers ethics should underpin each and every action: no issue, however small, should be considered 'beneath' the ethical debate.
>
> (Barker & Baldwin, 1991, quoted in Barker, 2011)

Other professions outside medical, psychological and criminal justice practice can struggle with similar issues. In the setting of anthropological fieldwork and ethics, Cassell and Jacobs (2006) wrote that:

> We do not wish to make ethics seem merely a matter of isolated choices in crucial situations. Much of our lives proceeds undramatically, and often our decisions are almost imperceptible, so that only with hindsight are we aware that our course of action had consequences that we had not foreseen and now regret. To improve the ethical adequacy of anthropological practice, we must consider not only exceptional cases but everyday decisions, and reflect not only upon the conduct of others but also upon our own actions.
>
> (Cassell & Jacobs, 2006, p. 1)

Approaches to dilemmas – problem-solving toolkits

There are a number of decision-making guides available in the literature on professional dilemmas in psychological practice and we will summarise them briefly here. What each has in common as a starting point is the identification of the problem or dilemma. What follows are thought processes that are usefully summarised as 'What are the useful questions to ask?'

Corey et al. (1993, in Scaife, 2001) suggest the following approach: identify the problem or dilemma; identify the potential issues involved; review the relevant ethical guidelines; discuss and consult with colleagues; consider possible and probable courses of action; list the possible consequences of each decision; decide what appears to be the best course of action. In such a formal process we would add the advice to document the reasoning for the decision.

Morrissey (2005) proposes an ethical decision-making procedure, also starting with problem identification. Morrissey expands on this with a set of questions including: Is this an ethical problem? What are the relevant facts, what is not relevant? What else do we need to know? To whom are we obligated? What resources are available to us? Morrissey goes on to recommend consultation with peers and supervisors to determine what ethical principles are relevant; to then determine 'ethical trap' possibilities; and frame a preliminary response while considering consequences. Linked to values-based practice Morrissey goes on to suggest that we ask ourselves how our values may be shaping our deliberations. Finally, prepare a resolution; get further feedback from peers or a supervisor; take action and follow up with an assessment of the outcome as this may require further refinements. It is helpful to our underlying thesis here regarding the invaluable role of reflective practice meetings that consultation with peers and supervisors receives such ringing endorsement. A further proposed model of ethical decision-making in forensic psychology is put forward by Bush et al. (2006) and follows much the same structure.

The similarities between all three procedures is striking, with only minor variations. It is not our intention to diminish these important decision-making considerations. However, in their abstraction of decision-making processes that apply across a range of settings they can appear reductionistic. It is in the everyday world of community practice that everyday conflicts of interest and duty must be resolved through pragmatic action. The development of ethical practice fit for a contemporary world might be assisted by academics and ethics experts 'but the key responsibility for shaping ethical practice lies with the practitioners themselves' (Barker, 2011, p. 46).

Team-based reflective practice

Kettles et al. (2002) highlight the need for supervision to support staff in the face of the stress of dealing with suicidal and potentially violent patients. Increasingly, perhaps with the pressure on resources, services have turned to team, case-based supervision, or what is commonly referred to as Reflective Practice (RP). Elsewhere such forums are referred to as 'work discussion groups' (Rubitel & Reiss, 2011). In mental health services generally, and forensic settings no less, there appears to have been a shift over time away from staff support groups to case-based team reflection as the modality of maintaining standards of practice and team development. This perhaps reflects shifts in the organisational ethos of forensic mental health work, but team-based reflective practice has grown in recognition as a key component of the matrix of professional support that maintains standards of professional practice. The Royal College of Psychiatrists' Quality Network Standards for Medium Secure Services and the more recently published Standards for Low Secure Services require that 'There are regular forums for all staff to reflect on their experience of the work', that 'regular staff support group, ideally weekly' takes place in in-patient settings, and that 'Frontline staff have regular supervision totaling at least one hour per week and are able to contact a senior colleague as necessary' (Tucker & Hughes, 2007; Tucker et al., 2012). The new Standards for Community Forensic Mental Health Services (Kenney-Herbert et al., 2013) seem less specific on the place of reflective practice, but refer to the need for 'regular multi-disciplinary team meetings for clinical formulation, risk analysis and decision-making' (B3.13) and all staff receiving regular supervision (B3.14).

A recently produced guide to delivering evidence-based forensic mental health services in Scotland identified 'formal opportunities for reflective practice for all frontline clinical staff' as one of the key developmental questions for services (Forensic Mental Health Matrix Working Group, 2011). Webber and Nathan (2010) highlight the role of reflective practice for the social work practitioner and texts on nursing, psychology and occupational therapy highlight similar priorities (Scaife, 2001; Tribe & Morrissey, 2005). In fact RP, as a mode of learning that is applicable across a huge sweep of professional settings, has burgeoned in recent years (Ghaye, 2010). While source texts such as Ghaye's outline tasks, competencies and goals for generic RP, there is little specific guidance on the skills, tasks and outcomes expected of RP in forensic practice. However, Vaughan and Badger (1995), writing before the term reflective practice became popular, highlight the role of small group supervision in shaping values and attitudes in practitioners who work with mentally disordered offenders in the community. We will set out below the potential value of RP in supporting forensic practitioners in the community to consider dilemmas and ethical conflicts, to evidence their reasoning processes in forming a judgement with a 'jury of their peers' and, in the process, to learn ethical reasoning skills.

All three authors are psychologists who work in part or wholly in community forensic mental health teams. Our roles include facilitating weekly team RP with the multidisciplinary teams that cover two large areas in the South of England. The RP meetings tend to follow referral and case management meetings. This is helpful because it creates a space for reflection and discussion following the team business meeting when clinical issues may be touched on but where there is insufficient time to allow for expansive discussion of them. Cases to be discussed are not decided in advance of the meeting. Team members can choose to bring a case for advice or to bring a dilemma, a complex assessment or a troubling development that makes a case 'hot'. Occasionally, when service pressures affect functioning, team and organisational dynamics that are not case-specific are addressed in the interests of restoring the team to equilibrium. Our working model of RP is that it should draw on theoretical models, but not be theory-driven. Its purpose is to achieve pragmatic ends, a reasoned, informed and defensible course of action, although in some cases the course may be 'inaction', but for very good reasons. It can thus be a translation of theory, as a sense-making exercise, into a footing for action. Ethical reasoning will always involve a process of reflection. There are facts that can contribute to the process of reasoning but ultimately decisions will be evaluative. RP therefore lends itself to being a tool to enable ethical practice, and so it is to a selection of dilemmas encountered in practice that we now turn.

Key theme: recognising practical challenges as ethical dilemmas

Decisions with great ethical implications are taken on an almost daily basis in forensic psychiatry, and so Adshead (2010) argues that ethical dilemmas and ethical reasoning are part and parcel of daily clinical work, 'the bread-and-butter of clinical practice' (p. 296). Reflective practice meetings are places in which these everyday clinical issues are considered. Of course, diagnostic and assessment questions arise and technical issues over practice too. However, when there are questions about what to do, in other words questions of action, there are inevitably questions of ethical import too. A key issue that has emerged in the course of our experience of RP meetings is the difficulty there can sometimes be in the members recognising when we are faced with a dilemma or an ethical decision. The dilemmas are typically not new as challenges of practice are invariably cyclical, however, they can appear novel. Dilemmas occur when there is a conflict over which outcome or course of action should be prioritised when the options are mutually exclusive and both potentially undesirable; in other words, both carry risks of adverse outcomes and positive outcomes. It is often less obvious that the conflict is underpinned by a clash of principles. All too often the tension is between a duty of care to a patient and a duty of care towards a member of the public, or simply a possible future victim. Risk assessment and management planning in the context of these dilemmas is a form of evaluative reasoning with ethical implications.

Exploring these dilemmas as ones that raise ethical questions can be a useful vehicle for teaching ethical awareness and maintaining ethical standards over time. Over time there have been many debates about the ideal way in which to teach ethical practice, with arguments as to how extensive or intensive teaching in ethics should be, how theoretically informed or how practice-based (Michels & Kelly, 1999; Morrissey, 2005). Current arguments reject the classroom as the place in which to learn about ethics in favour of the clinical setting, and an 'immersive' experience (Mokwunye et al., 2012; Spike, 2012). The 'trouble-case method' (Kaufert et al., 1984; Kaufert & Putsch, 1997) is employed in teaching across a range of disciplines, and can be turned to good effect in promoting ethical reasoning skills and supporting clinical teams to evidence the quality of their decision-making processes.

VIGNETTE 1: MATTHEW

Matthew is a man in his twenties with no previous convictions. He is referred to the forensic community team by a general psychiatrist because while being treated for anxiety, depression and personality problems he discloses that he fantasises about abducting and killing a stranger female. He reports that he has engaged in practice behaviours, such as following young women, but there is no objective evidence to corroborate his account. This raises ethical questions for the clinical team. Should time and resources be directed towards a preventative intervention when the client does not appear to meet the offence threshold or the diagnostic threshold for accessing the service? Will a contemporary, resources-led decision appear negligent to any future victim if the fantasies are enacted? Will the high likelihood of a false positive assessment of high risk result in a dis-service to the client? It was helpful to the team to consider not only the practical questions of resource allocation, but also the ethical dimensions of the situation. It was helpful to pose questions as to the value-base of each course of action, not only the resource-base, and to consider ethical obligations to stakeholders outside of the immediate concerns of the team.

Key theme: risk management or promoting recovery?

In our experience community forensic teams deal with two types of patients: treated and untreated. The 'treated' patient is typically recently discharged from a secure in-patient setting where questions of risk and intervention were dealt with within the containment of a perimeter fence and 24-hour nursing. The clinical and supervisory tasks with the treated patient are in the domains of consolidating treatment gains in a new environment with new psychosocial challenges (not to be underestimated), establishing the person in supported or independent living, supporting the person to navigate potential flashpoints for relapse (alcohol use, illicit drugs, exposure to high risk groups, associates, and interpersonal stress), maintain medication adherence and, ultimately, compliance with conditions of discharge. To this can be added support to access community resources, supported employment, education, training and other forms of meaningful activity. In theory, this is how it would work. In this respect the 'treated' patient has made considerable progress on a recovery journey, having addressed clinical recovery and offender recovery (Drennan & Alred, 2012) tasks in an in-patient setting. It would appear that the task of the community practitioners is to deepen social reintegration in the community. The realities are occasionally dramatically different as we will see below, but for now this serves to contrast with the 'untreated' patient.

The 'untreated' patient is the new referral from community-based services, such as probation, Youth Offending Service, police, other mental health services and primary care. They may also be referred from custodial settings, such as prisons or Young Offender Institutions or following brief admissions to secure facilities. The vignette of Matthew (Vignette 1) and that of Peter (Vignette 5) illustrate situations where their clinical needs as patients may be outside the model of service delivery and may exceed the resources available, requiring a multi-modal treatment to address offending behaviour and personality functioning difficulties. There is a risk that treatment may result in destabilisation and this may elevate their risk. In the assessment of suitability for the treatment of mental health difficulties, and particularly where there is a risk of suicide, there has been some consideration of the principles for non-intervention with psychological therapies (Frances & Clarkin, 1981). It is far less clear what evidence-based practice should be when it comes to assessing the risk of decompensation in individuals who are prone to violence, and hence almost by definition are psychologically fragile. The degree of risk already posed would need to support a judgement that, on balance, the risks of not intervening exceed the risks associated with offering an intervention and attempting to reduce the risks posed. In the absence of clear practice guidance, this is an ethical decision that will depend upon the particulars of each case.

In cases where the risk is of suicide, the risk to the clinician is reputational, emotional, professional and more besides. However, in cases where the risk is of physical violence towards the person, the risk to the professional is also that they may get caught up in being a target of such violence. In cases where there is a risk that the client may develop a paranoid or other form of pathological attachment towards the professional worker, the ethical responsibility of supervisors and team members is also towards the worker. It is not uncommon for questions regarding the safety of workers to be posed in forensic community teams as they are often the referral of last resort where mental health service users have formed risky attachments to previous workers. For example, counselling and psychotherapy patients who have engaged in stalking behaviour with previous therapists are more likely to be referred to the forensic community team for intervention. This presents a whole series of judgement calls that need to be made in relation to ongoing mental health intervention. Ways of working that can reduce the risk to the forensic practitioner such as co-working the case, attending to the gender of the worker or introducing additional checking-in and monitoring procedures may need to be devised.

VIGNETTE 2: SALLY

Sally is a woman in her thirties. She has been referred by a community mental health team with a history of forming inappropriate attachments to female workers and an ongoing very high level of psychological distress. Sally was severely abused as an adolescent and has significant trauma with dissociative states as a result. She engages in high levels of deliberate self-harm through cutting and other high risk behaviours associated with suicidality. She has a very caring and involved family who firmly assert her entitlement to treatment. Sally has tried to work with male therapists but becomes too anxious and fearful, and disengages. She has been assessed as too high risk for voluntary in-patient treatment but is not detainable under the MHA (2007). The question is: can she be offered psychological treatment by a female therapist from within the forensic team and are the risks that this would expose the therapist to amenable to adequate risk management to render the intervention ethically defensible? This required a set of practical safeguards to be put in place in order to address the ethical issues identified.

Occasionally, the ethics of an intervention are linked to resources in other ways. Very few community teams have the resources to offer systemic interventions, where it is not only the identified client who is the possible subject of an intervention, but also other significant persons who have a relationship with them (e.g. children, parents, spouses). The context of forensic mental health work can profoundly affect the issues that arise in relation to questions of systemic intervention. When a client's mental health is destabilised by factors in their relationships, it may require the 'system' around the client to be subject to an intervention. However, when, for example, intimate relationships, in other words not simply peer group pressures, may increase the potential for reoffending, this could point towards the need for a systemic intervention to address the offending behaviour risk of 'the system'. Significant ethical dilemmas may arise when a partner is possibly implicated in the offending behaviour but has not been identified as the 'index offender/patient'.

VIGNETTE 3: ADRIAN

Adrian is referred for psychological intervention to address problems associated with manic-depressive illness and online paedophile pornography offences. Adrian is in a civil partnership with a man who is not convicted for any similar offences, but Adrian's partner works for an IT company and his sophistication in the use of software and computer hardware far exceeds Adrian's. Adrian is subject to a period of probation supervision under licence and has expressed a willingness to engage in treatment for his emotional and psychological difficulties. He is not willing to include his partner in such an intervention. The effectiveness of the treatment intervention will be limited if it is not possible to also include his partner in the work as their relationship is a key driver in maintaining the psychological difficulties and the resulting offending. How should the team proceed?

Let us now return to the 'treated' patient on discharge from secure care. Unfortunately, it is a somewhat idealised picture to imagine that patients discharged from secure in-patient care have been adequately treated. With the pressures on services to reduce the numbers of 'bed days' occupied by a patient and specified commissioner targets to reduce length of stay, more patients are likely to be discharged into community settings who are 'partially treated'. These patients are likely to need more than the 'maintenance' interventions typically available in favour of needing ongoing, and even deepening, therapeutic work in the community. Some of these dilemmas of treatment arise when the 'clinical recovery' achieved as an in-patient is adequate to win a conditional discharge at a Mental Health Tribunal, but where their 'offender recovery' (Drennan & Alred, 2012) has not been sufficiently addressed. However, staffing models and staffing numbers may affect the safety of such an intervention, and community accommodation may not be ideal, with minimal after-hours support available. Challenging psychological interventions may risk destabilisation and recall to in-patient care. The patient and their legal representatives may not wish to provide consent to an intervention that carries such risks. This highlights that ethical dilemmas can frequently be a fundamental part of the community practitioner's clinical decision-making.

VIGNETTE 4: BARRY

Barry was detained in a high secure hospital for more than five years following conviction for manslaughter with diminished responsibility of a young woman. Barry underwent a number of group-based interventions to address offending behaviour needs but had relatively little individual treatment. A diagnosis of paranoid schizophrenia and anti-social personality disorder had been made and Barry was reasonably stable on a regime of anti-psychotic medication. However, on psychological assessment to inform risk management, it became clear that Barry's mental stability was fragile. Over the course of longer interviews he became more disorganised in his thinking and there was evidence of underlying animosity towards women with delusional intensity of feelings of entitlement to emotional and physical intimacy. It became evident on assessment that Barry's mental health stability prior to being granted a conditional discharge was based on a model of recovery that prioritised 'sealing over' of psychotic tendencies. This resulted in a seemingly stable but fragile equilibrium, which may yet prove to be inadequate, but where attempts to deepen Barry's insight and challenge his beliefs brought with them the risk of destabilisation too. There is the risk associated with the potential 'harm' to Barry should he decompensate in treatment and require readmission. There are the risks to possible victims should Barry act out in treatment. The ethical dilemmas seem to constellate around whether striving for more thorough-going recovery may appear to be a costly hubris on the part of the treating team should there be any number of adverse outcomes.

We have illustrated that there are a range of dilemmas and ethical questions that arise when community practice requires teams to balance risk management and the recovery needs of clients substantially 'treated', 'partially treated' or, for all intents and purposes, 'untreated' previously. In other words, what is 'good enough' recovery when managing the risk of offenders in community settings? It is possible that these difficulties are simply a version of the ethical challenges faced for many years by probation colleagues, with the imperative they have always had to find a balance between punishment and rehabilitation (Robinson & Crow, 2009; Silverman, 1993). However, Drennan and Alred (2012) have argued that the new recovery paradigm when applied to offender mental health requires additional thought and elaboration in order to spell out the implications for a new generation of professional workers and service clients. While writers such as Buchanan-Barker (2011) and Slade (2009) have begun to consider 'the ethics of recovery' in relation to non-offender recovery, it may be the case that an 'ethics of offender recovery' is also in need of articulation to assist community forensic practitioners in the dilemmas and challenges they face. Pouncey and Lukens (2010) make a similar argument in favour of multidisciplinary collaboration to develop deeper understanding of the ethical implications of recovery principles in forensic populations and settings. This is a complex and multifaceted task, ethics being only one aspect, and beyond the scope of this chapter.

Key theme: to accept or not to accept on to a caseload?

Another form of the 'untreated' patient is the client who is referred with offending behaviour, no evidence of mental illness, but with some degree of personality disorder or sexual offending. These clients are likely to be referred by Multi-Agency Public Protection Arrangement (MAPPA) agencies due to a presentation of high risk behaviours that appear to be in the context of some degree of emotional disturbance. This is the person about whom the question is often asked: mad or bad? Our argument is that they are neither. They are typically distressed or disturbed individuals who externalise their psychological conflicts through acting out on those around them, and to neglect their needs risks taking an unethical stance. The counter-argument is that by accepting such people on to a forensic mental health service caseload we would be guilty of the 'medicalisation of criminal behaviour'. This is also an ethical argument. It may be the case that our society and the individual are not well served when essentially medical services expend valuable resources on their rehabilitation when criminal justice agencies are better placed to address their needs and provide sanctions when the person's behaviour is criminal. Our position is that the dichotomy of medical/criminal is no longer tenable and that society invites us to consider such individuals in terms of the degree of their psychological disturbance. The arguments that previously excluded individuals with personality disorder are no longer accepted when the level of psychological and behaviour disturbance reaches diagnostic thresholds, the individual asks for help and there is an identifiable link between the offending behaviour and the psychological disturbance. It is increasingly difficult to argue that probation and police colleagues should manage the risk posed by personality disordered offenders under MAPPA when the risk management plan requires that the individual's psychosocial and mental health treatment needs are also attended to (Yakeley & Taylor, 2011). Nevertheless, in an age when resources are scarce and community forensic teams are required to transfer high risk patients with mental disorder back to supervision under generic mental health services, the use of valuable resources for men and women with personal difficulties and offending behaviour is a fraught one. The gatekeeping function described here is of course one about resources and service models, but our view is that it is also fundamentally tied to ethical decision–making processes.

VIGNETTE 5: PETER

Peter is a 48-year-old man convicted of an assault on a teenage girl who was unknown to him in a public place. There were also convictions for assault on a number of police officers who intervened at the time. He is sentenced, placed under MAPPA Level 3 supervision, and due for release on licence. Peter has made credible threats to fire-bomb a police station previously and has been in prison for angry violence before. He has also attempted to commit suicide on a number of occasions and had treatment for depression from a generic community mental health team in the local mental health trust. During this period of detention he asks his probation officer to help him to access psychological treatment to address his anger management difficulties. Peter has no evidence of mental illness and would not otherwise be accepted on to the forensic community caseload. By asking for psychological treatment in a situation in which he could be volatile and highly challenging, does the wish for psychological intervention justify acceptance on the community forensic team caseload, with all the care coordination and medical responsibilities that follow? Will accepting such clients on to the caseload open the door to many more such referrals? What impact could this have on other parts of the service, such as in-patient services and out-of-hours services? Once again, it was important for the team to consider together the ethical dimensions alongside the resource implications of each possible course of action.

Key theme: disclosure of confidential material to and with partner agencies

It is increasingly a core task for forensic community practice to acquire knowledge, skills and experience in managing the challenges of facing two ways: to have loyalties to the codes and practices of one's parent organisation and to have obligations with regard to other criminal justice system (CJS) organisations. Serious Case Reviews often highlight the need for cross-agency information sharing and increased multi-agency forums can create a perceived, and perhaps not unrealistic, pressure to share confidential information to alleviate both organisational and personal anxieties about carrying risk responsibility. Even disclosure of risk assessments from within the organisation may be fraught with difficulty, as teams hold concerns about the sharing of risk 'intelligence' with the offender patient. Clinicians often have little or no guidance or training on how to manage greater information sharing with their clients and as such fear compromising security or the safety of colleagues.

The disclosure of confidential information regarding a service user to others is no less a highly sensitive area for community practitioners. It would not be too much of an overstatement to suggest that it is perhaps the single most talked about aspect of community work, and the pressures around disclosure are likely to increase with the rise in so-called 'co-location' (Bradley, 2009), when mental health workers are based in the same offices as other criminal justice agencies. There are many guidelines and directives in place regarding disclosure of otherwise confidential information with the development of MAPPA and the duty to cooperate (MAPPA Guidance, 2012; Yakeley & Taylor, 2011). This remains an area of community forensic practice that throws up many dilemmas and conflicts for practitioners (Dowsett & Craissati, 2008; Young et al., 2005).

Disclosure is of particular concern for service users under section 37/41 of the Mental Health Act (2007), who are often the 'core business' clients in forensic community teams. Such patients typically have long periods of external monitoring from agencies, including the Ministry of Justice (MoJ), MAPPA, Sex Offender Register (SOR) and other criminal justice agencies. The complexity often lies within the challenge of trying to balance risk management with patient recovery tasks, as already highlighted. The disclosure of offending behaviour and requirements for supervision for this group of individuals often involves a complex set of judgements. Some of the service users we work with may have had lengthy institutional careers. Some may have committed their 'index offence' as much as 20 years previously. Questions arise as to where such individuals should sit on a 'scale of disclosure'; in other words how much information it is still relevant and necessary to disclose to potential employers, landlords and social contacts. Likely recidivism rates and time elapsed since the index offence are clinically relevant considerations in decisions to disclose; however, other criminal justice agencies may not apply such criteria. Positive risk-taking (Morgan, 2004; Slade, 2009) is often the very area that causes anxiety and ethical dilemmas for clinicians, although crucial in progressing a patient's recovery process.

In mental health settings, various recovery initiatives currently promote increased service user involvement in their own risk assessments and management plans (Ayub et al., 2013; Forensic ImROC Group, in preparation). Heilbrun (1997) notes that accountability and transparency in risk decision-making, as well as communication about dynamic risk, are more likely to enhance service user collaboration. Disclosure is best undertaken through open communication in a respectful and collaborative manner. If patients are part of the disclosure decision-making process it can be both productive and therapeutic. In fact if done collaboratively and sensitively with support and guidance the client can use the experience as an opportunity to develop skills, to challenge fears of social exclusion and stigma and hence to progress.

There are certain legal requirements of disclosure, for example to an employer, or under tenancy agreements, but disclosure outside of these areas may not need to occur and judgements have to be made. On the occasions when disclosure has to occur without the client's knowledge, for example if they do not have the capacity to consent or they are not willing to engage in the process of decision-making, clinicians need to remain mindful to promote the individual's dignity and well-being.

The obvious importance of public protection and patient safety requires disclosures of threats and perceived risk. However, disclosure can be a helpful tool in risk management as well as in therapeutic engagement. Ownership of the need for disclosure may be a way of engaging in a dialogue that supports the offender patient to take ownership of their own desistance processes (McNeill, 2006).

Multi-Agency Public Protection Arrangements (MAPPA) provide guidance on disclosure for clinicians whose patients are implicated in these public protection schemes; however complications arise when agencies have different criteria for disclosure. Criminal justice agencies may disclose more often than forensic mental health services would choose to.

VIGNETTE 6 : BILL

Bill is an 18-year-old man, with a mild learning disability, who as a minor had a contact sexual offence against a female minor at a time of considerable turmoil in his family. He was placed in residential supported accommodation until he turned 18 when he was referred to a forensic community team for anger management and care coordination. Bill lived independently, attended college and had a strong work ethic. He was managed by the local police under a Sex Offences Prevention Order (SOPO). Bill had several SOPO conditions and one in particular would be troubling for him: 'the individual must inform the police immediately if he enters into a relationship with anyone'. Bill struggled to differentiate levels of relationship, in spite of efforts to clarify it for him, and he was uncertain as to what he should report. Bill eventually understood this in terms of social networking sites as 'no sex talk' but any 'real contact' relationship with female peers remained uncertain for him. He was considered to be in Breach if he had even a platonic friendship with a female. These relationships would end due to police disclosures, often without Bill's knowledge, leading to increasing frustration and low self-esteem. Bill was also asked to leave his college following disclosure. How are the community team to maintain support for Bill's recovery needs and respect a duty to cooperate? How might have disclosure been handled more collaboratively? When there are competing ethical frameworks between different agencies, the task of working through the implications for their own ethical stance requires detailed consideration of each set of circumstances by a team.

Key theme: maintaining organisational boundaries within reflective practice

The set of dilemmas we wish to highlight here relate to the position of the RP facilitator as a member of the parent organisation. Some services contract with a consultant from outside the organisation to facilitate staff RP or versions of RP such as work discussion groups (Rubitel & Reiss, 2011). However, where the clinical expertise to facilitate RP exists within the staff team of the parent organisation, it is likely that psychologists, consultant nurses and other experienced staff will be called upon to provide RP. There are advantages and disadvantages to both models of provision and we will not rehearse these here exhaustively. Our experience has been in the model of providing RP to teams that we are also members of while being employed and managed by the parent organisation. This can involve a degree of 'positioning' in relation to the various constituencies in the organisation. This means that clinical expertise is not the only skill-set required. There is also a requirement to navigate the potential pitfalls of over-identification with one or other facet of the organisation. There are particular challenges presented when to be seen to support one position is interpreted as being in opposition to another. It will inevitably be the case that from time to time there are tensions between the expectations of management regarding ways of working and a clinical team's beliefs about how they should meet the needs of their client group. In an era where cost-savings are expected to be made, the significant reorganisation or new ways of working that this requires can generate tension between clinical teams and service managers. At another time the tensions may have a different locus; however, at the time of writing, the impact of cost-savings is a particular focus. This brings with it conflicts in teams about possible failures of duty of care towards the offender client and a potential victim when resources are allocated elsewhere. The interlinking of clinical dilemmas and resourcing issues are significantly present at the clinical coalface in ways that may not have been as prominent in previous eras, with implications for clinical practice across a range of settings (Ballatt & Campling, 2011). Berkowitz (2011), writing about her experience of facilitating a work discussion seminar as part of a training course, notes the strain imposed by the lack of reflection in students' work settings, and the considerable strain on the facilitator to sustain thinking and reflection in the group when hearing accounts of what may seem to be 'gross negligence or unethical behavior' in institutional settings (p. 213).

> Many of the problems are about inadequate supervision and management, stemming very often from supervisors and managers being overburdened themselves, or without adequate resources of personnel or staff. The consequences may be splits in the team, with the possibility of boundaries being breached, some staff full of rage and hatred for their seniors, at times feeling under threat of dismissal, and others too close and offered favours.
>
> (Berkowitz, 2011, p. 210)

Many dilemmas arise when the team members understand themselves as attachment figures for their clients (Adshead, 1998) where long-term, low intensity support maintains some degree of equilibrium in clinical stability and risk management. However, an apparently settled client is also likely to be one where there are questions about 'move on' in order to free up resources for new referrals.

A clinical team can look to the RP facilitator to take a position on discharges, care plans and new referrals that have implications outside of the meeting itself. It can be helpful to hold in mind the supervision imperative to 'do the work in the room' in order to manage pressures to act outside of the RP setting. However, if a practitioner team develops and sustains antipathy towards a management team, there can be expectations from the management team that this would be ameliorated through RP. Failure to do so can place the RP facilitator in an invidious position. This raises questions as to what level of qualification, skill-set or facilitator supervision is required to navigate these organisational dynamics. Cost pressures and their impact on staffing skill-mix can result in assistant psychologists and trainee psychologists facilitating such work groups. While this may be adequate to support teams with aspects of case work, it runs the risk that the junior member of staff will be overwhelmed when caught up in team splitting. This is itself a form of ethical dilemma for the trainee psychologist's supervisor and manager.

In the final analysis: wisdom and judgement

When confronted with a dilemma, ethical decision-making describes the process by which the advantages and disadvantages of a range of options for intervention are considered. There may seldom be judgements that are simply questions of one way being morally wrong and another morally and ethically right; but rather a range of scenarios that result from action. Each will have to have some degree of evidence as being risk assessed and that there is an adequate level of safeguards put in place, 'fail-safes', such that if a decision based on prediction proves to be incorrect, that the potential negative outcomes can be mitigated against.

Baum-Baicker and Sisti (2012) have drawn attention to the notion of clinical wisdom in mental health care, as having an important contribution to make to ethical dimensions of practice. They argue that it serves as a useful, often overlooked, tool in values-based practice. They propose that the features of clinical wisdom are pragmatic skills, such as an awareness of balance, the acceptance of paradox, and deep respect for the client in order to cultivate clinical wisdom. There will not always be an evidence-based decision available. When there are considerable pressures on our time and there may not be opportunities to consult widely, we have argued that team-based reflective practice forums can be an invaluable aid to the exercise of wisdom and good judgement. Personal experience and the capacity to think and feel with teams will often be the most important resources to hand. Decisions that are 'honest, informed, humane and thoughtful' (Adshead, 2010, p. 293) are as much as can be hoped for.

Acknowledgements

We wish to thank our colleagues in the Sussex Partnership NHS Foundation Trust community forensic outreach teams for sharing their thoughtful approaches to the dilemmas they face in their daily practice, as they have made this chapter possible. We particularly wish to thank Janet Bell and Dr Richard Noon for their helpful comments on an earlier draft of the chapter.

References

Adshead, G. (1998) Psychiatric staff as attachment figures: understanding management problems in psychiatric services in the light of attachment theory. *British Journal of Psychiatry*, 172, 64–9.

Adshead, G. (2010) Introduction to ethics. In A. Bartlett & G. McGauley (eds) *Forensic Mental Health: Concepts, Systems, and Practice* (pp. 293–4). Oxford: Oxford University Press.

Ayub, R., Callahan, I., Haque, Q. & McCann, G. (2013) Increasing patient involvement in care pathways. *Health Services Journal*, 3 June. (http://www.hsj.co.uk/home/commissioning/increasing-patient-involvement-in-care-pathways/5058959.article).

Ballatt, J. & Campling, P. (2011) *Intelligent Kindness: Reforming the Culture of Healthcare*. London: RCPsych Publications.

Barker, P. (2011) *Mental Health Ethics: The Human Context*. London: Routledge.

Barker, P. & Baldwin, S. (1991) *Ethical Issues in Mental Health*. London: Chapman and Hall.

Baum-Baicker, C. & Sisti, D.A. (2012) Clinical wisdom in psychoanalysis and psychodynamic psychotherapy: a philosophical and qualitative analysis. *Journal of Clinical Ethics*, 23(1), 13–27.

Beauchamp T.L. & Childress, J.F. (2001) *Principles of Biomedical Ethics*, 5th edn. New York: Oxford University Press.

Berkowitz, R. (2011) Work discussion group for trainees working in forensic settings. In A. Rubitel & D. Riess (eds) *Containment in the Community: Supportive Frameworks for Thinking about Antisocial Behavior and Mental Health* (pp. 203–16). London: Karnac Books.

Bloch, S., Chodoff, P. & Green, S.A. (1999) *Psychiatric Ethics*, 3rd edn. New York: Oxford University Press.

Bradley, The Rt Hon Lord (2009) *The Bradley Report: Lord Bradley's Review of People with Mental Health Problems or Learning Disabilities in the Criminal Justice System*. London: Department of Health. (http://www.rcpsych.ac.uk/pdf/Bradley%20Report11.pdf) (Accessed 6 May 2013).

Buchanan-Barker, P. (2011) Talking about recovery. In P. Barker (ed.) *Mental Health Ethics: The Human Context* (pp. 331–8). London: Routledge.

Bush, S.S., Connell, M.A. & Denney, R.L. (2006) *Ethical Practice in Forensic Psychology: A Systematic Model for Decision Making Forensic Ethics and the Expert Witness*. Washington, DC: American Psychological Association.

Cassell, J. & Jacobs, S-E. (2006) *Handbook of Ethical Issues in Anthropology* (No. 23). Washington, DC: American Anthropological Association. (http://www.aaanet.org/committees/ethics/toc.htm).

Dowsett, J. & Craissati, J. (2008) *Managing Personality Disordered Offenders in the Community: A Psychological Approach*. Hove: Routledge.

Drennan, G. & Alred, D. (2012) *Secure Recovery: Approaches to Recovery in Forensic Mental Health Settings*. London: Routledge.

Forensic ImROC Group (in preparation) Making recovery a reality in forensic settings.

Forensic Mental Health Matrix Working Group (2011) *'The Forensic Health Matrix' – A Guide to Delivering Evidence-based Psychological Therapies in Forensic Mental Health Services in Scotland.* (http://www.forensicnetwork.scot.nhs.uk/wp-content/uploads/2012/09/The-Forensic-Mental-Health-Matrix.doc) (Accessed 8 March 2013).

Frances, A. & Clarkin, J.F. (1981) No treatment as the prescription of choice. *Archives of General Psychiatry*, 38(5), 542–5.

Ghaye, T. (2010) *Teaching and Learning through Reflective Practice: A Practical Guide for Positive Action*, 2nd edn. London: Routledge.

Grounds, A., Gunn, J., Wade, C., Rosner, R. & Brusch, K.G. (2010) Editorial: Contemplating common ground in the professional ethics of forensic psychiatry. *Criminal Behaviour and Mental Health*, 20, 307–22.

Gutheil, T.G. (1999) Ethics and forensic psychiatry. In S. Bloch, P. Chodoff & S.A. Green (eds) *Psychiatric Ethics*, 3rd edn (pp. 345–62). New York: Oxford University Press.

Heilbrun, K. (1997) Prediction versus management models relevant to risk assessment: the importance of legal decision-making context. *Law and Human Behaviour*, 21, 347–59.

Kaufert, J.M. & Putsch, R.W. (1997) Communication through interpreters in health care: ethical dilemmas arising from differences in class, culture, language and power. *Journal of Clinical Ethics*, 8, 71–87.

Kaufert, J.M., Koolage, W.W., Kaufert, P.L. & O'Neil, J.O. (1984) The use of 'trouble case' examples in teaching the impact of sociocultural and political factors in clinical communication. *Medical Anthropology*, 8, 36–46.

Kenney-Herbert, J., Taylor, M., Puri, R. & Phull, J. (eds) (2013) *Standards for Community Forensic Mental Health Services.* (http://www.rcpsych.ac.uk/PDF/QNFMHS%20Standards%20for%20Community%20Forensic%20Mental%20Health%20Services%20-%20Final.pdf) (Accessed 10 June 2013).

Kettles, A.M., Woods, P. & Collins, M. (2002) *Therapeutic Interventions for Forensic Mental Health Nurses.* London: Jessica Kingsley Publishers.

LaFollette, H. (ed.) (2000) *The Blackwell Guide to Ethical Theory.* Oxford: Blackwell Publishing.

MacDuff, C., Gass, J., Laing, A., Williams, H., Coull, M., Addo, M. and McKay, R. (2010) *An Evaluation of the Impact of the Dissemination of Educational Resources to Support Values-Based and Recovery-Focussed Mental Health Practice.* Robert Gordon University, Aberdeen.

McNeill, F. (2006) A desistance paradigm for offender management. *Criminology and Criminal Justice*, 6, 39–62.

MAPPA Guidance (2012) (Version 4) Produced by the MAPPA Team National Offender Management Service Offender Management and Public Protection Group. (http://www.justice.gov.uk/downloads/offenders/mappa/mappa-guidance-2012-part1.pdf).

Michels, R. & Kelly, K. (1999) Teaching psychiatric ethics. In S. Bloch, P. Chodoff & S.A. Green (eds) *Psychiatric Ethics*, 3rd edn (pp. 495–509). New York: Oxford University Press.

Mokwunye, N.O., DeRenzo, E.G., Brown V.A. and Lynch, J.J. (2012) Training in clinical ethics: launching the Clinical Ethics Immersion Course at the Center for Ethics at the Washington Hospital Center. *Journal of Clinical Ethics*, 23(2), 139–46.

Morgan, S. (2004) Positive risk-taking: an idea whose time has come. *Health Care Risk Report*, 10(10), 18–19. (http://practicebasedevidence.squarespace.com/storage/pdfs/OpenMind-PositiveRiskTaking.pdf).

Morrissey, S. (2005) Teaching ethics for professional practice. In R. Tribe & J. Morrissey (eds) *Handbook of Professional and Ethical Practice for Psychologists, Counsellors and Psychotherapists* (pp. 291–302). Hove: Brunner-Routledge.

Pouncey, C.L. & Lukens, J.M. (2010) Madness versus badness: the ethical tension between the recovery movement and forensic psychiatry. *Theoretical Medicine & Bioethics*, 31, 93–105.

Rhodes, L.A. (1991) *Emptying Beds: The Work of an Emergency Psychiatric Unit*. Berkeley: University of California Press.

Robinson, G. & Crow, I.D. (2009) *Offender Rehabilitation: Theory, Research and Practice*. London: Sage.

Rubitel, A. & Riess, D. (eds) (2011) *Containment in the Community: Supportive Frameworks for Thinking about Antisocial Behavior and Mental Health*. London: Karnac Books.

Scaife, J. (2001) *Supervision in the Mental Health Professions: A Practitioner's Guide*. Hove: Brunner-Routledge.

Silverman, M. (1993) Ethical issues in the field of probation. *International Journal of Offender Therapy and Comparative Criminology*, 37(1), 85–94.

Slade, M. (2009) *Personal Recovery and Mental Illness: A Guide for Mental Health Professionals*. Cambridge: Cambridge University Press.

South London & Maudsley NHS Foundation Trust – Forensic Intensive Psychological Treatment Service. (http://www.slam.nhs.uk/media/398547/fipts%20info%20for%20services.pdf) (Accessed 6 May 2013).

Spike, J.P. (2012) Training in clinical ethics consultation: the Washington Hospital Center Course. *Journal of Clinical Ethics*, 23(2), 147–51.

Szmukler, G. (1999) Ethics in community psychiatry. In S. Bloch, P. Chodoff & S.A. Green (eds) *Psychiatric Ethics*, 3rd edn (pp. 362–82). New York: Oxford University Press.

Tribe, R. & Morrissey, J. (eds) (2005) *Handbook of Professional and Ethical Practice for Psychologists, Counsellors and Psychotherapists*. Hove: Brunner-Routledge.

Tucker, S. & Hughes, T. (2007) *Standards for Medium Secure Units*. CCQI: Royal College of Psychiatrists. (http://www.rcpsych.ac.uk/pdf/final%20standards%20for%20medium%20secure%20units%20pdf.pdf) (Accessed 8 March 2013).

Tucker, S., Iqbal, M. & Holder, S. (2012) *Standards for Low Secure Services*. Royal College of Psychiatrists: CCQI publication number: CCQI 130. (http://www.rcpsych.ac.uk/pdf/Standards%20for%20Low%20Secure%20Services.pdf) (Accessed 8 March 2013).

Vaughan, P.J. & Badger, D. (1995) *Working with the Mentally Disordered Offender in the Community*. London: Chapman & Hall.

Walker, H. & Langdon, D. (2012) Recovery evaluation: the Scottish Forensic Services. In G. Drennan & D. Alred (eds) *Secure Recovery* (pp. 186–201). Oxford: Routledge.

Webber, M. & Nathan, J. (2010) *Reflective Practice in Mental Health: Advanced Psychosocial Practice with Children, Adolescents and Adults*. London: Jessica Kingsley Publishers.

Yakeley, J. & Taylor, R. (2011) Multi-Agency Public Protection Arrangements (MAPPA): can we work with them? In A. Rubitel & D. Riess (eds) *Containment in the Community: Supportive Frameworks for Thinking about Antisocial Behavior and Mental Health* (pp. 161–86). London: Karnac Books.

Young, S., Gudjonsson, G. & Needham-Bennett, H. (2005) Multi-agency public protection panels for dangerous offenders: one London forensic team's experience. *Journal of Forensic Psychiatry & Psychology*, 16(2), 312–27.

4

INTERNATIONAL PERSPECTIVES

Natalie Woodier

Introduction

Globalisation and technological advances have brought countries closer together and aided travel and exchange across the European Union (EU) and international borders. With this comes the ease through which jurisdictions can develop and capitalise on international partnerships and practice exchange and look to one another for guidance and assistance in the justice arena. Working internationally expands perceptions of crime and justice and provides the opportunity for countries to identify innovative, effective and promising international policy and practice through collaborative relations with other jurisdictions and international bodies.

This chapter begins with a review of some of the background on international perspectives in probation and community justice and a brief look at how probation has developed internationally in the context of changing criminal justice landscapes and philosophies for punishment. This is followed by a focus on reintegration of ex-offenders across Europe and a review of some emerging themes and challenges in this field, such as exploring the possibilities for mutual EU-wide recognition of standardised reintegration strategies and practice.

The chapter offers an overview of themes within reducing reoffending and offender reintegration across Europe and internationally. These range from transfer and adaptation of effective practice, case management, significance of the staff–offender relationship in probation practice, the transfer of community penalties across EU borders and increasing the capacity for Europe-wide criminal justice organisations to work effectively with offenders. It is argued that addressing these themes requires collaboration and cooperation between countries to support mutual understanding in targeting reoffending and protecting communities.

Considering the growth of interest in comparative criminology and the broadening remits of criminal justice services across the world this chapter seeks to provide an overview of recent developments and good practice, specifically focusing on probation and community sanctions. It offers an introduction to some of the interesting and innovative work that is currently being undertaken in the field of international criminal justice.

Probation across the globe

There is no clear definition of probation across differing criminal justice systems and sectors. Hamai et al. (1995) suggest that probation is:

> A distinct organisation within the criminal justice system which has a judicial function and is based on a legal mandate . . . probation includes some element of supervision of offenders in the community.
>
> (Hamai et al. 1995)

The meaning of probation has shifted significantly from as far back as the nineteenth century. A form of probation began in some countries as voluntary in the 1870s and often consisted of religious or moral support to those who encountered the wrong side of the law. More recently, probation in many jurisdictions has developed into a sanction imposed by the state and in contemporary society is frequently a punishment in its own right; an alternative to custody.

Interest in probation across Europe and internationally has grown in recent years. Academics, scholars and even policy makers are interested in how other countries approach probation and manage offenders in the community as well as specifically looking for examples of effective practice that could be modified and adopted. As justice systems internationally are increasingly under pressure to work selectively and effectively with offenders, following a value for money approach, countries look across borders for examples of good practice in probation and resettlement services.

In Western Europe, probation has increasingly become embedded in criminal justice systems and is now further broadening its remit. Probation originally developed as a supervisory role for those individuals that courts decided not to punish. However, probation soon evolved to work with those convicted of offences and is now involved in the 'whole process': receiving the case pre-trial, following the defendant through the court, through their sentence and through the prison gate onto their resettlement. Probation organisations and related support services are key players in the criminal justice process, as community penalties and alternatives to custody gain more respect as being essential elements in reducing reoffending and supporting offender resettlement across the world.

Background

Probation was evident from the nineteenth century in countries such as Germany, Luxembourg and Ireland where religious institutions took it upon themselves to support detainees through material and immaterial support (Durnescu and Van Kalmthout 2008: 3). In England in the late nineteenth century pressure for penal reform was motivated by humanity and Christian principles. Police Court Missionaries were appointed through a donation from the Church of England to divert offenders away from drink by helping them find a place to stay. McWilliams (1985, in Vanstone 2004) acknowledges that a movement from this religious missionary to a professional probation service began from 1920; characterised by staff demands for training in specific tasks that were to define their roles as probation staff. Probation was an order of the court and those who chose not to comply were breached and sentenced instead. Early forms of aftercare (supporting offenders on release from prison) were voluntary and focused around social support in resettling offenders.

The first major developments in probation were initially across the western world. Probation aimed to rehabilitate individuals on release from prison through providing support and reforming them back into law-abiding members of society. In the twentieth century, the 'what works' debate took its place as one of the major stages in the history of correctional thinking across the world. Resulting from the proposed weak ideology of the rehabilitative ideal and its related practices in the 1960s and 1970s, Martinson (1974) prompted the 'nothing works' doctrine; this is thought to have built the groundwork for harsher criminal punishments and a movement towards the 'just deserts' penal ideology (Lösel 2007: 142). Criminal sanctions were increasingly seen to be purely for punishment purposes, and services such as those provided by probation organisations that aimed to rehabilitate and reform offenders were not viewed as effective or applicable to this emerging ideology.

Following Martinson's (1974) assessment of the effectiveness of rehabilitative approaches, critics began to review the evidence on which Martinson based his pessimistic conclusions. Positive findings began to emerge across Europe and the Atlantic implying that the sceptical view of 'nothing works' was incorrect; for example, Gendreau and Ross (1980, in Raynor 2007: 1070) found positive outcomes in a number of Canadian studies which reinforced a notion of effective rehabilitation. Other academics challenged Martinson's assertion by assembling new evidence-based practices to test the effectiveness of rehabilitative approaches within probation work. This resulted in improved theoretical understandings of how people behaved, systematic reviews of work with offenders and further developed and refined evaluations of this work. Lösel has commented (2007: 142) that this 'nothing works' later turned into the 'what works?' approach beginning in the 1990s.

The 'what works?' approach led to large-scale implementation of offending behaviour programmes and other interventions both within prisons and the community which were aimed at adjusting thinking and behaviours. This instigated the process of accreditation to ensure offender management services delivered high quality interventions in the community; accreditation is now evident in Canada, England and Wales, Scotland, Sweden and the Netherlands.

Contemporary probation

It has been suggested that criminal justice policy has generally been shifting altogether in punitive directions (Brown et al. 2005). Rising world prison populations appear to demonstrate this punitive direction and subsequently probation is seemingly carried along in the wake; with tougher penalties becoming more dominant, the ever more punitive style of probation can be taken as a credible alternative to custody. In addition, as public protection is evident as one of the primary aims of prison and probation services across different countries, this has arguably propelled probation into a tougher sanction: reassuring the public of their governments' ability to protect them from harm. In support of this punitive trend, whilst rehabilitation initiatives in England and Wales were previously identified as worthwhile ends in themselves, they are now increasingly having to provide clear and unambiguous evidence of their ability to reduce recidivism and/or protect the public (McNeill and Robinson 2004) to attract and sustain funding.

Criminal justice services in former Soviet States were previously largely characterised by a strict notion of imprisonment and therefore developments in probation have happened at a later stage than some other European democracies. The spread of probation services to Eastern European countries could be attributed to the notion that imprisonment inherited from former authoritarian regimes was no longer perceived as beneficial or affordable. In the 1990s many of these states established their democracies and reformed their approaches to criminal justice and the rehabilitation of offenders. The development of a probation service and the shift towards community-based sentencing as a more dominant model argu-ably facilitated the process of moving away from mass incarceration imposed by previous Soviet regimes (Raynor 2007: 1092). The Czech Republic was the first to experiment with probation in 1991, followed by Romania in 2001, Slovenia in 2002, Hungary in 2003 and Bulgaria in 2005 (Durnescu and Van Kalmthout 2008: 8).

The twenty-first century has seen a rise in probation services in many Eastern European countries. In Turkey the new penal code introduced in 2005 gave courts the power to impose community penalties instead of custody and thus the new Turkish Probation Service was launched. Supervised conditional release for prisoners was introduced and the probation service took on the role of providing reports on offenders at all stages of the criminal justice process (Perry 2006: 2). In Bulgaria, probation legislation came into force in January 2005; however preparation for a probation service began well before that in the 1990s when voluntary organisations began working with offenders in custody towards their resettlement (Pitts and Karaganova 2006: 6).

It is increasingly recognised that probation services across Europe are becoming more streamlined and regulated, specifically through the powers of bodies such as the European Commission and the Council of Europe. In addition, other non-governmental organisations (NGOs) such as the CEP (the European Organisation for Probation) support developments in probation across Europe and specifically the exchange of best practice within community justice. The Council of Europe Probation Rules[1] are a prominent example of the movement towards a European probation, introducing quality standards, rules and guidelines for European probation services to follow on the road to more effective services and organisations (Canton 2010).

Clearly developments such as these are not made without challenges. For example, upon Bulgaria's accession to the EU, developments in the Bulgarian Probation Service were required to ensure that their service was established to European standards as well as being tailored to Bulgarian practice (Pitts and Karaganova 2006: 6). Countries may wish to maintain some authority to deliver services and manage organisations how they see fit. However, if services are not appropriate for those who live, work and experience them then the core goals of such organisations may be undermined. Probation across the world differs hugely in language, culture, religion, surrounding politics and the economy, to name but a few factors. A further issue is that although a streamlined European style of probation may certainly increase mutual trust and sharing of best practice it is also important to celebrate the cultural diversity that allows countries to continuously develop and share new innovative working practices. Evidently, different justice systems and different ways of dealing with offenders lay the groundwork for comparative studies of criminology and provide a wider arena of innovative and effective criminal justice practice.

Employment and reintegration across Europe

The stated goal of the National Offender Management Service (NOMS) in England and Wales is to reduce reoffending and make communities safer through successful reintegration and rehabilitation of offenders. NOMS developed a good practice guide for skills and employment-related interventions in 2008 as a practical guide to assist those working directly with offenders (Ministry of Justice 2008). The guide supports the notion of working across government bodies to develop a coherent strategic framework within which providers and practitioners work. It accepts that more needs to be done to increase provisions, ensure they are flexible and relevant to individual offender requirements, and work across a number of issues and 'barriers' to reoffending. In addition, skills and employment interventions cannot exist in isolation and therefore the guidance reinforces the notion of working across different networks and for all involved to have detailed knowledge of the wider context within which offending occurs.

'The number of unemployed offenders in Europe is likely to run into millions', according to the European Offender Employment Forum (EOEF) report published in 2003 (EOEF 2003: 11). Rehabilitative strategies emphasising employment-related programmes are important for a variety of reasons. A number of studies have explored the significance of this area, considering how unemployment can lead to crime and identifying factors that need to be addressed to reduce this. It is also evident across Europe that unemployment and its commonly associated social exclusion are triggers for criminal activity in themselves and the subsequent reduction of this would also act as a crime prevention approach as well as reducing reoffending (EOEF 2003: 9). Webster et al. (2001) note how living circumstances such as insecure housing can act as a barrier for employment and could therefore subsequently have a link to offending. Furthermore, many offenders feel they are unemployed because they have a criminal record and the stigma of the label 'offender'; this further reduces their chances of successful integration and acts as a potential trigger for recidivism (Brazier et al. 2006: 14).

Considerable efforts are being made to further introduce employment-related interventions to prisoners and ex-offenders across the EU and a number of studies have sought to evaluate these. Prison work and vocational training 'do work' according to the criteria developed by Sherman et al. (1997). Further studies concerning the efficacy of job training and educational programmes by Bushway and Reuter (1997) and Lipsey (1995) also look to prove effectiveness. Many of these evaluations focus on success of the programmes in terms of numbers into employment, length in employment and skills development. Whilst this lacks the rigorous data to show a causal link between the intervention and reducing reoffending, these evaluations that test for programme success using employment as the outcome criteria provide valuable data with regards to 'what works'. They have also been useful in identifying some of the potential barriers to employment for ex-offenders. McGuire (1995) and Nuttall et al. (1998) suggest that addressing as many of these barriers as possible can pave the way for reducing reoffending outcomes; if barriers to employment are identified as triggers to reoffending and/or obstacles to desistance, then dissolving these moves jurisdictions one step closer to reducing recidivism (Brazier et al. 2006: 14).

Despite some studies demonstrating the links between unemployment and reoffending, more research, particularly to explore exactly *why* unemployment may impact upon reoffending, remains necessary. Davis et al. (2008) comment that there are several interesting and informative evaluations of community-based employment and skills training programmes, however 'none of these incorporate a sufficiently strong research design to clearly measure the effects of its programme on employment or recidivism' (Davis et al. 2008). This also suggests that we do not yet know enough with regards to what extent these programmes and inter-ventions meet both the needs of the (ex-)offenders as well as current labour market requirements. Tarling (1982) noted that the relationship between unemployment and crime is interactive; both problems being related to or being the effects of social and economic disadvantage (Hearnden et al. 2000); having a criminal record is both at the source of unemployment as well as a barrier to getting a job.

One element within criminal justice that all governments deal with is the range of diverse and complex needs in their offender populations that are not necessarily addressed by just one agency or one type of support. Research has suggested that offenders with multiple needs are more likely to be re-convicted and the more complex the needs identified, the greater the chance of re-conviction (McSweeney and Hough 2006: 111). Such individuals often slip through the net, as they may not meet the threshold of a given agency to trigger a full intervention, but the number of problems they experience is just as, if not more, detrimental to both the offender and the communities they live in. This signifies the origins of case management, whereby services and interventions are adapted and allocated to individuals based on an assessment of their individual risk and needs. Full assessment of initial needs and barriers to employment is therefore essential for case managers to identify the circumstances of the offender and apply interventions appropriately. These complex needs can act as 'barriers' to gaining work and employment if not addressed and supported.

The Ex-offender Community of Practice (ExOCoP)

Resettlement is evidently a key component in the reducing reoffending agenda. In 2006 NOMS identified seven pathways to reducing reoffending as part of their National Action Plan (Maguire 2007: 415). Education, Training and Employment (ETE) was one of the pathways; this highlighted the need for clearly defined ETE services to support offenders develop skills and qualifications to enhance their employability and reintegration into society.

The Ex-offender Community of Practice (ExOCoP) European learning network brought together over 40 European partners from a range of differing agencies (governments, NGOs, social enterprises). ExOCoP was initiated in 2009 and hosted its final policy forum in June 2012. The main goal of ExOCoP was to reduce reoffending in Europe by developing a clear Education, Training and Employment (ETE) pathway for prisoners and ex-offenders along which they can access strategic resettlement facilities. One of the primary outcomes of ExOCoP was the 'Berlin Declaration' on the reintegration of ex-offenders which at least seven countries currently support. The Berlin Declaration reinforced the networks' commitment to working towards reducing reoffending within differing criminal justice systems. It acknowledged ex-offenders' needs for education, skills development and employment and promotes ex-offenders' entitlement to receiving support to fully reintegrate back into society.

The heterogeneity of criminal justice systems across Europe imposes challenges for creating a common policy on ex-prisoner reintegration. The ExOCoP Berlin Declaration does go as far as laying out some of the key components and priorities for the provision of ETE and the reintegration of ex-prisoners across Europe. Due to the differing nature of justice systems it does not go as far as to try and align all services and provisions into a common European reintegration strategy. Each country has its own distinct legal framework, culture and administrative structures, and allocates responsibilities to a number of different offices or operational systems. The heterogeneity carries over into ETE provisions as countries provide a huge array of differing programmes and interventions which can be shared and exchanged across borders (ExOCoP 2012b: 1).

This project has seen the development of national and European initiatives that have tackled the employment, vocational training and labour market issues of ex-offenders, both inside prisons and in the community setting (for information on such projects refer to the programme information annex of the ExOCoP sub-evaluation report – ExOCoP 2012c: 73). However, many of these projects and interventions are not evaluated or are only evaluated through very basic localised measurements and feedback and therefore their effectiveness is extremely difficult to prove. An evaluation sub-project that formed part of ExOCoP focused on the link between employment and desistance. The initial aim was for the sub-project to contribute towards an enhanced EU understanding of 'what works' in improving offender resettlement across Europe. Primarily, it intended to demonstrate the importance of employment- and skills-related strategies in reducing reoffending and exemplify the importance of evidence-based practice in confirming 'what works'.

PROMISING PRACTICE EXAMPLE: GOL GROUPS – NORTHERN ITALY

The Gol groups that operate locally in the majority of the Italian provinces are just one example of innovative and experimental ways of engaging offenders in work-related activities which can follow them through to their release in the community.

These groups operate within the prison administration and have the majority of prisons across Italy as members. They aim to coordinate public and private interventions within both prisons and the community. The aim is to prepare the prisoners whilst incarcerated to engage in activities to support their desistance and subsequently continue their rehabilitation in the community upon release.

The groups consist of individuals such as prison officers, educators and social workers who actively address what needs to be done inside the prison to take care of the future release of offenders.

To date, they have stimulated businesses in prisons which produce branded biscuits sold by a fair trade label in Italy, they have developed furniture workshops in prisons where prisoners build wrought iron furniture and bookshelves for sale in the local communities and they have six greenhouses within prisons and the prisoners and managers work with cooperatives in the community to sell plants and flowers to the local communities.

Local evaluations have shown a high rate of resettlement for prisoners where the Gol groups operate and extremely low reoffending rates within three years.

One of the key conclusions from the evaluation sub-project was that resettlement is a complex, collaborative task and cooperation between institutions is crucial. National and EU policies at all levels must enable this collaboration and communication via an inter-agency approach and cross-governmental cooperation. Recommendations from ExOCoP suggest that consistent, inter-agency management is necessary to keep an offender on the right track and out of prison. A good resettlement strategy requires common, evidence-based policy, to enable different organisations to work towards an agreed goal in an effective way (ExOCoP 2012a: 10).

Emerging themes in probation practice

Transfer and adaptation

Programmes, interventions and further innovative practice are being transferred from one jurisdiction to another. The opening of borders and ease through which EU member states can cooperate and build relationships facilitates the exchange of evidence-based effective practice. The EU-funded STARR (Strengthening Transnational Approaches to Reducing Reoffending)[2] project evidenced the transfer of interventions and practice across borders, including processes related to risk–needs–responsivity, cognitive behavioural practice and human- and social-capital related desistance processes. These processes assist in bridging the gap between prison and probation across the EU. STARR research and learning emphasised that care must be taken to transfer and adapt practice, to ensure it reflects the culture and infrastructure of the recipient countries and also that programme integrity is maintained throughout.

Most significantly, opportunities to transfer and pilot interventions and practices in different jurisdictions provide a means for testing the feasibility of direct transfer and highlight any inadequacies to be addressed in order for them to be effective in differing cultures and infrastructures. This in turn makes products more transferable and more flexible to the wider European market. As countries become increasingly commercially minded there is more incentive for jurisdictions to develop evidence-based effective services that may appeal to and could be traded with other countries.

Multilateral projects provide an opportunity for European jurisdictions to collaborate towards the same end goal of facilitating offender reintegration and reducing reoffending. For example, the European Commission Directorates General of Justice, Home Affairs and Education and Culture provide funding in the form of grants to projects or organisations that assist in implementing EU policies. The European Commission works under the premise that a more open and secure Europe requires adequate funding directed to policy areas where there are increasing collective challenges. The NOMS Market and International Development team have led and partnered a number of EU projects to increase networking and exchange of best practice across Europe and in turn support European justice organisations to work more effectively with offenders.

The STARR project produced invaluable outcomes advising about the transfer and adaptation of interventions across EU member states. STARR was led by the London Probation Trust and project managed within NOMS, which identified the project's international themes and were responsible for project research and international partners. STARR aimed to improve the European Union's knowledge of 'what works' in reducing reoffending and offer an EU-wide view of good practice in community justice and subsequently inform and further develop models across the EU. One example of this was through facilitating the transfer and adaptation of interventions through identifying challenges to transfer and methods to overcome them. In addition there has previously been no systematic EU collation of evidence-based successful interventions in EU countries and therefore STARR drew out some of this research and disseminated it across EU project partners and further networks.

The implementation, delivery and research relating to STARR pilot programmes contributed to current knowledge on effective types of programmes when transferred from one country to another. This fits into the wider agenda of looking into 'what works' in reducing reoffending on a transnational scale, and specifically how programmes can remain effective whilst potentially requiring adaptation when transferred and embedded in differing infrastructures and surrounded by different cultural, political and economic values. In addition, the opportunity to pilot the transfer of programmes within this project allowed for them to be refined to become more EU applicable and flexible to differing jurisdictions.

CASE STUDY: Transfer of Aggression Replacement Training (ART) to Hungary

The objective of this pilot was to determine whether Aggression Replacement Training (ART), when transferred to Hungary, adapted and implemented, was effective in changing the attitudes and behaviour of young offenders. ART is a structured behavioural programme delivered to those individuals under probation supervision within the community. Eighteen probation staff were trained to implement and deliver ART to clients in the community throughout Hungary between April 2010 and January 2011. An evaluation methodology developed by STARR project researchers allowed for information to be gathered regarding the content, delivery and, most importantly, effects of the ART programme based on feedback from the clients who undertook it.

ART had previously been transferred from the UK to Turkey and Croatia; therefore the Hungarian pilot learnt from these experiences and the processes and implementation were adapted accordingly. This demonstrates how EU countries can cooperate and share their experiences, increasing the EU-wide exchange and development of best practice in working with offenders.

The Hungarian pilot generated a number of recommendations to improve delivery and implementation of interventions such as ART when transferred to a country with a different infrastructure and criminal justice process:

- Acknowledgement of the high workloads of probation staff and the movement of resources to ensure they have at least some resource to continue to run evidence-based effective programmes.
- The roll-out of evaluation across programmes throughout the whole country.
- Risk and needs assessments to be prioritised to ensure that suitable clients are directed to programmes; reports from probation staff to prosecutors and judges would aid this.
- Programme tutors should be informed of the risks of altering programmes at their discretion. Developers should obtain feedback from tutors and make alterations where appropriate across the whole programme to ensure programme integrity and quality are not compromised.
- Data collection should include those who complete the programme to allow for follow-up after one- and two-year intervals.
- A quality assurance checklist for developers and trainers to assist with the monitoring and consistency of the programme.

The planned Hungarian STARR work package is now being delivered in full. After reviewing and fine-tuning, a unified ART training manual for Hungary was developed, which took information and lessons from Dutch, UK and Turkish ART methods. When the STARR project ended in June 2011, the majority of ART tutors were beginning their second round of ART delivery to clients in the community.

Source: Full pilot report available online at:
www.starr-probation.org

STARR project research (Akoensi et al. 2013) conducted by a team from the Institute of Criminology, Cambridge University, and the experience gained from the project's pilot programmes highlighted a number of challenges to be addressed and overcome when transferring interventions across borders. Project outcomes instigated a sample of recommendations for transfer such as:

- The infrastructure in a country must be researched prior to programme transfer; processes such as data collection and follow-up which are integral to some evaluation procedures may not be supported by a different jurisdiction. It is important to ensure certain infrastructures are in place to support the programme and its additional requirements prior to transfer and implementation.
- Transfer must be flexible to the needs and requirements of recipient countries. A programme designed specifically for one country and its environment and infrastructure may not be directly applicable elsewhere.

- Adaptations may be necessary to ensure a programme is applicable in a new setting and accommodates new cultural, legislative and religious differences. However, when adaptations are made to programmes, quality assurance is paramount to ensure programme integrity is maintained. Allowing programme tutors to adapt the programme as they see fit undermines the evidence base used to design a programme to meet specific requirements. This raises an important issue when transferring programmes across jurisdictions: How do you 'adapt' a programme without going too far as to compromise its integrity? Any risks to programme integrity need to be considered whilst also recognising that some flexibility in programme design and delivery may be required. Likewise, the extent to which the conclusions from 'what works' literature may require a degree of cautious pragmatism in their application across different cultures needs further debate.

Case management

Case management is the process through which the different interventions and resources invested in our correctional systems are turned into individual programmes, mixed and matched to the needs and risks of each offender (CEP 2012). As noted in the section on employment and reintegration across Europe, case management ensures that offenders are supported appropriately and that correct interventions and services are applied based on individual assessments. The DOMICE (Developing Offender Management in Corrections in Europe) project was developed to view and analyse approaches to case management across Europe. DOMICE delivered in-depth research across European criminal justice systems to develop a picture of how approaches to case management differed across member states and identified areas of promising practice that could be disseminated across EU countries. The project produced a series of system maps clearly depicting and explaining the process an offender takes through the criminal justice system in each member state. The project's interesting findings and resources including the system maps were officially launched during the closing conference in September 2011 and are available on the DOMICE website.[3]

DOMICE found a general lack of coordination between the different stages of the case management process within a significant number of EU countries. Individualised case management could be identified in every system examined suggesting that, more often than not, arrangements are specific to particular providers, stages of the correctional system, sentences or projects and are not necessarily streamlined nationally. In not one country is case management designed and delivered as an integrated, system-wide function (CEP 2012). In addition, at a time when offenders are being transferred across borders and European probation measures are being prepared, there is little evidence to show that case management arrangements are understood between different countries. These are interesting findings that should be acknowledged as EU member states progress with the transfer of probation sentences across borders under the Framework decision 2008/947/JHA.[4]

One element of case management that has expanded with the 'what works' and desistance literature is the importance of the skills and characteristics of probation staff in changing offending behaviours and supporting desistance. McNeill (2006: 52) notes that probation staff should form legitimate and respectful relationships with their probation clients and conduct their work with empathy and genuineness. Staff qualities have been consistently mentioned in international literature but not always consistently transposed into policy and practice (Andrews and Bonta 2006; Bonta et al. 2010). NOMS started the Offender Engagement Programme (OEP) in early 2010 to improve effectiveness of one-to-one engagement between probation practitioners and offenders in order to reduce reoffending. The programme has introduced a range of methods to more effectively engage offenders, one example being Skills for Effective Engagement and Development (SEED) which focuses on the work practitioners undertake with offenders in supervision and provides skills training and development activities for staff. A study running for two years from December 2012 will aim to test the feasibility of transferring SEED to other European jurisdictions.

Evidence-led practice

A truly evidence-led culture would allow criminal justice worldwide to identify 'what works' with their offenders. It would ensure that resources, time and money are not wasted on ineffective interventions that could even be detrimental to offenders in the long term. During periods of diminishing resources when the emphasis is to do better for less it is paramount that justice organisations streamline their services and ensure that their work is effective and targeting the correct areas.

Research has highlighted the variability across the EU in the use of evaluation to develop evidence-based effective services. The STARR project found relatively sound evaluations in only five of 27 member states. The majority of member states evaluate their work in some way but this tends to be on an ad hoc basis using differing methods depending on the criteria for success. There are rarely data collection and follow-up processes in place to determine reoffending outcomes. STARR evidenced this disparity in evaluation and evidence-based practice between member states and identified the impact of infrastructure and culture on the type of evaluation or measurement they undertake. Developing an evidence-led culture would further promote the importance of effective practice throughout the EU and subsequently encourage the exchange of such practice and expertise.

The NOMS Market and International Development Team along with a number of other European partners are building foundations for a network that will disseminate knowledge about effective practice, how its implementation can be directed and how results can be identified. Evidence-led evaluation guidance would be the next step in encouraging and assisting EU-wide justice organisations to evaluate their work and be able to determine what truly is 'good' practice. Guidance would facilitate sharing of research and effective practice whilst remaining sufficiently flexible to accommodate diverse populations, cultures and contexts across EU criminal justice.

The European Probation Rules (EPR)[5] set out recommendations that should guide just and ethical policy and practice in correctional services across Europe. Guidance on evaluating practice and commissioning evidence-based services would support the implementation of the EPR and help EU-wide probation agencies further develop organisational policies and practice to work more effectively with offenders. Through evaluation of the implementation of EPR all member states would experience in a practical way the value of evaluation in delivering effective services. Agencies would subsequently be able to access recommendations on how organisational pre-conditions to effective working can be developed, as well as guidance on evaluating their practice.

Transfer of probation measures and alternative sanctions across borders

The EU Council Framework Decision 2008/947/JHA[6] came into force in December 2011. This Framework Decision (FD) aims to facilitate the social rehabilitation of convicted foreign national offenders by transferring sentenced persons from the EU member state in which they are sentenced to another country within the EU, in order to serve a community sanction or measure. Member states initially expressed concern and uncertainty regarding the practical consequences of implementing the FD. This uncertainty has the ability to create substantial risk for successful implementation and could negate not only the time and resources it has taken to reach the implementation stage, but also frustrate its primary aim: to apply the principle of mutual recognition of judgements and probation decisions between member states and so facilitate the social rehabilitation of convicted foreign national offenders and preserve family, linguistic, cultural and other ties, thus protecting victims and the public.

The National Offender Management Service (NOMS) lead on a two-year multilateral project which began in June 2011 and aims to support the implementation of the FD across EU member states. The ISTEP project (Implementation Support for Transfer of European Probation Sentences – JUST/2010/JPEN/AG/1531) aims to conduct a thorough investigation of community penalties and related infrastructures in all EU member states, building upon initiatives and data from research conducted by the Belgian Ministry of Justice and the Netherlands. It will produce a range of tools to facilitate European regional forums to support member states throughout the pre- and post-implementation phases; ultimately qualifying member states to supervise sanctions ordered in a different state.

Currently, there are over half a million prisoners in European custodial institutions. Of this group, over 100,000 do not have citizenship in the country they are detained in. This means that the average percentage of foreigners inside European prison populations is 19 per cent, although the numbers vary greatly between European countries, from over 22,000 in Germany to less than 100 in Latvia

(Hofstee-van der Meulen 2006: 4). The highest percentage of foreign nationals is in Luxembourg where 73 per cent of the prison population consists of foreigners. In Cyprus, Greece and Belgium the percentage is just above 40 per cent. Separate EU Council Framework Decisions regarding the transfer of prisoners (2008/909/JHA)[7] and regarding pre-trial detention (2009/829/JHA) have also been adopted by the European Union to support the movement of foreign national prisoners and those on remand back to their country of origin.

Next steps in probation across Europe

When considering current developments in community justice, it is important to look ahead and think about how such developments can be capitalised on and expanded in the future. We have talked about the transfer of knowledge and best practice, but how can this assist with developing probation practice in the future? As European probation organisations develop, they are increasingly learning from other jurisdictions' good practice and focusing even more prominently on working effectively with their clients and achieving their organisational aims and policy objectives.

Probation staff and work with offenders

With the significant and increasing proportion of EU nationals living and offending in other EU states, probation staff and services are faced with the challenge of responding to the growing complexity in the composition of their caseloads. In addition, staff are asked to become increasingly flexible in their roles as their remit widens and the type of individuals they deal with broadens. In a large number of EU countries, probation services are still under development and some are very much at the beginning stages of considering what a probation infrastructure may look like. Professionalism and effective working practices are important parts of this development. Under the umbrella of the European Organisation for Probation (CEP), whose remit goes beyond the EU, all EU jurisdictions are committed to focusing on and improving the quality of professionalism in the field of probation.

The Criminal Justice Social Work project, which was granted funding from the Education, Audiovisual and Culture Executive Agency (EACEA) of the EU, supports the professional training and development of European probation staff (CJSW 2011: 4). The project aims to ensure that probation workers across Europe can be trained with the skills, knowledge and values evident in the Council of Europe Probation Rules adopted by the Committee of Ministers in January 2010.[8] This also supports the notion of mainstreaming of methods within probation across Europe, which would evidently support the implementation of the Framework Decision 2008/947/JHA when transferring probation sentences across borders.

As ease of cross-border communication grows, probation staff will be increasingly contacting their opposite numbers in probation services throughout the EU just as they speak with criminal justice staff in their next town. The work of the London Probation Trust-led DUTT project[9] (Developing the Use of Technical Tools in Cross-Border Resettlement) in the use of video conferencing within the criminal justice system aimed to show how technology can better facilitate the interchange of information and assessment materials across EU borders and thus support the opening up of European probation. This in turn will facilitate exchange between EU member states when looking to transfer an offender across borders. Issues regarding breach of a community sanction, additional requirements to a community sanction and changes to the sanction to accommodate the legal code and policies of the executing state can all be discussed and resolved more efficiently via quick and effective video links.

Where structured programmes can be hard to transfer and lack the flexibility needed for ease of transfer to differing jurisdictions, offender management practices can be both flexible and adaptable through developing and expanding on the positive relationships that can form between offender managers and their clients. This is reflected within the NOMS Offender Engagement Programme (OEP), which takes a human capital approach to desistance: capitalising on positive engagement between staff and offenders as a means of reducing reoffending. One-to-one practices have acquired more attention and research recently, helped by the DOMICE project which reiterated the importance of successful case management processes (assessment, planning and continuity in support) in desistance. A body of evidence is developing with regard to both the effective processes to work directly with offenders and the recommended skills, characteristics and attributes for probation staff. It is expected this evidence base will grow further across Europe; with the aim of informing future policy and practice and encouraging supportive relationships as a means of working with offenders to aid desistance.

Risk and needs assessment

As networking throughout the EU strengthens, there is the growing opportunity to share new developments and good practice in assessing the needs and risks of offenders. NOMS have provided advice and information on risk and needs assessment tools to a number of countries and has established ongoing links with a number of probation services across Europe (Bulgaria, Hungary, Croatia and Turkey, for example). The UK remains keen to establish and strengthen ties with other European countries, as well as providing ongoing advice regarding the development and scoring of the actuarial systems.

The Offender Assessment System (OASys) in England and Wales is the assessment tool used to systematically assess and profile adult offenders to ensure they are targeted by the most appropriate services and interventions. In 2004, the OASys Data, Evaluation and Analysis Team (O-DEAT) in NOMS worked with the Norwegian Probation Service to establish OASys. OASys was integrated into the Norwegian Probation Service with great consideration of the differences between the UK and Norwegian criminal justice systems and was subsequently translated into Norwegian. Since then, the Norwegians have further developed their own, predominantly needs assessment tool. Furthermore, a probation team from the Netherlands developed their own assessment tool called RISc of which level 1 is based on OASys, and O-DEAT have conducted workshops in the Czech Republic to present some of the OASys data and provide an overview of risk assessment tools and how they could be transferred and adapted to the Czech situation (Moore 2006: 13).

Although maybe ambitious at this stage, the mainstreaming of risk and needs assessment processes across Europe would significantly aid the transfer of offenders across borders and assure jurisdictions that assessments conducted in other countries complement their processes and systems of acceptability. In the meantime, the sharing of research findings would help to maximise the potential of risk and needs assessment tools throughout Europe, and there is obvious scope for ground-breaking multinational comparative analysis.

Justice assistance

It is clear that administrations across the globe share many common challenges. These range from enhancing effective working practices and providing value for money, realising the importance of staff skills and engagement when working with offenders, meeting both local, national and international standards and at the same time continuing to provide an effective public service in crime prevention, reducing reoffending and protecting the public. Developing bilateral relations with specifically targeted countries across the globe provides a vital opportunity for jurisdictions to enhance their services in specific areas and gain support from countries where good practice has been identified.

Justice assistance is the means through which one jurisdiction has the opportunity to assist another through working closely with beneficiaries to design and deliver solutions that address their most important policy and strategic priorities. Furthermore, justice assistance can deliver tailored one-to-one support, building on the current strengths of the administration they are working with and tailoring assistance to legal systems and structures and keeping them realistic in line with available resources. Justice assistance should be mindful to build on international benchmarks and standards, draw on international evidence of effectiveness (and adapt to the individual jurisdiction) and significantly aim from the outset to build capacity and aid sustainability, inspiring effective and good value justice solutions. Justice assistance was evidenced in the funding for the 'Development of Probation Services in Croatia' (HR/2008/IB/JH/02) which was awarded to a consortium of both the UK and Czech Republic in 2008 by the European Commission Twinning Programme.[10]

NOMS has developed fruitful bilateral relationships with a number of Central and Eastern European Countries, and increasingly further afield. These relationships have predominantly been instigated by other jurisdictions seeking justice assistance from NOMS for the development of their probation services and surrounding systems. As NOMS has developed its expertise in this area, it has become apparent that the engagement of both stakeholders and the wider arena of criminal justice are of primary importance when building a probation service from scratch. Developing a sound infrastructure is a vital first step; this must pay specific attention to the wider policy agenda and public perceptions, addressing the frequent concern that probation may be perceived as a sign of the government becoming 'soft on crime'. Community engagement and a multi-agency approach have been identified by NOMS as significant in ensuring probation can meet aims of punishment, rehabilitation and reintegration whilst protecting the public from harm. However, this is not to say such priorities or approaches are the same in every bilateral relationship; it must be reiterated that justice assistance is tailored to the needs and requirements of differing jurisdictions.

Chapter summary

Evidently the notion of probation has undergone significant developments since its foundations in the nineteenth century. Traditional notions of probation as a social support mechanism for people who had seen the wrong side of the law grew into services that supported offenders to rehabilitate and resettle into the community. The 'nothing works' assertion was viewed as a turning point for probation practice across the world as academics strove to evidence rehabilitation methods and prove that programmes and interventions have a place in criminal justice and reducing reoffending. In contemporary societies, probation has slowly developed as an alternative to custody, a sentence in its own right that can be undertaken in the community with the support of probation staff. As countries develop their probation organisations (the more recent ones including Turkey, Bulgaria and Croatia) they tend to look at other jurisdictions' experiences to enhance their knowledge of 'what works' in probation and the reintegration of offenders into the community.

With the changes in the meaning behind probation over time, it is evident that jurisdictions across Europe are consistently trying to find ways to balance appropriately the different possible purposes of probation. These include: punishment, support, restoration, rehabilitation, resettlement, public protection and reducing reoffending. In addition, they must do this in light of their own histories, legislative and cultural traditions, resources, infrastructures and public and judicial preferences. As mutual trust grows and good practice is shared and transferred across borders, jurisdictions need to ensure that their practices remain tailored and applicable to their own embedded infrastructures and criminal justice policies.

Probation has developed across the globe into a means of punishing offenders, supervising them in the community and supporting their rehabilitation. This has generated a plethora of research and literature around case management practices. The significance of the process that the offender undertakes through the criminal justice system and the relationship between staff and offenders have gained prominence in recent years. A growing evidence base reflects the importance of the correct staff skills and characteristics when working with offenders and supporting their reintegration. The findings of the DOMICE project have been invaluable in informing us of the disparities in case management practices across Europe. The project highlighted the need for more communication and networking across jurisdictions regarding case management, especially with respect to the transfer of offenders and community sanctions across borders.

The transfer and mutual recognition of effective practice is becoming increasingly prominent throughout the world. Countries are under pressure to deliver effective services and reach performance targets with diminishing resources. This has paved the way for further exchange of practice across borders, as countries will look further and further afield to identify innovative and promising practice that can assist in delivering an effective service to their offending populations. The transfer of products and services is now increasingly evident, for example with OASys being transferred to Norway and the proposals for the Offender Engagement model SEED to be tried and tested in other jurisdictions. Piloting programmes and practices in other jurisdictions also allows for flaws and challenges to be drawn out and subsequently further refined and made more 'transferable' and desirable to other countries.

Notes

1 https://wcd.coe.int/ViewDoc.jsp?id=1575813&Site=CM
2 Refer to the STARR project website at: www.starrprobation.org
3 Website available at: www.domice.org
4 The Framework Decision 2008/947/JHA on Probation and Alternative Sanctions is addressed later in this section and can be found at http://eur-lex.europa.eu/LexUriServ/LexUriServ.do?uri=CELEX:32008F0947:EN:HTML
5 http://www.cepprobation.org/uploaded_files/CMRec(2010)1E.pdf
6 http://eur-lex.europa.eu/LexUriServ/LexUriServ.do?uri=CELEX:32008F0947:EN:HTML
7 http://eur-lex.europa.eu/LexUriServ/LexUriServ.do?uri=CONSLEG:2008F0909:20090328:en:PDF
8 https://wcd.coe.int/ViewDoc.jsp?id=1575813&Site=CM
9 JUST/2010/JPEN/AG/EG/1462 DUTT
10 http://www.fco.gov.uk/en/global-issues/european-union/eu-twinning-taiex-programmes/eu-uk-twinning-programme/

Bibliography

Akoensi, T., Humphreys, D., Koehler, J. and Lösel, F. 2013. A systematic review and meta-analysis on the effects of young offender treatment programs in Europe. *Journal of Experimental Criminology*, 9(1): 19–43.

Andrews, D.A. and Bonta, J. 2006. *The Psychology of Criminal Conduct*, 4th edn. Newark, NJ: LexisNexis.

Bonta, J., Bourgon, G., Rugge, T. and Gutierrez, L. 2010. Technology transfer: the importance of on-going clinical supervision in translating 'what works' to everyday community supervision. In McNeill, F., Raynor, P. and Trotter, C. (eds) *Offender Supervision: New Directions in Theory, Research and Practice*. Abingdon: Willan, 91–112.

Bosly, S., Flore, D., Honhon, A. and Maggio, J. 2012. *Probation Measures and Alternative Sanctions in the European Union*. Cambridge: Intersentia.

Brazier, L., Hurry, J., Parker, M. and Wilson, A. 2006. *Rapid Evidence Assessment of Interventions that Promote Employment for Offenders*. Research report RR747. London: Institute of Education, Department for Education and Skills.

Brown, D., Brown, M., Hallsworth, S. and Pratt, J. 2005. *The New Punitiveness: Trends, Theories, Perspectives*. London: Routledge.

Bushway, D. and Reuter, P. 1997. Labour markets and crime risk factors. In Sherman, L., et al. *Preventing Crime: What Works, What Doesn't, What's Promising*. Report to the US Congress. Washington, DC: National Institute of Justice, ch. 6.

Canton, R. 2010. European Probation Rules: What they are, why they matter. *EuroVista*, 1(2): 62–71.

CEP. 2012. DOMICE website launched: impressive resource on case management. CEP Newsletter article. 24 April. Available at: http://cep-probation.org/news/254/636/domice-website-launched-impressive-resource-on-case-management [Accessed 27 April 2012].

CJSW. 2011. Criminal Justice Social Work Project: kick-off letter. October. Breda, the Netherlands: CJSW.

Davis, R., Heaton, P., Kilmer, B., Rabinovich, L. and Rubin, J. 2008. A synthesis of literature on the effectiveness of community orders. Prepared for the National Audit Office: Rand Corporation.

Durnescu, I. 2011. Probation skills and characteristics: a critical analysis. Presentation at EU-funded STARR project final conference in Sofia, Bulgaria, 7 June. Available at: http://www.starr-probation.org/default.asp?page_id=224&name=Final%20Conference [Accessed 17 May 2012].

Durnescu, I. and Van Kalmthout, A.M. 2008. European probation service systems: a comparative overview. In Durnescu, I. and Van Kalmthout, A.M. (eds) *Probation in Europe*. Nijmegen, the Netherlands: Wolf Legal Publishers.

EOEF. 2003. What works with offenders: European networking for the identification of successful practices in preparing ex-offenders for employment integration. Brussels: European Social Fund.

ExOCoP. 2012a. *Core Messages*. The Ex-Offender Community of Practice European Network, Partial European Social Fund Project (unpublished). Available at: http://www.exocop.eu [Accessed 20 June 2012].

ExOCoP. 2012b. *The Berlin Declaration*. The Ex-Offender Community of Practice European Network, Partial European Social Fund Project (unpublished). Available at: http://www.exocop.eu [Accessed 10 June 2012].

ExOCoP. 2012c. *ExOCoP Sub-evaluation final report*. The Ex-Offender Community of Practice European Network, Partial European Social Fund Project (unpublished). Available at: http://www.exocop.eu [Accessed 29 June 2012].

Hamai, K., Harris, R., Hough, M., Ville, R. and Zvekic, U. 1995. *Probation around the World: A Comparative Study*. London: Routledge.

Hearnden, I., Hedderman, C., Hough, M., Nee, C. and Sarno, C. 2000. *Working Their Way Out of Offending: An Evaluation of Two Probation Employment Schemes*. Home Office Research Study 218. London: Home Office.

Heidensohn, F. 2007. International comparative research in criminology. In King, R and Wincup, E. (eds) *Doing Research on Crime and Justice*. Oxford: Oxford University Press.

Hofstee-van der Meulen, F. 2006. Foreign prisoners in Europe. *Probation in Europe: Bulletin of the Conférence Permanente Européenne de la Probation,* 37: 5–4.

ISTEP. 2011. ISTEP project overview: Implementation Support for Transfer of European Probation Sentences. Project newsletter (unpublished).

Lipsey, M. 1995. What do we learn from 400 research studies on the effectiveness of treatment with juvenile delinquents? In McGuire, J. (ed.) *What Works: Reducing Reoffending – Guidelines from Research and Practice.* Chichester: John Wiley.

Lösel, F. 2007. Doing evaluation research in criminology: balancing scientific and practical demands. In King, R. and Wincup, E. 2007. *Doing Research on Crime and Justice.* Oxford: Oxford University Press.

McGuire, J. (ed.) (1995) *What Works: Reducing Reoffending – Guidelines from Research and Practice.* Chichester: John Wiley.

McNeill, F. 2006. A desistance paradigm for offender management. *Criminology and Criminal Justice,* 6(1): 39–62.

McNeill, F. and Robinson, G. 2004. Purposes matter: examining the 'ends' of probation. In Mair, G. (ed.) *What Matters in Probation.* Cullompton: Willan.

McSweeney, T. and Hough, M. 2006. Supporting offenders with multiple needs: lessons for the 'mixed economy' model of service provision. *Criminology and Criminal Justice,* 6(1): 107–25.

Maguire, M. 2007. The resettlement of ex-prisoners. In Gelsthorpe, L. and Morgan, R. (eds) *Handbook of Probation.* Cullompton: Willan.

Martinson, R. 1974. What works? – Questions and answers about prison reform. *Public Interest,* 35: 22–54.

Ministry of Justice. 2008. *Skills and Employment Practice Guide.* ECOTECH Research and Consulting Ltd.

Moore, R. 2006. The Offender Assessment System (OASys) in England and Wales. *Probation in Europe: Bulletin of the Conférence Permanente Européenne de la Probation,* 37: 12–13.

Perry, D. 2006. Turkey launches new probation service. *Probation in Europe: Bulletin of the Conférence Permanente Européenne de la Probation,* 37: 2–3.

Pitts, S. and Karaganova, V. 2006. Establishing a probation service in Bulgaria. *Probation in Europe: Bulletin of the Conférence Permanente Européenne de la Probation,* 37: 6–7.

Raynor, P. 2007. Community penalties: probation 'what works', and offender management. In Maguire, M., Morgan, R. and Reiner, R. (eds) *The Oxford Handbook of Criminology,* 4th edn. Oxford: Oxford University Press.

Sherman, L., Gottfredson, D., Mackenzie, D., Eck, J., Reuter, P. and Bushway, S. 1997. *Preventing Crime: What Works, What Doesn't, What's Promising.* Report to the US Congress. Washington, DC: National Institute of Justice.

Stern, V. 1998. *A Sin against the Future: Imprisonment in the World.* Harmondsworth: Penguin.

Vanstone, M. 2004. *Supervising Offenders in the Community: A History of Probation Theory and Practice.* Aldershot: Ashgate.

Walmsley, R. 2008. *World Prison Population List.* Kings College London, International Centre for Prison Studies. Available at: http://www.prisonstudies.org/info/downloads/wppl-8th_41.pdf [Accessed 4 April 2012].

PART 2

Treatment approaches

5

WORKING WITH SEX OFFENDERS IN COMMUNITY SETTINGS

Derek Perkins

Sexual offending covers a wide range of behaviours, including rape, child sexual abuse, downloading child sexual exploitation material, and offences such as indecent exposure and voyeurism that mostly attract community disposals, as well as other sexually motivated offences ranging from theft to homicide that might not immediately appear to have a sexual motivation. Most sexual offenders will at some time – whether post-conviction or post-incarceration – be living in the community. This chapter considers factors that lead to and maintain sex offending, and the range of assessments and interventions that are relevant within the community setting.

Sexual offending in context

A hidden problem

A major barrier to gaining a full understanding of sexual offending, and therefore intervening appropriately to reduce it, is that it has a high 'dark figure', that is the proportion of sex offences that go unreported is much higher than for many other crimes (Stoltenborgh et al., 2011). It is estimated from self-report surveys that about one in ten children will be sexually abused at some time during childhood (Stoltenborgh et al., 2011) and that about 85 per cent of adult rapes go unreported (Wolitzky-Taylor et al., 2011). Reasons for non-reporting of offences to the police include: (a) the victim, or those responsible for the victim's welfare, not recognising that an offence has been committed, (b) lack of confidence that the offence will be believed and investigated, and (c) fear of the consequences of reporting, such as further direct aggression/sexual re-victimisation by perpetrators or being verbally threatened or abused on social networking sites.

Reporting and prosecutions

Sexual crimes are amongst the most difficult for the police to investigate and it is likely that sexual crime will continue to be a largely hidden phenomenon within society. The Sexual Offences Amendment Act of 1976, which enabled women alleging rape to remain anonymous in court proceedings, resulted in an increase in the number of rapes being reported. So too did the subsequent changes in police procedures for processing allegations of rape, with specially trained officers adopting a more victim-focused approach to processing complaints. Whilst such changes go a long way towards redressing factors that had previously deterred victims from reporting offences to the police, under-reporting/under-investigation/under-prosecution continues to be a deep-rooted problem. Various high profile cases have resulted in increased vigilance in the reporting of actual or suspected child sexual abuse to the police so that child and adult safeguarding procedures, and criminal prosecutions where feasible, can be mounted.

Public perceptions

Public stereotypes of the lone, predatory male sex offender attacking children or adults unknown to him, often reinforced by media reports and popular depictions, have given way to greater understanding that sexual abuse/offending is much more commonly embedded within existing or past relationships – partners, families and extended families, acquaintances and colleagues. Also, about 20 per cent of sexual perpetrators are under the age of 18, blurring categorical distinctions between victims and abusers (Barbaree & Marshall, 2006). Whilst most sex offenders are male – hence male terms will be used in this chapter – the proportion of known female perpetrators has increased over the last 20–30 years, with estimates currently being that they comprise about 5 per cent of all sex offenders (Cortoni et al., 2009).

Sex offender characteristics

Knowledge about sex offenders is largely drawn from research on convicted, mainly incarcerated, offenders rather than on the majority of sex offenders who remain unconvicted and living in the community. Reinforced by a media focus on extreme and dramatic stranger attacks, information from this end of the sex offending continuum has entered the public consciousness as being typical of sex offending, thereby disproportionately increasing fear of sexual crime, influencing political and policy prioritisations and deflecting attention from where most sex offending occurs.

Causation

Research on the nature of child sexual abuse and sexual violence towards women, as well as on rarer but equally traumatising sexual offences against men, has indicated a range of factors causing and/or being predictive of sexual offending.

Sex offence causation is now seen in terms of interactions between (a) biological predispositions/biological anomalies in brain functioning (Arrigo & Purcell, 2001; Cantor et al., 2008), (b) cultural norms and expectations, for example of male dominance and sexual entitlement (Beech et al., 2006), (c) early life experiences that sow the seeds of later offending, including insecure attachments, abuse experiences and neglect (Briere & Jordan, 2009) and (d) situational contingencies (e.g. parental separation, loss of friendships, lack of appropriate role models, and exposure to offence-supportive attitudes) that unfold during childhood and adolescence and shape individuals towards or away from offending behaviour. Offending behaviour is then either maintained (through reinforcements such as sexual gratification, feelings of agency and compensation for a lack of intimacy) or extinguished (through a lack of reinforcement of the behaviour and/or adverse consequences following the behaviours).

An inter-generational issue

There is now a better understanding of how sex offending/sexual abuse can be replicated and transmitted down the generations through processes of normalisation of the behaviour and/or secrecy within certain family, acquaintance, and (sub) cultural networks. Those caught up in such sexual abuse can be so tightly bound within these influences that information about the abuse does not come to light or, if it does, victims can be silenced by inducements, manipulation, threats or violence. Criminal justice and other agencies' operational or policy prioritisations can also play a part in directing resources to, or away from, certain classes of sexual offences, as illustrated in the recent Rochdale and Oxford child sexual abuse cases involving the grooming and manipulation of vulnerable teenage girls by networks of local male offenders.

Resistance to change

Once a pattern of sex offending is established, it is difficult to change because of both (a) the powerful forces of sexual and emotional gratification that maintain the offending behaviour and (b) the progressive removal from the offender's life of non-offending opportunities (e.g. for intimate relationships, satisfying work, enjoyable leisure time). This consequent lack of opportunities to develop non-offending behaviours leaves a gap in the offender's life that is readily occupied by sex offending, especially at times of emotional vulnerability or increased opportunity to offend. This in turn creates, for many offenders, its own negative consequences – such as fear, despondency, loneliness, shame or guilt – that further exacerbate their vulnerability to relapse into further offending.

Risk factors

Sex offence risk factors are typically characterised as 'static' or 'dynamic'. Static risk factors include elements such as the offender's age at first conviction, and the nature and diversity of previous offending – factors which by their nature cannot be modified – but which were characterised by Thornton as 'historical markers of long-term psychological vulnerability' (personal communication, 2004). Dynamic risk factors, in contrast, are features of the offender that interact with environment factors (e.g. ease of access to unprotected potential victims) and which can potentially be managed or modified by treatment or risk management procedures.

Dynamic risk factors have been subdivided into 'stable dynamic' risk factors, such as personality traits or mental disorders that are typically resistant to change, and 'acute dynamic' risk factors, such as becoming angry or depressed, which can change over a matter of minutes or hours. The two most powerful stable dynamic risk predictors for sexual recidivism have been consistently identified as psychopathic personality traits and offence-related sexual interest as measured by the penile plethysmograph (PPG) (Hanson & Bussière, 1998; Hanson & Morton-Bourgon, 2005). Individuals high on both sets of dynamic risk factors (psychopathic traits and sexual deviance) are more likely to reoffend than those with only one feature and particularly so for those who have neither (Hanson & Bussière, 1998; Hanson & Morton-Bourgon, 2005). Key *acute dynamic risk factors* have been identified as substance misuse, negative emotional states, and disengagement from treatment, supervision or support.

Personality disorder

Psychopathic personality traits are generally assessed by use of the Psychopathy Checklist revised (PCL-R) or other structured assessments of personality disorder such as the International Personality Disorder Examination (IPDE) or DSM-V and ICD-10 classification systems. Completion of these ideally requires access to official documentation such as offending history, and reports from clinical and criminal justice professionals, family members, work colleagues and friends. This information assists in highlighting which particular facets of personality disorder are most present and salient to offending. As well as the subdivision of the PCL-R into Factor 1 (interpersonal) and Factor 2 (lifestyle), it enables assessment of four facets of Interpersonal, Affective, Lifestyle and Antisocial traits, which can be useful in considering not only how these traits have contributed to offending but also how they will be likely to interact with risk management and treatment progress.

Offence-related sexual interests

Offence-related sexual interests cross-reference with paraphilias, as defined within DSM-V and ICD-10, for example paedophilia and sadism. These features, especially in combination with psychopathic personality traits, need to be accurately assessed so that relevant interventions can be put in place, and their effects accurately monitored. Sexual offenders can often be reluctant to reveal details of extreme sexual interests (e.g. raping children or torturing adults), either through shame about what they believe to be uniquely deviant fantasies, or through fear of the consequences of doing so, for example that they may receive a harsher sentence or be prevented from progressing out of prison/hospital. Although sexual fantasy disclosures can be achieved through rapport building, careful interviewing and psychometric assessments, these self-report based procedures are vulnerable to faking and minimisation.

Assessment and formulation

Current thinking suggests that a combination of actuarial instruments (e.g. Risk Matrix 2000, Static 99), structured clinical judgement (e.g. Risk for Sexual Violence Protocol (RSVP), Structured Assessment of Risk and Need for sexual offenders (SARN)) and an individualised formulation (e.g. Daffern et al., 2010) is required to fully assess sex offenders' risks and needs within risk management procedures (e.g. Multi-Agency Public Protection Arrangements (MAPPA) or rehabilitation programmes, such as Sex Offender Treatment Programmes (SOTP) in prisons and Circles of Support and Accountability (COSA) in the community).

The SARN, developed by Thornton (2002), is widely used in the National Offender Management Service (NOMS) and forensic mental health settings and comprises four broad areas of dynamic risk (and hence potential treatment targets): 'sexual interests', 'distorted attitudes', 'socio-affective factors' and 'self-management'. Through a review of file information combined with interviewing the offender, obtaining collateral information from relevant others, and using information such as psychological or psychophysiological test data, a detailed profile of risk factors and treatment needs within each of these four domains are identified.

It is important that these approaches draw from as wide a source of information as possible (past and present) and use multimodal methods of assessment, including case file data, interviews, information from relevant informants, psychometric assessments and other assessment methods targeted at specific risk and need factors (e.g. psychophysiological assessment of sexual interests). Offence-related sexual interests, personality traits and substance misuse are issues of particular relevance to risk management and treatment in the community but can only be addressed indirectly in institutional settings.

Recent years have seen increasing attention directed to young people who have committed sexually harmful behaviours, often peer-to-peer, with about 20 per cent of all sexual offences carried out by young people under the age of 18 (Barbaree & Marshall, 2006). The 'Assessment, Intervention and Moving on' (AIM) project was set up to improve professional practice with young people who exhibit sexually harmful behaviours. The philosophy was to deal with risk whilst avoiding stigmatisation and counter-therapeutic effects. The project established agreed inter-agency protocols and policies for multidisciplinary working with this group in Greater Manchester and implemented these within ten local authorities in 2001 (Griffin & Beech, 2004; Griffin et al., 2008). AIM provides a ten-step framework for initial assessment of young people with sexually harmful behaviours in which professionals join with the young people and their families/carers to identify both areas of high concern/risk and areas of strength/protective factors. By incorporating this strength-based review within the AIM assessment, practitioners could identify work programmes to build on assets as well as reducing risk. Evaluation of the interim framework was carried out using a combination of observational methods, conviction study data and feedback from participants and professionals. The results indicated that the framework was well received by those taking part, with high levels of implementation of assessment recommendations and key areas of good practice developed, for example utilisation of the multidisciplinary strategy meetings, enhanced staff training and refinements to the protocol to meet various additional needs of some young people taking part, such as in relation to their sexual orientation.

Substance misuse

Sex offenders' use of alcohol and drugs may be present (a) as a generic background risk factor associated with poor problem solving and poor self-control, which can thereby make offending more likely or (b) as a specific response to offence-related beliefs and urges. In the latter case, substance misuse may occur as part of the offender's struggle *against* offending or as a means of deliberately reducing inhibitions so as to *enable* offending. In either case, it results in offending being more likely, whether this is unintentionally or intentionally. Hair strand analysis technologies can provide feedback of what if any substances have been ingested by the subject over various time periods and to what levels. This can both serve as a public protection monitoring scheme and as an aid to offenders to maintain their relapse prevention plans.

In Finkelhor's (1986) model of child sexual abuse, substance use is one of the two main factors that are likely to 'overcome internal inhibitions to offending', the other being the presence of offence-supportive thinking. Similarly, in Arrigo and Purcell's (2001) model of sexual homicide, the role of substance misuse is seen as an important 'offence facilitator', along with offence-related pornography use. As well as being part of the aetiology of sexual offending and its escalation, substance use and pornography use are also described as factors that could, when present, combine with other factors to facilitate the commission of new offences.

Penile plethysmograph

Of the sexual interest assessment procedures that have been reviewed by Akerman and Beech (2012) and Snowden et al. (2011), the penile plethysmograph (PPG) emerges as the procedure most likely to produce results that identify the individual's sexual interest and be at least moderately resistant to attempts at faking. The PPG procedure involves the offender placing a small measuring device on his penis whilst sitting in a private room. He is then either listening to audio descriptions of sexual offending scenarios relevant to his offences and, for comparison, descriptions of consenting adult sexual activity, or watching still or moving images depicting offence-related and non-offence related sexual activity.

Some offenders undertaking the assessment will 'flat line', that is they will not respond to any of the stimuli. This is usually because of some or all of the following: (a) emotional states such as anxiety suppress the offenders' sexual arousal, (b) they are not responsive to the modality in which the material is presented (still images, stories, etc.), (c) the specific stimuli being used are not relevant to their sexual interests, (d) the material is relevant but not powerful or extreme enough to elicit sexual responses. Typically however it is possible to obtain a profile of relative sexual arousal to offence-related and non-offence related (adult consenting) sexual activity. This will, for example, enable the assessors to identify and work with the offender on the basis that he has, for example, a primary sexual preference for children as opposed to a primary preference for adults but has sexually offended against children for reasons such as social inadequacy with adults or a sense of greater 'emotional congruence' with children as described by Finkelhor (1986).

Given the complexities of undertaking PPGs, interest has developed in finding valid but simpler alternatives that are suitable for use in community settings. Banse and colleagues (2010) have developed the Explicit and Implicit Sexual Interest Profile (EISIP). This combines self-report measures of sexual interest with viewing time and implicit association tasks, the results from which are displayed in the form of an offender profile. The elements of the profile might be consistent or inconsistent (e.g. self-report and viewing time) and can be helpful in assessing different components of sexual interest in children and help guide therapeutic interventions. The assessment is carried out on a laptop and can easily be administered in a community setting in about an hour.

Another promising procedure is the Choice Reaction Time (CRT) procedure (Mokros et al., 2010), a similar procedure also described by Kalmus and Beech as a 'rapid serial visual presentation' task (Kalmus & Beech, 2005). Subjects are asked to respond when they see a dot appearing on the computer whilst various images are also presented on the screen. Child molesters have been shown to respond significantly more slowly than controls in this type of procedure. It appears to have the potential to overcome faking and could, like the EISIP, be of value in carrying out assessments of sexual interest in the community without the need for the complex laboratory procedures required for PPG assessments.

In similar vein, Perkins and Hogue (2011) have developed a prototype eye tracker system which is currently being piloted with sexually violent offenders and non-offender controls as a possible adjunct to PPG assessment, but one which may also have some independent diagnostic potential. Using a series of short moving images that depict consenting sexual activity, sexualised violence and non-sexual violence, the procedure involves analysing eye movements and lengths of gaze. At an earlier stage of development than the EISIP and CRT, the eye tracking procedures is currently being trialled alongside PPG assessments in a mentally disordered sex offender population (Perkins & Hogue, 2011).

As well as sexual deviance assessments, methods of assisting treatment compliance and offence desistance are needed. The Lucy Faithfull Foundation, for example, has developed and utilised a method that enables sex offenders' online activities to be remotely monitored and the offenders assisted to avoid inappropriate website access that might otherwise be a risk factor for reoffending.

Polygraph

Sex offenders in the community have also been involved in a number of related procedures designed to ensure safety and freedom from reoffending. Polygraph assessment, which is quite common in North America as part of enhancing disclosure at the beginning of treatment and as a treatment-compliance procedure as offenders work through their treatment and return to the community, has been piloted in the UK with good results (Grubin & Madsen, 2006). Typically, a sex offender will undergo a polygraph assessment during regular follow-up appointments with, for example, their probation officer and will be asked about their conduct and activities during the preceding weeks. Just as with any other assessment procedure, polygraph findings are not infallible but there is a sufficient relationship between offenders providing misleading information and the polygraph's ability to detect this that ex-offenders in the community are likely, and this has been shown to be the case, to reveal information which they may well believe the polygraph will identify if they are not honest during the interview. The results from these studies is such that professionals working with sex offenders rate the use of the procedure very highly and, interestingly, this is also true of the ex-offenders themselves. The majority reported during the pilot studies that they found the polygraph helpful in keeping them focused on living a non-offending life.

Offence-related pornography

With the growth of the Internet has come online access to a wide array of sexual material that covers every type of legal and illegal sexual behaviour including child sexual abuse. Pornography that depicts images and narratives supportive of previous offending behaviour (e.g. sexualised images of children or material describing sexualised violence towards adults) can serve both as (a) fantasy material which, when paired with orgasm, reinforces the likelihood of repeat offending and (b) a mechanism that normalises sexual offending.

In the UK, there was a 26-fold increase from 62 (1989) to 1,619 (2009) in convictions for the possession, exchange or production of child sexual exploitation materials. Those who access child sexual abuse imagery online may come to believe, because the material is so freely available, that it is 'normal', that they are not directly harming anyone, and that they are in any event unlikely to be punished because they believe their behaviour to be anonymous and undetectable. Although research to date has failed to establish a direct link between pornography use and sexual offending (Seto et al., 2001), the importance of mediating variables has been highlighted including antisocial beliefs, hostile masculinity, elevated sensation-seeking, and dysfunctional stress coping (Merdian et al., 2013).

Reducing sex offending

Statistically, the risk of sexual reoffending after one sexual conviction is low but this risk increases significantly for second, third and subsequent convictions. Sex offender treatment has typically been focused on offenders representing the higher levels of reoffending risk, as defined by higher scores on actuarial and structured clinical risk assessments (both static and dynamic). This is in line with the *risk–need–responsivity principles* set out by Andrews and Bonta (2006). That is, those with lower levels of risk generally receive little by way of intervention on the basis that they are unlikely to reoffend and that interventions with lower risk groups can be counterproductive.

Recidivist sex offenders become trapped in a cycle of reoffending, the consequences of which (e.g. loss of family or job) prompt responses (e.g. negative emotional states and use of alcohol) that in turn facilitate subsequent offending. The contingencies that maintain offending behaviour may, however, change with the individual offender's circumstances, for example forming a stable relationship, acquiring a satisfying work life, and developing supportive friendships, as well as through professional therapy and support.

Treatment and management

Sex offender treatment and management is now provided through criminal justice, forensic mental health and social care systems as well as through charitable and voluntary organisations such as the NSPCC (www.nspcc.org.uk) and the Lucy Faithfull Foundation (www.lucyfaithfull.org.uk) in ways that are more integrated, evidence-based and victim-focused than at any time in the past. The National Offender Management Service (NOMS) provides a range of treatment programmes for sex offenders both in prison and in the community. Most high risk sex offenders in treatment have convictions for child sexual abuse or rape/sexual assault of women, and attend a group-based sex offender treatment programme (SOTP). There are also a number of adapted programmes, for example for offenders with learning difficulties, or specialist programmes, for example addressing sexual homicide offences (generally carried out in prison) or non-contact offences as in the downloading of child sexual exploitation material from the Internet (mostly undertaken in the community).

Providing the most appropriate treatment and management strategies for sex offences requires as much information as possible on:

(a) the offender's history (including attachment experiences, and negative or positive early life experiences) that will, respectively, increase offending risks or act as protective factors against offending;

(b) current offending behaviour, including empirically determined (static and dynamic) risk factors as identified respectively by actuarial assessments such as RM2000 and structured clinical judgement protocols such as the SARN;

(c) ideographic risk and treatment need factors determined through a functional analysis of the offending behaviour using for example multi-modal functional analysis (Lord & Perkins, in press).

Major difficulties in intervening with the two major risk factors (psychopathic traits and sexual deviance) are: (a) the extent to which offenders may wish to mask their presence and (b) the fact that they are not easily observable or assessed without detailed collateral information. It is therefore important that methods are used to facilitate disclosure of relevant information in these areas. This will necessarily include the development of a positive therapeutic relationship with the offender (empathy and support for the offender whilst being clear on the unacceptability of the offending behaviour). Other specific techniques are also helpful, as indicated earlier.

For young people who engage in sexual offending or other sexually harmful behaviours, Multisystemic Therapy (MST) (Henggeler, 1999) has been used to good effect with its problem sexual behaviour variant (MST-PSB). MST-PSB involves a combination of family therapy and safety planning together with interventions directed at the sexual behaviour itself such as understanding effects of harmful behaviour on victims and the promotion of healthy sexual behaviour. The improvements in family functioning and parenting capacity are used to effect changes in the other areas of the young person's life such as their peers, school and community in order to break the cycle of offending behaviour. The twin approaches of risk reduction and strengths development is therefore consonant with the AIM assessment strategy for young people with sexually harmful behaviours outlined earlier.

'What works'

Much sex offender treatment over the last 20–30 years has flowed from the 'what works' approach (e.g. McGuire, 1995, 2013) of establishing the criminogenic factors associated with sexual offence recidivism and targeting these factors in treatment programmes using the risk–need–responsibility principle. This has produced better evidence for treatment success than the preceding approaches but has been recognised as being limited in its scope as it requires the next stages of generalisation to the community, which in turn raises questions about what other skills, strategies and resources sex offenders would need to be successfully and safely reintegrated within the community.

As noted previously, the Internet now permeates society and has the potential to facilitate sexual victimisation (child and adult) by removing various psychological and geographical barriers to offending and it is a matter of increasing international concern. A programme of treatment specifically designed for such offenders (iSOTP) is in use with the UK Probation Service. Research on the 'cross over' from the use of child exploitation material and contact offending has generated equivocal results. The Babchishin et al. (2011) meta-analysis which found a 3 per cent figure for online offenders who commit contact offences contrasts with Beier et al.'s (2009) finding that 42 per cent of self-reported child abusers in their clinic had also used child sexual exploitation material on the Internet.

'Good lives'

Treatment programmes have, until recently, focused on identifying sex offending risk factors and neutralising or ameliorating these through therapy or risk management/relapse prevention procedures. Over the last ten years or so, sex offender treatment has evolved from the targeting of empirically determined risk factors for offending into approaches that take a more rounded view of the sex offender and his/her need to live a healthy, satisfying and pro-social life. Ward and Stewart (2003) coined the term 'good lives' for this holistic approach, which focuses on offenders' interpersonal, educational, recreational and spiritual needs as well as offending behaviour. The 'good lives' approach is complementary to, rather than an alternative to, previous risk management approaches. It recognises that all people seek certain 'goods' such as group membership, emotional support, educational and spiritual engagement and that an absence of these goods not only impoverishes their lives but also serves to exacerbate risk factors for offending.

The aim is to encourage and help offenders to develop the skills and strategies needed to meet their needs in socially acceptable ways and thereby reduce the risk that offending behaviour will be used to compensate for these needs if they remain unmet. As Marshall et al. (1999) have noted, sex offenders typically engage in offence-related activities for only a small proportion of their day-to-day lives and it is therefore important to understand and reinforce factors that underpin their non-offending behaviour. Risk factors will, however, also continue to require specific interventions and monitoring, for example offence-related sexual interests and offence-supportive attitudes. If a 'good lives' approach is introduced early in the treatment process, this appears to enhance offenders' motivation to change and therapeutic commitment and result in better treatment outcomes (Willis et al., 2012).

Sex offenders returning to the community from prison or secure hospitals run the risk of relapse into sexual offending if the factors that lay behind their offending before conviction reoccur, for example living a lonely and unsatisfying life, having few positive activities and relationships, becoming preoccupied with thoughts and images of sexual abuse, amplifying and normalising such interests through the use of offence-related pornography, and use of substances that can inflame these thoughts or create behavioural disinhibition. Those with the highest levels of risk factors are most likely to be reconvicted. For many years, follow-up programmes have been used with discharged sex offenders, ranging from the fairly minimalist occasional appointment to see how things are progressing through to further intensive community-based treatment programmes.

Circles of support and accountability

A key concern in sex offender treatment has always been the extent to which treatment effects will generalise into the real world once offenders are back in the community and subject to the environments and influences (positive and negative) in which their offending originally occurred. Over the last ten years or so, an approach termed 'circles of accountability and support' (COSA) has been developed, initially in Canada but also now running in other countries including the UK. Based on the ideal of community reintegration, the concept of COSA is that the former sexual offender will be supported, monitored and maintained in the community. The 'supporters' comprise a mixture of professionals such as probation officers or police officers and specially selected and trained volunteers, who befriend the individual in full knowledge of the circumstances of their previous offending and risk factors. This approach both provides a network of trusted individuals to whom the ex-offender can relate, for example meet for meals and other social activities, and in whom he or she can confide if life is becoming difficult and risks of reoffending become more pronounced. The presence of these individuals around the ex-offender also enables them to recognise if risks are becoming heightened, for example if the individual is becoming disengaged from social contacts, drinking too much alcohol, or engaging in behaviour likely to put them at risk such as use of offence-related pornography.

Desistance

Recent years have also seen an interest in studying how (most) sex offenders come to desist from offending irrespective of formal interventions. Characterised by McNeill and Weaver (2010) as 'what matters' as opposed to 'what works', the approach sits well with the COSA model by emphasising the development of a non-offending persona and integration back into the community rather than a sole focus on offender risk management. It also links with the 'good lives' model in that it is focused on strengths and opportunuites. The underlining UK principles of safeguarding victims, which always requires the reporting of suspected offenders to the police, stands in contrast to a 'public health' approach to child sexual abuse that has been developed in Germany through the Dunkelfeld Project. Here, anonymous assessment and offence prevention treatment is provided for child sexual abusers, including online offenders (https://www.dont-offend.org/), and is producing some challenging results suggesting that this approach may ultimately achieve better results in reducing harm than the conventional model of treatment and risk management for child sexual abusers in the UK.

Treatment outcomes

Lösel and Schmucker's (2005) meta-analysis of 69 sex offender treatment evaluation studies, with a total sample of 22,181 sex offenders, showed a 37 per cent reduction for sexual recidivism but also a 44 per cent reduction for violent recidivism and a 31 per cent reduction for general recidivism. This suggests that the content of these well-designed and well-evaluated sex offender treatment programmes have positive effects not only on specifically sexual elements within the offending but also related issues that will be of relevance to nonsexual violence and general delinquency or antisociality.

Evidence on the effectiveness of COSA is very impressive when compared with sex offender treatment programmes. A study by Wilson et al. (2005) in Ontario compared 60 high risk ex-sex offenders on a COSA programme and 60 matched controls over a 4.5 year follow-up. COSA subjects reoffended significantly less on sexual convictions (5 per cent COSA vs. 17 per cent Controls), that is 70 per cent down, as well as on violence convictions (15 per cent COSA vs. 35 per cent Controls), 57 per cent down, and on all offences (28 per cent COSA vs. 43 per cent Controls), down 35 per cent. This is roughly equivalent to changes brought about by the most effective sex offender treatment programmes. These of course are not alternatives but complementing each other. In the UK, Bates and Wager (2012) carried out an evaluation of 13 COSAs and demonstrated a reduction in offence risk and changes in core member (sex offender) attitudes and beliefs using a Dynamic Risk Review (DRR).

Recent thinking has focused on the notion of seeing sexual crime in the same way that society would view a health problem that occurs across all sections of society. This notion, first most clearly set out by Laws and Ward (2010), requires a detailed understanding of how sexual abuse emerges and how it is maintained within society so that early preventative measures as well as post-offending interventions can be put in place, in much the same way that children may be inoculated against known physical illness risks as well as being treated if the illness occurs.

Research on sexual offenders' patterns of behaviour has also enabled knowledge about offending methods and strategies to be made more widely available so that potential victims can be alerted as to the real nature of risks that might apply in different situations and how to take preventative action. This of course does not and should not imply that potential victims are responsible for preventing sexual crime but simply that, in the same way people learn to understand the dangers of travelling about in a busy city centre or negotiating use of substances such as alcohol and cigarettes, they can be alerted to the range of issues facing them within the area of sexual behaviour and sexual crime.

Amongst the methods now used to do this are sessions within schools devoted to interpersonal relationships, sexual health and education, good citizenship and social skills. Carmody (2003) has developed a whole programme for young people for understanding and negotiating ethical sexual behaviour, which has now been made available to many groups of young people in Australia, with very promising results, and which is now being developed in other countries including the UK (Radford et al., 2011). The approach involves young people talking about their understanding and experiences of sexuality and sexual relationships, engaging in various exercises including role-playing about the nature of consent, and group discussion and sharing ideas about the principles and practice of an ethical approach to sexual conduct/relationships.

In considering these offence-preventative approaches, we have come full circle in highlighting that sexual offending and other types of sexually harmful behaviours emanate from within the society in which we live, within its family, educational, peer group and cultural influences. Whilst specialist sex offender treatment services undoubtedly have an important part to play in reducing sex offending as well as in adding to our knowledge about its causes and manifestations, offence reduction is ultimately embedded within society and its remedies as well as its causes will ultimately lie within the community.

References

Andrews, D. A. & Bonta, J. (2006) *The Psychology of Criminal Conduct* (4th edn). Cincinnati, OH: Anderson Publishing.

Akerman, G. & Beech, A. R. (2012) A systematic review of measures of deviant sexual interest and arousal. *Psychiatry, Psychology and Law*, 19(1), 118–43.

Arrigo, B. A. & Purcell, C. E. (2001) Explaining paraphilias and lust murder: toward an integrated model. *International Journal of Offender Therapy and Comparative Criminology*, 45(6), 6–31.

Babchishin, K. M., Hanson, R. K. & Hermann, C. A. (2011) The characteristics of online sex offenders: a meta-analysis. *Sexual Abuse: A Journal of Research and Treatment*, 23, 92–123.

Banse, R., Schmidt, A. F. & Clarbour, J. (2010) Indirect measures of sexual interest in child sex offenders: a multimethod approach. *Criminal Justice and Behavior*, 37, 319–35.

Barbaree, H. E. & Marshall, W. L. (eds) (2006) *The Juvenile Sex Offender* (2nd edn). New York: Guilford Press.

Bates, A. & Wager, N. (2012) Assessing dynamic risk in the community: the dynamic risk review and circles of support and accountability. *Forensic Update*, 108, 5–13.

Beech, A. R., Ward, T. & Fisher, D. (2006) The identification of sexual and violent motivations in men who assault women: implication for treatment. *Journal of Interpersonal Violence*, 21(12), 1635–53.

Beier, K. M, Neutze, J., Mundt, I. A., Ahlers, C. J., Goecker, D., Konrad, A. & Schaefer, G. A (2009) Encouraging self-identified pedophiles and hebephiles to seek professional help: first results of the Prevention Project Dunkelfeld (PPD). *Child Abuse & Neglect*, 33, 545–9.

Briere, J. & Jordan, C. E. (2009) Childhood maltreatment, intervening variables, and adult psychological difficulties in women: an overview. *Trauma Violence Abuse,* 10(4), 375–88.

Cantor, J. M., Kabani, N., Christensen, B. K., Zipursky, R. B., Barbaree, H. E., Dickey, R., et al. (2008) Cerebral white matter deficiencies in pedophilic men. *Journal of Psychiatric Research*, 42, 167–83.

Carmody, M. (2003) Sexual ethics and violence prevention. *Social and Legal Studies: An International Journal*, 12(2), 199–216.

Cortoni, F. & Gannon, T. A. (2009) Female sexual offenders. In A. Phenix & H. M. Hoberman (eds) *Sexual Offenders: Diagnosis, Risk Assessment and Management*. New York: Springer.

Daffern, M., Jones, L. & Shine, J. (eds) (2010) *Offence Paralleling Behaviour: A Case Formulation Approach to Offender Assessment and Intervention*. Chichester: Wiley.

Finkelhor, D. (1986) Explanations of pedophilia: a four factor model. *Journal of Sex Research*, 22(2), 145–61.

Griffin, H. and Beech, A. (2004) Evaluation of the AIM Framework for the assessment of adolescents who display sexually harmful behaviour. Available at: www.yjb.gov.uk/Publications/Resources/Downloads/AIM%20Full%20Report.pdf.

Griffin, H. L., Beech, A., Print, B., Bradshaw, H. and Quayle, J. (2008) The development and initial testing of the AIM2 framework to assess risk and strengths in young people who sexually offend. *Journal of Sexual Aggression*, 14, 211–25.

Grubin, D. & Madsen, L. (2006) Accuracy and utility of post-conviction polygraph testing of sex offenders. *British Journal of Psychiatry*, 188, 479–83.

Hanson, R. & Bussière, M. T. (1998) Predicting relapse: a meta-analysis of sexual offender recidivism studies. *Journal of Consulting and Clinical Psychology*, 66(2), 348–62.

Hanson, R. & Morton-Bourgon, K. E. (2005) The characteristics of persistent sexual offenders: a meta-analysis of recidivism studies. *Journal of Consulting and Clinical Psychology*, 73(6), 1154–63.

Henggeler, S. W. (1999) Multisystemic Therapy: an overview of clinical procedures, outcomes, and policy implications. *Child Psychology & Psychiatry Review*, 4, 2–10.

Kalmus, E. & Beech, A. R. (2005) Forensic assessment of sexual interest: a review. *Aggression and Violent Behaviour*, 10, 193–217.

Laws, D. R. & Ward, T. (eds) (2010) *Desistance from Sex Offending: Alternatives to Throwing away the Keys*. London: Karnac Books.

Lord, A. & Perkins, D. (in press) Challenges to recovery for mentally disordered sexual offenders. *Journal of Sexual Aggression*.

Lösel, F, & Schmucker, M. (2005) The effectiveness of treatment for sexual offenders: a comprehensive meta-analysis. *Journal of Experimental Criminology*, 1, 117–46.

McGuire, J. (1995) *What Works: Reducing Reoffending Guidelines from Research and Practice*. Chichester: Wiley.

McGuire J. (2013) 'What Works' to reduce reoffending: 18 years on. In L. A. Craig, L. Dixon & T. A. Gannon (eds) *What Works in Offender Rehabilitation: An Evidence Based Approach to Assessment and Treatment*. Chichester: Wiley-Blackwell.

McNeill, F. & Weaver, B. (2010) Changing lives? Desistance research and offender management. Glasgow: Scottish Centre for Crime and Justice Research. Available at: http://www.sccjr.ac.uk/documents/Report%202010%2003%20-%20Changing%20Lives.pdf.

Marshall, W. L., Anderson, D. & Fernandez, Y. (1999) *Cognitive Behavioural Treatment of Sexual Offenders*. Chichester: Wiley.

Merdian, H. L., Curtis, C., Thakker, J., Wilson, N. & Boer, D. P. (2013) The three dimensions of online child pornography offending. *Journal of Sexual Aggression*, 19(1), 121–32.

Mokros, A., Dombert, B., Osterheider, M., Zappalà, A. & Santilla, P. (2010) Assessment of pedophilic sexual interest with an attentional choice reaction time task. *Archives of Sexual Behavior*, 39(5), 1081–90.

Perkins, D. E. & Hogue, T. (2011) Phallometric responses to consenting sex, rape and violence in relation to eye movement responses. Paper presented at the Annual Conference of the Association of the Treatment of Sexual Abusers (ATSA), Toronto, November.

Radford, L., Corral, S., Bradley, C., Fisher, H., Bassett, l., Howat, N. & Collishaw, S. (2011) *Child Abuse and Neglect in the UK*. London: NSPCC.

Seto, M. C., Maric, A. & Barbaree, H. E. (2001) The role of pornography in the etiology of sexual aggression. *Aggression and Violent Behavior*, 6(1), 35–53.

Snowden, R. J., Craig, R. L. & Gray, N. S. (2011) Indirect behavioral measures of cognition among sexual offenders. *Journal of Sex Research*, 48(2–3), 192–217.

Stoltenborgh, M., van IJzendoorn, M. H., Euser, E. M. & Bakermans-Kranenburg, M. J. (2011) A global perspective on child sexual abuse: meta-analysis of prevalence around the world. *Child Maltreatment*, 16(2), 79–101.

Thornton, D. (2002) Constructing and testing a framework for dynamic risk assessment. *Sexual Abuse: A Journal of Research and Treatment*, 14, 139–53.

Ward, T. & Stewart, C. A. (2003) The treatment of sex offenders: risk management and good lives. *Professional Psychology: Research and Practice*, 34, 353–60.

Willis, G. M., Yates, P. M., Gannon, T. A. & Ward, T. (2012) How to integrate the good lives model into treatment programs for sexual offending: an introduction and overview. *Sexual Abuse: A Journal of Research and Treatment*. Online version, retrieved 12 July 2012.

Wilson, R. J., Cortoni, F. & McWhinnie, A. J. (2005) Circles of support & accountability: a Canadian national replication of outcome findings. *Sex Abuse*, 21, 412.

Wolitzky-Taylor, K. B., Resnick, H. S., McCauley, J. L., Amstadter, A. B., Kilpatrick, D. G. & Ruggiero, K. J. (2011) Is reporting of rape on the rise? A comparison of women with reported versus unreported rape experiences in the National Women's Study-Replication. *Journal of Interpersonal Violence*, 26(4), 807–32.

6

VIOLENT OFFENDING

Developments in assessment and treatment in the community

Matt Bruce

Overview

The current chapter focuses on violence between individuals (e.g. child maltreatment, intimate partner violence, elder abuse, youth violence and assault by strangers). Within the context of offending, a violent offence can be defined as the intentional and malevolent physical injuring of another without adequate social justification, resulting in conflict with the criminal justice system (Blackburn 1993). Although sexual offences technically fall within the definition of violence they shall not be the focus here. This chapter will begin by providing a brief overview of violence in order to highlight the scale of the problem. Attention will then be focused on assessment considerations and methods (both nomothetic and idiographic). Specific emphasis will be placed on the importance of examining the individual's motivation for violence, developmental origins, as well as the behavioural, affective and cognitive components in order to inform a robust idiographic formulation. The following section outlines ten best practice principles for effective 'high impact' community treatment. Single and multi-modal treatment programmes currently being delivered in community settings will then be reviewed. The section will conclude with a description of a multi-programme model known as the Positive Community Relationships Programme and evaluate it in light of the best practice principles.

The scale of the problem

An estimated 1.6 million people are killed each year as a result of violence, making it one of the world's leading causes of mortality (WHO, 2002). In UK communities, at least 1 in 10 people report physically assaulting or deliberately hitting someone within a five-year period (Coid et al. 2006). In 2012, approximately 2 million people living in England and Wales were victims of violent crime (Taylor and Bond 2012) costing the taxpayer in excess of £13 billion a year (Rubin et al. 2008). Whilst it is prudent to be cautious when interpreting crime figures (Hollin 2004), the financial burden associated with violent offending (e.g. legal fees, imprisonment costs, policing and security requirements, services for victims and their families) is enormous. Furthermore, the outcomes associated with violent offenders are equally sobering. They are more likely to demonstrate elevated rates of morbidity, self-harm, mortality and recidivism than their non-violent counterparts (Rubin et al. 2008; Capaldi et al. 2012).

Assessment

Assessment considerations

Persistent violent offenders, or individuals who exhibit 'habitual aggression' (Huesmann 1998), often come to the attention of community forensic services via orders, supervision directives or licence conditions. Their relationship to 'help' is often damaged and their aggressive behaviour is typically an indication that they perceive the world as a fearful or harmful place. This may be especially true for young people referred to Child and Adolescent Mental Health Teams/Professionals by Social Services or Youth Offending Teams. Such individuals are likely to be actively engaged in fearful, rejecting, and/or fragmented relationships. Rather than treatment-seeking, many violent offenders are considered treatment-rejecting (Tyrer et al. 2003) or, perhaps more accurately, treatment-fearing. Indeed, 'treatment' implies that an 'illness' has been exposed which requires a 'cure'. Arguably, for many violent offenders, aggression has served to protect their physical and psychological integrity and even provide them with a sense of worth, self-esteem and peer acceptance. Curing them of such a life-preserving or identify-affirming strategy is often far from appealing. Violent offenders are often resistant to admitting the extent of their offending, appreciating the impact on the victim, taking responsibility and committing themselves to change (Polaschek and Reynolds 2004). For many offenders, forensic mental health services in the community represent systems of authority and control, armed with expert law-abiding professionals, eager to expose weaknesses and fire derogatory labels at any unsuspecting victim that enters their doors. Accordingly, violence or treatment-oriented assessment can be a turbulent and challenging process for both offender and assessor.

It is therefore often advantageous to expose (and where appropriate dispel) these views from the outset of the assessment. This should be done in a non-accusatory, normalising manner to convey a wish to understand the individuals' situation. For many offenders, interviews are dangerous, anxiety-laden interactions where disclosures can have considerable punitive consequences upon them. It is therefore important to be clear about what the assessment will cover as well as what it will be used for and how it might be helpful to them. Most importantly, a good assessment is one that enhances the offender's engagement and readiness for change. A number of strategies are useful to integrate into any violence assessment:

- At the outset of the interview ask how they would prefer, or feel most comfortable, being addressed
- Expose and dispel any possible inaccurate beliefs that might impede the assessment process
- Avoid (if possible) referring to file information or scribing notes during the first session
- Ask about strengths, goals and aspirations and demonstrate an interest in these
- Enquire about skills and strategies that will help (or have helped) achieve these goals
- Explore (risk) factors that might delay or prevent achievement of these goals.

Integrating strengths-focused questions into violence assessment is critical for enhancing engagement and levels of agreement, reducing negative reactions, demonstrating and highlighting the individuality of the offender, as well as developing optimism for both offender and assessor. Such an approach is not designed to substitute but instead to facilitate subsequent assessment of risk. Table 6.1 outlines a number of strength-based questions (Saleebey 1997).

Assessment methods

The multifaceted nature of violence and aggression makes accurate assessment a notoriously challenging task. Indeed, more than 150 assessment tools currently exist worldwide (Fazel et al. 2012) to assist practitioners understand and assess violence.

TABLE 6.1 Examples of strength-focused questions

Strength domains	Example questions
Survival	Given what you have gone through for most of your life, how have you managed to survive so far?
Support	Who in your life has given you special understanding, support and/or guidance?
Possibility	What are your hopes and aspirations? What has been your biggest ambition in life?
Esteem	When people say good things about you what kinds of things do they say?
Exception	When things have gone well in your life, what do you think this has been down to?
Achievement	What things have you managed to achieve/do that others haven't?

Source: Adapted from Saleebey (1997).

Assessments often fall within two broad, but often related, categories of evaluation – retrospective and prospective. Retrospective assessments require that the assessor determine why an act of violence may have occurred and are often used to establish culpability in criminal cases. Prospective assessments involve the assessor determining the likelihood of future violence. This often includes detailing the nature, function, frequency, severity and even timing of potential violence acts in the future. Assessments can also be *nomothetic* – generalised or group-based such as the Risk Matrix 2000 (Thornton et al. 2003) and Violence Risk Assessment Guide (VRAG) (Harris et al. 1993), or *idiographic* – individualised and person-centred in nature. Recent years have witnessed a bridging between these historically distinct approaches to violence assessment such as the Historical, Clinical, Risk Management – Version 3 (HCR-V3) (Douglas et al. 2013; Scurich et al. 2012). The next section explores idiographic approaches to assessment of violence.

Idiographic approaches

Idiographic or individualised approaches to assessment enable clinicians to generate richer understanding of the nature and function of violence for an individual. Idiographic assessment of violence should therefore examine its: (i) motivation and/or function; (ii) developmental origins; and (iii) behavioural, affective and cognitive components. Utilising this information, a working idiographic formulation can be generated and shared with the individual and (where necessary) relevant professionals or agencies.

Assessing the 'motivation' for violence

Motivation is a psychological phenomenon that can be defined as the process that initiates, guides and maintains goal-oriented behaviours. Accordingly, assessment of the motivation for violence should always include detailed examination of all violent offences, including (wherever possible) those not resulted in conviction and near misses (violence was averted, curtailed, abandoned). Motives, planning, goals, victims and consequences should be noted and subjected to comparative analyses (i.e. how they compare structurally and functionally to previous patterns of violence).

Numerous motives underlying violent acts have been espoused in the aggression literature deployed to achieve a conscious or unconscious goal. Understanding the specific motives, rather than simply the risk correlates, is a crucial (yet often overlooked) component of violence assessment. Indeed, it has been argued there is increasing acceptance in describing aggression less by its nature and more by its motivation (Ireland 2009). Perhaps the best established are 'reactive' and 'proactive' aggression motives. Reactive (or hostile, expressive or angry) aggression refers to the drive to attack, harm or injure another in response to real (or imagined) frustrations, threats, provocations, aversive events and territorial instructions (Berkowitz 1993; Megargee 2011). It has been further characterised

TABLE 6.2 Examples of motivations for violence and offender statements

Aggression motivation	Examples of offender statements
Protection	He was out to get me.
Social recognition	I had to show that I wasn't a pussy.
Positive outcomes	I needed to win that argument.
Pleasure	I wanted to humiliate her.
Excitement	It was an adrenalin rush.
Compliance	I felt pressured to do it.
Provocation	He refused to get out of my way.
Financial	I needed the money for drugs.
Victim	I just wanted it to stop.
Hero	Nobody threatens my mates.
Professional	I had to do a job for someone.
Revenger	I had to put things right once and for all.

as emotionally driven, uncontrolled, impulsive and likely to occur in response to a blocked goal (Ireland and Ireland 2008). Conversely, proactive (or planned, instrumental, predatory) aggression refers to the conscious and controlled use of violence as a means of achieving desired goals (Buss 1961). These goals may include acquisition, self-defence, dominance, status, power and self-esteem (Megargee 2011). In recent years, the 'mixed-motive' aggressor has challenged this mutually exclusive dichotomy (Gendreau and Archer 2005). There have been a number of helpful developments which can be used to distinguish motives for violent offending (Gudjonsson and Sigurdsson 2004; Ohlsson and Ireland 2011; Youngs and Canter 2012), as summarised in Table 6.2.

Assessing the 'developmental' origins of violence

Assessment of any presenting problem requires understanding of its developmental course, thus charting violence across the individual's lifespan assists in the identification of its origin, function, habitual strength and most importantly its treatability. Contrary to popular belief, evidence suggests that aggression and violence is not a learnt behaviour. Observational studies indicate that aggression is present from birth, demonstrating a peak intensity at 3 years old (Tremblay et al. 2005) indicating individuals learn to become *non-aggressive* via the combined effects of socialisation and brain maturation (Vitaro et al. 2006). Accordingly, it might be deduced that life-course persistent aggressive behaviour reflects a number of developmental failures such as defective learning environments (both at home and/or school), family discord, parental psychopathology and individual neuro-cognitive deficits.

Developmental theories have linked the emergence of the reactive–proactive dichotomy to a number of environmental and individual childhood factors. Whilst reactive aggression is argued to proliferate in harsh, threatening and unpredictable environments or abusive parenting, proactive violence thrives in the context of supportive environments that demonstrate the value of aggression in resolving conflicts and advancing personal interests (Dodge et al. 1997). Reactive, but not proactive, aggression is associated with a temperamental disposition to anxiety, emotional dysregulation and distractibility as well as deficits in social and cognitive functioning (Vitaro et al. 2006). Arguably, the concept of psychopathy, with its emphasis on callous-unemotional traits, may well index those individuals who follow an exclusively proactive aggressive trajectory and thereby implicate a biological basis.

Assessing 'behavioural, cognitive and affective' components of violence

It is also important to assess the strength of violent responses or 'habits' (Megargee 2011) in order to understand how these have been reinforced both behaviourally and cognitively. Social learning (Bandura 1973) and information processing theories (Crick and Dodge 1994) provide useful frameworks to assess the nature and risk of proactive aggression, explaining how violent behaviours are acquired over the lifespan (via operant conditioning or reinforcement contingencies). Violent behaviours can be positively (e.g. securing goods, dominating others) and negatively (e.g. removal of stress, threat) reinforced via direct experience or through the observation of other aggressors. Furthermore, observational learning is thought to be most powerful when the observer values or identifies with the aggressor.

Cognitive and social-information processing theories of aggression (Gilbert and Daffern 2011) postulate that individuals with a propensity for violence hold more elaborate and accessible aggression-related cognitions. A useful way of assessing violence cognitions is through identifying aggression-related knowledge structures or schemas. Huesmann (1998) discusses two types of aggression-related schematic content, the first being *aggressive behavioural scripts* initially acquired through observation of others and which serve to define situations and guide behaviours. These scripts are subsequently deployed and reinforced over time until they become firmly established, well rehearsed and readily accessible. Whilst this process operates for non-aggressive scripts, habitually aggressive individuals tend to be unwilling and/or unable to deploy these. *Normative beliefs* constitute a further knowledge structure that influences the likelihood of aggression. These beliefs facilitate the use of aggression if perceived as appropriate and socially acceptable to the individual. Another factor responsible for the activation of aggressive cognitions is the *hostile attributional bias* (Crick and Dodge 1994) which refers to the tendency for some individuals to over-attribute hostile intent to others' behaviours even when the actual intent is benign or the situation is ambiguous (Gilbert and Daffern 2010). Accordingly, it is important to assess the presence and strength of aggressive behaviour scripts, the availability and effectiveness of non-aggressive scripts, the presence of normative beliefs in permitting and achieving goals via violent means and the tendency for hostile attributional biases.

Finally, the role of affective arousal should be considered in the activation of aggressive cognitions and behaviour. Anger, fear, anxiety and depression can activate related aggressive scripts, normative beliefs and attributional biases (Gilbert and Daffern 2010). Indeed, it is well documented that affective arousal can block or impair rational or non-aggressive cognitive processing resulting in only the most well-rehearsed scripts being retrieved and subsequently activated (Huesmann 1998).

Idiographic formulation

A number of theory-driven approaches to violence formulation provide very useful frameworks for developing individualised conceptualisations of offending behaviour, including the General Aggression Model (Anderson and Bushman 2002), 'Good Lives Model' (Ward and Brown 2004), Offence Paralleling Behaviour Approach (Jones 2008), Structured Professional Judgement (HCR-V3) (Douglas et al. 2013) as well as Functional Analytic Approaches (e.g. SORC: Lee-Evans 1994; ABC: Leslie and O'Reilly 1999; ACF: Daffern et al. 2007). A simple, yet multivariate idiographic approach, encompassing many aspects of aggression theory, is the 'Algebra of Aggression' (Megargee 1976, 2009, 2011). By way of illustration, the components of the model will first be described (see Table 6.3) and then applied to two case examples, of Rashid and Gary (see Table 6.4). Whilst both men were convicted of manslaughter, this multivariate approach assists the assessor to understand the idiographic origins and function of the violent act as well as provide opportunities to identify individual treatment targets and strengths.

Megargee proposes that at any given time, multiple responses, both aggressive and non-aggressive, are competing for expression. He describes this process as reflecting 'response competition' in which the behaviour that offers the *most* satisfactions at the *least* cost will be selected for expression. The 'reaction potential' (or net strength) of this reaction will be determined by subtracting those factors deterring it from those promoting an aggressive response. Megargee formulated a pseudo-algebraic formula representing this (Table 6.3).

TABLE 6.3 The Algebra of Aggression

Potential for Violence = $[A(t) + H + S(a)] - [I + S(i)]$		
A	=	Instigation to Aggression
t	=	Victim or target
H	=	Habit strength
I	=	Individual's inhibitions against violence
S(a)	=	Unique situational factors encouraging violence
S(i)	=	Unique situational factors inhibiting violence

Source: Megargee (1976, 2011).

Instigation to Aggression (A): individual factors promoting or instigating aggressive responses can be divided into 'intrinsic' and 'extrinsic' instigation to aggression. Intrinsic instigation is rooted in frustration–aggression theory (Berkowitz 1993) and relates to reactive aggression which can be traced to psychological (e.g. frustrations, provocations, threats and anger) and physiological (e.g. genetic predispositions, physical diseases, pain, psychoactive substances). Extrinsic instigation is related to social learning theory (Bandura 1973) which serves to achieve desired goals such as obtaining tangibles, self-esteem, power, social status.

Victim or target (t): refers to the actual and/or likely recipients of violence (e.g. specific individuals, groups or populations).

Habit strength (H): the reaction potential strength of aggressive responses is heavily dependent on habit strength. This takes into account learning history and can be explored in terms of social learning, operant conditioning and reinforcement contingencies. Individuals exhibiting persistent aggressive responses have developed strong, often unconscious, habit strength which is compatible with the social-cognitive notion of aggressive behavioural scripts and normative beliefs (Huesmann 1998).

Individual inhibitions against violence (I): a number of broad factors can be understood as deterring aggressive responses, including anxiety or conditioned fear of punishment, learned ethical prohibitions (these can be general or specific, lasting or temporary), empathy or identification with victim or target, physiological and physical factors as well as practical issues (e.g. the possible failure of the aggressive response).

Situational factors encouraging (S[a]) *and inhibiting violence* (S[i]): there are a number of situational factors which can enhance the reaction potential of aggressive responses. These can include a broad range of cultural or environmental factors such as political unrest, war zones, organised violence, gang conflicts and bystander provocation (Megargee 2011). Crowding, contagion, anonymity, architecture, access to potential victims and weapon availability are all empirically derived examples of situational factors that increase the potential for violence (Megargee 2009). Conversely, witnesses, physical barriers separating the aggressor and victim, surveillance technology, as well as intimidation by target, constitute a number of situational factors that may inhibit an aggressive response.

Arguably, the strength of this formulation approach is that it is broad enough to accommodate multiple factors and theories which attempt to explain the nature, origin and function of aggressive behaviour. Furthermore, it facilitates the development of individualised, action-oriented, narrative-based and ampliative (creation of new meaning) case formulations. Indeed, whilst Rashid and Gary were both convicted of manslaughter, the factors leading to the commission of their offences were very different and subsequently required distinct intervention and management strategies in the community. A further strength of this model is it explicitly draws the assessor's attention to individual and situational factors which are likely to protect the individual from responding violently, for example Gary's prosocial attitudes regarding the use of violence and his relatively weak habit strength and Rashid's religious faith and views about the use of violence on women as well as his fear of being caught. Disadvantages are that it does not offer a systematic framework with which to make final judgements about risk, discern levels of intervention required to manage it or address motivational issues for treatment.

Community treatment

Something works

The proliferation of meta-analytic studies published over the past few decades suggests that offender 'treatments', on balance, are positive for adults (Hollin 2004). A recent systematic review of 198 evaluating interventions for populations (age ≥16) at high risk of violent behaviour found a statistically significant advantage for interventions compared to the various comparators (Hockenhull et al. 2012). Moreover, the interventions targeted at mental health populations and particularly male groups in community settings were well supported as they achieved stronger effects than interventions with other groups. The latter finding has been observed in other meta-analyses (Redondo et al. 1999; Lipsey and Cullen 2007). These findings suggest that 'something works'.

Assessment, treatment and management of violent offenders in the community increasingly have come under focus and scrutiny for a number of reasons: (i) the introduction of new offender sentencing legislation such as Youth Justice Liaison and Diversion Schemes, Community Treatment Orders, Suspended Sentence Orders, Mental Health Treatment Requirements, and Drug Rehabilitation Requirements; (ii) increasing emphasis on 'convergence' working which emphasises the importance of multi-agency working (e.g. Multi-Agency Public Protection Arrangements – MAPPA) to manage high risk offenders; (iii) recent decommissioning of the Dangerous and Severe Personality Disorder (DSPD) programme and a reinvestment in community treatment and management of high risk offenders with likely personality disorder; (iv) Lord Bradley's (Bradley 2009) appeal for the provision of adequate community alternatives to custody and a national rehabilitation strategy for those leaving prison; and (v) encouraging findings that diversion to community services for adults and young people is associated with decreased costs, reduced reoffending and improved mental health (Sainsbury Centre 2009).

Perhaps the most established and accepted finding from meta-analytic studies is that treatments for violent offenders that conform to the risk, need, and responsivity principles (Andrews and Bonta 2006) demonstrate more superior effects to those that do not. This finding was also most significant in community versus secure

TABLE 6.4 Application of the 'Algebra of Aggression' to two case examples

Algebra of Aggression		Rashid	Gary
A	=	Instigation to Aggression	
	Intrinsic instigation	Rashid reported that prior to stabbing his victim he was stressed, tired and withdrawing from cocaine use. He also felt threatened and disrespected by the victim.	Gary reported that just before stabbing his victim he discovered she had been having sex with his friend. He was overcome with uncontrollable rage. He was also intoxicated.
	Extrinsic instigation	Although Rashid reported that he wanted money for drugs he stated that he also wanted to dominate the man who 'flaunted' his wealth and teach him a lesson.	Gary reported little to support the role of extrinsic instigation.
t	=	Victim or target	
		Male stranger	Wife
H	=	Habit strength	
		As a child, Rashid recalled that his father controlled the family with threats of violence. He also observed his elder brothers use violence to get food and money from his peers at school.	Gary recalled a very inconsistent and unpredictable mother who often mocked or invalidated his experiences. He could not recall either parents using violence.
		As Rashid matured he discovered that his own use of aggression both intimidated and impressed his peers. He also learnt that aggression allowed him to achieve his goals rapidly and offered immediate avoidance of unpleasant situations.	At school he was bullied and found it difficult to make friends. Occasionally he 'saw red', lost his temper and got into fights. He reported that he tended to bottle up his feelings rather than share them.

I	=	Individual's inhibitions against violence	Rashid reported that his religion condemned the use of violence. He believed that a man should never hit a woman. On the day of the offence he reported being physically exhausted.	Gary reported that he condemned 'thugs' who routinely used aggression. He did not associate with violent peers and avoided competitive sports. Gary reported that he loved his wife and could not understand the severity of his actions.
S(a)	=	Unique situational factors encouraging violence	Rashid's peers had encouraged him to obtain more cocaine. He also recalled that it was late at night and the streets were very quiet. It was heavily raining reducing visibility. Rashid carried a knife. The ATM was located in a small side street. The male victim who was wearing a suit refused to surrender his wallet, made derogatory remarks and tried to wrestle Rashid.	Gary recalled returning home early from work and entering his kitchen when he overheard his wife and friend having sex upstairs. There were knives on the worktop counter.
S(i)	=	Unique situational factors inhibiting violence	Rashid stated that he was aware of a small security camera. The victim was taller than him and holding a golfing umbrella.	There were very few situational factors which acted to inhibit Gary's response.

TABLE 6.5 Ten key principles for effective community treatment of violent offenders

	Principle	Descriptor
1	A cognitive-behavioural approach	Social learning theory, skills training, cognitive restructuring, differential association, behavioural system
2	Structured delivery programme	Programmes should have clear aims, objectives and measurable outcomes
3	Highly trained facilitators	Practitioners should be expertly trained and receive regular supervision
4	Programme integrity	Organisations should support, manage, audit and evaluate interventions
5	Matching treatment to risk posed	High risk offenders have increased difficulties requiring more intense interventions than their low risk counterparts
6	Focus on criminogenic risk factors	Such as negative emotions, antisocial attitudes, self-control, substance misuse and family factors
7	Responsive programme delivery	Taking into account individual differences in learning styles, personality, motivation, background and strengths
8	Continuity of service provision	Programmes span organisational settings to sustain coherence and maintain engagement and treatment gains
9	Collaborative high quality relationships	Maximising opportunities for, and valuing, good quality relationships between offender and therapist/facilitator
10	Interagency and community networks	Programmes should maintain positive relationships with other agencies involved (or likely to be) with the offender

settings. Current research evidence and expert experience suggest ten key principles for effective, 'high impact' (Hollin 2004) community treatment for violent offenders, which are summarised in Table 6.5.

Treatment programmes

Treatment programmes can be distinguished in terms of primary (offence-specific) or secondary (offence-related) targeting of violence. Community treatments may also differ from custodial programmes with respect to multi-modal working opportunities with the former more able to blend a number of interventions across different agencies utilising a specific social milieu (e.g. volunteering organisations, outpatient services, support groups, art projects, educational programmes).

Single and multi-modal models

Although the majority of treatment programmes for violent adult offenders have been widely disseminated and have acquired a substantial evidence base within custodial settings (Gilbert and Daffern 2010), few have established a solid empirical foundation for community delivery. Perhaps the most established programmes for treating violent offenders are anger management and cognitive skills programmes.

Anger management refers to a collection of cognitive-behavioural programmes which are often founded on the principles espoused by the stress inoculation–coping skills approach (Novaco 1975, 1997). These programmes include increasing self-awareness of anger traits and states, identifying triggers and addressing related behaviours. They also include cognitive restructuring, coping strategies, social skills training and relaxation training. Examples of these programmes are Controlling Anger and Learning to Manage It – Effective Relapse-Prevention Program (CALMER (Winogron et al. 2001), the successor of CALM) and Aggression Replacement Training (ART) (Glick and Goldstein 1987). These programmes have been delivered in residential, school and community settings spanning criminal justice and mental health settings. CALMER targets internal and external factors that trigger anger, arousal-reduction techniques, thoughts that lead to problematic behaviour, assertive communication skills, and development of a relapse-prevention plan (Winogron et al. 2001). Aggression Replacement Training (ART), originally designed for adolescents (and since adapted for violent adult offenders), is a psychoeducational treatment with three key components: social skills, anger control training and moral reasoning with evidence demonstrating its efficacy (Goldstein et al. 1998; Hatcher et al. 2008). However, there appears to be mixed support for the effectiveness of anger management programmes. Specifically, the reactive-aggressor focus of these programmes has been criticised for neglecting alternative motives for violence (e.g. pleasure, compliance and status-restorative functions) as well as important social–cognitive processes such as entrenched normative beliefs and aggressive behavioural scripts (Polaschek and Reynolds 2004; Gilbert and Daffern 2010).

Cognitive skills programmes may therefore command greater superiority for the treatment of violent offenders who exhibit entrenched instrumental aggression. A number of studies have demonstrated significant reductions in reoffending following completion of these programmes compared to controls (Robinson 1995; Lowencamp et al. 2006; Tong and Farrington 2006). Two well-established treatment approaches are cognitive skills and cognitive self-change programmes. Cognitive skills programmes encompass a number of interventions including Enhanced Thinking Skills (ETS; Clarke 2000), Reasoning and Rehabilitation (R&R; Ross et al. 1988; Porporino and Fabiano 2000) and Think First (McGuire 2000) and typically target problem-solving, interpersonal skills, impulse control and self-management, conflict resolution and critical thinking (Gilbert and Daffern 2010). These programmes have demonstrated treatment effects for moderate and higher risk offenders when delivered in the community (McGuire et al. 2008).

Evaluations of these programmes in the community have demonstrated significantly reduced rates of offending compared to controls, non-completers and non-starters (Hollin 2004, 2008; Palmer et al. 2008). The Cognitive Self-Change (CSC; Bush 1995) programme targets criminogenic attitudes, beliefs and thinking patterns in custodial settings over three distinct phases: the first phase involves group socialisation and programme orientation; the second phase supports offenders to identify their high risk thinking patterns, adopt alternative prosocial cognitions and develop a relapse-prevention plan; the third phase (completed in the community) involves weekly maintenance group meetings (Polaschek and Reynolds 2004).

The last decade has witnessed significant developments in interventions for violent offenders. In part these have emerged following a number of criticisms of anger management and cognitive skills programmes which include: the relatively narrow and insufficient understanding of emotions and cognition in programmes offered to violent offenders (Ward and Nee 2009); a lack of specificity to tackle entrenched aggressive scripts (Gilbert and Daffern 2010); inadequate programme duration and intensity ('dosage'); and a limited coverage of multiple criminogenic needs that underpin violent offending (Polaschek 2006; Ware et al. 2011). Multi-modal programmes that include a broad range of treatment targets have included the Violence Prevention Programme (Dixon and Polaschek 1992); the Violence Offenders Therapeutic Programme (Ware et al. 2011); and the Violence Reduction Programme (Wong et al. 2007). The suite of effective rehabilitative innovations has expanded beyond the risk–need–responsivity paradigm and incorporates contributions from other fields of psychology such as faith-based interventions (Burnside et al. 2005), therapeutic communities, 'strength-based' and Good Lives approaches (Ward and Stewart 2003), as well as Dialectical Behavioural Therapy (Evershed et al. 2003; Berzins and Trestman 2004). Two programmes that hold particular promise for helping individuals desist from violence is the Violence Reduction Programme (VRP) and Dialectical Behavioural Therapy (DBT).

The Violence Reduction Programme

The VRP (Wong et al. 2007) is a risk-reduction focused correctional programme, originally designed for institutional-based treatment, for violence-prone forensic clients. Embedded within risk–need–responsivity principles (Bonta and Andrews 2007) and the Transtheoretical Model of Change (Prochaska and DiClemente 2005) the programme is delivered within a three-phase model. Phase one (informed by the responsivity principles necessary for those in contemplation or preparation stage) aims to support the individual develop insight into past patterns of violence, identify treatment targets and enhance the therapeutic relationship. Phase two (driven by action-oriented principles) focuses on acquisition of alternative non-violent goal-oriented skills. Phase three (arguably pertaining to maintenance principles) tackles relapse-prevention strategies, skill consolidation and generalisation. The programme has demonstrated reductions in recidivism and violent institutional conduct as well as less serious violent reoffending (Di Placido et al. 2006).

Dialectical Behavioural Therapy

DBT (Linehan 1993) – borne from cognitive behavioural therapy, empirical evidence is accumulating to suggest that DBT represents a promising approach to the understanding and treatment of violent offenders (Berzins and Trestman 2004; Bosch et al. 2012). Indeed, the use of DBT with offenders both in the community and correctional settings has soared (McCann et al. 2000; Low et al. 2001; Trupin et al. 2002). Not only are the risk–need–responsivity principles easily realised within the DBT approach, but it also encompasses other positive psychology factors such as mindfulness, and explicitly addresses responsivity issues in a structured way (e.g. pre-emptive work around disengagement 'signatures'). Based on a modular framework, individuals are taught skills in mindfulness, emotional regulation, distress tolerance and interpersonal effectiveness (Berzins and Trestman 2004) in a weekly group format. Individuals also engage in one-to-one therapy where treatment targets are collaboratively identified and skills practice is discussed. Behavioural chain analyses of both violent and prosocial alternatives constitute key components of this approach.

A multi-programme model

The Positive Community Relationships Programme (PCRP; Kerr et al. 2013), although primarily designed for high risk violent offenders with personality disorder (PD), views all individuals with a propensity for violence to occupy different positions with respect to their relationship to 'help'. Participants can access the PCRP whilst living in the community and it is delivered in residential and outpatient settings. The PCRP model (see Figure 6.1) views engagement (or readiness to change) as a dynamic position, which is intricately linked to the individual's relationship to help and fluctuates over the course of the person's lifespan. This position will be influenced by a multitude of factors such as the individual's attachment style, personality functioning, self-awareness, peer and cultural influences, self-efficacy and perceived locus of control. Conceptually grounded in the Transtheoretical Model of Change (Prochaska and DiClemente 2005), Personal, Interpersonal, and Community Reinforcement (Andrews and Bonta 2006) and Good Lives (Ward and Brown 2004) principles, the PCRP aims to promote 'transformative' relational experiences with offenders at every stage of their pursuit of primary 'goods' in socially acceptable and personally meaningful ways. This model presupposes that interpersonal violence results from a restricted repertoire of choices, or adaptive plans, for achieving purpose and meaning in their lives. The PCRP is composed of discrete intervention programmes carefully sequenced and designed to target the individual's current readiness for change.

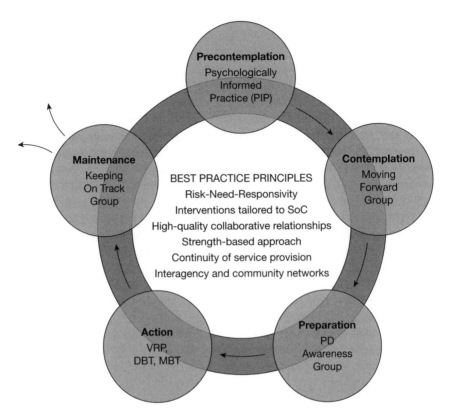

FIGURE 6.1 The Positive Community Relationships Programme (PCRP)

Precontemplation Stage of Change and Psychologically Informed Practice (PIP) Individuals in this stage are considered not yet able or willing to contemplate lifestyle change and therefore require consciousness raising, dramatic relief and environmental re-evaluation strategies (DiClemente et al. 1991). An intervention, referred to as a Psychologically Informed Practice (PIP), was developed for the purpose of generating 'transformative' relational experiences and targeting stage appropriate needs. This enabling approach is underpinned by the principles of Therapeutic Communities (see Jones 1962 for review) and Psychologically Informed Environments (see Johnson and Haigh 2010 for review) which focus on high quality relationships, prosocial modelling and positive environmental experiences. Staff groups in approved premises (providing temporary accommodation for high risk offenders) receive intensive training in personality disorder, relationship skills and psychologically informed interactions. The primary objectives of PIP are for residents to experience positive relationships as well as develop sufficient levels of self-awareness and motivation to enable movement to a contemplative stage of change.

Contemplation Stage of Change and Moving Forward Group Individuals who move to a contemplative stage of change, or those who already occupy this position, are encouraged to engage in a group. The Moving Forward Group aims to decrease the individual's feelings of ambivalence regarding change, improve their experiences of group working as well as develop motivation and self-efficacy. It is a brief seven-session programme devised from the principles of Motivational Interviewing (Miller and Rollnick 1991) and Good Lives Model (Ward and Stewart 2003) and encourages individuals to devise their own goals in order to increase personal ownership of change and optimise intrinsic motivation (Miller and Rollnick 2002). An important defining feature of this group programme is that it explicitly avoids references to offending. It is hoped that the content and process of this group will constitute a positive and enabling experience leading a number of individuals to move into a preparation stage of change.

Preparation Stage of Change and PD Awareness Group As many violent offenders have comorbid personality disorders, the aim of this group is to further develop awareness of these conditions and explore how they may impede the individual from achieving their goals or primary 'goods'. This six-session PD Awareness programme draws on a number of evidenced-based principles for motivating offenders to embrace and commit to change. The group hopes to enhance relational experiences, self-awareness, motivation and strengthen commitment to change.

Action Stage of Change and DBT or VRP Individuals who enter action, or those who are exhibiting observable but transient efforts to commit to change, are encouraged to take part in either the Violence Reduction Programme (VRP: Wong et al. 2007, as outlined in the previous section), Dialectical Behavioural Therapy (DBT: Linehan 1993; Berzins and Trestman 2004) programme or Schema Therapy (Young et al. 2003). Typically, individuals who exhibit persistent instrumental violence, with little reactive components, are encouraged to undertake VRP or Schema Therapy, whilst those individuals assessed as presenting with reactive or mixed-motive violence (frequently meeting criteria for Borderline Personality Disorder) are encouraged to attend the DBT group. In line with stage-specific targets, individuals are supported, via programme components, to seek and utilise positive social supports to reinforce change as well as substitute former antisocial cognitive and behavioural patterns for healthier adaptive alternatives (Prochaska and Levesque 2002).

Maintenance Stage of Change and Keeping on Track Group As follow-up sessions are important for sustaining the benefits of rehabilitative programmes (Day and Casey 2010), individuals deemed to be in maintenance following the successful completion of programmes (irrespective of where or when completed) are encouraged to attend the Keeping on Track Group. Consistent with Trans-theoretical, Good Lives and Personal, Interpersonal and Community Reinforcement principles, this group aims to maintain and support links with voluntary and community providers, facilitate ongoing prosocial relationships as well as promote and enhance a valued sense of personal identity and efficacy.

The PCRP model can be evaluated in light of the ten key principles for community treatment for violent offenders (see Table 6.5). With respect to Principles 1 to 4, the PCRP is conceptually grounded and structured within cognitive-behavioural approaches, each with a proven evidence base for use with violent offenders. Furthermore, the PCRP model and each stage-specific programme has an accompanying manual which details the aims, objectives, session-by-session content, facilitator/therapist qualifications, resources and outcome measures required for intervention delivery. All facilitators and therapists are required to undertake appropriate levels of training relevant to the programme or therapy being delivered and receive regular group and individual supervision. Programme integrity is monitored and maintained via regular audit and programme evaluation. In reference to Principles 5 and 6, offenders accessing each component of the PCRP model (with the exception of PIP) have been assessed with regard to risk–need principles (e.g. HCR-20/V3, VRP, SAPROF) and deemed to be at 'moderate–high', 'high' or 'very high' risk of violent reoffending. With respect to Principle 7, responsive programme delivery is the defining feature of the PCRP model with its emphasis on personality styles, relationships to 'help', motivation, readiness for change, strength-based assessment and 'Good Lives' approach. Principle 8, continuity of service provision, is partially met by the PCRP in so far as some of the model components are also delivered within the service's medium secure unit and a number of local approved premises. Accordingly, violent offenders may enter the PCRP whilst in approved premises or hospital and continue their engagement in other community settings. Principle 9, collaborative high quality relationships, is central to the PCRP model. All facilitators undergo specific training (co-facilitated by former service users) in working with individuals with complex and challenging interpersonal styles. Finally, with respect to Principle 10, interagency and community networks are indispensible components of the PCRP model. Many PCRP facilitators also work within other community service providers and agencies thereby having dual roles (e.g. care coordination, offender managers, project workers or occupational therapists) in order to maximise offender networks and opportunities for community integration.

Whilst this PCRP model holds promise with respect to its adherence to many of the ten key principles for effective community treatment for violent offending, it remains vulnerable to a number of limitations. First, the model requires sound strategic planning and investment so that it may function within a number of related but essentially distinct service providers, all of which may have competing philosophies, practices, funding streams and outcome targets related to this population. Second, the PCRP model, embedded within the community system, relies heavily on the quality and availability of local provision (e.g. substance misuse programmes and specialist employment agencies would be essential links in the model). Third, the model does not specifically address what tools are used to measure 'stages of change' or how (and when) an offender might be considered suitable for discharge.

Conclusions

In this chapter, violence has been conceptualised as a multifaceted construct stemming from a complex interplay of factors spanning biological, psychological and social systems. Accordingly, this chapter has attempted to stress the importance of effective practitioner engagement, idiographic assessment and formulation in order to ensure accurate risk assessment, treatment planning and service evaluation. As the understanding of violence evolves, so do the treatment practices and programmes designed to target this multifactorial construct. Unfortunately, compared to the evidence base for sexual offender programmes and interventions in secure settings, community-based programmes are at an early stage of development and require further outcome studies and systematic review. However, as outlined in the this chapter, there are a number of promising treatment programmes currently being delivered in community settings. The PCRP represents one such innovative community treatment programme that addresses violent offending in accordance with both the offender's stage of change and degree of community integration. This multi-programme model – similar to other emerging interventions – champions the importance of recognising protective factors and offender strengths. Indeed, where negativity has proliferated in the lives of many violent individuals, the facilitation of an increasingly optimistic and positive discourse appears to be transformative for both offenders and communities alike. Only time and systematic evaluation will be able to truly ascertain the merits of these new methods of forensic community practice.

References

Anderson, C. A. and B. J. Bushman (2002) 'Human aggression.' *Annual Review of Psychology* 53: 27–51.

Andrews, D. A. and J. Bonta (2006) *The Psychology of Criminal Conduct* (4th edn). Newark, NJ, LexisNexis/Matthew Bender.

Bandura, A. (1973) *Aggression: A Social Learning Analysis.* Englewood Cliffs, NJ, Prentice-Hall.

Berkowitz, L. (1993) *Aggression: Its Causes, Consequences, and Control.* New York, McGraw-Hill.

Berzins, L. and R. L. Trestman (2004) 'The development and implementation of dialectical behaviour therapy in forensic settings.' *International Journal of Forensic Mental Health* 3(1): 93–103.

Blackburn, R. (1993) *The Psychology of Criminal Conduct: Theory, Research and Practice.* Toronto, John Wiley.

Bonta, J. and D. A. Andrews (2007) *Risk–Need–Responsivity Model for Offender Assessment and Rehabilitation.* Ottawa, Ontario, Public Safety Canada.

Bosch, van den L. M. C., M. Hysaj and P. Jacobs (2012) 'DBT in an outpatient forensic setting.' *International Journal of Law and Psychiatry* 35(4): 311–16.

Bradley, L. (2009) *Lord Bradley's Review of People with Mental Health Problems and Learning Disabilities in the Criminal Justice System.* London, Department of Health.

Burnside, J., with N. Loucks, J. R. Adler and G. Rose (2005) *My Brother's Keeper: Faith-based Units in Prison.* Cullompton, Willan Publishing.

Bush, J. (1995) 'Teaching self-risk management to violent offenders.' In J. McGuire (ed.) *What Works: Reducing Reoffending.* Chichester, John Wiley.

Buss, A. H. (1961) *The Psychology of Aggression.* New York, Wiley.

Capaldi, D. M., N. B. Knoble, J. W. Shortt and H. K. Kim (2012) 'A Systematic review of risk factors for intimate partner violence.' *Partner Abuse* 3(2): 231–80.

Clarke, D. A. (2000) *Theory Manual for Enhanced Thinking Skills.* Prepared for the Joint Prison Accreditation Panel. London, Home Office.

Coid, J., M. Yang, A. Roberts, S. Ullrich, P. Moran, P. Bebbington, et al. (2006) 'Violence and psychiatric morbidity in the national household population of Britain: public health implications.' *British Journal of Psychiatry* 189: 12–19.

Crick, N. R. and K. A. Dodge (1994) 'A review and reformulation of social information-processing mechanisms in children's social adjustment.' *Psychological Bulletin* 115: 74–101.

Daffern, M., K. Howells and J. Ogloff (2007) 'What's the point? Towards a methodology for assessing the function of psychiatric inpatient aggression.' *Behaviour Research and Therapy* 45(1): 101–11.

Day, A. and S. Casey (2010) 'Maintenance programs for forensic clients.' *Psychology, Crime and Law* 16: 1–10.

Di Placido, C., T. L. Simon, T. D. Wittle, D. Gu and S. C. Wong (2006) 'Treatment of gang members can reduce recidivism and institutional misconduct.' *Law and Human Behavior* 30(1): 93–114.

DiClemente, C. C., J. O. Prochaska, S. Fairhurst, W. Velicer, M. Velasquez and J. Rossi (1991) 'The process of smoking cessation: an analysis of precontemplation, contemplation, and preparation stages of change.' *Journal of Consulting and Clinical Psychology* 59(2): 295–304.

Dixon, B. and D. L. L. Polaschek (1992) *The Violence Prevention Project Montgomery House.* Wellington, New Zealand, Psychological Services Division Report, Department of Justice.

Dodge, K. A., J. E. Lochman, J. Harnish, J. Bates and G. Pettit (1997) 'Reactive and proactive aggression in school children and psychiatrically impaired chronically assaultive youth.' *Journal of Abnormal Psychology* 106(1): 37–51.

Douglas, K. S., S. D. Hart, et al. (2013) *HCR:V3 Historical, Clinical, Risk Management (Version 3): Assessing Risk for Violence.* Vancouver, Canada, Mental Health, Law, and Policy Institute, Simon Fraser University.

Evershed, S., A. Tennant, D. Boomer, A. Rees, M. Barkham and A. Watson (2003) 'Practice-based outcomes of dialectical behaviour therapy (DBT) targeting anger and violence, with male forensic patients: a pragmatic and non-contemporaneous comparison.' *Criminal Behaviour and Mental Health* 13(3): 189–213.

Fazel, S., J. P. Singh, H. Doll and M. Grann (2012) 'Use of risk assessment instruments to predict violence and antisocial behaviour in 73 samples involving 24,827 people: systematic review and meta-analysis.' *British Medical Journal* 345: e4692.

Gendreau, P. L. and J. Archer (2005) 'Subtypes of aggression in humans and animals.' In R. E. Tremblay, W. W. Hartup and E. J. Archer (eds) *Developmental Origins of Aggression.* New York, Guilford Press: 25–47.

Gilbert, F. and M. Daffern (2010) 'Integrating contemporary aggression theory with violent offender treatment: How thoroughly do interventions target violent behaviour?' *Aggression and Violent Behavior* 15: 167–80.

Gilbert, F. and M. Daffern (2011) 'Illuminating the relationship between personality disorder and violence: the contributions of the General Aggression Model.' *Psychology of Violence* 1: 245–58.

Glick, B. and A. P. Goldstein (1987) 'Aggression Replacement Training.' *Journal of Counseling & Development* 65(7): 356–62.

Goldstein, A. P., B. Glick, et al. (1998) *Aggression Replacement Training: A Comprehensive Intervention for Aggressive Youth* (rev. edn). Champaign, IL, Research Press.

Gudjonsson, G. H. and J. F. Sigurdsson (2004) 'Motivation for offending and personality.' *Legal and Criminological Psychology* 9(1): 69–81.

Harris, G. T., M. E. Rice and V. Quinsey (1993) 'Violent recidivism of mentally disordered offenders: the development of a statistical prediction instrument.' *Criminal Justice and Behavior* 20: 315–35.

Hatcher, R. M., E. J. Palmer, J. McGuire, J. C. Hounsome, C. Bilby and C. R. Hollin (2008) 'Aggression replacement training with adult male offenders within community settings: a reconviction analysis.' *Journal of Forensic Psychiatry & Psychology* 19(4): 517–32.

Hockenhull, J. C., R. Whittington, M. Leitner, W. Barr, J. McGuire, M. Cherry, et al. (2012) 'A systematic review of prevention and intervention strategies for populations at high risk of engaging in violent behaviour: update 2002–8.' *Health Technology Assessment* 16(3): 1–152.

Hollin, C. R. (2004) To treat or not to treat? An historical perspective. In C. R. Hollin (ed.) *The Essential Handbook of Offender Assessment and Treatment*. Chichester, John Wiley: 1–13.

Hollin, C. R. (2008) 'Evaluating offending behaviour programmes.' *Criminology and Criminal Justice* 8: 89–106.

Huesmann, L. R. (1998) The role of social information processing and cognitive schema in the acquisition and maintenance of habitual aggressive behavior. In R. G. Geen and E. Donnerstein (eds) *Human Aggression: Theories, Research, and Implications for Policy*. New York, Academic Press: 73–109.

Ireland, J. L. (2009) Conducting individualised theory-driven assessment of violent offenders. In C. A. Ireland, J. L. Ireland and P. Birch, *Violent and Sexual Offenders: Assessment, Treatment and Management*. Cullompton, Willan Publishing: 68–93.

Ireland, J. L. and C. A. Ireland (2008) 'Intra-group aggression among prisoners: bullying intensity and exploration of victim–perpetrator mutuality.' *Aggressive Behavior* 34(1): 76–87.

Johnson, R. and R. Haigh (2010) 'Social psychiatry and social policy for the 21st century – new concepts for new needs: the "psychologically informed environment".' *Mental Health & Social Inclusion* 14(4): 30–5.

Jones, L. (2008) Offence paralleling behaviour (OPB) as a framework for assessment and interventions with offenders. In A. Needs and G. Towl (eds) *Applying Psychology to Forensic Practice*, Oxford, Blackwell Publishing: 34–63.

Jones, M. (1962) *Social Psychiatry in the Community, in Hospitals, and in Prisons*. Springfield, IL, Charles C. Thomas.

Kerr, R., Bruce, M., Chavura, K., Coulston, B., Russell, S., Brennan, F. and Sonigra, K. (2013) In R. Kerr (Chair), '*Engaging non-engagers: transforming the landscape of "treatment" for violent offenders*.' Symposium conducted at the British and Irish Group for the Study of Personality Disorder: 13th Annual Conference. Belfast, UK, February.

Lee-Evans, M. (1994) Background to behaviour analysis. In M. McMurran and J. Hodge (eds) *The Assessment of Criminal Behaviours of Clients in Secure Settings*. London, Jessica Kingsley Publishers: 6–34.

Leslie, J. C. and M. F. O'Reilly (1999) *Behavior Analysis: Foundations and Applications to Psychology*. Amsterdam, Harwood Academic Publishers.

Linehan, M. M. (1993) *Cognitive Behavioral Treatment of Borderline Personality Disorder*. New York, Guilford Press.

Lipsey, M. W. and F. T. Cullen (2007) 'The effectiveness of correctional rehabilitation: a review of systematic reviews.' *Annual Review of Law and Social Science* 3: 297–320.

Low, G., D. Jones, C. Duggan, M. Power and A. MacLeod (2001) 'The treatment of deliberate self-harm in borderline personality disorder using dialectical behaviour therapy: a pilot study in a high security hospital.' *Behavioural and Cognitive Psychotherapy* 29(01): 85–92.

Lowencamp, C. T., E. J. Latessa and A. Holsinger (2006) 'The risk principle in action: what have we learned from 13,676 offenders and 97 correctional programs?' *Crime and Delinquency* 52: 77–93.

McCann, R. A., E. M. Ball, et al. (2000) 'DBT with an inpatient forensic population: the CMHIP forensic model.' *Cognitive and Behavioral Practice* 7(4): 447–56.

McGuire, J. (2000) *Theory Manual for Think First*. Prepared for the Joint Prison Probation Accreditation Panel.

McGuire, J., C. Bilby, R. Hatcher, C. Hollin, J. C. Hounsome, and E. Palmer (2008) 'Evaluation of structure cognitive-behavioural treatment programmes in reducing criminal recidivism.' *Journal of Experimental Criminology* 4(1): 21–40.

Megargee, E. I. (1976) 'The prediction of dangerous behaviour.' *Criminal Justice and Behaviour* 3(1): 3–22.

Megargee, E. I. (2009) Understanding and assessing aggression and violence. In J. N. Butcher (ed.) *Oxford Handbook of Personality Assessment*. New York, Oxford University Press: 542–66.

Megargee, E. I. (2011) 'Using the algebra of aggression in forensic practice.' *British Journal of Forensic Practice* 13(1): 4–11.

Miller, W. R. and S. Rollnick (1991) *Motivational Interviewing: Preparing People to Change Addictive Behavior*. New York, Guilford Press.

Miller, W. R. and S. Rollnick (2002) *Motivational Interviewing: Preparing People for Change* (2nd edn). New York, Guilford Press.

Novaco, R. W. (1975) *Anger Control: The Development and Evaluation of an Experimental Treatment*. Lexington, KT, D. C. Heath.

Novaco, R. W. (1997) 'Remediating anger and aggression in violent offenders.' *Legal and Criminological Psychology* 2 77–88.

Ohlsson, I. M. and J. L. Ireland (2011) 'Aggression and offence motivation in prisoners: exploring the components of motivation in an adult male sample.' *Aggressive Behavior* 37(3): 278–88.

Palmer, E. J., J. McGuire, R. Hatcher, J. Hounsome, C. Bilby and C. R. Hollin (2008) 'The importance of appropriate allocation to offending behavior programs.' *International Journal of Offender Therapy and Comparative Criminology* 52(2): 206–21.

Polaschek, D. L. L. (2006) Violent offender programmes: concept, theory and practice. In C. R. Hollin and E. J. Palmer (eds) *Offending Behaviour Programmes: Development, Application and Controversies*. Chichester, Wiley 113–54.

Polaschek, D. L. L. and N. Reynolds (2004) Assessment and treatment: violent offenders. In C. R. Hollins (ed.) *The Essential Handbook of Offender Assessment and Treatment*. Chichester, John Wiley: 201–18.

Porporino, F. J. and E. Fabiano (2000) *Program Overview of Cognitive Skills Reasoning and Rehabilitation Revised: Theory and Application*. Ottawa, London, T3 Associates.

Prochaska, J. O. and C. C. DiClemente (2005) The transtheoretical approach. In J. C. Norcross and M. R. Goldfried (eds) *Handbook of Psychotherapy Integration* (2nd edn). New York, Oxford University Press.

Prochaska, J. O. and Levesque, D. (2002) Enhancing motivation of offenders at each stage of change and phase of therapy. In M. McMurran (ed.) *Motivating Offenders to Change: A Guide to Enhancing Engagement in Therapy*. New York, John Wiley: 57–73.

Redondo, S., J. Sanchez-meca and V. Garrido (1999) 'The influence of treatment programmes on the recidivism of juvenile and adult offenders: an European meta-analytic review.' *Psychology, Crime & Law* 5(3): 251–78.

Robinson, D. (1995) *The Impact of Cognitive Skills Training on Post-release Recidivism among Canadian Federal Offenders*. Ottawa, Correctional Service of Canada.

Ross, R. R., E. A. Fabiano and C. Ewles (1988) 'Reasoning and rehabilitation.' *International Journal of Offender Therapy and Comparative Criminology* 32: 29–35.

Rubin, J., F. Gallo and A. Coutts (2008) *Violent Crime: Risk Models, Effective Interventions and Risk Management*. Cambridge, National Audit Office.

Sainsbury Centre, The (2009) *Diversion: A Better Way for Criminal Justice and Mental Health*. London, Sainsbury Centre for Mental Health.

Saleebey, D. (1997) *The Strengths Perspective in Social Work Practice*. White Plains, NY, Longman.

Scurich, N., J. Monahan, and R. John (2012) 'Innumeracy and unpacking: bridging the nomothetic/idiographic divide in violence risk assessment.' *Law and Human Behavior* 36(6): 548–54.

Taylor, P. and S. Bond (2012) *Home Office Statistical Bulletin: Crimes Detected in England and Wales 2011/12*. London, Office of National Statistics.

Thornton, D., R. Mann, S. Webster, L. Blud, R. Travers, C. Friendship and M. Erikson (2003) 'Distinguishing and combining risks for sexual and violent recidivism.' *Annals of the New York Academy of Sciences* 989(1): 225–35.

Tong, L. S. J. and D. P. Farrington (2006) 'How effective is the "reasoning and rehabilitation" programme in reducing reoffending? A meta-analysis of evaluations in four countries.' *Psychology, Crime and Law* 12(1): 3–24.

Tremblay, R. E., D. S. Nagin, et al. (2005) 'Physical aggression during early childhood: trajectories and predictors.' *Canadian Child and Adolescent Psychiatry Review* 14(1): 3–9.

Trupin, E. W., D. G. Stewart, B. Beach and L. Boesky (2002) 'Effectiveness of a dialectical behaviour therapy program for incarcerated female juvenile offenders.' *Child and Adolescent Mental Health* 3: 121–7.

Tyrer, P., S. Mitchard, C. Methuen and M. Ranger (2003) 'Treatment rejecting and treatment seeking personality disorders: Type R and Type S.' *Journal of Personality Disorders* 17(3): 263–8.

Vitaro, F., E. D. Barker, M. Boivin, M. Brendgen and R. Tremblay (2006) 'Do early difficult temperament and harsh parenting differentially predict reactive and proactive aggression?' *Journal of Abnormal Child Psychology* 34(5): 685–95.

Ward, T. and C. A. Stewart (2003) 'The treatment of sex offenders: risk management and good lives.' *Professional Psychology: Research and Practice* 34: 353–60.

Ward, T. and M. Brown (2004) 'The good lives model and conceptual issues in offender rehabilitation.' *Psychology, Crime & Law* 10(3): 243–57.

Ward, T. and C. Nee (2009) 'Surfaces and depths: evaluating the theoretical assumptions of cognitive skills programmes.' *Psychology, Crime and Law* 15(2–3): 165–82.

Ware, J., C. Cieplucha and D. Matsuo (2011) 'The Violent Offenders Therapeutic Programme (VOTP) – rationale and effectiveness.' *Australasian Journal of Correctional Staff Development* 6: 1–12.

WHO (2002) *World Report on Violence and Health.* Geneva, World Health Organisation.

Winogron, W., M. Van Dieten and V. Grisim (2001) Controlling Anger and Learning to Manage It – Effective Relapse-Prevention Program (CALMER), North Tonawanda, NY, Multi-Health Systems Inc.

Wong, S. C. P., A. Gordon and D. Gu (2007) 'Assessment and treatment of violence-prone forensic clients: an integrated approach.' *British Journal of Psychiatry* 190(49): s66–s74.

Young, J. E., J. S. Klosko and M. Weishaar (2003) *Schema Therapy: A Practitioner's Guide.* New York, Guilford Press.

Youngs, D. and D. V. Canter (2012) 'Offenders' crime narratives as revealed by the narrative roles questionnaire.' *International Journal of Offender Therapy and Comparative Criminology* 57(3): 289–311.

7

LEARNING DISABILITIES

Dave Nash

There is a strong culture within the service provision for people with intellectual disabilities (LD) where perceptions of service users' perceived helplessness, passivity and vulnerability can have a disproportionate influence on practice. There is also a culture and tradition that embodies genuine caring attitudes, dedication, persistence and determination in service and care providers. These beliefs can however sometimes conceal the complexities of individual risk posed by some people with intellectual disability presenting a challenge to effective decision making and risk management. For example there may be a bias towards managing risks 'in-house' (by 'caring better') instead of reporting the concerns to outside agencies.

In this chapter we will examine LD and offending behaviour, particularly sex offending. The chapter will explore:

- The culture of not locating LD and offending in one person and the impact of this thinking on service development
- The lack of community services and also services that are linked to secure settings and provide 'step down' services
- Shortcomings and developments in current service and interventions
- Assessing and managing risks in the community
- Communication problems
- The future and conclusions.

Introduction

While attending a conference in the 1980s, I remember discussing with other delegates some work I was involved in at the time to try to design a service for a single sex offender we had in our old-fashioned learning disabilities service. Overheard by another delegate, he voiced the opinion that was common at that time that:

> A sex offender with mental handicap [learning/intellectual disabilities]?
>
> That's a contradiction in terms isn't it? Can't be both.

This was my first personal memory of how people's preconceptions about those with learning disabilities can sometimes blind them to their individuality to such an extent that it can be dangerous. More than 30 years later and it sometimes seems that similar sentiments continue to influence service development, decisions and practices.

Hopefully nowadays we do show more sophistication in our thinking and greater care in examining the information available informed by theory and research (mainly from mainstream offender work). My experience is that this chiefly only applies to those clinicians who are directly involved in the processes of assessment and therapy. Others, in my experience, tend to just avoid the topic because they do not have to address these issues as they do not encounter them. For those working in community-based treatment and for those with learning disabilities who abuse others the complexities of this work inevitably result in frequent and sometimes unacknowledged ethical and practice dilemmas.

Lyall et al. (1995) found that care staff showed a high tolerance of offending behaviour in service users with intellectual disability. Less than 25 per cent said they would always report sexually assaultive behaviour that they had encountered to the police. However, over more recent years, staff training in relation to Safeguarding of Vulnerable Adults (SOVA) has had some positive effects on reporting practices.

As this chapter will highlight, while there are some differences, many offenders with learning disabilities (like those without) have:

- insight and skill in covertly executing their abuses and offences,
- similar patterns of doubts and worries about who to trust,
- ambivalence about change,
- the same secret goals to fool people if they can or to escape from the need to address their abusive behaviour, and eventually,
- capacity to decide to stop.

The differences of course lie in cognitive limitations (recall, thinking, learning, decision making, etc.) and difficulties in communication but also in the cultural context of such work. By this I mean how someone with learning disabilities is perceived and how others therefore regard the apparent contradiction between a group of people who are often seen as vulnerable and/or dependent with being asked to consider some as having the capacity to deceive, threaten and pose significant risk of harm to others. Most challenging is the dissonance generated when all of these qualities are seen to coexist in the same individual. Then, only a genuine effort towards empathic understanding of that individual can help decision makers and clinicians regarding risk management and predicting the likely efficacy of therapeutic effort and in what forms.

Where a client goes through the criminal justice system there are opportunities, through prison or probation services, to receive some form of adapted treatment such as the Sex Offender Treatment Programme for Adults (SOTP). However their reconnection with community services afterwards can involve an uncoordinated and often inadequate response to the remaining risks. There are often insufficient appropriately competent professionals and services available to meet their needs.

Research on referral patterns with offenders with intellectual disability over the last 20 years has shown a wide variation in experience of referral practices, definitions and identification of intellectual disability. Uncertainty has existed regarding whether to include, for example, 'borderline' clients, those with autistic spectrum disorder, Attention Deficit Hyperactivity Disorder or specific learning difficulties and the national picture remains unclear. Lindsay et al. (2011) in a 20-year study of referrals in one service found around half of the offenders referred in that period were for sexual offences or abuse. The largest proportion of non-sexual offences was violence related. They also reported a very significant increase in referrals from criminal justice services and a similar decline from community services, which was considered, by the authors, possibly to:

> reflect changes in society whereby the Courts are becoming more comfortable with defendants with intellectual disabilities and services are more willing to involve the police when there are incidents of offending behaviour.
> (Lindsay et al. 2011, p. 513)

Others (e.g. Wheeler et al. 2009) found the opposite, with many clients already known to local community services being referred from community sources for offending behaviour, with Criminal Justice Service (CJS) referrals reported as scarce.

Lindsey et al. (2010, p. 537) looked at the relationship between assessed risk and service security level and found that,

> Despite an orderly relationship between assessed risk and level of security, the effect sizes are not large suggesting that factors may intervene to place some individuals of a high risk in community settings and others of a low risk in secure settings.

The factors suggested included aggressiveness, the level of development of services, practitioner confidence in dealing with such cases and judgements based on service abilities to manage or contain the problems. If a crime is reported to the police there are complications related to the process of interviewing the accused, his or her comprehension, suggestibility and mental capacity to make decisions and express himself or herself clearly in often 'bewildering' (Jones and Talbot 2010) criminal justice processes.

This is not to say that there is not some excellent work going on around the UK (e.g. Janet Shaw Clinic in Solihull (ASOTP), Northgate hospital programme near Newcastle, Bill Lindsay's programme in Scotland (see Lindsey 2009), community forensic service in East Kent, Wood Lea Clinic, Bedfordshire). However, something of a lottery exists as to whether an offender is connected with such a service in his or her locality and whether that service is meaningfully connected with other services that ought to form part of the pathway (e.g. whether community services are, in reality, ready to receive people who are ready to be discharged from low secure/locked rehabilitation services).

Early in the Bradley Report (2009, p. 9) it was readily acknowledged that progress since the Reed Report, 16 years earlier, had been slow and that its recommendations were still relevant in terms of the ongoing need for:

- a positive approach to the individual needs of patients;
- a flexible, multi-agency and multi-professional approach, the aim of which is to identify and meet most effectively the needs of mentally disordered offenders;
- improved access to more specialised services in mental health and learning disability services, and recognition of the role played by more general services in providing care and treatment for most mentally disordered offenders; and
- closer working between the police, health and social services to avoid unnecessary prosecution of mentally disordered suspects.

In his conclusions and next steps section Lord Bradley said (p. 149):

> I recognise that some of my recommendations will take longer than others to implement, but many can be implemented quickly. I would expect, therefore, that in the first six months following publication of my report there will be in place:
>
> - a clear national strategic direction;
> - the new governance arrangements at a national, regional and local level; and
> - a fully costed national delivery plan for all my recommendations, and progress on their implementation under way.

Suffice it to say that the latest update reports (e.g. Independent Custody Visiting Association Summer 2012 report) are not yet encouraging.

A person with intellectual disabilities arrested today may or may not have his/her disability recognised or an appropriate adult available to help with the police interview. In the case of young people an adult may be present but unaware of the learning disability or how this could impact on the process of arrest and questioning. Equally, a practitioner in the community who becomes aware that one of his/her clients may be sexually abusive may find it very difficult or impossible to find specialist help. The gap between what constructive action could be taken and practice does not yet seem to be narrowing.

Happily, over the last decade or two, a small body of research and expertise on treating and managing sex offenders with intellectual disabilities has been growing and provides a model of good practice for the future design of services for those with LD, especially when considered with the *context* of treatment, for example Keeling et al. (2006) found that for adults, group work combined with a therapeutic community, the development of living skills and treatments to help generalise group skills into the therapeutic community was an important combination. The first study to seek to identify the effectiveness of a cognitive behavioural therapy (CBT)-based treatment regime for men with intellectual disability was conducted by Glynis Murphy in her Sex Offender Treatment Services Collaborative – Intellectual Disability (SOTSEC-ID) project which reported in 2010. Therapists were recruited from around England to set up closed groups in their localities (two-hour weekly sessions for one year) sharing common inclusion criteria, core assessments and content. The content sections comprised:

a   group purpose and rule setting,
b   human relations and sex education,
c   the cognitive model (links between thoughts, feelings and action)
d   sexual offending model (after Finkelhor 1984)
e   general empathy and victim empathy, and
f   relapse prevention.

Cognitive simplification of content with the use of visual aids and role-play-based activities were strongly advocated to promote client comprehension and retention of the content. The mean IQ of participants was around 60, around 30 per cent had autistic spectrum disorder and offences of group members included stalking, sexual assault, indecent exposure and rape with both child and adult victims.

Results showed high levels of motivation, significant increases in SAKS (knowledge) scores, significant improvements in QACSO (attitudes) scores and improvements in VE (victim empathy) scores and service users commonly reported positive experiences and the helpfulness of the treatment. Sadly, funding limitations restricted follow-up measures beyond six months.

The risk–needs–responsivity (RNR) model is currently influential in sex offender treatment (Ward and Brown 2004) and has enormous face validity in work with intellectually disabled sex offenders where:

- *Risk* principle – the most effective treatments are those that match an individual's level of risk,
- *Needs* principle – treatments should directly target needs that are most closely related to the probability of reoffending, and
- *Responsivity* principle – treatments must match or fit with the learning styles of clients and take account of internal characteristics of the offender (e.g. intellectual and adaptive functioning, literacy and comprehension) such as the

use of drawings, videos and other visual aids, greater repetition of materials and reduced content for each treatment session. External factors that affect the client's successful engagement with the treatment process.

As one of the therapists involved in the SOTSEC-ID project, the many positive effects I found came from including carers in the process and from the relapse-prevention work. This both helped to establish an ongoing dialogue between client and others in their lives (professional and otherwise) regarding ongoing abuse-related thoughts and feelings in a way that encouraged openness and partnership regarding risk management, and kept motivations high and discouraged deceit.

WALTER – WHAT DO YOU MEAN THE TREATMENT IS OVER?

Walter, a 48-year-old with mild learning disabilities had been convicted of the sexual abuse of two boys in his flat and was detained under the Mental Health Act in a low secure setting. At the outset he expressed anger at his conviction, blamed his victims for getting him into trouble and took the view that he did not need any treatment. What he did, he said, was justified revenge for the ways the boys had treated him and he'd do it again, and although he could often appear belligerent and resistant, his ambivalence about his past behaviour also emerged in discussions. Eventually, through a motivational interviewing approach within the supportive and encouraging environment (provided by his carers who were closely informed of developments in 1:1 sessions) he cooperated with all assessment and pre-group preparation. This included being open about details of his thoughts, feelings and behaviour in relation to his index and other offences. Indeed, over the three months before his group started, he also *began* to reconsider whether his abusive behaviour was indeed, 'justified'.

He agreed to attend the group which explicitly did NOT require him to divulge details of his offending within group sessions as they had been revealed to the group leader previously in 1:1 sessions. He agreed to attend and did so reliably every week for a year and completed all homework tasks. However, his willingness to verbally contribute within group sessions was hampered, he said, by being nervous to talk in a group.

The last session was completed and the group was formally closed with the comment, 'Your group treatment is now over'. He immediately commented,

> What do you mean the treatment is over? I've only just started.
> I want to do it again but properly.

A private debrief after the session revealed that his quietness had been the consequence of constant fear that he was, in fact, going to be asked to confess in the group. 'I didn't realise you meant it when you said I didn't have to tell everyone [what I did] – can I do it again – only properly this time?' He could have done so as a new group was shortly to start.

In fact, we (he and staff) were soon to realise that despite his quietness and apparent lack of involvement in the group sessions, he had more than dutifully completed his homework tasks, had heard and retained much of the content and begun to apply it to his own thoughts about his feelings, relationships, future goals, etc. and although there were some aspects of the process he had missed or failed to comprehend that needed repetition, he was largely ready to engage with relapse-prevention planning despite his willingness to repeat the whole year again.

After completing his Relapse Prevention Plan and beginning to 'try it out' on the infrequent community outings that were available from his hospital, he needed to move to a setting that would allow daily community contact to develop and practise the plan further. Eventually, and after some difficulties, he found a placement in a community-based 'locked rehab' that could attempt to take the gains he had made and develop them further. Happily, and unexpectedly, his motivation did not appear to diminish over that time as staff kept him focused on slowly developing his plan.

A key issue with Walter, like so many others, is that of the helpfulness of keeping the client's carers informed and involved in the processes of change and therefore the importance of inviting and encouraging their active contributions. Without this, his initial refusal to engage, ongoing negative comments and low participation in the group could so easily have led to a view that Walter was not interested in change and insufficient encouragement and support.

It is clearly early days in achieving confident conclusions regarding effectiveness of group CBT-based treatment but early indications from this and other projects (e.g. Bruce et al. 2010) are most encouraging.

Managing risks in the community

Twenty years ago I was working in the clinical psychology service for a local learning disability community service. There was a modest but steady flow of around ten referrals per year of suspected sexual abusers into our service for 'assessment and recommendations'. Usually but not exclusively these were from a small number of community social workers in the LD team who had been approached by child protection or SOVA colleagues who were aware of the problems. It was then observed that the flow of referrals dwindled to two to three referrals per year for about two years and then all referrals just stopped. Closer examination revealed that most referrals had been coming from a small group of staff that had now been either redeployed in a major local authority reorganisation or had left the service.

The hope was that Multi-Agency Public Protection Arrangements (MAPPA) would be picking up those going through the CJS but the question remained as to who was monitoring the others? Some of those already identified and assessed were monitored by weekly or fortnightly visits from police or community nurses, but treatment in the community was unavailable.

The experience of setting up community-based services suggests they can be vulnerable to financial pressures and policy changes. For example an initiative to set up a county-wide treatment service network (based on SOTSEC-ID) in Cambridgeshire came to a close when the plans were suddenly terminated. Political and financial pressures meant that the purchasers were now unable to fund the service.

A review of this initiative did however provide some wider lessons for clinical practice which are worth considering. For example there was a substantial number of possible clients for treatment who were referred due to a lone social worker or community nurse perceiving risks of sexual abuse but the risks had not been assessed and the clients were receiving no services geared to sexual offending risks. Others had risk assessments and supervision arrangements in place but supervising staff were often doing what they could with no professional support, skilled guidance or 'clinical' supervision and in some cases were employed to supervise their client for a few hours of each day.

When interviewed, the clients in such situations were often (understandably) coy about how they spent their unsupervised times but from what they did reveal it was clear they recognised that daily opportunities to reoffend were occurring. The brief account of Darren is such an example. Darren's carers did what they could to manage the risks but Darren was occasionally unwilling to cooperate and usually unwilling to discuss the risks and how to avoid them. All his carers felt able to do was inform his social worker who would then try to visit within the week to try to persuade Darren to again work with his carers.

DARREN – PARTLY SUPERVISED

During the research to find clients in the community who may like to engage with an ASOTP I came across Darren, a young man with mild learning disabilities in his late twenties who lived on a smallholding around half a mile from a small one-street village with a playground and a primary school. This seemingly always quiet village was around 5 miles from the nearest small town. Darren shared a two-bedroom house (around 100m from the main farmhouse) with another rather reclusive man with learning disabilities who quietly went out to work very early each morning and returned home around 4.30 each afternoon. They both had limited skills in maintaining relationships and generally lived their lives in parallel rather than in any significantly connected way. They were both under the supervision of a husband and wife team, Mr and Mrs D (retired foster carers), who lived in the main farmhouse where they all (usually) ate breakfast and evening meals together on weekdays but not at weekends. During the day, Darren was directly supervised (them working together) or his movements monitored by Mr D making phone calls to check that Darren had arrived and departed his various places of learning and work on time. This happened until Mr D began suffering from back pain which often meant daytime supervision was only by phone calls. On non-work/non-college days Mrs D would encourage Darren to help her around the house and, happily, Darren was generally (but not always) willing to help. Closer questioning of Mr and Mrs D revealed that they both had significant insights into the likely thoughts, feelings and motivations of Darren regarding his risks of further abuse but as funding was only available for 8 hours per day, 5 days per week there were clear limitations on how effective the supervision arrangements could be.

Talking with Darren himself allowed me to also understand that he was aware that there were times in the week when he was unsupervised and was free to go anywhere he wished which included the nearby town to drink alcohol, visit his brother and sister-in-law and their young children and indeed to loiter around the local village playground and woods especially later in the afternoons or early evenings 'to watch the children and help them up if they fall over' – he carried a small first aid kit for the purpose. He said any parents who were around were usually very grateful to him.

Missing the risks

Providing SOTSEC-ID groups in low secure settings I discovered over three years that most participants had a single conviction but it was common to find an extensive history of suspected and alleged sexually abusive incidents before an appropriate risk assessment had been attempted or a report made to the police. In the community, I found it common to come across a parallel situation where clients were sometimes referred with no conviction (as yet) but a single initial suspected incident of abuse had triggered an assessment that then revealed a catalogue of others. In the majority of cases, clients would increasingly disclose long established careers as sex offenders that often surprised many of the other professionals involved regarding the number of abuses, the length of time it had persisted before decisive action had been taken (through CJS or otherwise) and the qualities (e.g. use of force or young age of victims) and apparent complexity of skills of the abuser (e.g. in terms of planning and avoiding detection).

Situations also became evident where clients had been transferred to new services where risks were better managed but their offending had never been discussed with them. This left many abusive clients with the understandable perception that they would never be prosecuted, their denial of responsibility was credible and they did not need to change their behaviour.

A further challenge to effective risk management can often be seen when attempting to adopt effective systems of risk communication especially when a client moves to a new carer. For example, situations have arisen where high quality risk assessments commissioned and completed even *before* a client's index offence occurred appear to have either been missed from the process of transition or misunderstood by or not made available to local services and their commissioners – they simply did not know about the risks that needed to be managed. Later investigation (after the index offence) revealed that the service system had become dependent on a key individual regarding such information and continuity was lost when that individual left.

As others have commented elsewhere (e.g. the No One Knows programme; Loucks 2006) there has been a culture in LD services for many years of seeing all inappropriate behaviour as 'challenging behaviour' with staff reluctant to see the illegal aspects of the behaviour as illegal or the individual as responsible. Add to this the additional reluctance to perceive the need to guide or even acknowledge the sexual development, needs and vulnerability of clients with intellectual disability and it is easy to imagine how more able and predatory clients could have ready access to many opportunities to abuse or exploit less able service users in group-living situations.

In a few cases I have known, where an investigation of one allegation by an alleged LD victim with high expressed emotion failed to produce corroborative evidence, the event was recorded in her client notes as 'made an allegation that was entirely without foundation' (rather than 'no evidence was found to support the allegation') and the complainant attracted the label of 'makes unfounded allegations' that lasted on her notes for many years but she continued to make allegations against the same man. Two years later a new staff member (unaware of the label) looked into a new complaint, found some supporting evidence and referred the alleged perpetrator to the local psychology service. It was in the course of this work mainly focused on antisocial behaviour that led to an admission of his covert illegal sexual activities.

'Strong suspicion' can often be the highest level of confidence most carers or police are able to achieve regarding inappropriate sexual behaviour because of inadequate staffing levels for effective observation and where victims were often those who were passive, compliant or simply unable to communicate effectively with their carers.

The high incidence of victimisation of people with intellectual disabilities in relation to sexual and physical abuse has been well reported (since Brown and Turk 1993) and, indeed, most of those abusers with intellectual disabilities I have assessed harboured the belief that those who have been victims before are most easily victimised again. Also, that those least able to communicate are those least able to report an offence. From a carer perspective, it is important also to realise that people with learning disabilities who already show the emotional and behavioural consequences of abuse previously suffered may not show clear additional signs when they suffer further abuse; evidence from this direction may be very difficult to notice especially in those who are already unassertive, passive or of limited verbal abilities.

The above scenarios highlight the potential for underestimating the risks that an individual with intellectual disabilities can pose through:

a   Assumptions that a suspicion or a single conviction indicates a low risk
b   Assumptions that intellectual disabilities predicts low level of skill as an offender
c   Fragile information passing systems that depend on one or very few staff
d   Carers seeing illegal behaviour as challenging behaviour to be managed in-house
e   Assumptions that 'no evidence' means 'no risks'
f   Difficulties in identifying behavioural changes in victims.

Finally, even when a risk has been identified, information shared and therapeutic work ongoing, the central importance of managing the risks can elude case-related decision makers. It seems ironic that therapists do so much to convince and encourage *the client* to acknowledge how vitally important it is to recognise his problem while those around him (e.g. service providers and care coordinators who are not closely involved in his therapy but aware of it) can so easily fail to include the 'problem' in their discussions with that individual about his future. The brief summary of 'George' illustrates many of these points.

GEORGE – CHARMING AND HELPFUL

George was regarded as a mild-mannered, helpful and essentially harmless man in his late teens when his family was split up by the criminal conviction of his father for violence and his elder brother for sexual crimes against children. Indeed it was he who, it was thought, had discovered his brother's activities and alerted the authorities to them. His intellectually disabled mother's alcoholism and George's inability to adequately take care of himself led to him being accommodated at a hostel for intellectually disabled adults where he soon gathered a reputation for being charming and helpful. Despite a speech impediment, that often rendered him very difficult to understand and made him appear more learning disabled than he was, he would always offer to help less able clients and indeed was eventually moved into a training flat with one of them. When he later moved out to a supported living environment, he also made friends with the single mum next door, did shopping for her and talked to her of how he used to look after his younger sisters when he was a child. Indeed, looking after her young children started on one occasion when she needed to leave for work early before the childminder arrived and it soon became a not infrequent event. Eventually, even the childminder would leave the children with George if she needed to 'pop out' for a short time. George was always willing to help and, on one occasion, took one of the children to the doctor's to get advice on treating 'a rash that was making him cry'.

What no one had known was that George had been involved in child sexual abuse with his brother and father in his early teens, and for some years with his sisters as his first victims. He had continued to abuse children and less able intellectually disabled women ever since as and when the opportunities arose and had learned that offering to help to provide care increased his opportunities.

It was only when he was suspected of sexually abusing a less able, non-verbal female resident in a care home that he was referred to a locked rehabilitation unit for assessment and possible treatment that he revealed his history as described above. Despite initial impressions, he was a very skilled abuser who had learned strategies to evade detection that played on the fact that as well as helpful, he was seen as 'disabled and vulnerable' himself. Indeed, his service purchaser was adamant that the information he had disclosed was unreliable and that as he had no previous convictions she could not justify spending funds on related treatment. Unknown to her and his recent carers until a thorough examination of his archived social service and health files, he had two previous convictions for sexual assault on children from before the Sex Offender's Act 1997 and so was therefore not on the sex offender register.

Clearly, problems such as these can inhibit the processes of gathering and weighing what evidence there is to help us assess risks much more accurately but they can also help us understand how day-to-day practices may still be failing to spot abuse in our services and therefore how we could make improvements.

However, not only are there missed opportunities for managing risks but when key decision makers view the client as an essentially vulnerable, suggestible victim, rather than as an individual who could potentially present a risk of harm to others, this can trigger demands for someone who poses significant risks to be allowed to 'exercise their rights to free movement and association' on the basis that they are innocent as they have not been proven guilty in a Court of law. What can be overlooked is:

1   Once an appropriate, positive working partnership and effective communication channels with the client have been established, information that is very helpful for risk assessment and management can often be gathered from the client and sometimes from the family and previous carers too.
2   The client's own perceptions and memories may not have been available to the legal system during interview if:

   • the client is told, by his legal representative, to say 'no comment' to any police questions, or

- an 'appropriate adult' has not been involved in the interview process to ensure the client's understanding of the questions posed (because one has not been available or the need for one has not been identified).

As an assessor and therapist, one often finds the client will gradually reveal information about their abusive behaviour in the course of assessment and treatment (and information about other offenders/offences) which concurs with past observations and suspicions that were inconclusively left at the time due to lack of evidence. This highlights the importance of proceeding with an open mind to both risks and reassurances but always making decisions on the basis of all the information available without assuming that there is no more information that can be accessed. Communication can often be the key.

The communication issue

Standardised programme approaches to treatment for an intellectually disabled population are likely to be much less effective than those adapted to the individuals receiving it. As with conducting assessment with learning disabled clients, the issues that can constantly interfere with progress in treatment regarding offending behaviour are:

- establishing effective communication with the client (finding the best ways to be understood and to interpret and understand the client), and
- managing his or her motivation to communicate and engage in the process of treatment.

Whenever one attempts the assessment or treatment of anyone with learning disabilities (before we overlay the issues related to working on forensic dimensions of a case) the almost universal issue that has to be constantly addressed from the outset is how to communicate effectively with the individual so that one does not make false judgements (positive or negative). This applies to how one needs:

- to ensure the attention of the individual is on the question, message or material concerned (and therefore need to deal with any distracting environmental, mood or preoccupation issues before proceeding),
- to modify one's speech (vocabulary, sentence structure and length, tone, speed, facial expression and gestures, etc.) to most effectively explain meanings or phrase questions so that one's intended meaning reaches the client, and then
- to be careful to accurately understand or interpret the responses of the individual which is often more difficult than expected and requires enormous care and skill in supplementary questioning.

There is enormous potential for wrongly assuming that a client has understood the questions asked and then, when one has carefully checked and been able to confirm his understanding, to misunderstand or misinterpret his response unless this too is checked with equal care.

The same applies whenever one is endeavouring to understand what a client is trying to say – the literal meaning of his words can be misleading as in the example of Alan.

ALAN – I DON'T DESERVE IT!

Alan had addressed his violent and destructive behaviour with considerable success despite only modest improvements in his assertiveness so far and he was now discharged from his Mental Health Act section. At his recent Care Programme Approach (CPA) review it was agreed:

- to work towards him moving out of his community hospital into supported living,
- this would happen when he felt he was ready and
- he would then go out directly from his current accommodation in the hospital (as he requested, *without* going through the pre-discharge unit 'Hillside View' despite his named nurse's efforts to persuade him otherwise).

A month later he said to his named nurse 'I want to move to Hillside View' and his nurse duly remade plans for his move in stages starting with Hillside View.

The day came for stage 1 (moving to Hillside View) and Alan became *highly agitated*, saying 'I don't want to do it, I can't do it, *I don't deserve it*', he became threatening and he left the hospital in an angry mood much to the confusion, frustration and concern of staff. Most puzzling was 'I don't deserve it' – was this some crisis of esteem?

On debrief, some hours later when he returned, through careful empathic questioning, we discovered what he meant.

1   'I want to move to Hillside View' – he was frustrated that since his Care Programme Approach (CPA) meeting, he felt he had not made any progress towards his move out of the hospital. He wanted progress and knew his named nurse had favoured the move to Hillside View and therefore would be unlikely to refuse him. He did not want to move to Hillside View – he just meant – '*I want to make some progress towards leaving*' and thought that was the only way.

2   'I don't want to do it' – this one we *could* take at face value but why? – he felt the plan was out of *his* control as his named nurse had made the plan *for* him rather than *with* him and in any case, he didn't actually want to move to Hillside View.

> 3 'I can't do it' – I just don't want to move there and I don't think I'll be able to keep myself in control, so I will fail and failure usually resulted in people judging that I'm not yet ready to leave. So he meant *It's too difficult and I'm going to fail and then I'll have to stay here longer.*
>
> 4 'I don't deserve it' – he felt he was being pressured to move via Hillside View and he meant '*I don't deserve to be pushed to move like this.*'
>
> Now read his original quote again. Once he felt understood, a calm mood was rapidly restored and a new plan could be agreed that reflected his wishes and feelings.

Alan's verbal abilities and very mild intellectual disabilities masked his persistent problems with assertiveness or even communicating that he needed help to work out what he wants when he is feeling anxious, depressed or angry. He would respond to being asked 'can I help?' but would still not ask for help when in an emotional state and avoided thinking about his problems when he was feeling OK.

The first mistake here was to take his first message '*I want to move to Hillside View*' at face value without examining why, especially given his previously expressed wish to go directly to his own place in the community. It would have been just as easy to assume that '*I don't want to do it*' meant 'I don't want' or 'I'm not ready to move out' instead of 'I don't want to move to Hillside View' and to see '*I can't do it*' in a similar light. If staff had not been so puzzled by '*I don't deserve it*' they might not have discovered the misunderstanding and simply put the planned move on hold (with predictable negative consequence to Alan's move and behaviour).

As assessors and therapists we need to continually adapt all communications to fit the needs of the individual(s) concerned and carefully check our understanding of the messages we are receiving bearing in mind that what the client says is only one possible intended meaning. Indeed, one of the great lessons of working developmentally or therapeutically with intellectually disabled clients is the need to adapt all communications, techniques, approaches and materials, so that they can be understood, retained and used by each individual. This apparently simple issue is still the one that poses most challenges to time-pressured professionals.

It can often be a mistake to assume that what a client says has only one possible meaning. The ways clients understand us can be very individual too and the ways we listen have to be empathic and checked with careful questioning of what is meant and why it is being said.

It is factors like these that render the work of police interviewers so difficult in steering the offender's experience of and progress through the early stages of the CJS (Howard and Tyrer 1998; Murphy and Mason 1999) with difficulties often encountered in helping a client to understand the caution, his legal rights or, indeed, the legal process as a whole. However, Murphy and Mason indicated that at least there appear to be improvements in identifying who is likely to have intellectual disability and needs special provisions by the use of screening by custody sergeants (e.g. using the Hayes Ability Screening Index; Hayes 2011).

Equally, therefore, any 'off-the-shelf' materials (to aid communication, comprehension or memory) have to be chosen to suit that individual or group. So, materials for group sessions will commonly need to be modified or redesigned or entirely designed to be effective and memorable for the client(s) concerned. The same of course applies to the design and use of flash cards as an aide-memoire for clients to retain and use important strategies during relapse-prevention work.

This often requires the reduction of the 'message' to its simplest cognitive or linguistic form and working with the client (who often has very limited if any reading abilities) to identify from picture and symbol collections those images that most accurately trigger (after brief learning) quick and accurate recall of the message. Without this personalisation, the triggers often do not work, can generate frustration and reduce motivation, but conversely when we 'pitch it right' the effects on recall and motivation can be invaluable.

Having considered the challenges presented by communication problems more generally, the additional complications presented in community forensic work will now be considered. For example situations often arise:

- when a client is genuinely unable to recall, unable to explain or fails to understand the question or is just reluctant to disclose
- when he says I don't want to go to sessions any more and establishing does he mean it, is he just angry, does it clash with another valued activity, has his father told him to keep quiet about the past?
- when he says something known or strongly suspected to be untrue is it simply his misperception, is it what he always says that works to avoid more difficult challenges or is it a deliberate attempt to mislead?

Then, finally, we often need to add to this the need to manage the challenging effects of those around the process (family, friends and also well-meaning colleagues) who, in their individual relationships with clients (who they may perceive more in a victim role than an offender) may risk validating the client's denial of their 'problem' especially when the client feels shame and vulnerability having made a disclosure. The case of Frank embodies many of these factors.

IRRITABLE 'VULNERABLE' FRANK

Frank was a 43-year-old man with limited abilities to express himself verbally and when he came to our male only service he had been suspected of sexually exploiting a less able woman with intellectual disabilities within the residential establishment where they had lived. He had been found in the undressed company of the woman who had *very* limited expressive abilities and while Frank was much more able than her there was no prosecution. There were uncertainties about risks however and an assessment process commenced.

It took four weeks of sessions for his assessor to satisfy himself that Frank had understood the rules on confidentiality, the idea of risk, the need to keep him and others safe and the conditions under which any information he gave would need to be passed on, i.e. if there was judged to be an immediate risk. Once done, reminders were conducted at the beginning of each session.

While initially, Frank was irritably defensive whenever the subject of his sexual history was broached in sessions and denied repeatedly that he had 'done anything' apart from the assault he was caught for, he soon settled into talking about the sexual behaviour of *others* he had known (including members of his family), his own ambivalence about abuses he said he had witnessed and then said he was willing to talk about the known incident about himself (which, as he explained ambiguously, was 'only just starting' when he was discovered). Over following sessions he then revealed the extent of his abuse of the woman on an almost daily basis over more than a year.

An hour or so after this disclosure, Frank became irritable and told one of his carers that the assessor was 'making him say things' and that these sessions were very upsetting and she complained saying that she felt it unfair to put him under what she described as 'such pressure' and she supported Frank's now expressed wish to discontinue sessions.

For two weeks Frank declined invitations to continue sessions but then, after a discussion with his psychiatrist, who supported the assessment process, Frank asked for them to continue. Over the next four months, Frank revealed a further extensive history of his sexual abuse of young children (male and female) and less able adults since he was a teenager. On the basis of this information more confident risk assessments became possible though his care coordinator remained sceptical and said that she saw such disclosures as unlikely to be 'true'.

Some months later Frank expressed the view that due to his learning disabilities he would never go to prison and the worst consequence he could foresee would be detention under the Mental Health Act and he didn't mind that and he later decided to disclose all to the police, reasoning to our surprise that if he was to stop offending, he didn't want to then be arrested for the crimes in his past.

One of Frank's ways of avoiding detection was to trigger sympathetic responses from others who see him as primarily vulnerable by complaining about or accusing those who caused him discomfort. The potential for Frank to 'split' care teams in ways that can interfere with assessment and therapy processes is also apparent.

Given the complexity of this combination of these communication issues it is, perhaps, unsurprising that it calls on the highest levels of skill by all those involved in the processes of arrest, charging, taking statements and the court processes.

The future

The current picture of service provision for offenders with intellectual disability is fragmented. Service provision has been beset with inadequate resources and limited research with which to confidently guide practice. However, despite these challenges, a growing evidence base is emerging which can inform practitioners in delivering increasingly effective risk assessment, risk management and risk reduction therapeutic processes.

The changes in practice called for which could potentially improve service provision include:

- improving professional carers' confidence in discussing and nurturing the development of appropriate social and sexual behaviour in those with intellectual disability
- improving reporting of offences/abuse so that appropriate actions can be triggered through developments in policies and staff training
- improving identification of defendants with intellectual disabilities by the police through the use of the available screening tools, e.g. Hayes Ability Screening Index and staff training regarding how best to respond to a positive result when limited specialist support is available
- improving access to CBT-based treatments in the community through specialist intellectual disability services including access to those who have not been convicted but where risk has been identified
- improved connectedness between those services that are available in a locality to ensure a more cohesive pathway
- better planning with individuals regarding their future accommodation, work, education, etc. specifically in relation to the need to manage offending risks both during post-treatment work and where treatment is unavailable. This could be seen in terms of maintaining treatment gains, further developing each individual's relapse-prevention strategies in response to life events and trying to ensure a good quality of life through assistance with developing a satisfying lifestyle.

To paraphrase Lord Bradley (2009, p. 149), some of these will take longer than others to implement, but many could be implemented relatively quickly, such as improving reporting, police use of screening assessments and better planning regarding service delivery decisions on an individual level.

Conclusion

There are a great many similarities between the assessment and treatment of learning disabled and non-learning disabled offenders but cultural perceptions, attitudes, biases and assumptions can often blind decision makers to the important differences. While there is some excellent treatment work in prisons, secure facilities and in some community services, many community services have a long way to go in providing treatment, supervising risks and in preparing to receive post-treatment clients who are ready for discharge to their home area.

The absence of a funded government strategy regarding the treatment of such abusers leaves something of a lottery regarding whether an individual's abusive behaviour is noticed, recorded, reported, stopped, treated or managed effectively.

References

Bradley, L. (2009) *The Bradley Report: Lord Bradley's Review of People with Mental Health Problems or Learning Disabilities in the Criminal Justice System*. London: Department of Health.

Brown, H. and Turk, V. (1993) 'Sexual abuse of adults with learning disabilities: results of a two year incidence survey.' *Mental Handicap Research* 6(3), 193–216.

Bruce, M., Collins, S., Langdon, P., Powlitch, S. and Reynolds, S. (2010) 'Does training improve understanding of core concepts in CBT by people with learning disabilities?' *British Journal of Clinical Psychology* 49, 1–13.

Finkelhor, D. (1984) *Child Sexual Abuse: New Theory and Research*. New York: Free Press.

Hayes, S. (2011) 'Hayes Ability Screening Index.' University of Sydney.

Howard, T.J. and Tyrer, S.P. (1998) 'Editorial: People with learning disabilities in the criminal justice system in England and Wales: a challenge to complacency.' *Criminal Behaviour and Mental Health* 8, 171–7.

Jones, G. and Talbot, J. (2010) 'Editorial: No One Knows: the bewildering passage of offenders with learning disability and learning difficulty through the criminal justice system.' *Criminal Behaviour and Mental Health* 20, 1–7.

Keeling, J.A., Rose, J.L. and Beech, A.R. (2006) 'An investigation into the effectiveness of custody based cognitive behavioural treatment for special needs sex offenders.' *Journal of Forensic Psychiatry & Psychology* 17(3), 372–92.

Lindsay, W. (2009) *The Treatment of Sex Offenders with Developmental Disabilities: A Practice Workbook*. Chichester: Wiley (see particularly Chapters 9–20).

Lindsay, W., Carson, D., O'Brien, G., Holland, A.J., Johnston, S., Taylor, J.L., et al. (2010) 'The relationship between assessed risk and service security level for offenders with learning disability.' *Journal of Forensic Psychiatry & Psychology* 21(4), 537–48.

Lindsay, W., Hant, F. and Steptoe, R. (2011) 'Referral patterns of offenders with intellectual disability: a 20 year study.' *Journal of Forensic Psychiatry & Psychology* 22(4), 513–17.

Loucks, N. (2006) *No One Knows – Offenders with Learning Difficulties and Learning Disabilities – Review of Prevalence and Associated Needs*. London: Prison Reform Trust.

Lyall, I., Holland, A.J. and Collins, S. (1995) 'Offending by adults with learning disabilities and the attitudes of staff to offending behaviour: implications for service development.' *Journal of Intellectual Disability Research* 39(6), 501–8.

Murphy, G. and Mason, J. (1999) 'People with developmental disabilities who offend.' In Bouras N. (ed.) *Psychiatric and Behavioural Disorders in Developmental Disabilities and Mental Retardation*. New York: Cambridge University Press, pp. 226–45.

Murphy, G., Sinclair, N., Hays, S.-J., Heaton, K., Powell, S., Langdon, P., et al. (2010) 'Sex Offender Treatment Services Collaborative – Intellectual Disabilities (SOTSEC-ID): effectiveness of group cognitive-behavioural treatment for men with intellectual disabilities at risk of sexual offending.' *Journal of Applied Research in Intellectual Disabilities* 23(6), 537–51.

Ward, T. and Brown, M. (2004) 'The good lives model and conceptual issues in offender rehabilitation.' *Psychology, Crime and Law* 10(3), 243–57.

Wheeler, J.R., Holland, A.J., Bambrick, M., Lindsay, W.R., Carson, D., Steptoe, L., et al. (2009) 'Community services and people with intellectual disabilities who engage in anti-social or offending behaviour: referral rates, characteristics and care pathways.' *Journal of Forensic Psychiatry & Psychology* 20(5), 717–40.

8

ADDRESSING SUBSTANCE MISUSE

Developments in community-based interventions

Matthew Gaskell

Introduction

Over the last two decades interventions for substance misusing offenders in the community have arisen following raised government priority and the subsequent targeting of resources. Crime reduction has been a key part of successive government's agendas since that time, and with evidence suggesting a link between high volume acquisitive crimes and funding substance misuse, initiatives aimed at reducing crime rates by tackling substance misuse amongst the criminal justice population became commonplace. Studies across the western world show that between 70 and 80 per cent of the offender population have substance use patterns in need of some kind of intervention, and over 50 per cent of offenders acknowledge that substance use is related to their index offence. Substance misuse represents one of the most criminogenic factors which contribute to offending behaviour (Weekes et al., 2013). Early intervention with young people is also a priority. Evidence suggests that offending begins before drug use starts, and well before dependence takes hold, then escalates dramatically as the cost of maintaining a heroin or crack cocaine habit increases (Makkai & Payne, 2003; Pudney, 2002).

The initial priority of service providers (which remains in place today) was tackling the link between largely heroin and crack cocaine dependence and acquisitive crime. Attention is now also being given to addressing the link between alcohol misuse and violent crime. According to Singleton et al. (1999), 63 per cent of adult male sentenced prisoners are hazardous drinkers. Following on from North American data demonstrating that substance misuse intervention can reduce the risk of reoffending (Ball & Ross, 1991; Hubbard et al., 1989), the comprehensive National Treatment Outcome Research Study (NTORS; Gossop et al., 2005) in the United Kingdom offered further encouragement that intervention is a worthwhile enterprise, for the individual offender, society and for the economic benefits that result.

This chapter will outline the link between substance misuse and crime and the theory and models employed to address substance misuse in the community. It will focus on developments in community-based interventions, and will draw upon the available evidence of 'what works' in reducing substance-related offending behaviour.

The nature of substance misuse

Substance misuse is a perplexing business: for the user, their significant others, society, as well as policy makers, services and practitioners attempting to intervene. Where substance misuse may have arisen out of strong social and personal reinforcement value, the user typically becomes caught in motivational conflict between the countervailing forces of incentive and restraint: emotional attachment and impulsive desire for a reward-seeking behaviour which has powerful effects on the central nervous system on the one hand, and a growing recognition that harm is ensuing as a result of impaired control over the behaviour, on the other. These effects can be devastating for the individual, yet even significant health, familial, relational, criminal justice, psychological or social consequences may be insufficient to undermine the normal checks and balances that operate to prevent undesirable behaviour patterns from taking hold and continuing. These patterns include offending behaviour. The user may experience repeated failures to refrain from the behaviour despite prior resolutions to do so. They may live in an environment where availability for the behaviour is high, where social networks are built around engaging in the behaviour, where environmental conditions create distress, where emotional vulnerability and/or psychiatric problems make the user susceptible to the reinforcing effects of the drug, and where incentives to change and restraints for the behaviour are weak (Orford, 2001; West, 2006).

There is no agreed definition of addiction but a contemporary view is captured by West (2006), seeing it as 'impaired control over a reward-seeking behaviour from which harm ensues'. Definitions tend to acknowledge the compulsion the user feels to engage in the activity, the excessive priority it takes in their life, and the difficulty stopping the activity or maintaining abstinence. Addiction is not all-or-none but a matter of degree, and the term 'substance misuse' is a useful one within criminal justice settings, allowing for the variety of use patterns, and defined by the UK National Institute for Health and Care Excellence (NICE) as 'intoxication by – or regular, excessive consumption of and/or dependence on psychoactive substances leading to social, psychological, physical or legal problems'. Intoxication and so-called 'binge' patterns of use are linked to offending behaviour, not just more continuous patterns of use. It is imperative for psychologists to measure the severity of dependence, as this has important implications for the intensity of intervention required and the risk the offender poses. Those with the most severe patterns tend to be polydrug using and the extent to which substance abuse and criminal behaviour are linked increases dramatically with the severity of offenders' problems (Gossop et al., 2005). Of those offenders with severe dependence 97 per cent reported they used on the day of the offence; 87 per cent reported that substance abuse was associated with their crimes over the course of their criminal history. Offenders with more severe problems are more likely to be readmitted to custody following release (Weekes et al., 1999). Treatment should not be a 'one size fits all' as it needs to reflect these diverse use patterns with its scope and intensity.

Dependence is diagnosed by examining a set of symptoms but both the World Health Organisation's ICD-10 and American Psychiatric Association's DSM-IV have struggled to encompass the wide variety of addictive behaviours and observations seen, and it is possible for two 'addicts' to have completely different symptoms (see Rounsaville, 2002, for a discussion of the problems with the diagnostic criteria). Measurement of its severity is done via clinical interview and the use of questionnaires. Historically addiction was seen at its core as a state of neuroadaptation to the presence of a drug in the body so that absence of the drug leads to physiological dysfunction (i.e. withdrawal symptoms). When you see an alcohol-dependent person shaking uncontrollably or a heroin addict in severe physical discomfort, it is easy to see why this view is persuasive to some. While this still holds sway in some quarters, addiction is better characterised as a psychological phenomenon, with physiological factors better viewed as ante- cedents and consequences rather than defining the phenomenon itself. Contem- porary views focus on psychological factors to better capture the nature of dependence, such as: a preoccupation of thinking about substance use, the salience the behaviour has in a person's day, perceived inability to abstain, planning and decision making, using in a manner to achieve a specific reinforcing effect, a stereotyping of behaviour, perceived loss of control, using to avoid the loss of the drug effect or to avoid other unpleasant effects, and a perceived inability to cope without the use of the drug.

Theories of substance misuse

There are a variety of addiction theories. There is no theory which seems to account for all the big observations seen in substance misuse, but the most common are listed in Table 8.1.

The model favoured in contemporary criminal justice intervention is the social cognitive theory. Social cognitive theory is the most comprehensive theory of them all and it is a well-tested approach with abundant evidence of such pro- cesses being involved in the development and maintenance of substance misuse problems.

TABLE 8.1 Theories of substance misuse

Theory	Central tenets
Medical/disease model	Addiction is a chronic, progressive illness. Considered a disease of the brain resulting in behavioural impairment. Assumes impaired control and craving are irreversible and there is no cure for addiction. Only total and lifelong abstinence from mind-altering drugs can arrest the problem. AA, NA and the Minnesota 12-Step model are treatments consistent with this perspective.
Moral model	Addiction is seen as the individual's own fault due to their weak moral character. Addiction is the result of poor choices, which addicts make because of a lack of willpower or moral strength. Substance misusers are anti-social and rather than offering treatment, they should be punished. This perspective has been traditionally favoured within the criminal justice system.
Psychodynamic model	Substance misuse is seen as 'self-medicating' due to underlying psychological problems. These models link the cause of addiction to ego deficiencies, inadequate parenting, attachment disorders and the like. Drug use is a maladaptive coping strategy. Substance misusers need to resolve internal conflict, and when they do, substance misuse will be unnecessary.
Social cognitive theory	Primary motivation is the reinforcement of the behaviour by a powerful reward, which may be a positive feeling such as euphoria or confidence (positive reinforcement) or the alleviation of negative emotions or physical discomfort (i.e. negative reinforcement). Addiction is seen as a learned behaviour as a result of classical and operant conditioning, modelling, and a variety of internal cognitive processes such as outcome expectancies and self-efficacy. Such learned behaviour can be unlearned by the same processes and replaced by more adaptive patterns of behaviour. Cognitive-Behavioural Treatment (CBT) is the treatment of choice for this perspective.

Links between substance misuse and crime

Drugs and crime

There is an obvious link between drug misuse and crime, but the association is more complex than meets the eye.

In young people the evidence (e.g. Pudney, 2002) suggests that criminal behaviour begins before starting to take drugs (typically recreational cannabis and drinking alcohol) and that early intervention efforts should focus on addressing criminal behaviour, delinquency, social exclusion and lifestyle rather than drug use. For a small number of young people use escalates to 'harder' and costlier drugs (typically heroin and crack cocaine in their late teens) and this can lead to a propensity to offend to fund the habit as dependence unfolds in their twenties. This link between dependent patterns of drug use in adolescents and adults and acquisitive crime is well established, but it does not account for all links.

There also exists an association between violence and drug use. Some drugs may facilitate or inhibit violence, and systemic violence exists with some forms of drug trafficking, distribution and supply. For example, according to Mexican government data between January and September 2011 there were 12,903 drug-related violent deaths, mostly near the USA border where organised crime related to drug supply is concentrated. Violence and intimidation is also used by organised criminals in Britain, fighting for territory in the illicit drug trade. However, community interventions in Britain focus on adult drug users committing high volume acquisitive crime. This association is often strongest where drug misuse involves the regular and dependent use of heroin and crack cocaine (Gossop et al., 2005). It is also worthy of note that modern substance misuse behaviour patterns typically involve polydrug use. A combination, for example, of heroin, crack cocaine, non-prescribed use of methadone and benzodiazepines, and alcohol misuse is not uncommon. Almost two-thirds of the NTORS sample was using three or more substances at admission to treatment.

A review paper by Hough, McSweeney and Turnbull (2001) drew the following conclusions about the nature of the drug–crime link:

- Of the four million people using illicit drugs in Britain each year, most is relatively controlled 'recreational' use of cannabis and ecstasy.
- A very small proportion of users – less than 5 per cent of the total – have chaotic lifestyles involving dependent use of heroin, crack/cocaine and other drugs.
- An even smaller proportion of users – perhaps around 100,000 people – finance their use through crime.
- The majority of those who steal to buy drugs were involved in crime before their drug use became a problem for them.
- This group are involved in high volume acquisitive crime to finance their drug use.

It is on this very small group that the government has concentrated its intervention efforts, and mostly this has been done to date in prison settings rather than in the community. However, it is not simply reducing drug use that will arrest criminal behaviour in this group. Targeting this group is rightly viewed as worthwhile though, as involvement in, and the number of, criminal activities during periods of substance misuse far exceed that committed during periods of non-addiction (Gossop et al., 2005).

Alcohol misuse and crime

Alcohol is associated with a wide range of criminal offences, including drink driving and drunkenness, where drinking and excessive drinking define the offence. It is public order offences and in particular violent crime in the entertainment areas of towns and cities that have drawn most government attention. There also exists a notable link between alcohol misuse and domestic violence, as well as murder.

The Labour government introduced the Licensing Act in 2003 and the National Alcohol Harm Reduction Strategy for England in 2004 in an attempt to address the problem. Nine out of ten perpetrators of violent crimes are male, with over half (53 per cent) being between the age of 16 and 24 (Flatley et al., 2010). Young men are also the ones who are most likely to drink to intoxication (Robinson & Lader, 2007). In population studies more violence occurs in northern Europe where binge drinking is more prevalent, compared to the Mediterranean. Binge drinking (with intoxication the common feature) is seen as more risky than a steady regular consumption of alcohol (Room & Rossow, 2001). Looking at the prison context is instructive. Of sentenced male prisoners, 63 per cent are hazardous drinkers. They are more likely than non-hazardous drinkers to be young, and held for a violent offence. Of sentenced women, 39 per cent are hazardous drinkers (Singleton et al., 1999). In terms of longitudinal studies, Fergusson and colleagues (Fergusson et al., 1996; Fergusson & Horwood, 2000) followed a New Zealand cohort of 1,265 and found, controlling for shared risk factors, heavy drinkers are three times more likely to be violent than light drinkers. Gilchrist et al. (2003) found that alcohol was consumed prior to the offence in 62 per cent of domestic violence cases, with almost half (48 per cent) being alcohol dependent.

Summarising the current data McMurran (2007b) states that those most likely to be involved in alcohol-related violence in the UK are young males who drink to intoxication in places where drunk people gather together (so-called 'trouble spots' such as particular entertainment areas on a weekend), and when provocations are most likely (such as closing time, a taxi queue or at a fast food outlet). Walker et al. (2006) found that 17 per cent of all violent offences occur in or around pubs and clubs in England and Wales.

Why is alcohol related to violence?

When intoxicated the pharmacological effect of alcohol tends to decrease the cues a person can attend to. They attend to 'dominant cues' such as perceived threat, and inhibitory cues such as consequences become less salient: so-called 'alcohol myopia' (Giancola et al., 2010). It has also been found to impair access to socially appropriate problem-solving strategies in threatening situations, instead preferring default aggressive responses when provoked (Hoaken et al., 2003). Alcohol expectancy effects seem to also play a role. Holding alcohol–aggression expectancies predicts aggression (Giancola, 2006), and the popular alcohol expectancy of 'alcohol makes me feel socially confident' may mean that a number of overconfident young males find themselves in close proximity, thus increasing the risk for violence (McMurran, 2007a).

Given the above it is no surprise that interventions for alcohol tend to prioritise men who commit alcohol-related violent offences. Seeing as data has revealed that violence is more likely to occur where a large number of male binge drinkers congregate, there is also much to be done to change and control such drinking situations.

It is also worth noting that alcohol misuse problems are very common among the modern drug misusing population. Too often these problems are considered separately and dealt with by different agencies (usually due to commissioning arrangements). About one-fifth of the NTORS sample was severely alcohol dependent, drinking the equivalent of a bottle of spirits per day (Gossop, 2005). Alcohol misuse may well worsen outcomes if it goes unaddressed.

Community-based interventions for drug misusing offenders

Drug treatment for offenders in the community has increased in availability over the last decade. For adults this has been achieved in the main through the introduction of the Drug Interventions Programme (DIP) and the Drug Rehabilitation Requirement (DRR). The Drug Interventions Programme, funded by the Home Office, brings together a range of agencies including the police, courts, prison and probation services, treatment providers, government departments and drug action teams (DATs) to provide tailored treatment for offenders with drug problems. The DRR, which is issued by the court, is run by probation and locally commissioned treatment agencies.

Drug Interventions Programme (DIP)

Introduced in April 2003 as part of the government's 10-year drug strategy for adults, the Drug Interventions Programme or DIP is designed to follow the offender at all parts of their journey through the criminal justice system (arrest and court referral; during bail; in prison and in the community), redirecting the offender at key points into treatment. Key points of intervention are following a positive drugs test on arrest, following a community sentence involving a 'Drug Rehabilitation Requirement' (of between six months and three years) handed down by the courts and following release from prison. DIP's operational Handbook puts the figure invested in this service at £900m. Interventions within the programme include a mandatory drug test on arrest if one of the listed 'trigger offences' has been committed (refusal can lead to a three-month custodial sentence), a 'required assessment' with a drugs worker if the drug test is positive, and a bail requirement by the court to attend their local DIP for treatment, designed to prevent offending while on bail. The DIP drug worker's role is a holistic one, with care plans targeting housing, employment, mental and physical health, education and training, and access to benefits, as well as targeting substance misuse directly.[1]

Does DIP work?

A Home Office evaluation study by Skodbo et al. (2007) followed a DIP cohort of 7,727 and found the overall volume of offending was reduced by 26 per cent following DIP identification. However, a quarter of the cohort increased their offending rates following DIP contact, and the study lacked a comparison group. This is quite typical of the lack of methodological rigour in evaluating substance misuse interventions in the UK.

Drug Courts and the Drug Rehabilitation Requirement

There has been much discussion and debate in the field about whether treatment for offenders ought to be coerced or voluntary. In part this has been driven by ideological differences between the criminal justice system and treatment providers, who recognise that intrinsic motivation to change is an important element in the change process (Miller & Rollnick, 2002). While the evidence is somewhat mixed it is generally accepted that getting offenders into treatment, and retaining them in treatment, is more important than how they get into treatment (Bean, 2008).

The current sentencing and treatment of substance misusing offenders in Britain is coerced in varying degrees of severity. There are some who argue that change is more likely when an individual is intrinsically motivated to change, or alternatively has hit 'rock bottom'. Criminal justice treatment tends to involve the interaction of internal motivation with a level of external pressure (i.e. coercion). Coercion represents a variety of options, from a probation officer's recommendation to enter treatment, a drug court judge offering a choice between prison or treatment, to a judge's requirement that the offender enters treatment as a condition of a community order. The use of coercion can be traced back to the success of Drug Courts in the United States, first developed in the late 1980s, which set out legally mandated treatment to drug offenders with the aim of stopping the 'revolving door' of addicts who were seen as clogging up the judicial system and overcrowding prisons. The treatments ordered by these courts were generally high-intensity, abstinence-oriented programmes, involving frequent drug testing and the constant involvement of the court. The judge was intimately involved at every stage of the process. Underlying the model is the belief that drug-related offending requires social and therapeutic interventions rather than legal sanctions.

Six pilot Dedicated Drug Courts (DDCs) were introduced in magistrates courts in England and Wales from 2004. The four features of the drug court model in the USA form part of the UK's Drug Rehabilitation Requirement (DRR), and they are:

- Early, continuous, and intense judicially supervised treatment
- Mandatory periodic drug testing
- Community supervision
- The use of appropriate sanctions and other rehabilitation services.[2]

A DRR lasts between six months and three years, and gets offenders to:

- Identify what they must do to stop offending and using drugs
- Understand the link between drug use and offending, and how drugs affect health
- Identify realistic ways of changing their lives for the better
- Develop their awareness of the victims of crime.

The system in Britain cannot be referred to as drug courts in the American sense, and it contains different, some would say, weaker, elements of this system. Bean (2008) outlines his criticisms of the British drug court model and the DRR:

- The British approach is harm reduction, whereas the American one is abstinence
- In Britain the Probation Service conducts the supervision; in America it is the judge
- In Britain treatment providers are employed by the Probation Service; in America they are employed by the court
- The features of the DRR are poorly integrated
- The DRR is overly reliant on drug testing, it is not integrated effectively into treatment programmes, and on its own is a poor deterrent
- Continuity is lost in that the offender can appear before a different bench of magistrates when the treatment order is being assessed along its journey
- DRR review hearings lack the firmness of purpose of the drug courts. In the drug courts all those involved in the offender's case management are required to be present which is not the case with the DRR. Sanctions are imposed immediately and the judge has multiple sanctions at his disposal; the DRR has breach proceedings at a later date
- Drug court judges concentrate on drug offenders and they become somewhat specialist in the area of addiction; in Britain the judges retain the full range of offenders
- The American drug testing system aims to have a testing system free of all possible errors; in Britain the possibilities of error are endless. Criticisms include a lack of supervised testing; infrequent testing and then testing on scheduled days; some programmes have so few controls it is easy to avoid detection; even if an offender tests positive the most likely response is to do nothing; if the violation is known to the court it is likely to be a long time after the test.

Bean (2008) also highlights the unsatisfactory pilot study results of the DRR (formerly the Drug Treatment and Testing Order – DTTO) and concludes: 'Clearly the DTTO is the government's flagship to deal with the problem of drug abuse and crime. It has within it certain flaws and, as such, it will, in my judgement, be a failure' (Bean, 2008: 128).

The number of DRR orders increased from 4,854 in 2001–2 to 16,607 in 2007–8. Completion rates were only 28 per cent in 2003 and improved to 43 per cent in 2007–8 (National Offender Management Service Drug Strategy 2008–11).

Case study

John, a 37-year-old man, was awarded his third Drug Rehabilitation Requirement (DRR) by the court which would last for nine months, a so-called medium level DRR. The Probation Officer referred him to the substance misuse service to carry out the DRR. He was mandated as part of his DRR to attend weekly sessions with his substance misuse case worker, to be drug tested twice per week, and to attend a group session once per week. The group was not an accredited programme, but one developed in-house by the substance misuse service. In addition John was asked by his substance misuse worker if he would like to take advantage of a range of other activities within the service such as photography, football, attending the gym, and art. He was also required to attend regular appointments with his offender manager.

John has been on a methadone prescription since 2006, with a couple of breaks when he relapsed into heroin dependence. At assessment he reported using, in addition to his methadone prescription, heroin, crack cocaine, illicit diazepam and pregabalin, and drinking 100 units of alcohol per week. He was also hepatitis C positive. He was convicted for shoplifting and subsequently for assaulting the police officer who arrested him. He complained of low mood and was prescribed an anti-depressant by his GP. His partner is a non-user and has two children under 18 from a previous relationship. John considered himself a step-father to the two children. He was in debt to drug dealers and was concerned that his family was at risk from this. He shoplifted in order to fund his drug use, but had assaulted the police officer while under the influence of alcohol. Misusing alcohol was a new feature and had not been reported during his previous DRRs.

Within the holistic treatment plan the following was agreed:

- To complete the mandated elements of his DRR including providing negative urine samples for illicit drugs
- To address his substance use and achieve abstinence
- To detoxify him from alcohol
- To provide motivational interviewing and subsequently cognitive-behavioural therapy by his substance misuse case worker as a means to achieving abstinence
- Access hepatitis treatment once abstinent
- To refer him to a housing worker to help move his family out of harm's way
- To include a home visit with the offender manager to monitor any safeguarding children concerns and to involve his partner in John's treatment
- For John to attend the Narcotics Anonymous group
- Towards the end of the DRR to offer John some job skills training.

The above treatment plan is representative of the holistic approach to addressing the needs of offenders with substance misuse problems. It benefits from having a variety of services provided within a criminal justice service. In John's case his offender manager, substance misuse case worker, prescriber, safeguarding lead, housing worker and job skills worker all work within the same building and therefore have the opportunity to communicate together.

After a period of engagement John began to make progress and started providing negative urine samples for illicit drugs. His methadone dose was increased and his prescriber placed him on a reducing dose of diazepam. However this progress did not last and he began to regularly provide positive samples for illicit drugs and he continued to drink alcohol. His engagement at appointments suffered and he was brought before the magistrates involved in his case on different occasions to review his order. At these sessions both his offender manager and substance misuse case worker were not present, which is not uncommon. John described the pressure he was under escaping drug dealers and the difficulties in addressing his substance use while looking after two children. The magistrates chose to adopt a lenient view. He continued to make the majority of his appointments with his case worker and offender manager but his drug use continued throughout the order. Most of the time with his case worker was spent discussing his substance use and his positive drug tests. He reoffended and was given an additional three-month term on his existing DRR, so he ended up completing a twelve-month DRR. Six months after the completion of his DRR he was before a judge again for further substance-related offences.

Conclusions

The case of John illustrates some of the strengths and limitations of current service provision. One of the key benefits is the variety of interventions in the care plan, and the access to a variety of specialists who all liaise with the case worker and offender manager. The case also illustrates some of the problems. For example, the lack of negative consequences for ongoing illicit drug use (addiction thrives where there is opportunity and few constraints). This also had a knock-on effect to meetings with the case worker, which were taken up by discussing positive tests, rather than following an evidence-based behaviour change intervention.

Psychological interventions

The following evidence-based psychological interventions are all offered in the community to substance misusing offenders. They tend to target the offender's substance misuse but should also be integrated to simultaneously address a criminal lifestyle. The following are typically offered on a one-to-one basis, but are also integrated into group programmes. They can be applied to drug and/or alcohol misuse.

Motivational interviewing (MI)

Motivational Interviewing (Miller & Rollnick, 2002) departs from traditional psycho-educational and behavioural interventions, which typically rely on advice giving, information provision and skill building. So instead of trying to persuade offenders of the need to change or insert motivation or skills, it holds the implicit assumption that offenders have inherent motivation and the resource capabilities to engage in positive change. It combines client-centred and directive strategies and encourages the active and strategic elicitation of intrinsic motivations to change. Thus the arguments for change and the plans for change come from the offender, not the practitioner. It is especially helpful in a criminal justice population where offenders are often ambivalent about their substance misuse and offending behaviour, and where they can present as being 'resistant' to change. Its effectiveness in addressing alcohol and drug misuse and other behaviour changes has been demonstrated (Hettema et al., 2005) and its application in secure forensic settings are outlined in Gaskell and Mann (2008). It is a difficult method to use competently and relies on good training, ongoing coaching and feedback, video recorded practice, and a culture of using the model in the agency. Changes are often seen in one to three sessions and so it is also attractive to agencies with limited resources. Employing this method as a general style of interaction with offenders in community settings may also strengthen engagement, retention, as well as outcome.

Cognitive-behavioural therapy (incorporating relapse prevention)

This is largely a behavioural treatment with some cognitive elements. It is designed for offenders at the 'action' stage of change (Prochaska & DiClemente, 1983). Once a commitment to change has been made, the practitioner typically completes a functional analysis of substance misuse with the offender, identifying antecedent cues to substance misuse, contemporaneous thoughts and feelings, and short- and long-term consequences of use. A cognitive-behavioural treatment plan is agreed and followed which addresses:

- the cues identified in the functional analysis (via cue avoidance and response prevention)
- the need for alternative reinforcement to compete with reinforcement from substance misuse
- the need for alternative modelling and access to abstinent role models
- substance-related beliefs including outcome expectancies and self-efficacy beliefs
- skill building to strengthen coping confidence in the face of high risk substance use situations.

The method relies on the offender practising a variety of skills within their community environment which are first shaped in the treatment room, as well as being able to make changes to their environment and following an alternative lifestyle. CBT/relapse prevention has been commonly used in the addiction field since the 1980s, has a large evidence base for both adults and young people (Marlatt & Donovan, 2008; Porporino et al., 2002), and again relies on a highly skilled workforce.

Contingency management

Contingency management strategies involve the systematic application of behavioural management principles underlying reward and punishment to encourage reductions in substance use and offending behaviour. These strategies, proven effective in community settings, use voucher-based incentives or rewards (to be exchanged for goods or services of the service user's choice or privileges such as take home methadone doses), to reinforce abstinence (measured by negative drug tests) or to shape progress towards other treatment goals, such as programme attendance or compliance with pharmacological treatment (Lussier et al., 2006).

It is most effective when the contingent reward closely follows the behaviour being monitored. Graduated sanctions can be an effective tool in conjunction with drug testing. The first response to drug use detected through urinalysis should be a clinical one – for example increasing treatment intensity. Behavioural contracting is used in advance, which specifies proscribed behaviours and associated sanctions, as well as positive goals and rewards for success. This method is typically employed within methadone maintenance treatment. Recent studies have shown it to be a superior treatment to cognitive-behavioural therapy (Rawson et al., 2006), and it shows promise with dual diagnosis clients in addressing their substance use, improving psychological functioning and reducing hospitalisations (McDonell et al., 2013).

While the methods are well tested the application of the methods varies widely. Despite its effectiveness its systematic use is relatively uncommon in community addiction treatment in the UK. The most prevalent objections to incentive programmes are that they cost too much, reward clean urine rather than drug abstinence, fail to address the underlying problems of addiction, and do not address multiple behaviours (e.g. Kirby et al., 2006). In addition outcomes tend not to be maintained once the incentive is removed.

Evidence-based pharmacological treatment

Pharmacotherapy intervention is a key part, but only a part, of addressing both opiate and alcohol misuse problems. There are no current evidence-based pharmacological treatments for cocaine use. It may be obvious to say it but these medications are only useful if users take them, and there is an underground market for these drugs so diverting them can be a problem. Psychosocial intervention in tandem with pharmacotherapy is desirable in supporting motivation for change and lifestyle change, and evidence suggests that both together achieve better outcomes than pharmacotherapy alone. Notably, these medications work at the psychological and behavioural, as well as pharmacological, level.

Pharmacotherapy for heroin dependence

For heroin dependence there are two commonly prescribed 'substitute' drug therapies, methadone and buprenorphine. These drugs are prescribed for both maintenance and detoxification. Methadone is a potent synthetic opiate agonist, typically prescribed to a level that saturates the opiate receptors, thus giving the user the opiate drug effect. It has a very long half-life and is less intoxicating than heroin. Taking one daily dose should mean the user does not suffer opiate withdrawal effects. Users experience less euphoria and impairment compared to heroin. Methadone maintenance treatment (MMT) was intended as a maintenance medication much like insulin is for diabetes.

Methadone prescribing can leave the gate open for continued, albeit reduced, heroin use on top of the prescription. There are a variety of problems with drug testing to police heroin use, and consequences for using that are built into the DRR are not always metered out. If practitioners are not careful they can be caught in a situation where services are adding to, rather than addressing, a drug-using lifestyle, and one where risks of drug-related death are heightened by adding this potent drug to the mix. Critics of criminal justice MMT would say there has been a tendency to 'park' a number of offenders on large long-term doses of methadone with little, if any, additional meaningful intervention. Supporters of its use point to the reductions in criminal activity and the positive health benefits of arresting heroin use. The new government drug strategy (2010) is focused on achieving abstinence, which could mean short/medium-term methadone prescribing, with a focus on detoxification thereafter.

The data on reducing criminal behaviour via methadone treatment is strong. Hunt et al. (1984) report crime reduction by addicts in methadone maintenance treatment when compared to comparable groups of addicts not in treatment. A study by Ball and Ross (1991) revealed a 20 per cent reduction in the number of offences committed by participants compared to pre-treatment levels. Retention in methadone treatment is linked to reductions in both heroin use and offending behaviour (Flynn et al., 2003). Higher methadone doses are also linked to reductions in crime (Bellin et al., 1999). Within the NTORS community sample (consisting of methadone reduction and methadone maintenance treatment) rates of acquisitive offending had halved at one year, and had been maintained at the 4–5 year follow-up (Gossop et al., 2005).

Buprenorphine is a relatively new evidence-based treatment for opiate dependence. Although less frequently prescribed, it is a mixed agonist/antagonist opioid with high affinity to opiate receptors. Therefore it has the important added advantage of rendering heroin use on top of the prescription pointless. It is long acting, is relatively safe, and it is easier to detox from than methadone. Now that it is less expensive than it used to be it could be more advantageous for services to provide than methadone.

From a psychological perspective, pharmacotherapy for heroin use has the potential for eliminating withdrawal as a cue for using heroin, extinguishing a variety of cues associated with heroin use and reducing the number of expectancies associated with heroin use. It provides the reinforcing drug effect, and it prevents the punishing consequences of heroin dependence for the individual, and for society.

Pharmacotherapy for alcohol misuse

Roberts et al. (2007: 14) observed 'There has been no research on pharmacological treatments for alcohol misuse in offender settings' and went on to conclude that there was a general need to conduct clinical trials of new and existing alcohol interventions in the UK.

Pharmacotherapy is, however, common as part of approaches to address alcohol misuse problems in the general population. There are drugs available to aid the achievement of abstinence goals, for both detoxification and relapse-prevention purposes. These medications have been rigorously evaluated within general substance misuse populations and should be routinely considered within the alcohol misusing offender population. Abstinence is the obvious goal for offenders whose alcohol misuse is linked to violence, and having access to these pharmacological treatments can enhance psychological approaches.

Accredited Criminal Justice Group Treatment Programmes in the community

Accredited programmes are delivered in probation areas in England and Wales, usually as part of a Drug Rehabilitation Requirement (DRR). The aim is a reduction in crime by targeting substance misuse as a key underlying factor in the offender's risk of reoffending. While Addressing Substance Related Offending (ASRO) and Offender Substance Abuse Programme (OSAP) have been replaced by an equivalent programme they are included here as the replacement programme, Building Skills for Recovery (BSR), has only recently begun.

Addressing Substance Related Offending (ASRO)

This is a cognitive-behavioural programme consisting of 20 two-and-a-half-hour sessions. Offenders selected for the programme are at medium–high risk of reoffending and their substance misuse is stabilised. There needs to be an identified link between substance misuse and offending behaviour. It aims to enhance motivation to change, strengthen self-control, develop strategies to avoid relapse to problem substance use, and encourage lifestyle change to reduce the risk of a return to substance use and offending. A 2008 survey (McSweeney et al., 2009) reported that 16 of the 41 probation areas in England and Wales were using the programme. Palmer et al. (2011) completed an evaluation independent of the criminal justice system. They sampled 319 male participants, of which 141 entered the programme as part of a court order. Another 178 offenders made up a comparison group who had substance misuse problems and similar sentences. The findings are not favourable in terms of demonstrating the programme's effectiveness: even offenders who completed the 20 group sessions (29 per cent of the sample) were reconvicted over the following year no less often (after other factors had been taken in to account) than the comparison group. The authors conclude, 'the completed programme failed to significantly better a sentence which did not include the programme at all, even though it presumably benefited from the likelihood that offenders who completed were relatively stable and committed to staying out of trouble – a so-called "selection" effect' (Palmer et al., 2011: 1078).

Offender Substance Abuse Programme (OSAP)

This is a 26-session cognitive-behavioural accredited programme for those at a medium–high risk of reoffending. This programme aims to address drugs or alcohol misuse, using cognitive methods to change attitudes and behaviour to prevent relapse and reduce offending. It has been rigorously evaluated in Canada (where it is used in institutions rather than as a community programme) where it was found that completers are less likely to be readmitted to prison one year after release compared to matched control groups and programme non-completers (Porporino et al., 2002).

Building Skills for Recovery (BSR)

The latest development in community interventions is the BSR programme. A recent review of National Offender Management Service (NOMS) substance misuse interventions found too much similarity between different programmes such as ASRO and OSAP so they have been amalgamated into one new programme, BSR, which has recently been accredited by the Correctional Services Accreditation Panel (CSAP). This is available for adult men and women offenders and is suitable for drug and alcohol problems related to offending behaviour. There are 16 sessions, and it includes active ingredients of effective treatment, including skills training. It targets varying offender needs including:

- Emotional management
- Problem-solving and decision making
- Self-control
- Self-efficacy
- Harm minimisation
- Self-support systems

- Motivation and engagement
- Effective communication
- Substance use management and control
- Relapse prevention
- Impulsivity.

This is likely to become the flagship programme for drug and alcohol misusing offenders in the community. It is too early for any evaluation data.

A note on outcome research of substance misuse offending behaviour programmes

Palmer et al. (2011) criticise government evaluation research of substance misuse programmes aimed at reducing reoffending. They note that while some of the outcomes described appear positive, the research methodology upon which it is based can have serious limitations, including the lack of comparison groups. This means, they say, that according to current evidence, accredited cognitive-behavioural programmes in the community aimed at reducing substance-related offending cannot be relied upon to do that job.

Alcohol interventions for offenders in the community

Interventions follow the models of care for alcohol misuse (Department of Health, 2006) and should primarily be based on assessed need. The following is a selection of key available interventions.

Alcohol Treatment Requirements (ATRs)

These have been available since 2005, and can be imposed as part of community sentences of up to three years. Offenders are typically alcohol dependent, have co-morbid problems, and require tier 3 and 4 intervention from the National Treatment Agency (NTA) models of care framework (i.e. detoxification, day pro-grammes, residential rehabilitation and integrated care involving a range of agencies). Their offending is usually alcohol related and violent in nature. A report by McSweeney et al. (2009) of probation areas found a number of problems with the implementation of ATRs across probation areas. They found a lack of:

- resources and dedicated funding for alcohol treatment
- guidance and protocols to inform the targeting of available interventions
- appropriate and accessible alcohol treatment provision
- staff confidence, skills and training, and
- success influencing commissioners to afford greater priority to treatment for alcohol misusing offenders.

Moore (2008) reported that only 8 per cent of dependent drinkers starting community sentences in 2007/8 were on an ATR. Within the McSweeney (2009) report they found that only one in four of the areas reporting to the national survey that they were delivering ATRs were doing so in a manner consistent with existing guidance. With such an enormous shortfall in alcohol treatment provision for offenders, with budgets squeezed for the foreseeable future, and with serious questions regarding implementation where treatment is happening, we are a long way off meeting the needs of alcohol misusing offenders in the community.

Simple brief interventions

This is typically five minutes of advice given to 'hazardous drinkers' by an offender manager following screening at the pre-sentence report stage, or during supervision.

Extended brief interventions

These are 3–12 structured sessions of 20–30 minutes' duration delivered to harmful or binge drinkers. They are delivered within probation or the voluntary sector, via what are called 'activity requirements' or as part of a 'supervision requirement'. Brief interventions are in line with the NTA's guidelines on effective practice.

Cognitive-behavioural programmes

OSAP and ASRO have been available for alcohol misusing offenders. As already mentioned these programmes have been replaced by Building Skills for Recovery (BSR), and it is available for alcohol misusing offenders.

Lower Intensity Alcohol Programme (LIAP)

For adult male and female offenders assessed as not sufficiently meeting the criteria for BSR then a number of probation areas run the Lower Intensity Alcohol Programme (LIAP).This is a 14-session programme combining cognitive-behavioural and educational approaches, and it targets consequential thinking, addressing triggers for relapse, problem-solving and goal setting. It is not suitable for those with severe alcohol dependence. At the time of writing it was provisionally approved by CSAP, and awaiting full accreditation.

COVAID

This CSAP-accredited programme is for male offenders who are aggressive or violent after drinking. It is ten 2-hour sessions of cognitive-behavioural therapy and aims to alter positive alcohol outcome expectancies, binge drinking, drinking in risky environments, impulsive decision making, and hostility and aggression. In a pilot study, short-term reconviction data favoured COVAID over a group of non-starters and non-completers (McMurran & Cusens, 2003).

Drink Impaired Drivers (DID) Programme

This is aimed at offenders who have committed a drink-drive related offence. It consists of 14 group sessions and combines cognitive-behavioural and educational approaches. The programme aims to enable offenders to reflect on the effects alcohol will have on their driving ability and the dangers this presents to both themselves and others. Very limited evidence is available as to its effectiveness. Sugg (2000) completed a small-scale evaluation of DID in South Yorkshire and found a reduction of two percentage points for drink-related offences for the treatment group compared to those who received a custodial sentence.

Mutual aid groups

Alcoholics Anonymous (AA) and its equivalent for drug misusers, Narcotics Anonymous (NA), are often utilised by community offenders. These groups are very popular, although evidence as to their effectiveness is limited. McCrady et al. (1996) reported on the three randomised controlled trials which compare AA with another treatment. Of the three none were found to be better than the comparison treatment. In fact two of the three studies found a better response to the comparison treatment than to AA. Evidence does exist for specific types of 12-step approaches to treatment. Project Match (Project Match Research Group, 1997) found long-term positive outcomes for a highly structured programme with detailed treatment protocols and supervision of practice. SMART Recovery self-help groups are a relatively new initiative and provide a secular, science-based, cognitive-behavioural framework as the driving treatment philosophy. This can be an alternative to those who might engage less well with the disease and 'higher power' perspective of the AA and 12-step groups.

Treatment for young substance misusing offenders

The government strategy launched in December 2010 seeks to ensure early identification and intervention to prevent the escalation of use and harm. The objectives are for all young offenders to:

- Be screened for substance misuse
- Those with identified needs to receive specialist assessment within five working days
- Following assessment, access to early intervention and treatment within ten working days.

The bulk of intervention occurs on a one-to-one basis within Youth Offending Teams (YOTs), by YOT substance misuse workers and by specialist young people's substance misuse treatment services. There are over 200 specialist drug workers and services working with YOTs in England and Wales. There exists a Youth

Rehabilitation Order (YRO) which can specify a Drug Rehabilitation Requirement (DRR), a Drug Testing Requirement (DTR) and/or an Intoxicating Substance Treatment Requirement. Treatment can be residential or non-residential. Treatments include harm reduction as well as psychosocial and pharmacological treatment.

Summary of evidence-based treatment

Treatment can, and does, work. Within the NTORS comprehensive research study at one year, acquisitive crimes were reduced to one-third of intake levels, and involvement in crime was reduced to about half of intake levels (Gossop et al., 2000). Notably, these reductions in crime were maintained through to the five-year follow-up. A body of evidence exists of 'what works' in gaining positive outcomes to guide us. This evidence base has told us:

- Crime reduction group treatment programmes based on the principles of risk, need and responsivity (Andrews et al., 1990) are most likely to work.
- Crime reduction treatment programmes are most likely to work when they follow evidence-based implementation protocols and have programme integrity at heart. This includes having a skilled workforce who deliver treatment consistently and as intended (Bonta, 1997).
- Interventions are most likely to work when they consist of the 'active ingredients' of substance misuse interventions. For example, structure, goal-direction, social support, motivation to change, alternative reinforcement and skills training (Moos, 2007).
- Treatment programmes with a cognitive-behavioural orientation appear to be most effective, as well as multisystemic therapy for young substance misusing offenders.
- Therapeutic communities are effective.
- Retaining offenders in treatment is important. Drop-outs and non-completers fare worse.
- Integrating aftercare with the main treatment programme reduces relapse rates and should be offered within community sentences, as well as following a prison term.
- Offering holistic intervention is important, which, in addition to addressing substance misuse, should include housing, benefits, education and employment interventions.
- Randomised controlled trials of pharmacological treatments have told us that they are effective treatments for heroin and alcohol misuse. These ought to be integrated into treatment planning and psychological approaches.
- Randomised controlled trials of psychosocial interventions for substance misuse problems have shown us that interventions such as motivational interviewing, cognitive-behavioural therapy and contingency management are effective.

- Evidence from the United States that 'Drug Courts' and coerced treatment for the criminal justice population works. The Youth Justice Board has introduced treatment along similar lines for young offenders.

Conclusions and future directions

There is little doubt that successive governments have recognised the link between substance misuse and crime, and made resources available to tackle the problem. Interventions are drawn from the principles of 'what works' in addressing offending behaviour; active ingredients of substance misuse interventions are generally holistic in approach, and offenders are organised within the community so they have every opportunity to engage in, and be retained within, treatment services. However, community interventions for substance misusing offenders are best seen as a work in progress. There are a number of challenges in providing more effective intervention and the following future directions may strengthen our efforts to address the challenge of substance-related offending:

1 More significant resources ought to go into researching current and future interventions. Much of the available research is methodologically weak, lacks independence and is often unable to tell us what is making the difference. Research is questioning the effectiveness of some interventions (e.g. Palmer et al., 2011) and it is vital to know if they are not working, or whether they are poorly implemented or simply poorly evaluated.

2 In addition, focusing on outcomes such as whether individuals reoffend within one or two years may be too simplistic a measure, particularly as we know that offending is multi-factorial and many substance misusing offenders were criminals before and separately to their substance use. What may be preferable is a focus on abstinence-based treatment and outcomes (at least from drugs and alcohol where there is a crime link).

3 The Drug Intervention Programme and DRR/ATR, evidence suggests, is not stringent enough in constraining drug or alcohol use or providing immediate and robust punishment for violations of treatment orders. The system may need reform. Addictive behaviour thrives where opportunity and incentive for it outweighs restraints for the behaviour.

4 There should be a move away from long-term methadone maintenance for the majority of offenders, towards abstinence-based treatment and effective aftercare.

5 There should be a greater focus on abstinence-based treatment for drinkers who commit violent offences.

6 Treating substance misusing offenders has tended to fall upon a workforce sometimes ill-equipped and supported to meet the challenge. More effective staff training, supervision, and continued professional development of addiction workers, and other professionals involved in addiction work, is arguably needed. There have been some improvements with the introduction of a

competency framework, but there is more work to be done to create a consistently effective professional workforce across the country. These practitioners should work within a culture of using only evidence-based practice, and have their practice regularly coached and video monitored for fidelity purposes. Substance misusing offenders have complex needs and can be challenging to work with, and addiction workers need more substantial support. There seems to exist a culture of 'chat' in the substance misuse field and, more worryingly, when practitioners say they are using treatment as usual or evidence-based interventions, independent raters of sessions find evidence of these 'virtually undetectable' (Martino et al., 2008; Santa Ana et al., 2008, 2009). When sessions are examined, evidence suggests that therapist-initiated discussion of issues clearly unrelated to any service user problem or issue is observed more frequently than any evidence-based practice (Martino et al., 2009; Bamatter et al., 2010). Psychologists should play a more central role in front-line addiction treatment.

7   Alcohol misuse ought to be treated within the same services as drug misusing offenders. Alcohol is common among drug misusing offenders and it makes little sense to have separate services.

8   The huge problem of alcohol misuse and its strong link to violent crime has been largely ignored over the years in terms of government funding and service provision. Alcohol treatment for offenders, including use of the ATR, has increased but more widespread intervention is needed.

9   There is too much focus on mandatory drug testing within drug treatment. This has limitations in terms of its ability to detect patterns of drug use and, according to Bean (2008), there is a low rate of punishment for violations.

Notes

1   Please see page 15 of *Breaking the Link: The Role of Drug Treatment in Tackling Crime*, NHS National Treatment Agency for Substance Misuse (August 2009) to illustrate the pathway and the way offenders are organised into treatment.

2   Please see page 2 of *The Dedicated Drug Courts Pilot Evaluation Process Study* by Jane Kerr, Charlotte Tompkins, Wojtek Tomaszewski, Sarah Dickens, Roger Grimshaw, Nat Wright & Matt Barnard of the National Centre for Social Research, Ministry of Justice Research Series 1/11 (January 2011) for an illustration of this process.

References

Andrews, D.A., Bonta, J. & Hoge, R.D. (1990) Classification for effective rehabilitation: rediscovering psychology. *Criminal Justice and Behaviour*, 17, 1, 19–52.

Ball, J. & Ross, A. (1991) *The Effectiveness of Methadone Maintenance Treatment*. New York: Springer.

Bamatter, W., Carroll, K.M., Anez, L.M., Paris, M., Ball, S.A. & Nich, C. (2010) Informal discussions in substance abuse treatment sessions with Spanish-speaking clients. *Journal of Substance Abuse Treatment*, 39, 353–63.

Bean, P. (2008) *Drugs and Crime*. 3rd edn. Cullompton: Willan Publishing.

Bellin, E., Wesson, J., Tomasino, V., Nolan, J., Glick, A.J & Oquendo, S. (1999) High dose methadone reduces criminal recidivism in opiate addicts. *Addiction Research*, 7, 19–29.

Bonta, J. (1997) *Offender Rehabilitation: From Research to Practice.* Ottawa: Public Works and Government Services Canada.

Department of Health (2006) Models of care for alcohol misusers (MoCAM). London: Department of Health.

Fergusson, D.M. & Horwood, L.J. (2000) Alcohol abuse and crime: a fixed effects regression analysis. *Addiction*, 95, 1525–36.

Fergusson, D.M., Lynskey, M.T. & Horwood, L.J. (1996) Alcohol misuse and juvenile offending in adolescence. *Addiction*, 91, 483–94.

Flatley, J., Kershaw, C., Smith, K., Chaplin, R., Moon, D. (2010) *Crime in England and Wales 2009/10.* Home Office Statistical Bulletin 12/10. London: Home Office http:// webarchive.nationalarchives.gov.uk/20110218135832/rds.homeoffice.gov.uk/rds/pdfs10/ hosb1210.pdf.

Flynn, P.M., Porto, J.V., Rounds-Bryant, J.L. & Kristiansen, P.L. (2003) Costs and benefits of methadone treatment in DATOS. Part 1: discharged versus continuing patients. *Journal of Maintenance in the Addictions*, 2, 129–49.

Gaskell, M. & Mann, R. (2008) Motivational Interviewing. In Towl, G.J., Farrington, D.P., Crighton, D.A. & Hughes, G. (eds) *Dictionary of Forensic Psychology.* Cullompton: Willan Publishing.

Giancola, P.R. (2006) Influence of subjective intoxication, breath alcohol concentration, and expectancies on the alcohol–aggression relationship. *Alcoholism: Clinical and Experimental Research*, 30, 844–50.

Giancola, P.R., Josephs, R., Parrott, D. & Duke, A. (2010) Alcohol myopia revisited: clarifying aggression and other acts of disinhibition through a distorted lens. *Perspectives on Psychological Science*, 5, 265–78.

Gilchrist, E., Johnson, R., Takriti, R., Weston, R., Beech, A. & Kebbell, M. (2003) Domestic violence offenders: characteristics and offending related needs. *Home Office Findings*, 217.

Gossop, M. (2005) Treatment outcomes: what we know and what we need to know. Treatment Effectiveness 2. London: NHS National Treatment Agency for Substance Misuse.

Gossop, M., Marsden, J., Stewart, D. & Rolfe, A. (2000) Reductions in acquisitive crime and drug use after treatment of addiction problems: one year follow-up outcomes. *Drug and Alcohol Dependence*, 58, 165–72.

Gossop, M., Trakada, K., Stewart, D. & Witton, J. (2005) Reductions in criminal convictions after addiction treatment: 5 year follow-up. *Drug and Alcohol Dependence*, 79, 295–302.

Hettema, J., Steele, J. & Miller, W.R. (2005) Motivational intervewing. *Annual Review of Clinical Psychology*, 1, 91–111.

Hoaken, P.N.S., Shaughnessy, V.K. & Pihl, R.O. (2003) Executive cognitive function and aggression: Is it an issue of impulsivity? *Aggressive Behavior*, 29, 15–30.

Hough, M., McSweeney, T. & Turnbull, P. (2001) Drugs and crime: What are the links? Evidence to the Home Affairs Committee Enquiry into Drugs Policy. London: Drugscope.

Hubbard, R.L., Marsden, M.E., Rachal, J.V., Harwood, H.J., Cavanaugh, E.R. & Ginzberg, H.M. (1989) *Drug Abuse Treatment: A National Study of Effectiveness.* London: Chapel Hill.

Hunt, D.E., Lipton, D.S., Goldsmith, D. & Strug, D. (1984) Street pharmacology: uses of cocaine and heroin in the treatment of addiction. *Drug and Alcohol Dependence*, 13, 4, 375–87.

Kirby, K.C., Benishek, L.A., Dugosh, K.L. & Kerwan, M.E. (2006) Substance abuse treatment providers' beliefs and objections regarding contingency management: implications for dissemination. *Drug and Alcohol Dependence,* 85, 19–27.

Lussier, J.P., Heil, S.H., Mongeon, J.A., Badger, G.J, & Higgins, S.T. (2006) A meta-analysis of voucher_based reinforcement therapy for substance use disorders. *Addiction*, 101, 2, 192–203.

McCrady, B.S., Epstein, E.E. & Hirsch, L.S. (1996) Issues in the implementation of a randomised controlled trial that includes Alcoholics Anonymous: studying AA-related behaviors during treatment. *Journal of Studies on Alcohol*, November, 605–12.

McDonell, M.G., Srebnik, D., Angelo, F., McPherson, S., Lowe, J.M., Sugar, A., et al. (2013) Randomised controlled trial of contingency management for stimulant use in community mental health patients with serious mental illness. *American Journal of Psychiatry*, 170, 1, 94–101.

McMurran, M. (2007a) The relationships between alcohol–aggression proneness, general alcohol expectancies, drinking, and alcohol-related violence in adult male prisoners. *Psychology, Crime and Law*, 13, 275–84.

McMurran, M. (2007b) An intervention for alcohol-related violence. *Mental Health Review*, 12, 3, 7–9.

McMurran, M. & Cusens, B. (2003) Controlling alcohol-related violence: a treatment programme. *Criminal Behaviour and Mental Health*, 13, 59–76.

McSweeney, T., Webster, R., Turnbull, P.J., & Duffy, M. (2009) *Evidence-based Practice? The National Probation Service's Work with Alcohol-misusing Offenders*. London: Ministry of Justice.

Makkai, T. & Payne, J. (2003) *Drugs and Crime: A Study of Incarcerated Male Offenders*. Research and Public Policy Series No. 52. Canberra: Australian Institute of Criminology.

Marlatt, G.A. & Donovan, D.M. (eds) (2008) *Relapse Prevention: Maintenance Strategies in the Prevention of Addictive Behaviours*. 2nd edn. New York: Guilford Press.

Martino, S., Ball, S.A., Nich, C., Frankforter, T.L. & Carroll, K.M. (2008) Community programme therapist adherence and competence in motivational enhancement therapy. *Drug and Alcohol Dependence*, 97, 37–48.

Martino, S., Ball, S.A., Nich, C., Frankforter, T.L. & Carroll, K.M. (2009) Informal discussions in substance abuse treatment sessions. *Journal of Substance Abuse Treatment*, 36, 366–75.

Miller, W.M. & Rollnick, S. (2002) *Motivational Interviewing: Preparing People to Change*. 2nd edn. New York: Guilford Press.

Moore, R. (2008) *Offenders Identified as 'Dependent Drinkers' and Levels of Provision (Valid 2007/08 OASys assessments): Explanatory notes on the O-DEAT workbook. Series*, 13/09. Internal paper (unpublished). London: Ministry of Justice.

Moos, R. (2007) Theory-based active ingredients of effective treatments for substance misuse disorders. *Drug and Alcohol Dependence*, 88 (2–3), 109–21.

Orford, J. (2001) *Excessive Appetites: A Psychological View of Addictions*. 2nd edn. Chichester: Wiley.

Palmer, E., Hatcher, R., McGuire, J., Bilby, C., Ayers, T., & Hollin, C. (2011) Evaluation of the Addressing Substance Related Offending programme (ASRO) for substance using offenders in the community: a reconviction analysis. *Substance Use & Misuse*, 46, 1072–80.

Porporino, F., Robinson, D., Millson, B. & Weekes, J. (2002) An outcome evaluation of prison-based treatment programming for substance users. *Substance Use & Misuse*, 37, 1047–77.

Prochaska, J.O. & DiClemente, C.C. (1983) Stages and processes of self-change of smoking: toward an integrated model of change. *Journal of Consulting and Clinical Psychology*, 51, 3, 390–5.

Project MATCH Research Group (1997) Matching alcoholism treatments to client heterogeneity: Project MATCH post-treatment drinking outcomes. *Journal of Studies on Alcohol*, 58, 1, 7–29.

Pudney, S. (2002) The road to ruin. Sequences of initiation into drug use and offending by young people in Britain. Home Office Research Study 253. London: Home Office.

Rawson, R.A., McCann, M.J., Flammino, F., Shoptaw, S., Miotto, K., Reiber, C., & Ling, W. (2006) A comparison of contingency management and cognitive-behavioral approaches for stimulant-dependent individuals. *Addiction*, 101, 267–74.

Roberts, A.J., Hayes, A.J., Carlisle, J. & Shaw, J. (2007) *Review of Drug and Alcohol Treatments in Prison and Community Settings. A Systematic Review Conducted on Behalf of the Prison Health Research Network*. Manchester: University of Manchester.

Robinson, S. & Lader, D. (2007) Smoking and Drinking in England & Wales. http://www.ons.gov.uk/ons/re/ghs/general-household-survey/2007-report/rpt---smoking-and-drinking-among-adults-2007.pdf

Room, R. & Rossow, I. (2001) The share of violence attributable to drinking. *Journal of Substance Use*, 6, 218–28.

Rounsaville, B.J. (2002) Experience with ICD-10/DSM-IV substance use disorders. *Psychopathology*, 35(2–3), 82–8.

Santa Ana, E., Martino, S., Ball, S.A., Nich, C. & Carroll, K.M. (2008) What is usual about 'treatment as usual': audiotaped ratings of standard treatment in the Clinical Trials Network. *Journal of Substance Abuse Treatment*, 35, 369–79.

Santa Ana, E.J., Carroll, K.M., Anez, L., Paris, M., Ball, S.A. & Nich, C. (2009) Evaluating motivational enhancement therapy adherence and competence among Spanish-speaking therapists. *Drug and Alcohol Dependence*, 103, 44–51.

Singleton, N., Farrell, M. & Meltzer, H. (1999) *Substance Misuse among Prisoners in England and Wales*. London: Office for National Statistics.

Skodbo, S., Brown, G., Deacon, S., Cooper, A., Hall, A., Millar, T., Smith, J., & Whitham, K. (2007) The Drug Interventions Programme (DIP): addressing drug use and offending through 'Tough Choices'. Home Office Research Report 2, November. London: Home Office.

Sugg, D. (2000) South Yorkshire Impaired Drivers Scheme. *National Probation Service Briefing*. Issue 4, July.

Walker, A., Kershaw, C. & Nicholas, S. (2006) *Crime in England and Wales 2005/06*. Home Office Statistical Bulletin 12/06. http://news.bbc.co.uk/1/shared/bsp/hi/pdfs/17_07_07.pdf, also available at http://www.northamptonshireobservatory.org.uk/docs/doccrime englandandwales2006060804092423.pdf.

Weekes, J.R., Moser, A.E. & Langevin, C.M. (1999) Assessing substance abusing offenders for treatment. In Latessa, E.J. (ed.) *Strategic Solutions: The International Community Corrections Association Examines Substance Abuse*. Lanham, MD: American Correctional Association Press.

Weekes, J.R., Moser, A.E., Wheatley, M. & Matheson, F.I. (2013) What works in reducing substance-related offending? In Craig, L.A., Dixon, L. & Gannon, T.A. (eds) *What Works in Offender Rehabilitation: An Evidence-Based Approach to Assessment and Treatment*. First edn. Chichester: John Wiley.

West, R. (2006) *Theory of Addiction*. Oxford: Blackwell Publishing.

PART 3

Management in the community

9

MANAGING RISK IN THE COMMUNITY

Simone Fox and Richard Latham

Introduction

Risk assessment, prediction and management aims to prevent harm: harm by the individual to themselves through suicide or self-harm, or harm to another such as a sexual or serious violent assault. The use of mental health professionals within civil and criminal courts in the assistance of assessment of dangerousness and risk of future violence has increased (Yang et al., 2010). For example, expert witnesses may be asked to provide reports regarding risk for the purpose of sentencing or parole which will have implications on the liberty of a perpetrator. This chapter will focus primarily on risk assessment, prediction and management in relation to violent offenders and other serious offenders.

The law by necessity treats the concept of 'dangerousness' as binary, that is either someone is dangerous or they are not (Criminal Justice Act, 2003). From the clinical perspective, however, the risk of harm is dynamic and depends at any given time on the interaction between the individual, and their circumstances. For example, the risk of antisocial behaviour in an adolescent will increase when they are associating with other negative peers (Coleman & Hagell, 2007). In order for management and intervention to be most effective it is necessary to predict which individuals are at high risk of violence and under what conditions violence is more likely to occur (Yang et al., 2010). This model has been applied successfully in the reduction of future violence among offender populations (Andrews et al., 1990) and high risk adolescents (Lipsey & Wilson, 1998). Thus, the aim of a risk assessment for violence is to evaluate the interaction between the individual offender, their psychological state and their environmental circumstances so as to develop a management plan to minimise the risk of violence.

It is in everyone's interests – professionals, relatives, society, the government and (usually) the individual themselves – for harm to be prevented, particularly very serious harms such as murder. This strong desire tends to lead to the expectation that it will be possible to predict when such a harm might occur, for example, 'if we don't detain this man with command auditory hallucinations today, he will leave and kill his wife'. However, such detailed prediction of something as complex, multi-factorial and often over-determined as human behaviour is impossible, at least at present. Because harm cannot be predicted accurately, there will always be false positives, that is situations in which action is taken against people who would not have caused harm on that occasion – as well as false negatives, in which action is not taken and harm results (Monahan, 1981).

Approaches to risk assessment

There has been ongoing debate about the various approaches to the prediction of violence (Doyle & Dolan, 2008). The traditional focus of violence risk assessment has been on risk factors: meaning those factors that increase the probability of an individual engaging in future violence (Desmarais et al., 2012). There is limited research on what factors would protect against or decrease the risk amongst adults (Webster et al., 2006). The literature of the adolescent offender has a much stronger emphasis on the inclusion of protective factors in the violence risk assessment process.

There are various approaches to risk assessment: pure clinical approach alone, actuarial approach and a combination of the two, structured professional judgement.

Clinical approaches

Unstructured clinical or professional judgement is historically the most common approach to risk assessment (Doyle & Dolan, 2008). Clinical approaches are based upon the judgement of an individual clinician or a team of clinicians, preferably from different disciplines. Findings suggests that risk management decisions are made more upon clinical judgement than risk assessment tools (Hilton & Simmons, 2001; Sturidsson et al., 2004; Stubner et al., 2006). Research looking at purely clinical approaches to risk assessment has tended to show that risk predictions are only slightly better than chance and the competence varies between clinicians (Lidz et al., 1993). This approach has been criticised for being subjective, unstructured, informal and impressionistic (Grove & Meehl, 1996).

Actuarial approaches

The last two decades have seen a rise in the development of specialised tools for both the prediction and management of violence across a range of populations (Heilbrun et al., 2009). The use of actuarial risk assessment tools has now become an accepted standard of forensic risk assessment practice (Monahan et al., 2001). Actuarial tools consider static factors, which produce a statistical probability of recidivism (Hart, 1998). This probability must be considered as the rate of recidivism in a group of people (convicted of a violent offence) and not the probability of that individual reoffending. Elbogen et al. (2005) found that there is disagreement amongst clinicians about when to use actuarial assessment tools and Hilton et al. (2008) found that there is disagreement amongst clinicians about what non-numerical descriptive terms about risk assessment mean.

Actuarial approaches have been found to predict recidivism more accurately than unstructured clinical assessment alone (Monahan, 1981; Dawes et al., 1989;

TABLE 9.1 The advantages and disadvantages of unstructured clinical and actuarial approaches to risk assessment

Advantages	Disadvantages
Clinical judgement	
• Includes risk factors that are amenable to change in a way that is assumed to impact on risk	• No systemic empirical support – low agreement (unreliable), low accuracy (unvalidated) and foundation is unclear (unimpeachable)
• Flexible – easily adapted to new cases and contexts	• Justification for imposing structure requires inductive logic (belief that the specified components will build a picture that defines that risk potential)
• Idiographic – meets the needs of courts and tribunals	
• Relevant to professional practice – rationally guides management decisions, consistent with professional standards, supports professional liability management promoting transparency in decision making	• There are no explicit decision-making rules
	• Lack of consistency and agreement across assessors – low inter-rater reliability
• Requires limited training and technology	• Reasons for the decision may not be explicit, making it difficult for others to question that decision
	• Assumes risk can change
Actuarial	• They have a low positive predictive value, partly because the low prevalence of relevant harms (e.g. serious violence in the case of the PCL-R)
• Risk factors have an established empirical association with violent outcome	
• Designed to predict violence more accurately than clinical judgement alone	• They are unable to define and measure independent factors, both in the individual and the environment, in sufficient detail or specificity to be of clinical use
• Have better receiver operating characteristics	
	• Limited by their reliance on static factors and limited use of dynamic factors and therefore cannot measure changes in risk
	• Mostly ignore protective factors that reduce risk
	• They are more focused on prediction of risk as opposed to management of risk

Ægisdóttir et al., 2006). However there have been a number of criticisms of actuarial approaches alone: they tend to focus on a limited number of factors which are static and take no account of dynamic variables, and they tend to be optimised to predict a specific outcome over a specific time period in a specific population which may not be generalised to other populations (Gottfredson & Gottfredson, 1986).

Structured professional judgement

As can be seen from Table 9.1, both clinical and actuarial approaches have a number of advantages and disadvantages. A range of approaches is needed, and always will be, because undue reliance on lists of small numbers of static risk factors is too restrictive, as well as being scientifically and ethically dangerous. A structured clinical approach can act merely as an aide-memoire or can incorporate some actuarial elements. Some actuarial tools have been designed to assist, not replace, clinical evaluations of risk across a broad range of populations and settings. Structured professional judgement encompasses a varied assessment approach which is embedded in evidence that has mainly been validated by research (Douglas et al., 1999). When used alongside an individual knowledge of the offender and their environment, structured clinical risk assessments, like the Historical Clinical and Risk – 20 items (HCR-20), have been shown to improve clinical decision-making.

Risk assessment tools

A variety of assessment instruments have developed over time. Some tools are purely actuarial in that they provide a probabilistic estimate of violence risk in a specified period of time, and others allow for a professional judgement to be made on level of risk, such as low, medium or high, after taking into account the presence or absence of a predetermined set of factors (structured clinical judgement instruments). The latter tend to consider a range of static and dynamic risk factors, the precise formulation of the factors depending on the development of the instrument, and often on the population on which it was normed or for which it was intended. There are over 150 different risk assessment instruments currently in existence (Singh et al., 2011). Many of the tools are time-consuming and resource-intensive, requiring the cooperation of various different professionals (Vijoen et al., 2010) and many require training and are expensive.

It is important to note that risk assessment tools are not sufficient on their own for the purposes of risk assessment (Fazel et al., 2012). In some criminal justice systems, the scores from these instruments have been used in a simplistic way to estimate an individual's risk of future offending by some expert witnesses (Janus, 2004). The risk assessment tool should form part of the wider clinical risk assessment process and assist in the development of risk management plans in high risk groups (Fazel et al., 2012).

Table 9.2a summarises the most common adult violence risk assessment instruments and Table 9.2b summarises those for adolescents. Many of the risk prediction instruments overlap, for example the HCR-20, the SORAG and the VRAG include the PCL-R. Care must always be taken to ensure that the instrument is appropriate for use on the group to which the individual belongs. Risk assessment tools for sex offenders are summarised in Tables 9.3a (adults) and 9.3b (adolescents).

Risk management

The main aim of risk management is to minimise harm to others and the individual. In contrast, the main aims of treatment are to benefit the offender by improving quality of life or delaying death. Although risk management may benefit the offender, at least in some ways (e.g. avoiding an incident of serious violence and consequent prosecution and incarceration may improve the offender's quality of life during what would otherwise have been the period of incarceration), it can also conflict with what is in the offender's interest, at least as they see it (e.g. mandatory attendance on an offender treatment programme run by the Probation Service may reduce the risk of reoffending, but reduces liberty and free time). This irreducible ethical tension between the interests of the offender and the interests of others means that risk management cannot be done automatically and without thought, but only with careful consideration of whether the measures proposed, and the impact they may have on the offender, can be justified.

Many of the structured professional judgement tools described above necessitate completion of a risk management section with explicit questions about actions and interventions. Any actions or interventions should flow from the identification of the salient risk factors in the assessment process. Attention to understanding the nature and extent of the risk is an integral part of the management but there should also be consideration of whether important factors in determining risk can be appropriately supported or ameliorated. This might take the form of bolstering protective factors (e.g. assisting with education or employment) or reducing risk factors (e.g. providing support for decreasing use of drugs). This process also allows for acknowledgement of the limitations of the risk management plan in relation to specific risk factors (e.g. age and gender cannot be changed but there might be limits in terms of other factors such as re-housing). Interventions have not consistently demonstrated efficacy in reducing risk of recidivism (Maguire, 2002).

Multi-agency working

Forensic mental health professionals will often need to work with the police and other agencies as part of a risk management plan. Although there may be a shared goal to reduce the levels of risk, health services and criminal justice agencies may have different goals which may conflict. For example, the probation service may wish to prevent the individual from reoffending and protect the public, whereas the mental health professional may wish to promote the individual's welfare and

TABLE 9.2A Adult violence risk assessment instruments

Structured professional judgement

Offender Assessment System (OASys; Home Office, 2002)
- Standardised process for the assessment of offenders jointly developed by the National Probation Service and Prison Service
- Measures the risks and needs of criminal offenders under supervision
- Comprises a series of computer-based forms on which clinical evaluations are made, and supervision and sentence plans are recorded

Historical/Clinical Risk Scale (HCR-20; Webster et al., 1997)
- 20 items in 3 domains (Historical, e.g. 'early maladjustment'; Clinical, e.g. 'negative attitudes', and Risk, e.g. 'plans lack feasibility')
- Assesses clinical evaluations of risk of violence across a wide range of populations and settings
- Monitors clinical and situational factors that may be relevant to violence
- Includes emphasis on scenario planning based upon risk factors
- For use with psychiatric patients

Short Dynamic Risk Scale (SDRS; Quinsey, 2004)
- 8 items rating dynamic factors on 4-point scales, e.g. hostile attitude, coping skills and consideration of others

Emotional Problems Scale (EPS; Prout & Strohmer, 1991)
- Rates 12 items on 5-point scales, e.g. anxiety, depression, self-esteem, verbal aggression, physical aggression
- Validated for people with learning difficulties

Risk Assessment Management and Audit Systems (RAMAS; O'Rourke et al., 1998)
- An integrated approach to risk assessment. This includes a Risk Assessment Checklist component

Spousal Assault Risk Assessment (SARA; Kropp et al., 1999)
- 20 items assessing risk of future violence in men for spousal assault

Violence Risk Scale – second edition (VRS-2; Wong & Gordon, 2006)
- Risk of violent recidivism in incarcerated offenders: 6 static and 20 dynamic factors
- Integrates violence assessment, prediction and treatment
- Designed to be used in forensic patients

Purely actuarial tools

Violence Risk Appraisal Guide (VRAG; Webster et al., 1994)
- 12-item actuarial tool including factors relating to antisocial behaviour, e.g. childhood behaviour problems, history of personality disorder, history of non-violent offending
- Uses a linear approach

Psychopathy Checklist – Revised (PCL-R; Hare, 1991, 2003)
- 20-item scale measuring psychopathy rather than risk assessment, but has been shown to have good predictive power
- PCL-SV is a screening version with predictive validity in institutional and community patients

Offender Group Reconviction Scale 3 (OGRS 3; Howard et al., 2009)
- A statistical reconviction scale used by probation officers in pre-sentence reports

TABLE 9.2A *continued*

Purely actuarial tools

- Allows probation, prison and youth justice staff to produce predictions of risk for offenders when the use of dynamic risk assessment tools is not possible

Level of Service Inventory – Revised (LSI-R; Andrews & Bonta, 1995)
- 54-item tool that predicts general criminal offending
- Used with adult offenders

Note: It is important to note that most risk assessment tools have been standardised in male offenders, and their generalisation to female offenders is doubtful. The base rate for violence in females is so low, that predictive risk factors are much harder to establish.

TABLE 9.2B Child and adolescent violence risk assessment instruments

Structured professional judgement

Onset (Centre for Criminology, 2003) and Asset (YJB, 2000)
- Structured risk assessments used by Youth Inclusion and Support Panels (YISPs), Youth Offending Teams (YOTs)
- The Onset referral and assessment framework was designed for the Youth Justice Board (YJB) to promote their prevention strategy by helping to identify risk factors to be reduced and protective factors to be enhanced – for use with young people aged 8–13 years
- Assets must be completed for all young offenders who come into contact with the criminal justice system
- Information gathered can be used to inform court reports so that appropriate intervention programmes can be drawn up

Structured Assessment of Violent Risk in Youth (SAVRY; Borum et al., 2002)
- 24 items in 4 domains (historical, social/contextual, individualised/clinical and protective factors)
- For use with male and female adolescents aged 12–18 years
- There are no numerical values

Purely actuarial tools

Psychopathy Checklist – Youth Version (PCL-YV; Forth et al., 2003)
- A version of the PCL-R (see above) modified for use in adolescents. There are ethical controversies about its use

Offender Group Reconviction Scale 3 (OGRS 3; Howard et al., 2009)
- See Table 9.2a

Early Assessment Risk List for boys and girls (EARL-20B and EARL-21G; Augimeri et al., 2001)
- 20 items (child, family and responsivity) measuring risk of violence in children under 12

Youth Level of Service/Case Management Inventory (YLS/CMI; Hoge & Andrews, 2002)
- 42-item risk–need assessment measure developed specifically for youths
- Follows principles of risk–needs–responsivity to inform community supervision and case management to manage risk and prevent recidivism

TABLE 9.3A Adult sexual violence risk assessment instruments

Structured professional judgement

Risk of Sexual Violence Protocol (RSVP; Hart et al., 2003)
- 22-item risk assessment for adult sexual offenders
- Uses formulation and scenario planning

Sexual Violence Risk – 20 (SVR-20; Boer et al., 1997)
- 20 items assessing violence risk in sexual offenders
- Includes 11 items around social adjustment, 7 items around sexual offences and 2 on future plans

Purely actuarial tools

Rapid Risk Assessment of Sexual Offender Recidivism (RRASOR; Hanson, 1997)
- 4-item screening instrument (any male victims, any unrelated victims, age less than 25, and prior sexual offences)
- Relies purely on file information
- Superseded by Static 2002

Static – 99/2002 (Hanson & Thornton, 1999, 2003)
- 10 items including all 4 items from RRASOR plus items concerning relationship history, violent offences and stranger victims
- For use with male offenders only

Risk Matrix 2000 (RM2000; Thornton, 2000)
- Uses static factors to predict risk up to 15 years later for adult offenders with at least one sexual offence conviction
- Mainly used by probation
- Consists of 3 scales (sexual reconviction, violent reconviction and combination of both)

Minnesota Sex Offending Screening Tool – Revised (MnSoST-R; Epperson et al., 2003)
- 21 items assessing risk of recidivism in incarcerated rapists and child sex offenders

Sexual Offending Risk Appraisal Guide (SORAG; Quinsey et al., 1998)
- 14 items assessing risk of recidivism in incarcerated rapists and child sex offenders

well-being. Integrated Offender Management (IOM) is the umbrella term used by government and criminal justice bodies in England and Wales for the overarching framework of managing offenders in a coordinated way. IOM relies on local policies and procedures being agreed between agencies. The main agencies are considered to be police, probation services and local authorities but the guiding principles suggest involvement of other organisations including health and the voluntary sector. By January 2011 almost all areas had IOM procedures. IOM has five overarching policies:

1   *All partners tackling offenders together* – local partners, both criminal justice and non-criminal justice agencies, encourage the development of a multi-agency problem-solving approach by focusing on offenders, not offences.

TABLE 9.3B Child and adolescent sexual violence risk assessment instruments

Structured professional judgement

Estimate of Risk of Adolescent Sexual Offence Recidivism (ERASOR; Worling & Curwen, 2001)
  • Uses both static and dynamic factors
  • Historical sexual assaults, sexual interests, attitudes and behaviour, psychological functioning and treatment

Purely actuarial tools

Juvenile Sex Offender Assessment Protocol, version 2 (J-SOAP-II; Prentky & Righthand, 2003)
  • 28-item checklist to aid in the systematic review of risk factors associated with sexual and criminal offending
  • Designed for boys aged 12–18 years convicted of sexual offences or with a history of sexually coercive behaviour

2 *Delivering a local response to local problems* – all relevant local partners are involved in strategic planning, decision-making and funding choices.
3 *Offenders facing their responsibility or facing the consequences* – offenders are provided with a clear understanding of what is expected of them.
4 *Making better use of existing programmes and governance* – this involves gaining further benefits from programmes such as the public and other priority offender programme (PPO), drug intervention programme (DIP) and Community Justice, to increase the benefits for communities. This will also enable partners to provide greater clarity around roles and responsibilities.
5 *All offenders at high risk of causing serious harm and/or reoffending are 'in scope'* – intensity of management relates directly to severity of risk, irrespective of position within the Criminal Justice System or whether statutory or non-statutory.

Consent and confidentiality

The various agencies involved with an offender will have different issues around disclosure. The ultimate aim to prevent crime might be seen as a ticket to universal access to medical and social care records but this is not the case. For a mental health professional, the legal and ethical duties that apply to normal clinical work continue to apply when working jointly with other agencies (General Medical Council, 2009). There is a duty of confidentiality to the individual and confidential information cannot be disclosed about them to partner agencies without their consent, or unless one of the statutory or public interest exceptions applies. Other agencies are not subject to the same duties as the mental health professional, and they may· use information or assistance provided to them for purposes that would amount to breaches of the mental health professionals' duty to their patient. Inquiries into serious incidents including Lord Laming's inquiry into the death of Victoria Climbié and the evolving collection of homicide inquiries have led to government recommendations in relation to information sharing (HM Government, 2008). This guidance emphasises that duties in relation to confidentiality are not a barrier to sharing relevant information but suggests information that is shared should be 'necessary, proportionate, relevant, accurate, timely and secure'. The National Health Service and social care services will have access to a Caldicott guardian who will be a senior person within one of these organisations. Their role is to ensure the highest possible standards for confidentiality and handling patient information. This acts as protection for careless sharing of information when it does not meet the threshold described above (Department of Health, 2010).

National Offender Management Service (NOMS)

In England and Wales NOMS is an executive agency of the Ministry of Justice incorporating the commissioning of prison and probation services. These services are commissioned from both the public and private sector. A number of initiatives exist under the umbrella of NOMS with the intention of managing (particularly high risk) offenders in the community.

Prolific and other priority offenders (PPOs) are identified locally and are one of the main facets of IOM. In broad terms these are the people considered to be at highest risk of reoffending. Between April 2009 and March 2010, of 680,000 offenders identified nationally approximately 8,000 were being managed under local PPOs at some point. Approximately 75 per cent of these reoffended within a one-year period. Multi-agency working and sharing of information underpins the PPO approach, with a focus on intensive supervision. PPOs have an average of 47 convictions and tend to be young men.

Drug interventions programmes (DIPS), introduced in 2003, are another component of IOM. The management of offenders who use drugs has three major components: identification, assessment and case management. DIPS include, but are not restricted to, community management. The interventions are usually delivered through Criminal Justice Integrated Teams (CJITs). The CJIT caseworker will have involvement with people with and without statutory supervision requirements.

Public Protection Arrangements: MAPPA

In the three UK jurisdictions, the process of inter-agency cooperation for protecting the public has been formalised under the Multi-Agency Public Protection Arrangements (MAPPA) for England and Wales, and Scotland, and the Public Protection Arrangements for Northern Ireland (PPANI). Under this statutory scheme,[1] the so-called Responsible Authorities (RA) – the police, probation and prison services[2] – must jointly manage offenders deemed to pose a 'serious risk of harm to the public', and are entitled to cooperation from other relevant agencies, such as health, housing, education and social services.

Identification of offenders to be supervised is generally determined by the offender's offence and sentence, but also by assessed level of risk. There are three formal categories: sex offenders, violent offenders and potentially dangerous offenders. Agencies can also cooperate in the management of offenders not covered by MAPPA, under informal arrangements. Public Protection Panels focused on the management of sexual offenders initially but non-sexual violent offenders were subsequently incorporated.

MAPPA promotes information sharing between all the agencies, resulting in more effective supervision and better public protection. Victims' needs are represented, and additional measures are put in place to manage the risks posed to known victims. MAPPA enables resources and attention to be focused on offenders who present the highest risk (most MAPPA offenders do not present a serious risk to the public).

MAPPA offenders should be managed at one of three levels. While the assessed risk is an important factor, it is the degree of management intervention required which determines the level.

- *Level One*: involves normal agency management – generally offenders managed at this level will be assessed as presenting a low or medium risk of serious harm to others.
- *Level Two*: often called local inter-risk agency management – most offenders assessed as high or very high risk of harm.
- *Level Three*: known as Multi-Agency Public Protection Panels (or MAPPPs) – appropriate for those offenders who pose the highest risk of causing serious harm or whose management is so problematic that multi-agency cooperation and oversight at a senior level is required with the authority to commit exceptional resources.

There is no clear conclusion that can be drawn about how effective MAPPA has been. Annual reports produced by the Ministry of Justice are difficult to evaluate. An attempt to compare reconviction rates prior to and subsequent to the implementation of MAPPA demonstrated a reduction although conclusions were tentative in relation to the direct effect of MAPPA (Peck, 2011).

Voluntary organisations

Voluntary organisations are supported by an umbrella organisation called Clinks. There are over 450 organisations under their auspices. For example:

- NACRO is the largest charity in England and Wales dedicated to reducing crime. Their stated aims incorporate prevention initiatives but they are largely concerned with offender management and resettling of prisoners. Offender management interventions are described as 'working with people in prison, on post-release licences and on community sentences. We challenge them to stop offending, provide positive skills, help them find a suitable home and create chances for people to move on from crime and to give something positive back to their communities' (NACRO.org.uk). They have approximately 2,000 staff working for and volunteering for their initiatives.

- Circles UK is a registered charity aimed at reducing sex offending. Their focus is in assisting sex offenders reintegrate into the community. They provide support and a safety mechanism for offenders (referred to as Core members) and the local community. The 'circle' is a group of volunteers from a local community (4–6) who provide a supportive social network for the Core member but still requiring them to take responsibility for their own risk management. They work in conjunction with other agencies but offenders must enter into the Circle voluntarily.

Statutory supervision of offenders in the community

Management of risk in the community might be supported by legal requirements, if the person has been convicted of an offence. People convicted of an offence will broadly be in one of four groups in the community:

- Community sentence via a Community Order with a Drug Rehabilitation Requirement (DRR) attached
- Community sentence via a Community Order with no DRR attached
- Release from prison and subject to statutory supervision under licence
- Release from prison and not subject to statutory supervision.

Probation is organised into 35 probation trusts and one of the roles of probation is to take responsibility for overseeing offenders on community sentences or released from prison on licence. Probation trusts also manage approved premises for offenders with a condition on their licence relating to residence. Probation use the OASys risk assessment and management tool (see Table 9.2a).

Probation services were subject to a new 'what works?' initiative in the late 1990s. This was with the intention of pursuing evidence-based interventions to reduce offending. The programme was not restricted to community risk management but led to reconsidering the nature of programmes aimed at reducing reoffending. Probation services continue to provide community-based interventions aimed at reducing reoffending risk. There have been systematic attempts to evaluate these interventions (both community and prison based). The reduction of violence as the main outcome is consistently demonstrated in studies, particularly in relation to emotional self-management, problem-solving in social situations and management of relationships (McGuire, 2008).

Mentally disordered offenders who have been sentenced to hospital might also have been the subject of a restriction order under section 41 of the Mental Health Act 1983 (if it is considered necessary to protect the public from serious harm). This restriction order means that discharge from hospital will invariably be accompanied by conditions. These will commonly relate to residence, concordance with supervision appointments, abstinence from drugs and/or alcohol and compliance with recommended psychotropic medication. Restriction orders have been shown to be a significant protective factor for recidivism in people discharged from medium secure hospitals (Coid et al., 2007)

Managing sex offenders

Sex offenders are not excluded from the various management strategies described in this chapter (the majority of sex offenders are managed under MAPPA arrangements) but there are some specific management strategies. Psychological interventions are discussed in more detail elsewhere. In 1997, the sex offender register was introduced by the Sex Offenders Act. The Sexual Offences Act 2003 introduced some additional powers under the heading Notification Orders, including: the registration of overseas sex offenders registering on their return to the United Kingdom; a requirement for offenders to confirm their details annually including their national insurance number; and a reduction in the timescale required for notification of a change of name or address from 14 days to three. The police have additional powers to enter the house of a person on the sex offender register since the Violent Crime Reduction Act 2006. The main power is in relation to the requirement to notify the local police of name, aliases, date of birth, address and national insurance number. Registered people must also notify of any changes or plans to travel abroad.

The sex offender register is maintained and monitored by the police and includes the names of all people convicted of offences since 1997. There is no public access to the register but the police can share information with other professionals. The database containing the details of people's records is referred to as ViSOR (the Violent and Sex Offender Register). The duration of notification is determined by the sentence with indefinite notification requirements for the most serious sexual offences. The Supreme Court found in 2012 that this was incompatible with the European Convention on Human Rights because there is no procedure for this requirement to be reviewed.

A Sexual Offences Prevention Order (SOPO) is a civil order introduced to replace Restraining Orders and Sex Offender Orders by the Sexual Offences Act 2003. The order is made with the intention of 'protecting the public or any particular members of the public from serious sexual harm'. The orders can be made at sentencing or by application to a magistrate's court. The police are responsible for the application but supporting information might come from other professionals. The SOPO can prevent an individual doing certain things that can be justified: contact with children; accessing the Internet; going to schools or parks; travelling on public transport. SOPOs must be necessary and proportionate. There have been a number of appeal court judgements in relation to the limitations of the conditions although they did not provide absolute guidance. Complete prohibition of Internet or computer use is not permitted for example. SOPOs last for a minimum of five years.

Foreign Travel Orders were also introduced in the 2003 legislation and provide that a person convicted of specified sexual offences against children can be prevented from travelling overseas. The application is made by the police.

The Child Sex Offender Disclosure Scheme started in 2008 and allows access to information about child sexual offences. Anyone can make an application to the police about a person known to have some form of contact with a child or children. They do not need to justify any concern or suspicion before making a request. The disclosure might not be made to the person making the request but to a more appropriate person such as a parent. If the subject of the request has convictions for child sexual offences or is considered to pose a risk to the child concerned then it is likely that information will be disclosed. This scheme augments other duties on professionals to disclose risks (Home Office, 2008).

Types of intervention to manage risk

Restorative justice

This is an approach that is centred on the needs of victims. Victims are given an opportunity to discuss how they have been affected by the crime and can decide what should be done to repair the harm. This may initiate a dialogue between the person who has inflicted the harm and the person who has been hurt. Whilst professionals within the Criminal Justice System (CJS) may have a secondary role in facilitating the restorative justice process, it is the citizens who must take up the majority of the responsibility in healing the pains caused by the offence (Braithwaite, 2002). Restorative justice is a balance between the therapeutic and the retributive models of justice, the needs of the victim and the right of the offender, and the duty to protect the public and the need to rehabilitate the offender (Braithwaite, 2002). An advantage of this approach is that it involves the victim and the community to work collaboratively with the offender to find a resolution. However the process is lengthy and both parties need to be committed in order to achieve the best outcomes.

Early interventions

There are a range of early interventions that may be applied to offenders when they first come into contact with the CJS, particularly if the risk is viewed as low. An Acceptable Behaviour Contract (ABC) may be made against an offender as an early intervention strategy. It is a written agreement between the offender, the local housing office and the local police in which it specifies what behaviour the individual is expected to abide by (Bullock & Jones, 2002). It generally follows two warnings before an Antisocial Behaviour Order (ASBO) is applied. Most ABCs are given to young people, although they may be used against adults (Campbell, 2002). The contract is drawn up by the agencies in conjunction with the offender and breach of an ABC is often used as evidence to support an application for an

ASBO. The latter is a civil order that is designed to deter antisocial behaviour without having to resort to criminal sanctions, although a breach can result in criminal proceedings (Campbell, 2002). The majority of ASBOs were applied to those under 21 years (74 per cent) (Campbell, 2002). Although a review of the use of ASBOs indicated that they were being used inconsistently between areas and agencies, there was evidence to suggest that they had been used successfully in a number of areas both to stop existing criminal behaviour and as a deterrent to future acts (Campbell, 2002). ASBOs are likely to be replaced in the near future.

Intensive programmes managed by Youth Offending Teams (YOT) or Probation

Accredited offending behaviour programmes are an integral part of the work carried out by NOMS. They are accredited by the Home Office and are provided by the YOT or probation service. There are over 40 programmes currently approved by NOMS' Correctional Services Accreditation Panel. Accreditation shows that these programmes are evidence-based and consistent with the 'what works' literature (Ministry of Justice, 2012). Table 9.4 shows some examples of accredited offending behaviour programmes that may be offered to serious offenders. The strengths of these programmes are that they are standardised and manualised, thus can be offered by a range of professionals with specific training in their implementation. However they are not individualised to the needs of each particular offender and may not be suitable for all offenders, for example those with a learning disability, acquired brain injury or serious mental health issues.

There are few examples of well-evaluated specialist programmes for violent males, and even less for violent females and mentally disordered offenders. Most interventions consist of a time-limited programme that is targeted at a single factor (e.g. anger management) or longer multi-factorial programmes that typically focus on cognitions, skills development and relapse prevention.

TABLE 9.4 Some accredited offending behaviour programmes for violent offenders

- Aggression Replacement Training (ART)
- Controlling Anger and Learning to Manage it (CALM)
- Enhanced Thinking Skills (ETS)/Juvenile Enhance Thinking Skills (JETS; carried out by YOTs)
- One-to-One
- Think First
- Community Domestic Violence Programme (CDVP)
- Integrated Domestic Abuse Programme (IDAP)
- Sex Offender Group Work Programme
- Internet Sex Offender Treatment Programme

Recommendations from homicide inquiries

Over the last 18 years there have been mandatory independent inquiries (Department of Health, 1994) in relation to all homicides by patients under the care of mental health services. These inquiries have been variable in quality (Petch & Bradley, 1997), methodology (Buchanan, 1999) and depth, but focus on one (or occasionally more than one) homicide and examine in detail the clinical assessment and management. They have been criticised largely on grounds that apply to any inferences drawn from a single case report (Crichton, 2011). Alongside these reports the National Confidential Inquiry Into Suicide and Homicide (NCISH) provides a systematic analysis of homicides by people with recent contact with mental health services and attempts to provide general recommendations. In one of their first reports, *Safer Services* (Appleby et al., 1999) they made recommendations in the following areas:

- Training in the recognition, assessment and management of risk
- Simplification of documentation relating to risk and Care Programme Approach (CPA)
- Patients with a history of violence should receive the highest level of care under CPA
- Information relating to violence should be available to mental health services
- Compliance with medication and specific planning for non-compliance
- Engaging people who disengage
- Making provisions for people with co-morbid drug or alcohol use
- Multidisciplinary teams should review cases after homicides.

These areas were revisited and led to the development of *12 points to a safer service* (Appleby et al., 2001). In addition to the points listed above, specific recommendations led to changes in community management:

- All patients followed up within seven days of discharge from hospital
- Prompt access for patients in crisis
- Assertive outreach teams to prevent loss of contact with high risk patients.

The NCISH has continued to publish annual reports and more recently has reported on thematic analysis of independent inquiries. This work resulted in recommendations in 15 areas:

- Review of the application of CPA policy
- Regular review of risk assessment with use of appropriate tools
- Guidelines and procedures should be developed for patients on leave
- Development of dual diagnosis services
- Training in assessment of personality disorder should be provided

- Local and national consideration of offenders who change their name and/or address
- Home visits should only be done following consideration of risk
- Trusts should address non-attendance rates
- Referral pathways should be free from unnecessary obstacles
- Discharge planning should be multidisciplinary and shared
- Consideration of whether restriction orders should be lifelong
- There should be avoidance of reliance on agency staff
- Services should develop clear information-sharing policies
- Health and social care should work with domestic violence and child protection agencies
- Serious untoward reviews should be open and independent.

The subsequent review by NCISH in 2010 included further recommendations that reflect common themes seen throughout systematic reviews and individual inquiries in relation to CPA, clear procedures in relation to better communication and information sharing, risk management, engaging difficult patients, involvement of family and carers, better multidisciplinary and interagency working, training and supervision.

Summary and future directions

Managing the risk of violence in the community must be underpinned by a thorough risk assessment. The use of structured professional judgement provides a balance of empirical foundation with practical utility and is recommended as the standard approach.

There is a need for different agencies to share information when appropriate and to communicate effectively. There has been an emergence of opportunities for this over the last two decades in forums such as MAPPA. Training and supervision of professionals are commonly identified as deficiencies following serious incidents and this should be a part of all professional development.

There have been changes in criminal justice agencies towards identifying causes of offending and trying to address those factors. The future will hopefully pursue this principle over the temptation to employ more punitive measures. This chapter and the majority of resources are targeted towards people who have already been violent or committed a serious offence but if violence is viewed as a public health matter then it will be large-scale projects targeting the most powerful predictors of violence in primary prevention schemes that hold the most promise. There has been significant investment and attempts to disseminate programmes targeted at effective parenting particularly in children with conduct problems (Scott, 2010). There are programmes targeted at young people with the aim of preventing domestic abuse in the next generation. Social inclusion and family support are not conventionally described as crime prevention strategies but they start to address some of the most potent factors associated with violence as early as possible.

Notes

1 Brought in by the Criminal Justice and Courts Services Act 2000 and extended under the Criminal Justice Act 2003 for England and Wales; and brought in elsewhere in the UK by the Criminal Justice (Northern Ireland) Order 2008 and the Management of Offenders (Scotland) Act 2005.
2 Except in Scotland, where the responsible authorities are the police, prison service, social services and health boards.

Bibliography

Ægisdóttir, S., White, M. J., Spengler, P. M., Maugherman, A. S., Anderson, L. A., Cook, R., et al. (2006) The meta-analysis of clinical judgement project: fifty-six years of accumulated research on clinical versus statistical prediction. *The Counselling Psychologist*, 34, 341–82.

Andrews, D. & Bonta, J. (1995) The level of service inventory – revised. Toronto: Multi-Health Systems.

Andrews, D. A., Bonta, J. & Hoge, R. D. (1990) Classification for effective rehabilitation: rediscovering psychology. *Criminal Justice and Behavior*, 17, 19–52.

Appleby, L., Shaw, J., Amos, T., McDonnell, R., Harris, C., McCann, K., et al. (1999) *Safer Services*. Report of the National Confidential Inquiry into Suicide and Homicide by People with Mental Illness. London: Stationery Office.

Appleby, L., Shaw, J., Sherratt, J., Amos, T., Robinson, J., et al. (2001) *Safety First*. Report of the National Confidential Inquiry into Suicide and Homicide by People with Mental Illness. London: Stationery Office.

Augimeri, L. K., Koegl, C. J., Webster, C. D. & Levene, K. S. (2001) *Early Assessment Risk List for Boys (EARL-20B); Version 2*. Toronto: Earlscourt Child and Family Centre.

Boer, D. P., Hart, S. D., Kropp, P. R. & Webster, C. D. (1997) *Manual for the Sexual Violence Risk-20: Professional Guidelines for Assessing Risk of Sexual Violence*. Vancouver: Mental Health Law and Policy Institute.

Borum, R., Bartel, P. & Forth, A. (2002) *Manual for the Structured Assessment of Violence Risk in Youth (SAVRY), Version 1*. Tampa: University of South Florida.

Braithwaite, J. (2002) *Restorative Justice and Responsive Regulation*. Oxford: Oxford University Press.

Buchanan, A. (1999) Independent Inquiries into homicide. *British Medical Journal*, 318, 1089–90.

Bullock, K. & Jones, B. (2002) *Acceptable Behaviour Contracts Addressing Antisocial Behaviour in the London Borough of Islington*. London: Home Office.

Campbell, S. (2002) *Implementing Anti-social Behaviour Messages for Practitioners*. London: Home Office.

Centre for Criminology (2003) Onset. www.justice.gov.uk/youth-justice/assessment.

Coid, J., Hickey, N., Khatan, N., Tianqiang, Z. & Yang, M. (2007) Patients discharged from medium secure forensic psychiatry services: reconvictions and risk factors. *British Journal of Psychiatry*, 190, 223–9.

Coleman, J. & Hagell, A. (2007) *Adolescence, Risk and Resilience: Against the Odds*. Chichester: John Wiley.

Crichton, J. (2011) A review of published independent inquiries in England into psychiatric patient homicide, 1995–2010. *Journal of Forensic Psychiatry & Psychology*, 22(6), 761–89.

Criminal Justice Act (2003) Chapter 5. London: HMSO.

Dawes, R. M., Faust, D. & Meehl, P. E. (1989) Clinical versus actuarial judgement. *Science*, 243, 1668–74.

Department of Health (1994) *Guidance on the Discharge of Mentally Disordered People and their Continuing Care in the Community*. HSG(94)27. London: Department of Health.

Department of Health (2010) *The Caldicott Guardian Manual 2010*. London: Department of Health.

Desmarais, S., Nicholls, T. L., Wilson, C. M. & Brink, J. (2012) Using dynamic risk and protective factors to predict inpatient aggression: reliability and validity of START assessments. *Psychological Assessment*, 24(3), 685–700.

Douglas, K., Cox, D. & Webster, C. (1999) Violence risk assessment: science and practice. *Legal and Criminological Psychology*, 4: 149–84.

Doyle, M. & Dolan, M. (2008) Understanding and managing risk. In Soothill, K., Rogers, P. & Dolan, M. (eds) *Handbook of Forensic Mental Health*. Cullompton: Willan Publishing.

Elbogen, E. B., Huss, M. T., Tomkins, A. J. & Scalora, M. J. (2005) Clinical decision making about psychopathy and violence risk assessment in public sector mental health settings. *Psychological Services*, 2(2), 133–41.

Epperson, D. L., Kaul, J. D., Huot, S., Goldman, R. & Alexander, W. (2003) Minnesota Sex Offender Screening Tool – Revised (MnSOST-R) technical paper: Development, validation, and recommended risk level cut scores. http://www.psychology.iastate.edu.

Fazel, S., Singh, J. P., Doll, H. & Grann, M. (2012) Use of risk assessment instruments to predict violence and antisocial behaviour in 73 samples involving 24,827 people: systematic review and meta-analysis. *British Medical Journal*, 345–57.

Forth, A. E., Kosson, D. S. & Hare, R. D. (2003) *Hare Psychopathy Checklist: Youth Version Technical Manual*. Toronto: Multi-Health Systems.

General Medical Council (2009) http://www.gmc-uk.org/guidance/ethical_guidance/confidentiality_contents.asp. (Accessed 3 August 2012).

Gottfredson, S. & Gottfredson, D. (1986) Accuracy of prediction models. In Blumstein, A. et al. (eds) *Criminal Careers and Career Criminals*. Washington, DC: National Academy Press, 212–90.

Grove, W. & Meehl, P. (1996) Comparative efficiency of informal (subjective, impressionistic) and formal (mechanical, algorithmic) prediction procedures: the clinical–statistical controversy. *Psychology, Public Policy and Law*, 2, 293–323.

Hanson, R. K. (1997) The development of a brief actuarial risk scale for sexual offense recidivism. Department of the Solicitor General of Canada, Public Works and Government Services Canada. http://www.defenseforsvp.com/Resources/Hanson_Static-99/RRASOR.pdf.

Hanson, R. K. & Thornton, D. (1999) *Static-99: Improving Actuarial Risk Assessments for Sex Offenders*. User Report 99–02. Ottawa: Department of the Solicitor General of Canada.

Hanson, R. K. & Thornton, D. (2003) *Notes on the Development of Static-2002*. User Report 2003–01. Ottawa: Department of Solicitor General of Canada.

Hare, R. D. (1991) *The Hare Psychopathy Checklist – Revised*. Toronto: Multi-Health Systems.

Hare, R. D. (2003) *The Hare Psychopathy Checklist – Revised* (2nd edn). Toronto: Multi-Health Systems.

Hart, S. D. (1998) The role of psychopathy in assessing risk for violence: conceptual and methodological issues. *Legal and Criminological Psychology*, 3: 121–37.

Hart, S. D., Kropp, R., Laws, D. R., Klaver, J., Logan, C., Watt, K. A. & Fraser, S. (2003) *The Risk for Sexual Violence Protocol; Structured Professional Guidelines for Assessing Risk of Sexual Violence*. Vancouver: Institute Against Family Violence.

Heilbrun, K., Yasuhara, K. & Shah, S. (2009) Violence risk assessment tools: overview and clinical analysis. In Otto, R. K. & Douglas, K. S. (eds) *Handbook of Violence Risk Assessment* (pp. 1–18). New York: Routledge.

Hilton, N. Z. & Simmons, J. L. (2001) The influence of actuarial risk assessment in clinical judgements and tribunal decisions about mentally disordered offenders in maximum security. *Law and Human Behaviour*, 25(4), 393–408.

Hilton, N. Z., Carter, A. M., Harris, G. T. & Sharpe, A. (2008) Does using the nonnumerical terms to describe risk aid violence risk communication? *Journal of Interpersonal Violence*, 23, 171–88.

HM Government (2008) *Information Sharing: Guidance for Practitioners and Managers*. London: Department for Children, Schools & Families and Communities and Local Government.

Hoge, R. & Andrews, D. (2002) *Youth Level of Service/Case Management Inventory*. Toronto: Multi-Health Systems.

Home Office (2002) *OASys User Manual, Volume 2*. London: National Probation Directorate.

Home Office (2008) *The Child Sex Offender (CSO) Disclosure Scheme Guidance Document*. Home Office: London.

Home Office (2010) *Integrated Offender Management: Key Principles*. London: Home Office.

Home Office (2011) http://www.homeoffice.gov.uk/publications/crime/reducing-reoffending/IOM-Survey-Exec-Summary (Accessed 3 August 2012).

Howard, P., Francis, B., Soothill, K. & Humphreys, L. (2009) *OGRS 3: The Revised Offender Group Reconviction Scale*. London: Ministry of Justice.

Janus, E. (2004) Sexually violent predator laws: psychiatry in service to a morally dubious enterprise. *Lancet*, 3664, 50–1.

Kropp, P. R., Hart, S. D., Webster, C. D. & Eaves, D. (1999) Spousal assault risk assessment guide. Toronto: Multi-Health Systems.

Lidz, C., Mulvey, E. & Gardner, W. (1993) The accuracy and predictions of violence to others. *Journal of the American Medical Association*, 269, 1007–11.

Lipsey, M. W. & Wilson, D. B. (1998) Effective intervention for serious juvenile offenders: a synthesis research. In Loeber, R. & Farrington, D. P. (eds) *Serious and Violent Juvenile Offenders: Risk factors and Successful Interventions*. Thousand Oaks, CA: Sage, pp. 313–45.

McGuire, J. (2008) A review of effective interventions for reducing aggression and violence. *Philosophical Transactions of the Royal Society*, 363, 2483–622.

Maguire, M. (2002) Criminal statistics: the 'data explosion' and its implications. In Maguire, M., Morgan, R. & Reiner, R. (eds) *The Oxford Handbook of Criminology* (3rd edn). Oxford: Oxford University Press.

Ministry of Justice http://www.justice.gov.uk/offenders/before-after-release/obp (Accessed August 2012).

Ministry of Justice (2012) Proven reoffending statistics. *Quarterly Bulletin, April 2009 to March 2010*. London: Ministry of Justice.

Monahan, J. (1981) *Predicting Violent Behaviour*. Beverley Hills, CA: Sage.

Monahan, J., Steadman, H., Silver, E., Appelbaum, P., Robbins, P., Mulvey, E. & Banks, S. (2001) *Rethinking Risk Assessment: The MacArthur Study of Mental Disorder and Violence*. New York: Oxford University Press.

O'Rourke, M., Hammond, S.M., Smith, S. & Davies, E.J. (1998) *Risk Assessment, Management and Audit System: Professional Manual*. London: RAMAS.

Peck, M. (2011) *Patterns of Reconviction among Offenders Eligible for Multi-Agency Public Protection Arrangements (MAPPA)*. London: Ministry of Justice.

Petch, E. & Bradley, C. (1997) Learning the lessons from homicide inquiries: adding insult to injury? *Journal of Forensic Psychiatry*, 8, 161–84.

Prentky, R. & Righthand, S. (2003) *Juvenile Sex Offender Assessment Protocol – II; Manual*. Washington, DC: US Department of Justice, Office of Justice Programs, Office of Juvenile Justice and Delinquency Prevention.

Prout H. T. & Strohmer D. C. *(1991) Emotional Problems Scales. Professional Manual for the Behaviour Rating Scales and the Self-Report Inventory*. Lutz, FL: Psychological Assessment Resources.

Quinsey, V. L. (2004) Risk assessment and management in community settings. In Lindsay, W. R., Taylor, J. L. & Sturmey, P. (ed.) *Offenders with Developmental Disabilities*. Chichester: Wiley, pp. 131–42.

Quinsey, V. L., Harris, G. T., Rice, M. E. & Cornier, C. A. (1998) *Violent Offenders: Appraising and Managing Risk*. Washington, DC: American Psychological Association.

Scott, S. (2010) National dissemination of effective parenting programmes to improve child outcomes. *British Journal of Psychiatry*, 196, 1–3.

Singh, J. P., Serper, M., Reinharth, J. & Fazel, S. (2011) Structured assessment of violence risk in schizophrenia and other psychiatric disorders: a systematic review of the validity, reliability and item content of 10 available instruments. *Schizophrenia Bulletin*, 37, 899–912.

Stubner, S., Groß, G. & Nedopil, N. (2006) Inpatient risk management with mentally ill offenders: results of a survey on clinical decision-making about easing restrictions. *Criminal Behaviour and Mental Health*, 16(2), 111–23.

Sturidsson, K., Haggard-Grann, U., Lotterberg, M., Dernevik, M. & Grann, M. (2004) Clinicians' perceptions of which factors increase or decrease the risk of violence among forensic out-patients. *International Journal of Forensic Mental Health*, 3(1), 23–36.

Thornton, D. (2000) *Scoring Guide for Risk Matrix: 2000*. Unpublished manuscript.

Vijoen, J. L., McLachlan, K. & Vincent, G. M. (2010) Assessing violence risk and psychopathy in juvenile and adult offenders: a survey of clinical practices. *Assessment*, 17, 377–95.

Webster, C. D., Harris, G., Rice, M., Cormier, C. & Quinsey, V. (1994) *The Violence Prediction Scheme: Assessing Dangerousness in High Risk Men*. Toronto: University of Toronto, Centre of Criminology.

Webster, C. D., Douglas, K. S., Eaves, D. & Hart, D. (1997) *HCR-20 Assessing Risk for Violence: Version II*. Burnaby, BC: Mental Health, Law & Policy Institute, Simon Fraser University.

Webster, C. D., Nicholls, T. L., Martin, M. L., Desmarais, S. L. & Brink, J. (2006) Short-Term Assessment of Risk and Treatability (START): the case for a new violence risk structured professional judgment scheme. *Behavioral Sciences & the Law*, 24, 747–66.

Wong, S. & Gordon, A. (2006) The validity and reliability of the Violence Risk Scale: a treatment friendly violence risk assessment tool. *Psychology, Public Policy and Law*, 12(3), 279–309.

Worling, J. R. & Curwen, T. (2001) *Estimate of Risk of Adolescent Sexual Offense Recidivism* (Version 2.0: The 'ERASOR'). In M. C. Calder, *Juveniles and Children Who Sexually Abuse: Frameworks for Assessment*. Lyme Regis: Russell House Publishing, pp. 372–97.

Yang, M., Wing, S. C. P. & Coid, J. (2010) The efficacy of violence prediction: a meta-analytic comparison of the nine risk assessment tools. *Psychological Bulletin*, 136(5), 740–67.

Youth Justice Board (YJB) (2000). Asset. www.justice.gov.uk/youth-justice/assessment.

10

FAMILY INTERVENTION

Multisystemic Therapy

Zoë Ashmore

Finding effective treatment for young people to reduce reoffending and prevent imprisonment or placement into the care system has been a challenge for forensic practitioners in the past. Research evidence for interventions that work has been in short supply. Multisystemic Therapy (MST) is unusual as it is a well-researched effective alternative to expensive and often ineffective custodial sentences.

In this chapter the MST theory of change, the model and nine principles are explained. The practice of MST, the strong emphasis on implementation fidelity and the rigorous quality assurance measures to ensure that all MST delivered to families is adherent to the MST model are discussed. The UK pilot, which introduced MST to nine areas initially and the START trial that is evaluating the effects in these areas, is described. The introduction of MST to more parts of the UK and the setting up of a UK-based network partnership is detailed and the growth of MST in Europe outlined. The effectiveness of MST is examined by looking at a range of randomised control studies (RCT) carried out in the USA and Europe over the past 30 years. Typically MST is compared with the services young people and their families would have received if they had not had MST, termed 'usual services' by the researchers. Three long-term studies are outlined. A recent RCT which compares MST with a control group receiving interventions from the Youth Offending Service in a UK sample is also described. The difference in the way MST is delivered and operates compared with traditional services in the Criminal Justice Service is contrasted and the costs compared. Finally the future challenges in delivering an evidenced-based treatment such as MST are discussed.

MST is an intensive community based programme for young people who are at risk of entering prison custody or care due to their anti-social behaviour or crime. MST engages with their families, primarily their parents. It aims to help parents become more effective in their role and improve family functioning. The aim of

TABLE 10.1 Risk factors for young people involved in crime and antisocial behaviour

System	Risk factors
Family	• harsh and inconsistent discipline • lack of parental monitoring supervision • family conflict • lack of parental involvement
Community	• high crime rates • community disorganisation • transitions and mobility
School	• low expectations from teachers • poor attendance • academic failure exclusions
Peer	• involvement with deviant peers • anti-social friends reinforce disruptive behaviour • a delinquent peer group make anti-social behaviour more likely to occur • young people make riskier decisions when in peer groups

MST is to keep young people living safely at home, free from offending and successfully engaging in education, training or work.

The MST model (Figure 10.1) addresses the risk factors, drawn from multiple systems, for young people (Table 10.1) who are becoming involved in criminal or anti-social behaviour. This framework is drawn from empirical evidence suggesting the importance of family, community, school and peers as well as individual factors in reducing reoffending with young people. For example, McCarthy and colleagues found that family factors that impact on children include harsh and inconsistent discipline, lack of parental monitoring and supervision, family conflict and a lack of parental involvement (McCarthy et al., 2004). Community risk factors cited were high crime rates, community disorganisation, transitions and mobility. At school low expectations from teachers, poor attendance, academic failure and exclusions were found to be important. Family maltreatment, adverse contexts and involvement with deviant peers were risk factors for developing conduct problems (Dodge et al., 2008). Anti-social friends continue to reinforce disruptive behaviour and a delinquent peer group make anti-social behaviour more likely to occur (Coleman & Hagell, 2007). Young people make riskier decisions when in peer groups than when alone (Gardner & Steinberg, 2005).

What is Multisystemic Therapy?

MST focuses on the role of family functioning in impacting on the multiple systems around the young person, primarily the school, the peer and the community systems, to reduce anti-social behaviour and crime. It is an empirically based programme which uses a clear model of treatment and nine treatment principles to guide clinicians rather than a rigid programme which must be followed for every treatment session. In practice every course of MST is different, being individually tailored to the needs of the young person and the family. MST is flexible, within the applied model, and is focused on the identified risk factors in the family, the peer group, the school, the community and the individual for each young person. MST standard, as it has become known and which is described in this chapter, is a licensed programme which ensures the model is applied as indicated from the extensive research into its effectiveness. A number of MST adaptations have also been developed for specific areas such as problem sexual behaviour, child abuse and neglect and substance misuse.

MST is for young people aged 11 to 17[1] and is delivered by teams with three[2] or four therapists drawn from a range of staff with professional qualifications and experience in areas such as social work, psychology, mental health and youth offending or probation. The supervisor for the team is typically an applied psychologist, family therapist or a previous MST therapist with knowledge and experience of group and individual supervision. MST supervisors have experience of delivering a range of psychological therapies including cognitive therapy, evidenced-based parenting programmes, family therapy, cognitive behavioural therapy, social skills and behaviour therapy.

Treatment is provided flexibly with on-call support available to all families 24/7. Therapists hold between four and six cases and have intensive contact with families at times most convenient to them. Typically around 60 hours of treatment would be provided within three to five months. Treatment can be provided every day with the expectation that most families will need around three home visits a week at least in the beginning few months which can include visits and meetings at school or in the community. If treatment goes according to plan this would be decreased in the final months as MST closes and families prepare to increase their role in managing without any further statutory support but drawing instead on friends and wider family and using the skills they have developed.

Multisystemic Therapy theory of change

The MST theory of change is based on the theory of social ecology (Bronfenbrenner, 1979), which describes the multiple systems that impact on the young person and focuses on the interdependencies of these systems. These include the family, the peer group, school, the neighbourhood and the community. Bronfenbrenner sees the young person living in a social ecology of interconnected systems that impact upon their behaviour both directly, for example within their family home, and indirectly, such as their parent's workplace. These influences act in both directions so the young person affects settings in which he or she spends time as well as being affected by these systems. Bronfenbrenner depicts the environment as a series of layers or systems around the young person with each playing a key role in their life.

The MST theory of change is that improved family functioning will affect the other systems, the peer group, the school and the community and so anti-social behaviour and crime will be reduced. The young person's anti-social behaviour is influenced by the interconnected systems around them such as their family, school, neighbourhood and friends. By working through the parents or caregivers to create 'an environment of alignment and engagement of family and key participants' (Henggeler et al., 2009, p. 17), MST is able to affect the young person's multi-determined problems. MST targets individualised risk factors from the systems around the young person such as the family system or the school system. For example 'within' systems by reducing family conflict in the home and 'between' systems such as improving the interaction between school and home or by enhancing the parents' knowledge about their son or daughter's peer group with whom they are offending. The parents are the main conduits of change so in MST there is a focus on their empowerment to make them more effective in managing their young person and reducing anti-social behaviour and crime.

Social ecological theory places an emphasis on ecological validity. Behaviour does not happen in a vacuum and can only be understood by viewing it in its naturally occurring context. This is important in MST. MST is undertaken at home or in school where the behaviour occurs naturally, not in a clinic or Youth Offending office. The therapist views the young person's anti-social behaviour in the settings where it normally occurs and engages with those who interact with the young person directly, for example parents and teachers. The MST interventions are delivered where the problems are occurring for example in the neighbourhood or with the young person's extended family and are ecologically valid (Boer, 2009) as a home-based model of delivery is used.

The nine principles

The MST model of change does not incorporate session-by-session rigid plans of what the therapist should do with each family. Treatment is individually tailored to each young person and their family and so MST therapists have to be able to intervene successfully and flexibly across complex systems. In the absence of a rigid protocol or manual therapists are guided by nine treatment principles. These are described in Table 10.2 (Henggeler et al., 2009).

Multisystemic Therapy analytical process

As well as the nine principles, the MST analytical process, usually referred to as the 'Do loop', provides the guide for the treatment process. This is a step-by-step model of the stages to follow in order to conceptualise the case and to provide treatment (Figure 10.1) (Henggeler et al., 2009, p. 17).

Young people who are living at home are referred because of concerns about their behaviour which would place them at risk of being taken into care or placed in custody. Typically the referral behaviours consist of family conflict or violence

TABLE 10.2 The nine treatment principles

1 *Finding the fit*
The primary purpose of assessment is to understand the factors (called drivers) from the different systems that are impacting on the behaviour. This is called 'the fit' in MST. The 'fit' portrays, in a drawing of the 'fit circle', how the identified problems are maintained within the broader systemic context (see Figure 10.2).

2 *Positive and strength focused*
Therapeutic contacts should emphasise the positive and should use systemic strengths as levers for change. These are the drivers that are reducing the problem behaviour.

3 *Increasing responsibility*
Interventions should be designed to promote responsibility and decrease irresponsible behaviour among family members.

4 *Present-focused, action-oriented and well-defined*
Interventions should be present-focused and action-oriented, targeting specific and well-defined problems.

5 *Targeting sequences*
Interventions should target sequences of behaviour within and between multiple systems that maintain identified problems.

6 *Developmentally appropriate*
Interventions should be developmentally appropriate and fit the developmental needs of the young person.

7 *Continuous effort*
Interventions should be designed to require daily or weekly effort by family members.

8 *Evaluation and accountability*
Intervention efficacy is evaluated continuously from multiple perspectives, with providers assuming accountability for overcoming barriers to successful outcomes.

9 *Generalisation*
Interventions should be designed to promote treatment generalisation and long-term maintenance of therapeutic change by empowering caregivers to address family members' needs across multiple systemic contexts.

which is connected to the young person's behavioural difficulties. Common concerns are family breakdown, school attendance and/or behaviour problems, anti-social behaviour or crime, running away and substance misuse.

Initially the therapist asks family members and other key participants such as the social worker, the Youth Offending officer or the school to provide their desired outcomes for the young person. They are described in behavioural terms in their own words. MST works with the key stakeholders, such as family members, social workers and Youth Offending officers, to develop agreement of the main over-arching goals to treatment. Typically three or four goals would be developed from desired outcomes and an overarching goal addressing family conflict might be:

> "J. will not engage in physical aggression in the home as evidenced by no fighting and pushing or throwing of objects and damage to property as reported by parents and youth offending."

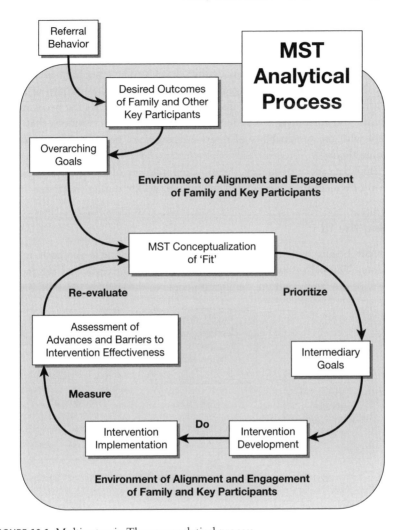

FIGURE 10.1 Multisystemic Therapy analytical process

Source: Henggeler et al. (2009, p.17). Reproduced with kind permission from Guilford Press.

The therapist starts by completing a genogram with the family across three generations building a picture of the young person within their extended family. This can show where relationships are strong and where more support could be forthcoming. It allows family members to tell the therapist about their family and work together to understand patterns and events that have reoccurred or have significance.

Building further on the systemic assessment, the strengths and needs are collated in every system, that is the individual, the family, the school, the peer group and community. In line with principle 2, building on strengths helps to identify protective factors, for example supports in the local community or other family members that will lead to better interventions which are more likely to be sustained when MST ends. Further strengths and needs will be added to this as treatment progresses. At the beginning the therapist is looking to inform therapy with information from the family and other stakeholders of the positive aspects of each system. Individualised interventions are then developed levering on these strengths to keep the young person from engaging in the identified referral behaviours which are placing him or her at risk of care or custody. In this process the needs in each system are also identified and added so that barriers to interventions that could interfere with the sustainability of positive changes are noted and plans made to overcome them.

Baseline data about frequency, duration and intensity of each referral behaviour which is of concern is collected and monitored weekly during treatment.

Finding the fit

Treatment begins with a drawing of the systemic fit circle for each referred behaviour. The behaviour is put in the middle of the fit circle and the therapist works with the family and the significant people in the systems around the young

FIGURE 10.2 Substance abuse fit

person in order to build up a picture of the factors, referred to as drivers, that are maintaining the referral behaviour. For example if the referral behaviour is substance misuse, some of the drivers identified across the different systems around the young person could be that some of his peer group are using drugs, he is not attending school, he has sufficient funds to purchase drugs, he has easy access to drugs in the community, there is a lack of monitoring and supervision and there is family conflict. The fit will be well defined to reflect the specific drivers for J, illustrated in the example in Figure 10.2.

These drivers would then be prioritised by applying the following criteria to the identified drivers referred to as 'the 4 Ps'. They are:

- *Proximal* (how close they are to the referral problem)
- *Powerful* (drivers that are occurring across a number of fits are described as powerful meaning that tackling them makes it more likely to achieve the desired goals and give the biggest changes)
- *Participants'* goals (drivers that are closely aligned with the family's overarching goals)
- *Prerequisite* (drivers that need to be tackled first before we are able to tackle other areas).

The priority drivers are drawn together to form the hypothesis about why the behaviour, for example substance misuse in the example above, is occurring and so it can be tested.

Using the nine principles in treatment

Building on the identified strengths (principal 2) from each system the therapist develops interventions to meet the intermediary goal (IG). The IG is simply the 'flip side' of the identified priority goal. For example if a priority driver was 'most of the young person's peer group are using drugs' the IG would be to increase their peer group with those who are not using drugs. Developing the intervention could build on the strength that there are some peers who are not using drugs so it could include helping the parents to identify the peers who do not use drugs, supporting the parents to contact the parents of these peers and work together to increase the time spent with these peers.

The therapist would help the parents implement these interventions in a range of different ways individualised to their needs. This could be by breaking down each stage of the task, supporting and using principle 3, which is helping the family increase their responsibility in carrying out the work. Typically therapists would guide them through the process of identifying the pro-social peers, perhaps using exercises developed for this purpose. They would then be encouraged to contact them using their knowledge of their son or daughter's network and drawing on a range of methods which have previously been found to be effective in MST. Typically plans would be tested perhaps by role-playing likely scenarios.

They will develop interventions which are 'present-focused and action-oriented' (principal 4) and often 'target sequences of behaviour between the multiple systems that maintain the difficulties' (principal 5). The way interventions are developed and implemented will differ according to the developmental stage of the young person and also of their parents (principal 6). For example increasing monitoring and supervision for a 12 year old will require a different type of intervention than for a 17 year old. In order to meet the MST assumption that change can be achieved quickly, everyone – that is all family members, friends, the wider extended family, the MST therapist and other professionals involved – will be required to make an effort and a contribution daily or weekly (principal 7). Progress is evaluated continuously from different perspectives to identify the positive results and there are a range of informants to the process of change and clear accountability for overcoming barriers (principal 8).

Following the MST analytic process, the therapist and the family would then assess the effectiveness of the intervention and re-evaluate their progress by identifying advances and barriers. This information would then inform the new fit and the whole process could start again until sufficient drivers had been addressed to stop the drug abuse. Then a positive fit would be completed identifying all the drivers that were sustaining the positive change aiding generalisation and long-term maintenance of the improvement (principal 9).

Working with families where there are serious concerns can be challenging and staff can become overwhelmed by the entrenched difficulties that the family have been struggling to manage for some time. Families can feel both judged by professionals and hopeless which can make engagement in treatment collaboration difficult. Retaining a strengths focus throughout the whole process of MST (i.e. with the family, in supervision and consultation and within the wider group of MST stakeholders) is important in sustaining progress. Building feelings of hope and positive expectations is linked to favourable outcomes (Greenberg & Pinsof, 1986).

Supervision and consultation

Following the MST model and adhering to the nine principles is supported by the MST expert through consultation, quality assurance and staff development. Coaching and training MST teams is a critical part of this work. Therapists prepare paperwork weekly on each family showing how they are using the 'Do loop' and indicating their plans for the next week. The supervisor of the team reviews the plans and conducts on-site group supervision with all therapists where every family is discussed, beginning with the families that have the greatest needs. New referrals will be given more time in order to review strengths and needs and the initial referral fits. Other team members who may cover 'on call' for the new family will also need to know this information as well as contributing to and understanding the plans for treatment this week. Supervision is also supported by remote consultation by the team's MST expert by telephone for an hour, following soon after the on-site supervision. Again every family is discussed with those with the greatest needs being taken first.

The supervision and consultation process emphasises equipping therapists to engage families and design and implement interventions using the MST model and the nine principles. The therapists and supervisor are accountable for outcomes. Preparation for supervision and consultation reflects this responsibility with paperwork showing the current stage of the MST analytic process. This is in contrast to the more usual 'diary entries' which describe communications with and about the family, common in many social work and mental health settings. The style of supervision, which is present-focused, action-oriented and targeting specific areas of concern (principle 4), does not spend much time on a description of what has happened that week. Instead the focus is on analysing how events for the family that week have changed the multisystemic fit, identifying strengths which can be used as levers for change, anticipating barriers and developing strategies to overcome them. Often role-play is used to help therapists practise the skills they will need to implement the interventions with the families as planned.

Quality assurance and implementation fidelity

Quality assurance is critical in MST in order to evidence adherence to the MST model which has been found to be effective and to ensure replication of these conditions. There are a range of measures that contribute to implementation fidelity.

Every month each family completes a Treatment Adherence Measure–Revised (TAM-R; Henggeler & Borduin, 1992), reporting back on a range of questions about their experience of MST. The questions reflect the family's view of the extent to which the therapist is following the MST analytical process and the nine principles. The MST Services website allows teams to collate this information and it can then be used for clinician and team development as well as making it possible to compare their scores with those obtained in different parts of the world. TAM-R scores have demonstrated that adherence is 'a robust predictor of reductions in youth behaviour problems through one year post treatment with MST' (Schoenwald et al., 2008, p. 391). Scores also predict reductions in anti-social behaviour generally and improvements in family functioning (Henggeler et al., 2009; Schoenwald et al., 2004).

Similarly there is a Supervisor Adherence Measure (SAM) (Henggeler et al., 2009) and a Consultant Adherence Measure (CAM) (Schoenwald et al., 2004). The SAM is completed by therapists on their supervisor every two months. Findings indicate that supervisor adherence affects therapist adherence and MST outcomes (Henggeler et al., 2009).

CAMs are completed every two months by the whole team following a consultation with their MST expert. Perceived expert competence in MST and alliance with therapists predicted therapist adherence. However experts with low competence predicted low therapist adherence even with high alliance. Although a good alliance may help teams attend consultation it does not have to be present for therapist adherence. It is competence that is needed from experts to improve outcomes for young people in MST (Schoenwald et al., 2004).

Implementing an evidence-based programme like MST with fidelity is not easy and there is considerable organisational support made available. This is in setting up the service initially, engaging stakeholders, recruiting staff with the right skills and competencies to run it and continuing support to maintain adherence to the model and achieve the expected outcomes. An organisational manual specifies how MST is to be delivered to maintain its effectiveness and ongoing programme implementation reports monitor each programme's adherence to these criteria. Once the service is running the MST expert allocated to work with the MST team will provide or access the organisational support and initial and ongoing booster training. In MST many of the experts have previously worked successfully as supervisors and their role is to train and support their team to effectively implement MST.

How effective is Multisystemic Therapy?

MST started out as a clinical research programme in 1986 in the USA led by Scott Henggeler (Henggeler et al., 2009) and it has retained close links with its developers. He compared the effectiveness of a 'family–ecological treatment' given to 57 young people who had offended and their families with 23 offenders who were given an alternative treatment and with 44 adolescents and their families who acted as developmental controls. He reported decreases in conduct disorders and association with anti-social peers, warmer mother–adolescent and marital relations and the young person was more involved in family interaction in the families receiving this early form of MST. The alternative treatment group showed no positive change and deterioration in relations. The developmental controls changed in a way that was consistent with normal adolescent behaviour.

In a randomised control trial (RCT) Henggeler et al. compared MST given to 84 families with a young person who had a violent and serious offending history with those receiving usual services (Henggeler et al., 1992). Young people who had MST were found to have fewer arrests and self-reported offences and spent on average ten fewer weeks in custody compared to those receiving usual services. They also reported increased family cohesion and less aggression in the young people's peer relationships.

Further RCTs showed similarly positive results. In the Missouri Delinquency Project (Borduin et al., 1995) young people with violent and serious offending were given MST or individual counselling and after four years the MST group were found to have improved family relations, decreased psychiatric symptomology and 69 per cent decrease in recidivism. In another RCT in a similar population (Henggeler et al., 1997) MST was compared with usual youth offending services and a decrease in custody by 47 per cent at 1.7-year follow-up was found. An absence of ongoing treatment fidelity checks were thought to account for why the findings for decreased offending were not as high as had been seen in previous studies of MST.

MST has been closely linked with research into its effectiveness since its initial development and many of the early studies involved a researcher who had also been involved in the development of the MST model. The first independent RCT not involving an MST model developer in the USA (Timmons-Mitchell et al., 2006) examined the effectiveness of MST in a real-world mental health setting with juvenile offenders who were at imminent risk of placement. They found a significant reduction in re-arrest rates and an improvement in the functioning for the young people who received MST.

In Sweden another RCT which did not involve an MST model developer (Sundell et al., 2008) evaluated the effectiveness of MST for 156 young people with conduct disorder with treatment as usual. There was a general decrease in psychiatric problems and anti-social behaviours across treatment groups but no significant differences between the two groups. MST treatment fidelity measures were lower than in other studies. The results are discussed in terms of the differences in the way young people are processed in Sweden which uses a child welfare approach and the USA which uses a juvenile justice system. It is also thought that differences in other social factors such as poverty, crime and substance misuse may also moderate the effects on the rates of rehabilitation.

In Norway, a study independent of an MST model developer followed up MST after two years, comparing 75 adolescents who were randomly assigned to MST or regular child welfare services at four sites. Using a range of assessments they found MST was more effective than regular services in reducing out-of-home placement and behavioural problems (Ogden & Hagen, 2006).

Other RCTs have been conducted outside the USA by researchers not connected with the development of the MST model. For example the impact of MST on 100 Norwegian young people with serious anti-social behaviour (Ogden and Halliday-Boykins, 2004) and with 108 British young offenders (Butler et al., 2011). In Norway seriously anti-social young people were assigned to MST or usual child welfare services. Data was collected from teachers, parents and young people before and after treatment. The results for MST were positive with decreased 'out-of-home' placements, increased youth social competence and increased consumer satisfaction; however results differed across sites, with the sites that achieved the highest treatment adherence getting the best outcomes, which is a similar finding to Henggeler et al. (1997), showing that outcomes are linked with treatment fidelity.

In the British sample both Youth Offending Service (YOS) interventions and MST reduced reoffending but MST gave significantly greater reductions in non-violent reoffending after 18 months. This study was regarded as 'the first RCT of MST that contrasts it with the current protocols for youth offenders in the United Kingdom' (Butler et al., 2011, p. 1221). The use of the statutory YOS interventions as the comparison group for 'usual services' makes it possible to compare MST's effectiveness with a clearly defined alternative treatment rather than 'services as usual' which may vary considerably across different countries and within the control group. This means that the effectiveness of MST can be clearly measured and compared. In the last six months of the study only 8 per cent in the MST group against 34 per cent in the YOS group had one or more further non-violent convictions.

Long-term outcomes for MST have also been investigated. A 13.7-year follow-up of the same sample of families in the Missouri Delinquency Project found that MST continued to produce reductions in reoffending for serious crimes and fewer days in custody for those who had undertaken MST compared with individual therapy. The young people who had MST were now 28 years old on average showing that MST was reducing offending behaviour through early adulthood (Schaeffer & Borduin, 2005).

A further study then went on to examine criminal and civil court outcomes on average 21.9 years later when the young people who had taken part in the original research trail were now 37.3 years old (Sawyer & Borduin, 2011). They found that rates of serious reoffending were significantly lower for those who had MST compared to individual therapy, 34.8 per cent compared to 54.8 per cent and that the frequency of offending was five times lower for the MST participants than for those who undertook individual therapy. They also compared family-related civil suits during adulthood and again the families who had experienced MST were involved in only half the family-related civil suits. The authors see this as consistent with MST's focus on family interventions. It would seem that improved family relations were still persisting well into mid-life.

In the UK the Systemic Therapy for At Risk Teens (START) trial began in 2010 to evaluate MST in the UK context in nine pilot sites (Fonagy et al., 2013). The START research project is led by University College London in collaboration with Cambridge University and Leeds University to carry out the largest RCT ever undertaken in the UK (n = 684). The study is being backed and funded by the Department for Education working with the Department of Health. All sites have recruited families for the research which is due to report in 2014.

The research is a randomised control study designed to compare MST with Management as Usual (MAU), the usual services young people would have received if MST were not available. Every suitable referral allocated to MST will be compared with a suitable referral allocated to MAU. Building on the work of Butler et al. (2011) in their evaluation of MST at the Brandon Centre, the independent researchers are looking at the effectiveness of MST in routine practice when it is not part of a demonstration project working closely with the developers.

The START trial will add to our understanding of the effectiveness of MST, particularly in a UK setting. However the wealth of sound RCT evidence already built up over 30 years has consistently demonstrated that MST is an effective community treatment, reducing reoffending and custodial sentences for young people at risk of being placed into custody due to serious anti-social behaviour or crime. The effectiveness has been demonstrated by independent researchers in the USA and Europe and the effects of MST have been shown to endure for over 21 years after the 3–5-month treatment has ended. Recently published National Institute for Health and Clinical Excellence (NICE) (2013) guidelines for conduct disorder have concluded that Multisystemic Therapy should be offered to children and young people aged between 11 and 17 years for the treatment of conduct disorder.

Developments in Europe

The initial results obtained at the end of MST have been very encouraging. In the UK, for example, results presented at the first European conference for MST in Norway in 2012 indicated that 92 per cent of young people were living at home, 83 per cent were in education, training or work and 76 per cent were not re-arrested. Results presented from across Europe show a similar pattern of outcomes at the end of treatment with over 90 per cent at home. For education, work or training results ranged from 75 per cent to 83 per cent and the number not re-arrested was even higher than the UK result achieved.

At the first European conference it was also reported that since 1999 there were 92 MST teams in Europe. These included the standard teams, which this chapter is describing, but also MST adaptations for problem sexual behaviour, child abuse and neglect and substance misuse. MST is present in Europe in Belgium, Denmark, the Netherlands, Sweden, Switzerland, Iceland and Norway. Many organisations with a strong track record of starting and successfully sustaining MST have collaborated with MST Services to become Network partners (www.MST services.com/index.php/teams/network-partners). They include a number of different organisations in the USA, Canada, New Zealand and Australia; and in Europe, the Netherlands, Denmark, Norway, Sweden, and most recently the UK have taken this route.

The Network partner organisations ensure MST treatment integrity in order to achieve the best possible outcomes as evidenced by the research and findings to date and they play a key role in shaping research on effectiveness in their country. The Network partnership enables the teams to have professionals from their own locality taking the lead in starting and implementing MST and local MST experts supporting the consultation, quality assurance and regular booster training for teams. There are advantages in embedding this knowledge and expertise in the workforce of the organisations delivering MST as well as reducing costs and increasing the opportunity to share organisation-specific learning and collaboration across sites with much in common. In Europe it has enabled organisations to conduct most of their business in their own language. MST Services maintains an ongoing close relationship with its Network partners and focuses particularly on developing staff in their new roles and implementing quality improvements and quality assurance so that MST can be successfully transported to community practice settings with outcomes similar to those of university-based trials. Network partners can also learn much from each other about the successful dissemination of MST, for example into European settings.

Challenge to traditional services

The challenge to traditional services from an evidenced-based community service such as MST is how current services can be transformed in their delivery and their adherence to a model of effective practice based on the evidence (Ashmore and Fox, 2011). For example services would need to be individually designed around the needs of service users and not around the needs of services and staff. Also many services for young people who are engaging in serious anti-social behaviour or crime are not available in the community but in secure settings, often not close to their home thus making the involvement with families difficult.

Reconviction rates for young people leaving secure establishments are very high. In 2010/11, for example, 72.6 per cent leaving a Youth Offending Institution were reconvicted within a year (Ministry of Justice, 2013). One-year reconviction rates are higher for adults and young people leaving custody who reported previously experiencing violence in the home (58 per cent compared with 48 per cent) (Ministry of Justice, 2010).

Custody is a particularly expensive option, estimated at around £4 billion for policing and criminal justice for under 18 year olds alone and around one-fifth of all arrested and followed through are in this age group (Ministry of Justice, 2012, p. 38) (Independent Comission on Youth Crime, 2009). It is not only costly in terms of money but also in human terms if serious offending is not stopped during adolescence.

The rate for custody use for juveniles varies greatly across the UK from 19.9 per cent to less than 1 per cent in 2009/10 and the variation cannot be explained solely by the crimes the young people have committed but appears sensitive to a range of factors including diversion (Bateman, 2011). There is an opportunity then to challenge the systemic factors that lead to high rates of custody and to further extend the provision of well-researched alternatives such as MST. It is estimated that in the USA about 96 per cent of the eligible population is not receiving an evidenced-based treatment (Henggeler, 2003).

Young people placed in institutions with others who have committed crimes will be affected by their influence. Low parental monitoring and association with deviant peers have been shown to be strong proximal predictors of engagement in an array of problem behaviours at two-year follow-up (Ary et al., 1999). More worrying are findings from longitudinal research that peer interventions carried out in groups increase adolescent problem behaviour and negative outcomes when they become adults compared to a control group. High risk youth are particularly vulnerable (Dishion et al., 1999).

MST is very different to traditional approaches to working with young people who offend. The process of engaging families in therapy, the intensive individualised therapy delivered in the family home or local community, and the quality assurance systems all pose challenges to traditional services (Ashmore & Fox, 2011). Service users who have presented challenges for traditional services to keep engaged in treatment have indicated that they prefer many aspects of the MST service.

Approaches such as the home delivery at a time that is convenient for the family, the 24-hour 7-day-a-week support available from the MST team and the single therapist carrying out all therapeutic work with the family have been reported as some of the features that have enabled successful treatment engagement (Tighe et al., 2011).

For many young people who offend where community treatment is offered it will be in the company of other young people with similar problems. They may also be expected to attend settings for treatment where they mix with others who have been involved in crime and anti-social behaviour. Often they will be educated not in mainstream settings but in special schools where others have similar problems and so mixing with a pro-social peer group will be made more difficult. Services have been slow to respond to the clear, consistent message from the evidence that bringing young people together with others who are behaving anti-socially will often increase anti-social and offending behaviour (Dishion et al., 1999). All too often services are arranged in a way that makes them easier for the organisations doing the delivery rather than for the families who are trying to access the services.

Cost of Multisystemic Therapy

MST is sometimes seen as being expensive or 'relatively high cost' (Hughes et al., 2012, p. 54) but without looking at the comparative costs of an out-of-home placement such as care or custody and the long-term results of these interventions any comparisons are largely invalid. Also when compared with other statutory or commissioned services there is a dearth of evidence that these services are achieving the results that both the public and policy makers expect.

If change is to happen, commissioners would need to divert money from statutory services which they have always funded to evidenced-based services, not yet available in every area. In the UK where many services for children and young people are delivered through the local authority, services would need to be transformed. Often current practice involves removing young people who are behaving anti-socially from mainstream services for example in education and providing them with separate services together in another site. There is significant evidence that interventions of this type are not effective and this policy has been shown to make outcomes worse (Dishion et al., 1999). In tougher economic times especially, funding needs to be diverted to evidence-based treatments where results are shown to follow.

In the UK the steady growth of MST from four sites in 2008 to over 30 in 2013 has largely been due to the recognition of the evidence for MST's effectiveness, the tapered start-up funding, the organisational support from the Department of Health and the Department of Education working in partnership with the Youth Justice Board and the hard work of committed teams and stakeholders with a belief that young people and their families deserve better. The UK has become a 'Network partnership' which means that it can develop a locally controlled group who are fully trained in effectively developing the programme by MST Services who maintain an ongoing working relationship with the organisation. This is to work on staff development, quality improvement and quality assurance to ensure that the promised results can be delivered by the UK staff using experts drawn from the UK teams which have been in existence for five years.

Conclusion

Forensic practice needs to put what we know about 'What works?' into practice in the settings where the anti-social behaviour and crime happens and where it can be stopped. This chapter argues that this can be most effectively undertaken in the community.

MST achieves this by adherence to a model and through a comprehensive range of quality assurance measures and ongoing training and support which enables experienced professionals to implement the interventions in a way that is consistent with the evidence. This is something that needs to be done with every intervention. Too often the approach is to 'train and hope' (Stokes & Baer, 1977, p. 351). Other well-researched interventions could work in this way if they were delivered as found to be effective from the evidence and had ongoing measurement, training and support to keep delivering to this standard continuously.

The challenge for community forensic practice is no longer in finding effective interventions for young people who are committing anti-social behaviour or crime. It is to work out how to take the evidenced-based treatments we have found and effectively get them established into routine practice in the community.

Acknowledgements

The author would like to thank Lori Moore, MST Services, Manager of Network Partnerships, and Grant Nolan for their input into earlier drafts of this chapter.

Notes

1   The range 11 to 17 refers to the target age in the UK. In other countries this may vary by a year. MST Services describes the 'typical' MST young person as aged 14 to 16 years old.
2   In the UK teams are made up of three or four therapists, elsewhere there may also be teams of two therapists.

References

Ary, D. V., Duncan, T. E., Duncan, S. C. & Hops, H. (1999) Adolescent problem behaviour: the influence of parents and peers. *Behaviour Research and Therapy*, 37(3), 217–30.

Ashmore, Z. & Fox, S. (2011) How does the delivery of Multisystemic Therapy to adolescents and their families challenge practice in traditional services in the Criminal Justice System. *British Journal of Forensic Practice*, 13(1), 25–31.

Bateman, T. (2011) Child imprisonment: exploring 'injustice by geography'. *Prison Service Journal*, 197, 10–15.

Boer, D. (2009) Ecological validity and risk assessment: the importance of assessing context for intellectually disabled sex offenders. *British Journal of Forensic Practice*, 11(2), 4–9.

Borduin, C. M., Mann, B. J., Cone, L. T., Henggeler, S. W., Fucci, B. R., Blaske, D. M. & Williams, R. A. (1995) Multisystemic treatment of serious juvenile offenders: long-term prevention of criminality and violence. [Clinical Trial Comparative Study Randomized Controlled Trial Research Support, Non-U.S. Gov't]. *Journal of Consulting and Clinical Psychology*, 63(4), 569–78.

Bronfenbrenner, U. (1979) *The Ecology of Human Development: Experiments by Nature and Design*. Cambridge, MA: Harvard University Press.

Butler, S., Baruch, G., Hicklet, N. & Fonagy, P. (2011) A randomised controlled trial of MST and a statutory therapeutic intervention for young offenders. *Journal of the American Academy of Child and Adolescent Psychiatry*, 50(12), 1220–35.

Coleman, J. & Hagell, A. (2007) *Adolescence Risk and Resilience: Against the Odds*. Chichester: Wiley.

Dishion, T. J., McCord, J. & Poulin, F. (1999) When interventions harm: peer groups and problem behaviour. *American Psychologist*, 54(9), 755–64.

Dodge, K., Greenberg, M., Malone, P. & Conduct Problems Prevention Research Group. (2008) Testing an idealized dynamic cascade model of the development of serious violence in adolescence. *Child Development*, 79(6), 1907–27.

Fonagy, P., Butler, S., Goodyer, I., Cottrell, D., Scott, S., Pilling, S., et al. (2013) Evaluation of Multisystemic Therapy pilot services in the Systemic Therapy for At Risk Teens (START) trial: study protocol for a randomised controlled trial. *Trials*, 14, 265.

Gardner, M. & Steinberg, L. (2005) Peer influence on risk taking, risk preference and risky decision making in adolescents and adults: an experimental study. *Developmental Psychology*, 41(4), 625–35.

Greenberg, L. S. & Pinsof, W. M. (1986) *The Psychotherapeutic Process: A Research Handbook*. New York: Guilford Press.

Henggeler, S. W. (2003) Advantages and disadvantages of MST and other evidence-based practices for treating juvenile offenders. *Journal of Forensic Psychology Practice*, 3(4), 53–59.

Henggeler, S. W. & Borduin, C. M. (1992) *Multisystemic Therapy Adherence Scales*. Unpublished instrument. Charleston: Department of Psychiatry and Behavioral Sciences, Medical University of South Carolina.

Henggeler, S. W., Melton, G. B. & Smith, L. A. (1992) Family preservation using Multisystemic Therapy: an effective alternative to incarcerating serious juvenile offenders. *Journal of Consulting and Clinical Psychology*, 60, 953–61.

Henggeler, S. W., Melton, G. B., Brondino, M. J., Scherer, D. G. & Hanley, J. H. (1997) Multisystemic Therapy with violent and chronic juvenile offenders and their families: the role of treatment fidelity in successful dissemination. [Clinical Trial Randomized Controlled Trial Research Support, U.S. Gov't, P.H.S.]. *Journal of Consulting and Clinical Psychology*, 65(5), 821–33.

Henggeler, S. W., Schoenwald, S. K., Borduin, C. M., Rowland, M. D. & Cunningham, P. B. (2009) *Multisystemic Therapy for Antisocial Behavior in Children and Adolescents* (2nd edn). New York: Guilford Press.

Hughes, N., Williams, H., Chitsabesan, P., Davies, R. & Mounce, L. (2012) *Nobody Made the Connection: The Prevalence of Neurodisability in Young People who Offend*. London: Children's Commission.

Independent Comission on Youth Crime (2009) Responding to Youth Crime and Antisocial Behaviour: A Consultation Paper. London: Independent Comission on Youth Crime.

McCarthy, P., Laing, K. & Walter, J. (2004) *Offenders of the Future Assessing the Risk of Children and Young People Becoming Involved in Criminal or Anti-social Behaviour*. (RR545). London: Department for Education.

Ministry of Justice (2010) *Compendium of Reoffending Statistics and Analysis*. London: Ministry of Justice.

Ministry of Justice (2012) *Youth Justice Statistics 2010/11*. London: Ministry of Justice.

Ministry of Justice (2013) *Youth Justice Statistics England and Wales*. London: Ministry of Justice.

National Institute for Health and Clinical Excellence (2013) *Anti-social Behaviour and Conduct Disorders in Children and Young People*. London: NICE.

Ogden, T. & Halliday-Boykins, C. A. (2004) Multisystemic treatment of antisocial adolescents in Norway: replication of clinical outcomes outside of the US. *Child and Adolescent Mental Health*, 9(2), 77–83.

Ogden, T. & Hagen, K. A. (2006) Multisystemic therapy of serious behaviour problems in youth: sustainability of therapy effectiveness two years after intake. *Journal of Child and Adolescent Mental Health*, 11, 142–9.

Sawyer, A. M. & Borduin, C. M. (2011) Effects of MST through midlife: a 21.9 year follow up to a randomised clinical trial with serious and violent juvenile offenders. *Journal of Consulting and Clinical Psychology*, 79, 643–52.

Schaeffer, C. M. & Borduin, C. M. (2005) Long-term follow-up to a randomized clinical trial of Multisystemic Therapy with serious and violent juvenile offenders. [Clinical Trial Randomized Controlled Trial Research Support, N.I.H., Extramural Research Support, Non-U.S. Gov't Research Support, U.S. Gov't, P.H.S.]. *Journal of Consulting and Clinical Psychology*, 73(3), 445–53.

Schoenwald, S. K., Sheidow, A. J. & Letourneau, E. J. (2004) Toward effective quality assurance in evidence-based practice: links between expert consultation, therapist fidelity, and child outcomes. [Comparative Study Research Support, Non-U.S. Gov't Research Support, U.S. Gov't, P.H.S.]. *Journal of Clinical Child & Adolescent Psychology*, 33(1), 94–104.

Schoenwald, S. K., Carter, R. E., Chapman, J. E. & Sheidow, A. J. (2008) Therapist adherence and organizational effects on change in youth behavior problems one year after Multisystemic Therapy. [Research Support, N.I.H., Extramural]. *Administration and Policy in Mental Health*, 5(5), 379–94.

Stokes, T. F. & Baer, D. M. (1977) An implicit technology of generalization. *Journal of Applied Behavior Analysis*, 10(2), 349–67.

Sundell, K., Hansson, K., Lofholm, C. A., Olsson, T., Gustle, L. H. & Kadesjo, C. (2008) The transportability of Multisystemic Therapy to Sweden: short-term results from a randomized trial of conduct-disordered youths. [Randomized Controlled Trial]. *Journal of Family Psychology*, 22(4), 550–60.

Tighe, A., Pistrang, N., Cadagli, L., Baruch, G. & Butler, S. (2011) Multisystemic Therapy for young offenders: families's experience of therapeutic processes and outcomes. *Journal of Family Psychology*, 26(2), 187–97.

Timmons-Mitchell, J., Bender, M. B., Kishna, M. A. & Mitchell, C. C. (2006) An independent effectiveness trial of Multisystemic Therapy with juvenile justice youth. [Randomized Controlled Trial]. *Journal of Clinical Child & Adolescent Psychology*, 35(2), 227–36.

11

OFFENDING BEHAVIOUR PROGRAMMES

Managing the transition from prison into the community

Richard Shuker and Andrew Bates

Introduction

An inherent problem for those undertaking risk assessments and carrying out interventions in secure forensic settings is that behaviour displayed and observed in one setting can often be discrepant with that exhibited within another. Behavioural change, treatment progress and risk reduction observed in a secure setting may be limited to a specific set of conditions particular to that environment. This presents clear challenges to those practitioners working within secure settings. It is incumbent on those who have a responsibility to deliver interventions and risk assessments to ensure that their utility and relevance extends beyond the prison or hospital setting. Attending to the relevance of the environment in which an offender is to be eventually at liberty becomes a priority for all practitioners involved in offender treatment, risk assessment and management. This chapter will outline the challenges and the opportunities available to practitioners when managing the transition of their clients from secure to community settings. It will explore the difficulties that clinicians face when attempting to equip their clients with the necessary skills, provide the required support and establish the conditions needed to maintain attitudinal and behavioural change following the transition to the community. It will highlight some principles for effective practice and suggest a framework for sustaining change.

Secure settings and effective programme delivery

In-session behaviour

The delivery of Offending Behaviour Programmes (OBPs) in secure settings may provide practitioners with some advantages but can also present some significant challenges. One question asked of programme deliverers concerns the relevance of behaviours observed within the treatment setting as indices of risk reduction. Shine (2010) emphasises the limitations of focusing on in-treatment behaviour, arguing that a more meaningful method of assessing the impact of an intervention on risk is to consider the offence-paralleling behaviours occurring outside of the immediate treatment setting.

Individual versus contextual factors

Another criticism of treatment approaches, which particularly applies within secure settings, concerns the weaknesses of adopting a risk reduction and management approach which focuses primarily on individual factors and neglects wider systemic factors such as family, community, school and peer group. For example Webster et al. (2001) identify how risk management for violence needs to be attentive to a range of lifestyle and contextual factors, stating that 'it is probably not too great an over-statement to say that much undue aggression and violence comes about from a disproportionate emphasis on the individual as distinct from circumstances' (p. 125). The delivery of interventions in isolation, or without a consideration of the anticipated context in which the offender is likely to find him or herself, may well render therapeutic progress largely irrelevant. Theories such as social ecology (Bronfenbrenner, 1979) which emphasise the multi-determined nature of human behaviour have also provided an impetus to pay attention to the wider systems in which the offender is located (see Chapter 10 in this volume).

Recent risk management frameworks have emphasised the importance of individual (i.e. attitudes, appraisals, beliefs), situational (i.e. lifestyle, circumstances) and environmental (i.e. familial, social) factors on post-release behaviour (Douglas et al., 2013). Risk is influenced by an interaction of factors such as ongoing supervision, availability of treatment, monitoring and victim safety planning. Risk management strategies need to attend equally to all these areas. However Augimeri (2001) has highlighted the discrepancy that continues to exist in the extent to which the risk–need–responsivity principles (Andrews & Bonta, 2010) have actually informed an understanding of offender rehabilitation. For example features of programme delivery which tend to be seen as the priority by practitioners focus primarily on protecting the quality of delivery; far less emphasis is generally placed on systems to help consolidate progress post-release. Augimeri argues that whilst implementing well-designed and delivered group-based interventions is essential, the impact of these interventions is greatly reduced if there is inadequate follow-up or support in the 'day to day life of that individual'.

Young people face particular challenges which highlight this issue. Some families can be reluctant to accept the young person back into the family home after a custodial sentence. There have often been familial difficulties prior to custody (such as for example stealing, violence in the home, drug use) and families can be reluctant to agree that the young person can return home on release. Often professionals working with young people – social workers or young offending teams (YOTs) – have limited options available (17 year olds may have hostel accommodation in some parts of the country). However professionals are often still trying to secure a suitable place for the young person to live days or weeks before release meaning that little planning or preparation is in place at release.

Some suggestions have been made regarding ways of supporting the generalisation of skills learnt in treatment delivered in psychiatric settings. For example Cohen et al. (1985) have suggested a set of behaviourally based principles. These include emphasising the use of natural reinforcers within the environment which may include social, financial or material rewards, a focus on enhancing intrinsic motivation, the provision of instruction including self-evaluation and reward, the application of behavioural methods to learning, and assisting in goal setting. Whilst useful these have not been translated into practice guidelines which can inform practitioners within the community.

Treatment context

Livesley (2001) identifies a set of core therapeutic factors necessary for effective interventions with personality disordered offenders. One such factor was the need to provide opportunities for the generalisation of skills taught within treatment groups. The efficacy of prison OBPs can potentially be undermined by the lack of suitable learning opportunities or the overemphasis on individual/psychological factors which neglect the role of skill practice and development. The 'What works' (see Andrews & Bonta, 2010) literature has consistently emphasised that programme efficacy is dependent on a number of features being in place; one key element, which tends to be given secondary recognition within programme design and delivery, is identifying clinical procedures to support the transition and continuity of treatment progress into the community. Whilst in some ways it may be easier to deliver OBPs in secure settings, severe limitations will be placed on their long-term value without this component being in place.

Whilst secure settings can overcome some of the more practical issues such as ensuring client attendance, McIvor (2001) suggests that the prison environment is far from an ideal setting to acquire and develop pro-social skills, arguing that 'the behavioural changes which are adaptive in prison settings may have limited relevance to an individual's ability to sustain a law-abiding lifestyle on release'. Whilst coordinated through-care, which supports continuity, may be hard to achieve (McIvor & Barry, 1998), effective programming does need to ensure that prison-based OBPs include a clear structure and practical link to allow the transition from prison into the community. This post-release follow-up component of treatment is where the strongest treatment effect has frequently been found (Gendreau & Andrews, 1990).

Treatment delivery in the community

Since the mid-1990s, a range of (latterly accredited) OBPs are run in the community, primarily by probation trusts operating in the UK. These OBPs have been similar in theoretical premise and structure to those run in custodial settings. In recent years there have been initiatives within the National Offender Management Service (NOMS) to bring custodial and community OBPs together to better link the two areas of practice. For instance the community cognitive skills programme named Think First was redesigned to become the Thinking Skills Programme (TSP) which is run identically in community and custodial settings. A range of interventions have also been developed for young people leaving prison which address areas such as substance misuse, and 'thinking skills'-based interventions. This has helped streamline treatment provision so that offenders were not repeating OBPs in both custodial and community settings, thus wasting resources. To some extent the restriction and reallocation of staffing resources in central NOMS has meant that the planned programme to bring together community and custodial OBPs became somewhat stalled over recent years. Also as a consequence of the economic cutbacks affecting all public sector services probation trusts have re-evaluated their previous prioritisation of OBPs, which tend to be expensive to run due to the deployment of specialist staff and stringent audit processes which govern their application. As a result of this probation trusts in the UK have been diverting resources away from OBPs and into retraining their core offender management staff with skills to enhance offender engagement, supporting desistance from offending over time (McNeill, 2010), reflective practice and enhancing professional judgement. While the impact of these new initiatives is not yet known, it is hoped that a more individually focused offender management approach might both enhance offenders' transition back into community settings while also maintaining a clear focus on public protection.

Opportunities for offence-paralleling behaviours, which may have been significantly limited whilst the offender is incarcerated, expand greatly once they are released into the community, to the extent that the offender is able to (and unfortunately sometimes will) actually commit further offences. In this regard the careful monitoring and supervision of offenders undertaking OBPs by probation staff becomes paramount in community forensic practice and potentially problematic. Offenders in such settings are fully susceptible to stresses in their lifestyle which may be directly or indirectly linked to their offending behaviour. An example here would be a man undertaking a Community Domestic Violence Programme who remains living in a relationship with the victim of his offence and is therefore at risk of repeating assaults upon her. Such risks presented by men to female victims may increase particularly during the period of treatment when the offender's attitudes and beliefs are subject to scrutiny and challenge within the group setting, with a possible immediate negative emotional impact on him. For this reason a key element of such a treatment programme is the provision of a Woman's Safety Worker whose role is to liaise closely with the partner of a domestic violence perpetrator undertaking treatment to reduce the risk of their being re-victimised. Currently Domestic Violence group interventions are only provided for male offenders. The significantly smaller numbers of convicted female perpetrators of domestic violence generally undertake individualised interventions within their supervision sessions with a probation officer.

Even in cases where the risk of reoffending may not be so imminent, community treatment OBPs are conducted within the context of various complicating factors which are absent from custodial settings. These range from problems to do with housing, finances or family commitments to simple practical issues such as the need to travel long distances at problematic times of day (e.g. evenings) in order to attend the treatment group. Such factors add to the risks associated with community treatment as offenders may be undertaking and then leaving sessions at times when professional support from agencies is not available.

CASE STUDY ONE

This first case study illustrates the possible negative outcomes when correct information about an offender's past behaviour is not assimilated in order to fully inform a risk management and treatment plan. Furthermore, adverse outcomes can occur when information regarding risky behaviours is either not identified or not shared in a timely manner with relevant public protection partners during an offender's sentence both in and outside custody.

Mark is a 34-year-old married man with two children, a boy aged 6 and a girl aged 4. He was convicted for wounding in June 2009 and given a five-year prison sentence. The victim was a man he had accosted in a pub who he accused of having an affair with his wife Alison and then attacked with a knife. Mark has a lengthy history of violence against Alison evidenced by nine call-outs of the police Domestic Abuse Unit (2002–8) and a previous conviction for battery where she was the victim (2006). Alison told him their relationship was over when he began his prison sentence. Shortly after this time Mark's offender manager had asked the prison to monitor his mail and telephone calls as he had issued threats of violence to his partner during a previous custodial sentence. However this request was not responded to as Mark was not convicted for an act of domestic violence on this occasion. Mark completed an Enhanced Thinking Skills programme in prison but no work to address his domestic violence history. The offender manager had asked the prison for a psychological assessment to address Mark's wider treatment needs including those relating to his domestic violence and a suspected personality disorder but this was not proceeded with due to resource limitations and a focus on assessment for those serving life and Indeterminate Public Protection Sentences. In 2012 Mark was decategorised to open conditions, where he went absent without leave for two days and travelled back to his home town where he was seen by his ex-partner watching her home from a distance. This information was not communicated to his offender manager and Mark was not returned to closed conditions. Despite his qualifying for Multi-Agency Public Protection Arrangements (MAPPA) due to the nature of his conviction (for a violent offence for which he received more than a year's custodial sentence), Mark's offender manager did not refer him to MAPPA within the required six months prior to his release but only one month before release. This did not allow for the correct and timely processing of Mark as a Level 2 MAPPA case due to his assessment of high risk of harm to a known adult (his ex-partner) and the involvement of more than one key risk management agency in the community (probation, police Domestic Abuse Unit and social services due to risks of indirect violence presented by Mark to his two children). Mark was placed in Probation Approved Premises on his release from custody, with an exclusion order covering the town where Alison and their children live, although with only a standard curfew which allowed him to be away from the Approved Premises for much of the day as the incident where he had been seen outside Alison's home had not been shared with his offender manager. However a week after his release Mark travelled to Alison's home and forced his way in, began arguing with her about his access to the children then hit her in the face in front of both of their children. Neighbours called the police who arrive and arrest Mark for assault by beating.

Communication and liaison

Communication between custodial treatment providers and those operating in the community has sometimes been problematic. As a practice example, treatment reports produced by forensic psychologists working in custodial settings may make recommendations for community follow-up which are not realistic due to limited knowledge of available community services. There are major regional differences in community forensic provision, dependent, in part, on whether or not a probation area employs a forensic psychologist, where the majority do not. Given the very small number of forensic psychologists working in the probation service their roles tend to focus around consultancy and case formulation and the capacity of individual practitioners to respond to specific requests for various forms of follow-up treatment following prison interventions will be very limited. Similarly variable is the provision of community forensic services under the auspices of the National Health Service, where there is no funding provision for the training of forensic psychologists. Where some Forensic Mental Health services provide a range of services to the wider community which can be accessed by local probation services, many others restrict their practice primarily to the management of patients either currently or previously sectioned under the Mental Health Act, with little provision for referral from primary or secondary health services (e.g. general practitioners or general psychiatry).

Conditions for learning

Whilst the effective delivery of OBPs in the community may be associated with certain difficulties there are some recognised advantages (McGuire, 1995). A main strength is the opportunity they offer for learning and skill generalisation which is not present within secure settings. Furthermore, OBPs structurally linked into the community are able to harness and support the engagement of families, and progress is also less likely to be eroded by the influence of anti-social peers (Shine, 2010).

This point can be illustrated when considering the accredited sex offender treatment programmes which were introduced to the UK in 2001. All the OBPs were cognitive-behavioural in their theoretical perspective and covered broadly similar areas of treatment including a key focus on reduction of denial, increased insight into offending behaviour and victim empathy and relapse prevention (Beckett, 1998). The crucial difference between community and custodial treatment is that in the former the offender is exposed to the risks of reoffending which are only theoretical when they are in custody. In community Sex Offender Groupwork Programmes (SOGPs) the relapse prevention element of treatment becomes arguably the most crucial as the offender is applying what they learned about the attitudes and behaviour which contributed to their offending to their everyday experiences relating to employment, accommodation and relationships. It is within this context that risk factors that were previously only considered theoretically become very real.

The demands of transition

On release from prison key factors come into play which may not have been fully prepared for by the offender. The focus on the regaining of their liberty can often be made without considering that the anticipated enthusiasm and excitement may be linked with inevitable problems and disappointments, and that their positive feelings in regaining their freedom may be short-lived once the problems and frustrations of community living once again become apparent. This can be of particular significance for those who have become institutionalised over years of custodial sentences whereby prison life, although often condemned and berated, in fact becomes more familiar and psychologically as well as physically secure than the community. For those who are thus institutionalised blaming 'the system' which contains them can allow for the avoidance of taking responsibility for their behaviour and their future. In more practical terms accommodation for those released from prison can be difficult to access, especially for those with a history of sexual offending and arson. These problems can be further enhanced for young people coming out of custodial settings who are not able to hold a tenancy agreement until they are aged 18 and, even after this age, usually have no history of successful independent living and thus struggle to maintain such tenancies. Unfortunately the possibility of them living with their family of origin, which might have some advantages, may have ceased due to the impact of their past offending and possible risk to other family members including children. For higher risk of harm offenders the first six months after a prison sentence are likely to be spent in Probation Approved Premises (AP) or hostels. Such placement allows the offender a period of time to reacclimatise to living in the community in a supported and monitored environment which is especially necessary after long custodial sentences. Simple tasks such as shopping for food, dealing with new technology and moving among crowds of people can present challenges even for the most 'rehabilitated' offender (e.g. one who has been observed to participate in and gain from prison OBPs) and AP staff provide vital assistance in these areas through key-working. Most of all, the offender will now have to approach their life as their own responsibility and not what is dictated for them by an institution. Offenders released from prison will often miss the structure of the prison regime and can have difficulty organising their own finances and accommodation on eventually moving on from APs. Social exclusion and isolation can also cause longer-term problems which reduce the deterrent effect of custody which can act as a familiar if negative environment compared to an excluded community existence. For younger offenders accessing schooling following a custodial sentence can prove very problematic due to long histories of school exclusion.

Further problems for the offender can occur around the use of alcohol. Genuinely believed insights around the perils of alcohol use developed in the prison environment may fall by the wayside once alcohol and other substances become accessible again in the community. Probation staff can refer the offender to community alcohol treatment agencies in order to assist them in managing alcohol and drug use but the ready availability of alcohol (legally) and drugs (illegally) will inevitably elevate risk. While in the AP the offender, although receiving structured resettlement assistance from staff, will also be subject to various controls such as signing-in requirements (as often as hourly for a high risk of harm offender recently released from prison) and curfews. Offenders who have convicted sexual offences against children may have a licence requirement to remain within the AP during the time when children are travelling to and from school. In some cases these restrictions cause anger and resentment among offenders who thought that once released from prison their movements would be free. In fact restrictions in place in APs when a high risk offender is first released from prison are often greater than those at most Open Prisons, although the intention is that such restrictions are reduced as quickly as possible once the offender has demonstrated that their risk is manageable in the community. APs provide a vital link between custody and eventually living unrestricted in the community.

The role of the offender manager (OM), in part, is to provide the link between custody and the community for the offender. This will involve receiving information arising from treatment undertaken by the offender and other sources within the prison. In this respect the probation officer is updated on progress the offender is making in custody. This information can be incorporated into their Offender

Assessment System (OASys), a computerised document encompassing relevant information about the offender, the ownership of which is passed from prison to probation services when the offender is released. In recent years the advent of the offender supervisor (OS) role within the prison has been seen to significantly improve links between custody and the community. The OS (often a prison officer) will be the conduit through which information on sentence and risk will pass to the OM (who ideally will hold the case from the point of sentence until release into the community, to ensure continuity and the understanding of risk and welfare issues pertaining to the offender). The OS can assist the OM by arranging prison visits or Videolink interviews as well as the sharing of treatment reports produced after the completion of accredited OBPs.

CASE STUDY TWO

This second case study shows that good communication between custodial and community treatment providers can lead to a more streamlined approach to treatment and risk management. It also illustrates that progress made in one treatment setting does not always follow through into another when social and emotional pressures increase and opportunities for different behaviours become available. It highlights the need for ongoing monitoring regardless of apparent progress in treatment.

Jason is serving a five-year prison sentence for sexual abuse of a neighbour, a 10-year-old girl, who he groomed over a period of months after befriending her parents and offering to babysit for her. In prison Jason undertook the Core and Booster Sex Offenders Treatment Programmes (SOTPs). At the end of his treatment a case review meeting was held in the prison which was attended by his probation officer (PO). It was considered that Jason had made good progress in his treatment, acknowledging the full extent of his sexually abusive behaviour and a recognition that he might be at risk of reoffending if his mood and social circumstances worsened as had happened prior to his current offence. The PO received a copy of the Structured Assessment of Risk and Need report from the prison psychology department which she passed on to the treatment manager (TM) of the community Sex Offender Treatment Programme. From this report and the feedback from the PO the TM identified that Jason only needed to complete the Better Lives section of the community programme. Three months after his release from prison while resident in Probation Approved Premises (AP) it was discovered that Jason had sent a birthday card to a female child of an old friend of his and a love poem to the child was found in his room in the AP. This information was passed on to the PO who interviewed Jason to discuss this issue who said he was only being friendly to the child because he missed his own children. At this point Jason had been a Level 1 MAPPA case as his risk of harm was assessed as medium, although there was multi-agency management in his case (additional to police public protection and probation) from social services who were involved in child protection arrangements regarding Jason's own two daughters with whom he was seeking contact. Despite his positive treatment progress in prison the letter to the child was deemed a significant setback although recall to prison did not follow. Instead it was agreed with the TM that Jason should complete the full community treatment programme to better manage his current risk, and he was escalated to a Level 2 MAPPA case presenting high risk of harm to children given recent events.

Risk communication

A key development in offender management over recent years has been the establishment and evolution of the Multi-Agency Public Protection Arrangements (MAPPA). This framework has become a mutual reference point for custody and community practice with the prison, probation and police services all having statutory responsibility to ensure it is applied. MAPPA applies to three groups of offenders: registered sex offenders, those serving more than a year's custodial sentence for a violent offence and any other person with a conviction in their history who presents a high risk of harm to others using a recognised risk assessment methodology and require multi-agency risk management. MAPPA has required that greater communication takes place regarding the risks presented by these offenders between custodial and community practitioners. This includes sharing information about custodial behaviour incurring disciplinary breaches which indicate changes in general risk levels as well as issues to do with specific victims. In such communication the Victim Liaison Units located within probation services have a key role to play, relaying information to victims of sexual and violent offenders to increase their safety and well-being by the imposition of exclusions zones which perpetrators have to maintain once released from custody. The prison service is required to provide information for those MAPPA offenders who are subject to active multi-agency review and this process is essential in ensuring that accurate, up-to-date risk assessments are recorded for offenders being released into the community. Despite the clear benefits that the MAPPA has brought to community safety some limitations in practice have remained – specifically the limited amount of information that is often available on offenders who have failed to engage in treatment for various reasons including low motivation, denial or low IQ. Often these untreated offenders remain an 'unknown quantity' when released into the community and the focus of prison psychological work within OBPs has, in the past, limited the availability of detailed risk assessment reports for those who have not engaged in treatment. A shift in the role of forensic psychologists in custodial settings away from purely programme-based work has been welcomed by those who manage the risks of offenders in the community and significant changes in practice in this regard have become apparent.

The challenges of implementing community-based treatments

It is recognised that delivering OBPs within the community may yield more effective results than those delivered solely in closed settings (Lipsey, 1989; Andrews & Bonta, 2010). Whilst results for some cognitive-behavioural therapy (CBT) interventions delivered in custodial settings have produced inconsistent findings (Friendship et al., 2002; Cann et al., 2003), those delivered in community settings have generally produced more positive findings (Hollis, 2007; Hollin et al., 2008, Palmer et al., 2007). Furthermore research has also found that interventions offering an after-care component which mirror the treatment delivered within secure settings are shown to considerably enhance the effectiveness of the intervention. For example, Lipton et al. (2002) found that the treatment effects of intensive, custodial interventions for substance misusers were considerably weakened without treatment comprising a community-based follow-up component. Similarly Muller-Isberner (1996) found that the delivery of post-release intervention was an important variable in reducing later rates of reoffending in a sample of mentally disordered offenders.

Whilst the delivery of treatment for offenders in community settings makes intuitive as well as empirical sense (see, however, Dishion et al., 1999, for critique of community-based group work interventions with young offenders), attempting to deliver OBPs effectively in community settings presents practitioners with considerable challenges; Kemshall (2008) comments that 'the Criminal Justice System has developed a highly credible set of OBPs . . . however there is no doubt that delivering treatment in secure settings is, by and large, much easier than in the community' (p. 121). Difficulties can often be encountered when attempting to plan, implement and deliver follow-up interventions designed to support and consolidate progress made within secure settings. These difficulties are often evident in the high rates of attrition frequently seen in community programmes and present a dilemma for community treatment providers. Whilst treatment attrition presents a general problem with forensic populations (Cann et al., 2003; McMurran & Theodosi, 2007), this problem is heightened within the community. Rates of non-completion in community treatment OBPs have routinely found extremely high attrition rates. Non-completion rates of around 70 per cent have been reported (Hollin et al., 2004, 2008; Palmer et al., 2007) in certain OBPs targeted at general offending behaviour.

In addition to the lack of physical or institutional containment, Dowsett and Craissati (2008) point to other factors associated with positive treatment outcome within prisons which are not afforded within the community. They argue that for some offenders the capacity to adhere to and sustain motivation for treatment they are offered within the community demands skills and attributes they may not possess. They also observe that offenders who have presented as compliant and motivated within the prison setting often behave in a markedly different way within community treatment. This is particularly the case for those with personality disorders where motivation, treatment compliance and engagement may fluctuate more rapidly within the community than within the relative stability that custodial environments provide. Practitioners need to incorporate some flexibility in order to respond to these challenges, while at the same time being able to respond to the risk-related behaviours that emerge during the course of treatment. Kemshall (2008) identifies a similar problem of 'false compliance' which offenders can present with during treatment. This can be an undesirable and unplanned consequence of treatment where prisoners who are allocated treatment inappropriate to their needs and learning style acquire the 'required responses', presenting superficially whilst giving reassurances that risk and behaviours associated with risk are reducing.

McIvor and Barry (1998) highlight a further problem that can arise in the context of post-release supervision: a disparity between the goals of offenders and those supervising them has the potential to create conflict and tension. For example, offenders' priorities typically concern seeking practical assistance related to finance and accommodation. A discrepancy of expectations can emerge where supervisors are more likely to place an emphasis on the consolidation of treatment goals and focusing on individual risk management. The risk of eroding what can be an already precarious relationship between ex-prisoners and community supervisors needs to be avoided, by clarifying and negotiating any incompatibility of goals, expectations and demands.

A risk management framework for sustaining change

The risk management literature provides an important contribution to the understanding of how the learning derived from OBPs delivered within secure settings can remain reinforced and relevant within the community. Dowsett and Craissati (2008) argue that a psychologically informed risk management strategy needs to avoid the risk of the 'fragmentation' of the individual and adopt a more holistic approach, with the ultimate aim of post-release risk management being to enable offenders to integrate back into society with progressively decreasing restrictions on their autonomy. This inclusive approach, which focuses on social functioning, mental health and individual risk, should guide effective offender assessment and management (Thomas-Peter, 2002).

The difficulties of sustaining an individual's engagement with the treatment plans and goals established pre-release presents significant challenges; this provides one potential explanation for the limited efficacy of some OBPs. Borum et al. (2001) suggest a risk management model for promoting post-release treatment adherence which emphasises three components:

- the development of a strong and collaborative therapeutic alliance
- identifying any practical or attitudinal barriers to compliance
- having in place comprehensive monitoring procedures.

In their analysis of risk management strategies, Webster et al. (2001) argue that mechanisms such as monitoring and surveillance can be effectively used to support engagement and compliance by providing supportive, preventive or deterrence functions.

Belfrage and Fransson (2001) argue that the intention and ability to follow through pre-release risk management plans are critical factors in programme outcome and that these can be strengthened in a number of ways. They suggest that one of the most important components in pre-release planning aimed at maintaining adherence is the involvement of professionals and family members outside of the institution. Where this does not feature in the planning process, and where there is little collaboration in release planning between secure and community-based agencies, the likelihood of successful continuation of learning will be reduced. This practice is routine in the management of young offenders where collaboration between the young person, family and supervising officers from both within and outside the institution is seen as necessary practice for effective transition.

Dowsett and Craisatti (2008) suggest that the tools for risk management should ideally range from 'internally driven to externally driven controls' and argue that the risk management, aimed at consolidating treatment progress, can be framed within three paradigms:

- *The attachment paradigm*, which is rooted in the principle that offenders require a safe, collaborative and secure alliance where providing a consistent and secure approach is an important condition in the alleviation of anxiety and promotion of stability (Adshead, 1998).
- *The behavioural paradigm*, which relies primarily on external controls such as supervision and surveillance provided by the police and probation services – this is enhanced by openness and transparency, with clear rules and boundaries and the offender having a degree of certainty about the likely sanctions should these boundaries be breached.
- *The environmental paradigm*, which focuses on ensuring that offenders are supported in environments associated with risk reduction.

This latter approach is identified by Tyrer and Bajaj (2005), referring to the notion of 'Nido' (meaning nest) therapy. Nido therapy focuses on changing a person's environment rather than their personality. They argue that some environments are likely to exacerbate the expression of anti-social behaviour for personality-disordered offenders, whilst others are likely to reduce both emotional distress and anti-social behaviour. Interventions should, they suggest, emphasise the importance of identifying the environments, as well as the therapeutic approach, which are likely to reduce distress. The emphasis on changing systems and its importance in risk management is also a key focus of the Multisystemic Therapy (MST) model when intervening with young people in the community (see Chapter 10 in this volume).

A key current development in community forensic practice is seen with the implementation of the new Personality Disorder (PD) strategy in the UK.

This has evolved since the turn of the century with the publication of the document 'Personality Disorder: No Longer a Diagnosis of Exclusion' (National Institute for Mental Health in England, 2003). Significant developments in community mental health practice have followed this publication including the creation of 'Complex Needs' services providing long-term and intensive psychotherapy services for those with PD in the community. These treatment approaches have referenced the Therapeutic Community approaches which have been practised in some custodial settings for many years (Shuker & Sullivan, 2010). Connected to this new initiative has come the creation of Psychologically Informed Planned Environments (PIPEs) which have been piloted in custodial settings – primarily as sites where offenders who have been through custodial treatment can be housed in settings that allow them to practice skills and approaches learned in treatment. One key objective of the PIPE is to avoid scenarios where such skills may be lost if the offender has to return to other custodial settings where the skills may have less currency and therefore become extinguished. PIPEs are also planned for the community to be run in AP settings, where additional clinical support from forensic and clinical psychologists will be made available to support offenders more systematically post-release. This has a strong focus on a workforce development component (stemming from the Knowledge and Understanding Framework (KUF) initiative, a national training initiative around Personality Disorder covering a range of depths from Introductory awareness training to Master's degree level) and is designed to lead to better practice in managing high risk, high need offenders who might be diagnosed with a personality disorder in other contexts. Although in its infancy in terms of practice, the focus of PD services away from high and medium security forensic services out into community settings represents a significant development and sea change in practice in the UK. Another aspect of this development in this regard will be the provision of funding for additional clinical support (mainly delivered by psychologists) for probation trusts to assist in the risk assessment and case management of high risk offenders who might be classed as having a personality disorder. This strategy will markedly increase the presence and influence of forensic psychology in community settings.

Good lives and post-release follow-up

The Good lives model (Ward et al., 2007) emphasises the importance of enabling offenders to work towards positive, personally meaningful goals and an improved quality of life. Drawing on this, risk management strategies that attend to individual goals and values as well as risks are likely to be those that are most effective. Ward et al. argue that a collaborative focus on goals congruent with the individual's wider values is likely to lead to greater investment in treatment and risk management strategies. Playing to an individual's strengths whilst identifying and anticipating possible barriers to compliance (whether in the form of practical problems or negative attitudes towards treatment), needs to be considered prior to treatment plans being implemented. Wong and Gordon (2004) argue that the risk–need–responsivity principles are acutely relevant as a means of guiding the delivery of services in the transition from secure to community settings. They suggest a risk–readiness model of post-treatment risk management where addressing deficits in treatment readiness and making a comprehensive risk assessment are pivotal to planning intervention and supervision. They argue that 'attention to both risk and readiness variables are just as important during as they are after treatment' (p. 154). More recently developments in our understanding of offender desistance suggest the importance of non-offending personal identities or 'narratives' (see Chapter 13 in this volume) in maintaining pro-social behaviour.

Summary

In this chapter we have provided an overview of the challenges that can arise for offenders who have completed treatment, and those responsible for their management, when making the crucial transition from secure institutional settings back into the community. Whilst challenges remain for the different agencies involved in this process to improve their knowledge, communication and understanding of one another's work, innovations and improvements in practice are also identified. These include the streamlining of offending behaviour pro-grammes across custodial and community settings, the role of the offender supervisor in prison settings and the revised national strategy which aims to reallocate resources from high secure mental health settings into the community. Whilst this will allow for earlier identification of PD cases and improved case management throughout the criminal justice pathway, a continued focus on collaborative working could also go some way to ensure that risk reduction seen in prison-based programmes can be more effectively consolidated and sustained upon transition to the com-munity. Furthermore, a renewed emphasis on developing constructive ways to engage offenders, focusing on strengths as well as risk management, and reinforcing a non-offending personal narrative may go a significant way in helping offenders achieve meaningful life goals; this is likely to provide further opportunities for effective programme transition. In the authors' view, interventions that are able to sustain a collaborative focus on attaining a valued and valuable life provide considerable promise in helping offenders achieve long-term desistance.

References

Adshead, G. (1998) Psychiatric staff as attachment figures. *British Journal of Psychiatry*, 172, 64–9.

Andrews, D. A. & Bonta, J. (2010) *The Psychology of Criminal Conduct* (5th edn). New Providence, NJ: Anderson Publishing/LexisNexis.

Augimeri, L. K. (2001) Providing effective supports. In K. Douglas, D. Webster, S. Hart, D. Eaves & J. Ogloff (eds) *HCR-20 Violence Risk Management Companion Guide*, pp. 135–46. Burnaby, BC: Mental Health, Law and Policy Institute, Simon Fraser University.

Beckett, R. (1998) Community treatment in the United Kingdom. In W. Marshall, Y. Fernandez, S. Hudson & T. Ward (eds) *Sourcebook of Treatment Programs for Sexual Offenders*, New York: Plenum Press.

Belfrage, H. & Fransson, G. (2001) Creating feasible plans. In K. Douglas, D. Webster, S. Hart, D. Eaves & J. Ogloff (eds) *HCR-20 Violence Risk Management Companion Guide*, pp. 119–24. Burnaby, BC: Mental Health, Law and Policy Institute, Simon Fraser University.

Borum, R., Swartz, M., Swanson, J. & Wiseman, S. (2001) Compliance with remediation attempts. In K. Douglas, D. Webster, S. Hart, D. Eaves & J. Ogloff (eds) *HCR-20 Violence Risk Management Companion Guide*, pp. 147–54. Burnaby, BC: Mental Health, Law and Policy Institute, Simon Fraser University.

Bronfenbrenner, U. (1979) *The Ecology of Human Development: Experiments by Nature and Design*. Cambridge, MA: Harvard University Press.

Cann, J., Falshaw, L., Nugent, F. & Friendship, C. (2003) Understanding What Works: accredited cognitive skills programmes for adult men and young offenders. *Findings*, 226. London: Home Office.

Cohen, B. F., Ridley, D. E. & Cohen, M. R. (1985) Teaching skills to severely psychiatrically disabled persons. In H. A. Marlowe & R. B Weinberg (eds) *Competence Development: Theory and Practice in Special Populations*, pp.118–45. Springfield, IL: Charles C. Thomas.

Dishion, T. J., McCord, J. & Poulin, F. (1999) When interventions harm: peer groups and problem behavior. *American Psychologist*, September, 755–64.

Douglas, K. S., Hart, S. D., Webster, C. D. & Belfrage, H. (2013) *HCR-20: Assessing Risk for Violence, Version 3*. Burnaby, BC: Mental Health, Law and Policy Institute, Simon Fraser University.

Dowsett, J. & Craissati, J. (2008) *Managing Personality Disordered Offenders in the Community: A Psychological Approach*. London: Routledge.

Friendship, C., Blud, L., Erikson, M. & Travers, R. (2002) An evaluation of cognitive behavioural treatment for prisoners. Home Office Research Findings No. 161. London: Home Office.

Gendreau, P. & Andrews, D. A. (1990) Tertiary prevention: what the meta-analyses of the offender treatment literature tell us about 'what works'. *Canadian Journal of Criminology*, 32(1), 173–84.

Hollin, C., Palmer, E., McGuire, J., Hounsome, J., Hatcher, R., Bilby, C. & Clark, C. (2004) *Pathfinder Programmes in the Probation Service: A Retrospective Analysis*. London: HMSO.

Hollin, C. R., McGuire, J., Hounsome, J., Hatcher, R. M., Bilby, C. & Palmer, E. (2008) Cognitive skills offending behaviour programs in the community: a reconviction analysis. *Criminal Justice and Behavior*, 35, 269–83.

Hollis, V. (2007) Reconviction Analysis of Interim Accredited Programmes Software (IAPS) Data. Research Development Statistics, National Offender Management Service, London.

Kemshall, H. (2008) *Understanding the Management of High Risk Offenders*. Maidenhead: Open University Press.

Lipsey, M. W. (1989) The efficacy of intervention for juvenile delinquency: results from 400 studies. Paper presented at the 41st annual meeting of the American Society of Criminology, Reno, Nevada, November.

Lipton, D. S., Pearson, F. S., Cleland, C. M. & Yee, D. (2002) The effects of therapeutic communities and milieu therapy on recidivism. In J. McGuire (ed.) *Offender Rehabilitation and Treatment: Effective Programmes and Policies to Reduce Re-offending*, pp. 39–77. Chichester: Wiley.

Livesley, W. J. (2001) A framework for an integrated approach to treatment. In W. J. Livesley (ed.) *Handbook of Personality Disorders: Theory, Research, and Treatment*. New York: Guilford Press.

McGuire, J. (ed.) (1995) *What Works: Reducing Reoffending. Guidelines from Research and Practice.* London: Wiley.

McIvor, G. (2001) Treatment in the community. In C. R. Hollin (ed.) *Offender Assessment and Treatment*, pp. 551–65. London: Wiley.

McIvor, G & Barry, M. (1998) *Social Work and Criminal Justice Volume 7: Community-based Throughcare.* Edinburgh: The Stationery Office.

McMurran, M. & Theodosi, E. (2007) Is offender treatment non-completion associated with increased reconviction over no treatment? *Psychology, Crime, and Law*, 13, 333–43.

McNeill, F. (2010) Travelling hopefully: desistance research and probation practice. In J. Brayford, F. Cowe & J. Deering (eds) *What Else Works? Creative Work with Offenders.* Cullompton: Willan Publishing.

Müller-Isberner, J. R. (1996) Forensic psychiatric aftercare following hospital order treatment. *International Journal of Law and Psychiatry*, 19(1), 81–6.

National Institute for Mental Health in England (2003) *Personality Disorder: No Longer a Diagnosis of Exclusion.* National Institute for Mental Health in England, Best Practice Guidance.

Palmer, E. J., McGuire, J., Hounsome, J. C., Hatcher, R., Bilby, C. & Hollin, C. R (2007) Offending behaviour programmes in the community: the effects on reconviction of three programmes with adult male offenders. *Legal and Criminological Psychology*, 12, 251–64.

Shine, J. (2010) Working with offence paralleling behaviour in a therapeutic community setting. In M. Daffern, L. Jones & J. Shine (eds) *Offence Paralleling Behaviour: A Case Formulation Approach to Offender Assessment and Intervention*, pp. 203–14. Chichester: Wiley.

Shuker, R. & Sullivan, E. (2010) *Grendon and the Emergence of Forensic Therapeutic Communities: Developments in Research and Practice.* Chichester: Wiley-Blackwell.

Thomas-Peter, B. (2002) *Forensic Service Models.* London: Department of Health.

Tyrer, P. and Bajaj, P. (2005) Nidotherapy: making the environment do the therapeutic work. *Advances in Psychiatric Treatment*, 11, 232–8.

Ward, T., Mann, R. E. & Gannon, T. A. (2007) The good lives model of offender rehabilitation: clinical implications. *Aggression and Violent Behavior*, 12, 87–107.

Webster, C. D., Eaves, D. & Halpin, P. (2001) Building stable environments. In K. Douglas, D. Webster, S. Hart, D. Eaves & J. Ogloff (eds) *HCR-20 Violence Risk Management Companion Guide*, pp. 125–34. Burnaby, BC: Mental Health, Law and Policy Institute, Simon Fraser University.

Wong, S. C. P. & Gordon, A. E. (2004) A risk-readiness model of post-treatment risk management. *Issues in Forensic Psychology*, 5, 152–63.

12

COMMUNITY RISK MANAGEMENT FOR HIGH HARM PERSONALITY DISORDERED OFFENDERS

Phil Minoudis

Introduction

There are particular anxieties associated with community management of high harm personality disordered offenders. High profile inquiries arising from tragic cases of homicides, although intended to facilitate learning, have done little to decrease the fear of culpability for poor practice. Reviews of the findings from these inquiries therefore provide a good starting point, if we are to take a risk management approach which avoids repeating past mistakes (e.g. Crichton, 2011). These include failures of risk assessment/management, communication, liaison with external agencies, staff support/supervision and care planning. Recommendations for the future prevention of homicides included focusing on transition from in-patient to community, aligning the Care Programme Approach with risk and responding when a care plan breaks down (e.g. by assertive contact) (NCIS, 2006). Whilst learning from inquiries provides a helpful foundation for best practice, there have been calls to demystify the risk management process (Eastman, 1996). A recent best practice guide, although immensely helpful, may not be sufficient to implement a transparent and replicable process (Department of Health, 2007).

This chapter focuses on management of personality disordered offenders in the community in light of a new personality disorder pathways strategy (Department of Health, 2011). The strategy is clear in outlining the dual responsibility of probation and mental health in managing risk and psychologists in particular will need to be well versed in risk management approaches as they will be called upon to provide on-the-spot consultation. Core objectives include early identification of personality disordered offenders, formulations to inform treatment and intervention pathways, facilitating entry into and completion of programmes, providing evidence of improvement, planning safe return to the community and ultimately reducing risk of serious offending. A pilot project informed the service specification for this strategy, consisting of a psychological consultation model to probation to identify personality disordered offenders, consult via case discussions, formulate and co-work complex cases (Minoudis et al., 2012). It is expected there will be a significant increase in this work as the strategy is rolled out nationally.

The aim of this chapter is to illustrate aspects of best practice in risk management for high harm personality disordered offenders (for male offenders, the strategy defines high harm as sexual or violent offending) in the context of the pathways strategy, outlining a step-by-step approach to increase transparency and confidence for working with this group, whilst ensuring throughout that one is making good decisions about risk (see Table 12.1). Case studies drawn from experiences of piloting the community pathways specification are used to elaborate implementation. The core principles underpinning best practice in risk management are cited as a summary of all identified risks. A formulation is then made of likely risk situations and action plans for practitioners and service users at times of increased risk (Department of Health, 2007). The fundamental ethos of positive risk management is based on a human rights principle of the least restrictions necessary to minimise or prevent harm (Ward & Stewart, 2003) – that people have the right to live their lives to the full as long as they do not stop others from doing the same (Department of Health, 2007).The goal is to achieve sustainable results in a humane manner whilst avoiding risk aversive practice driven by anxiety, short-term gains and poor understanding of risk. Whilst there may be a temptation to affix procedure as a defence against anxieties of making mistakes, there is justification in outlining a systematic approach based on encouraging involvement with this group. A framework should allow enough flexibility for creative thinking with the aim of making it less intimidating to manage high risk of harm personality disordered offenders in the community

The chapter begins by briefly introducing a model for risk management. This model guides subsequent sections ordered as they would occur in practice, beginning with assessment and formulation, developing a crisis management plan and elaborating five components of risk management in turn. This should not be considered an exhaustive overview of risk management approaches, which are described more fully in Chapter 9. Risk of harm to self and risk related to mentally ill offenders is not within the scope of this chapter.

TABLE 12.1 Criteria for good decision-making about risk

1   Does the decision conform with guidelines?
2   Is it based on the best available information?
3   Has the decision been documented?
4   Have the relevant people been informed?
5   Does the severity, imminence and likelihood of risk necessitate action?

Source: Department of Health (2007); Hart & Logan (2011).

Model for risk management (including legislative arrangements and multi-agency involvement)

Figure 12.1 illustrates key stages to consider in a suggested order – however, it should be noted risk management is a dynamic process and new information, developments or arrangements may occur at any point, requiring a reassessment of related stages. Legislative arrangements occur following contact with the criminal justice system and to some extent dictate the parameters of risk management in terms of the powers available to health and criminal justice services. A summary of relevant legislation is reviewed in detail elsewhere (e.g. Dowsett & Craissati, 2008). The key agencies responsible for the case and ancillary agencies involved in risk management should be noted early on, for pre-emptive planning of who should be informed about crises and what level of information is likely to be shared. Organisations include the police, court, prison, probation, mental health, social services, child protection, substance misuse, education/employment and housing.

It is important to explore the approaches taken to assessment and formulation of personality disordered offenders as these directly inform the recommendations for the risk management plan. Whilst there may be no single approach, there are accepted methods that guide best practice and interesting recent developments in formulation for personality disordered offenders are discussed. Collaboration and

FIGURE 12.1 Risk management model

information sharing occur in different degrees of formality depending on the risk level, relationships between agencies and their individual roles. Decisions about information sharing can be complex and examples are discussed below. The crisis and risk management approaches outlined are amalgamated from prominent approaches and result in five areas which are discussed individually (Department of Health, 2007; Hart & Logan, 2011; Dowsett & Craissati, 2008).

Assessment and formulation

It is generally accepted that one must draw on a range of clinical and psychometric methods in the assessment of a personality disordered offender. Risk assessment should be representative of professional opinion and steer clear of unstructured clinical judgements (Dowsett & Craissati, 2008). Pure actuarial approaches focusing only on statistical factors associated with increased risk, while aiding risk prediction, provide little practical assistance with prevention (Hart & Logan, 2011). Structured clinical judgement is the preferred approach, including an assessment of relevant factors supported by research, clinical knowledge, experience of the offender and the individual's own view of their experience. In this process, psychometric tools should be an aid to clinical decision-making and not over-relied upon as a substitute for it (Department of Health, 2007). A full assessment should include a clinical interview and psychometric tools aiding assessment of personality and risk. This often complex array of diverse information is linked together via a formulation.

Clinical interview

Beyond the standard approach to a clinical interview, the assessor should have a sound understanding of the development of personality disorder, to be able to focus questioning on key areas. Single theory approaches have given way to a biopsychosocial view, incorporating the importance of gene–environment interactions. Several clear accounts can be found in the literature (e.g. Paris, 1998; Craissati et al., 2011; Bateman & Fonagy, 2007). In summary, it is a developmental disorder, beginning in infancy and developing through adolescence, where personality is shaped by innate temperament reacting to parental style, cultural influences, social environment, intelligence and adverse events (e.g. trauma). Infants vary in temperament in terms of activity, sociability and emotional reactivity. These are considered 'constitutionally based individual differences, influenced over time by heredity, maturation and experience' (Rothbart & Ahadi, 1994).

The temperament of the child interacts with caregivers' capacity for parenting to influence personality development. In psychopathy, for example, a temperament of high impulsivity and high behavioural activation interacts with parental capacity to limit behaviour and supervise. Attachment to the primary caregiver affects the development of a reflective function and disturbances in attachment increase vulnerability to recover from later adverse experiences. Social factors are thought to increase risk or buffer against individual vulnerability, altering the threshold at which other risks influence the development of personality disorder. For example, poverty is not related to persistent crime when families are functioning well (Paris, 1996). Adolescence offers opportunities to select one's environment and becomes a key stage where belief systems about self, others and the world are consolidated. In cases of personality disorder, maladaptive patterns of relating to others repeat and become fixed. Individuals with personality disorder struggle to adapt these patterns due to consistent difficulties with the accurate interpretation of the thoughts, feelings and intentions of others, leading to relationships activating intense emotional states which are difficult to self-regulate (Bateman & Fonagy, 2007).

Incorporating an understanding of personality disorder and violence partly as the result of environmental failures in the socialisation process ameliorates the tendency to focus exclusively on trauma and aversive experiences. Fonagy (2004) stated this simply by noting the importance of understanding the natural propensity for violence – that it is unlearned rather than learned. From the point of view of assessment, it is important therefore to include early experiences that restrict opportunities for socialisation, such as poor supervision and limit setting, alongside traumatic exposure to violence and other abuses. Key areas to assess in personality disordered offenders include attachment experience, family relationships, romantic relationships and psychosexual history, drug and alcohol history, mental health history, offending history, educational and occupational history, progress on custodial and community sentences and a review of completed interventions. There can often be a mass of information on complex personality disordered offenders and knowledge of epidemiological research and empirically supported factors associated with an antisocial trajectory can assist with selecting the more relevant factors for inclusion in the formulation. Key findings from prospective longitudinal studies, such as early onset versus late onset offenders (Moffitt, 1993) and summary explanations of offending (Farrington, 1991) provide simple frameworks for identifying salient information. The personality disorder strategy prioritises identification of personality disorder early in an offender's sentence. This sometimes demands a brief assessment of the case, which is assisted by reference to research evidence to support decisions. An example of case identification is outlined in Vignette 1.

VIGNETTE 1: CASE IDENTIFICATION

As part of the community pathways project, psychologists work into probation screening large caseloads of offenders for personality disorder. With 50–60 offenders per caseload and approximately 2,000 cases per local delivery unit, cases can be hard to distinguish from one another. At least 50 per cent are likely to meet criteria for personality disorder (Shaw et al., 2012) and of those it can be hard to identify which might be persistently problematic and deserving of more attention. This is particularly challenging with gang-related crime, where social influences and individual vulnerability are not easily differentiated.

Whilst screening a probation officer's caseload, two co-defendants were discussed. The offence occurred during a Saturday night, when a group of youths in their late teens were kicked out of a party for becoming rowdy after getting into a dispute with a rival group over a girl. The former continued to drink and consume drugs in a park, returning to the party in the early hours of Sunday morning, as the last revellers were leaving. One of the rival group was singled out and, following a short chase, was stabbed several times, including wounds to the face and genitals. Both the co-defendants were convicted of manslaughter, but it was not clear who had stabbed the victim.

In a discussion about the two perpetrators, case A had a history of minor offending from 10 years old, including shoplifting, burglary and street robberies. There was a suggestion of domestic violence in the home and repeated truancy from school had culminated in permanent exclusion. Case B had left school at 15 years old without qualifications, lived at home with his mother, step-father and academic sister, who was applying for university. He had one previous offence for possession of cannabis. The probation officer intuitively suspected case A of committing the stabbing, however felt she was judging him speculatively and thought for either case the offence presented a marked escalation in seriousness.

Drawing on key findings from research, the psychologist focused on which offender was more likely to persist with criminal behaviour rather than speculating who may have committed the stabbing. Salient information included age at onset of offending from 10–12 years old (Moffitt, 1993) and risk domains spanning family, school and community in the absence of obvious promotive factors (Stouthamer-Loeber et al., 2002). Case A was screened in for possible personality disorder and a more intensive therapeutic intervention at a prison-based democratic therapeutic community was added to his sentence plan.

Personality disorder assessment tools

Assessment tools available for assisting with personality disorder diagnoses range from self-report questionnaires, informant report, checklists and structured interviews. Tyrer et al. (2007) outline developments in assessment methods and Dowsett and Craissati (2008) provide a detailed account of the available tools. In practice, which you select may depend on the nature of the assessment. Where diagnosis is less contentious and there is adequate and reliable collateral information reporting on behaviours across the lifespan – as can sometimes be the case with antisocial personality disorder – a supplementary self-report personality disorder questionnaire (e.g. Millon et al., 1994; Morey, 1991) alongside a clinical interview and collateral information should be sufficient. At the other end of the scale, where the pathology is less overt (e.g. Cluster A diagnoses), collateral information is patchy, and access to a specialist personality disorder service hinges on a diagnosis, a more in-depth personality disorder assessment tool, such as the Structured Clinical

Interview for DSM-IV (SCID-II) (Spitzer et al., 1987) or International Personality Disorder Examination (IPDE) (Loranger et al., 1987) may be warranted.

Identifying psychopathy is of particular importance in forensic settings, given the association between high scores on the psychopathy checklist-revised (PCL-R) (Hare, 1991) and serious harm offending. The psychopathy checklist remains the tool of choice and at a minimum the screening version should be used in a comprehensive assessment of personality disorder and risk. Prevalence of personality disorders in prison suggest higher rates of antisocial personality disorder, followed by paranoid and borderline personality disorders (Singleton et al., 1998). In practice, any of the personality disorders may be encountered. Assessment and diagnosis of personality disorder is a contentious and much disputed issue and this section does not attempt to broach several unresolved areas of inquiry, such as dimensional approaches, severity and functions of personality.

Risk assessment tools

There is a temptation to be over-reliant on risk assessment tools for high harm offenders, perhaps in an unconscious attempt to distance oneself from the decision-making process so looking to the risk assessment tool to make the decision instead. An understanding of the purpose, limitations and range of risk assessments available for the desired population is necessary. Dowsett and Craissati (2008) provide a good overview of the essential areas to consider. The primary purpose of static risk assessment is to predict the likelihood of reoffending, often assigning offenders to a categorical risk banding. Some authors would claim risk prediction adds little to the risk management process as it can make no proposals for addressing changeable areas (Hart & Logan, 2011). However, according to the risk–needs–responsivity model, assigning a risk level is useful in determining the level of resource allocation. Indeed, a statistically low recidivism risk for a low harm offence is a sound basis on which to make a risk management recommendation for not allocating to treatment, which itself may have a low level of effectiveness. Static risk can also be a simple method of communicating risk levels to other professionals, which can assist in disentangling risk from challenging interpersonal styles (see Vignette 3). Assessment of dynamic risk is primarily to aid prevention and provides the main tools for informing risk management approaches by identifying the key areas to focus on.

Commonly used static risk assessment tools for high harm personality disordered sexual offenders include the Static 99/02 (Hanson & Thornton, 1999) and Risk Matrix 2000 (Thornton et al., 2003) and for dynamic risk the Stable and Acute 2007 (Hanson & Harris, 2000). The HCR-20 (Webster et al., 1997), VRS (Wong & Gordon, 2000) and PCL-R (Hare, 1991) are the most commonly used risk assessments for violence. The tests alone cannot inform how the risk factors influence the person and interact to increase risk. In essence, they are a guide to ensure consideration of known areas related to risk. A crucial element in the use of these tests lies in their incorporation into a formulation, where their influence in terms of sequential order and function to predispose, trigger or maintain risk is elaborated.

Refining assessment information

Offender typologies provide an additional method of refining assessment information, by offering frameworks that select, link and sequence risk factors. Typologies
subdivide offenders variously according to offence, background characteristics,
motivation and victim type. These assist in developing hypotheses for an explanation
of offences and help to focus on the most salient risk factors common to subgroups
of offenders. References for leading typologies include sex offending (Knight &
Prentky, 1990; Ward, 2002), stalking (e.g. Meloy, 2001; Mullen et al., 2000),
domestic violence (Hamberger & Hastings, 1990; Hilton & Harris, 2005), fire-
setting (Quinsey et al., 1998) and general violence (Cornell et al., 1996; Howard,
2011). Familiarity with these models aids understanding and increases confidence
that explanations of the offending are based on the best available evidence, one of
the elements of confident risk decision-making (see Table 12.1).

Prominent research findings offer an additional method of refining assessment
information. These include: epidemiological evidence (e.g. Moffitt, 1993; Farrington, 1991), the 'big four' criminogenic factors (Andrews & Bonta, 2003), gradations
of antisociality (Stone, 2000), domestic violence lethality factors (Browne &
Williams, 1989) and common risk factors for violence (Department of Health, 2007,
appendix). They provide a quick reference point to inform understanding and prove
a practical aid in consultations with other professionals.

Formulation

Formulation adds substantially to the management of complex personality disordered
offenders; providing ideas for alternative interventions where programmes have
failed, incorporating risk alongside personality to reduce disengagement, helping
to prioritise and sequence interventions to enhance effectiveness, clarifying
understanding to reduce the likelihood of overly-restrictive risk management and,
when multiple agencies are involved, providing a consensus on how to proceed
(Hart et al., 2011). Recent attempts to evaluate formulation offer guidelines against
which one can evaluate adequacy (e.g. Sturmey & McMurran, 2011; Hart et al.,
2011). These include (amongst others) a narrative structure, incorporating critical
evidence, consistency with accepted theory, spanning the past, present and future,
generating new understanding, and leading to actions.

In practice, an approach to formulation requires the flexibility to be both
evidence-based and pragmatic – sometimes conflicting purposes. Hart and Logan
(2011) distinguish orthodox and latitudinal approaches to formulation, the latter
accepting that the incomplete evidence base requires inference/intuitive reasoning
to reach the best explanation of complex behaviour. It is certainly the case when
mental health work alongside probation managing high volumes of personality
disordered offenders that the foundation of information is often incomplete,
making a strictly orthodox approach impractical and necessitating inference to the
best explanation based on the available evidence. A framework for formulation is

systematic in guiding the selection, ordering and linking of assessment information (e.g. BPS, 2011). This should be sufficiently flexible to account for variation in the breadth of available information, whilst ensuring adherence to accepted psychological theory. Common frameworks used in mental health include the 'five Ps' (Weerasekera, 1996) and Hart's HCR-20 method of risk formulation (Hart & Logan, 2011). The research findings and typologies mentioned above increase the validity of formulations for forensic personality disordered populations – methods that at the same time help to simplify and re-complexify the data (Hart et al., 2011).

The high harm personality disorder strategy stipulates formulation-led management and a clinically justifiable link between personality disorder and risk (Department of Health, 2011). A formulation must broach this issue in attempting to provide an explanation of the offence. Dowsett and Craissati (2008, p. 38) have suggested motivation as the link between personality disorder and offending. This is on the basis that any sexual or violent offence is interpersonal in nature and has meaning to the individual in terms of how they relate to others. A mentalization-based approach considers motivation in terms of the task of appraising the thoughts, feelings and intentions of others in deciding to act – a process that is disrupted in personality disorder (Bateman & Fonagy, 2007). Motivation is proximal to the offence and acts as a driver for the behaviour, meaning it is instrumentally related to risk. However, motivation should not be considered as the exclusive link; using the five Ps model of formulation, one should also consider personality functioning in terms of how it contributes predisposing (e.g. early maladjustment), precipitating (e.g. relationship breakdown, or substance misuse) and perpetuating factors (e.g. avoidance as a coping strategy for emotional distress, or anti-authority attitudes preventing engagement with services).

VIGNETTE 2: FORMULATION DURING A TEAM CASE CONSULTATION IN PROBATION

During a probation service team meeting, a case was presented of a man in his late twenties, previously of good character and with no history of offending, who had grabbed a woman in the street in the early evening, dragged her into an alleyway and raped her. He was described as 'callous and audacious' for asking for her telephone number afterwards and whether she had any money for food. The probation officer managing the case was uncertain how to explain the rape given the lack of a history of offending and the unusual behaviour after the rape. A pre-sentence report was due in a week, in which she was required to write a plausible offence analysis. The team looked to the psychologist facilitating the case discussion, as if to ask, 'Why did he do it?'

During the discussion, further information about the background of the perpetrator came to light. He came from a high functioning family – his siblings all had successful careers in respected professions and there were no obvious problems in the family, such as criminality, abuse in the home or alcoholism. His relationships with his parents were not particularly remarkable. He had described his mother in glowing terms, saying she was the most caring person you could hope to know. He fearfully respected his father, whom he described as critical and with high standards. Prior to the offence, the perpetrator had inexplicably dropped out of his undergraduate degree during the final year and complained his 'true love' had cheated on him. He was described by his probation officer as 'perfectly charming', with good manners and a 'healthy disregard' for the other offenders he was 'forced' to associate with in prison.

In formulating the case, the psychologist drew on typologies of sex offenders to hypothesise about the motivation for the rape. The lack of a clear abuse history and no previous offending made the most common antisocial rape subtype unlikely. The academic failure (in contrast to his siblings) and romantic relationship difficulties were suggested as precipitants to the offence, perhaps serving as a significant challenge to his otherwise high self-regard, inducing shame. The combination of potentially having been treated as special by one parent and criticised by another, the hint of exclusivity in his relationship with his mother, his smooth presentation and sense of superiority supported a hypothesis of narcissistic traits. The seemingly oblivious comprehension of the impact of the rape and apparent desire to form a relationship with the victim fitted with a narcissistic linking fantasy (Kernberg, 1984) where, to the perpetrator, the victim only exists as an extension of his 'love' fantasy. The motivation for the rape was therefore suggested to be a shame-induced rage reaction, associated with a brittle narcissistic personality structure, the latter having collapsed following significant personal failures.

Risk management: information sharing and crisis management plan

There are different but overlapping approaches to risk management. The best practice guidance (Department of Health, 2007) states a plan should include what to do when warning signs emerge, listing examples of 'general aspects of management' such as monitoring, interventions, appropriate placements and employment needs. Hart and Logan (2011) identify strategies for violence risk management relating to monitoring, supervision, treatment and victim safety planning. Dowsett and Craissati (2008) make a distinction between risk assessment, information sharing and risk management. They suggest the latter be considered along a continuum of internal, relational and external controls, depending on the capacity and motivation for the individual to exercise self-control over behaviour. This leads to a risk management approach specific to personality disordered offenders consisting of attachment, behavioural controls and environmental management.

Combining these approaches, a management plan would prepare a stance on information sharing, including which agencies should be informed and the amount of information to be shared – incorporating plans on managing the anxieties these individuals evoke in other agencies. The plan should anticipate what to do when monitoring and supervision identifies a change in risk, ranging from no action to invoking a predetermined crisis management plan. Specific strategies can be considered in five domains: restrictions, treatment, environmental planning, victim safety planning and interpersonal strategies (see Figure 12.1). These are discussed in turn in the next section, with case examples to illustrate implementation.

Information sharing

Key clinical messages summarised from a review of independent investigations after homicides committed by mental health patients included sharing information about risk between all individuals, professionals and agencies involved (NCIS, 2010). The main services include police, probation, mental health and social services. They may also include court, prison, child protection, substance misuse, education/employment and housing. Past tragedies have cited the complex nature of personality disorder demanding cooperation between services to address multiple needs which cannot be met by one service alone (NHS South East Coast, 2006). Fragmentation is central to personality disturbance and splitting can be moderated by integrating services' approaches via effective communication. Expressions of distressing material, communications suggesting an elevation in risk and strong countertransference feelings evoke anxieties in agencies. These can be managed by sharing experiences and understanding via inter-agency communication. The purpose of sharing information should be carefully considered before deciding what information to disclose. Anticipating the response of both the agency and the offender and the likely impact on risk should be considered. Static risk measures can sometimes be useful in the information-sharing process, helping to differentiate a challenging personality presentation from the risk level, as discussed in Vignette 3.

VIGNETTE 3: SHARING CLIENT INFORMATION AT A MULTI-AGENCY PUBLIC PROTECTION PANEL (MAPPP) MEETING

At a MAPPP meeting, a middle-aged offender assessed at level 2 was discussed. He had been convicted of possession of indecent images of children at his place of work, where several members of staff had access to the same computer. He did not have a prolific offending history, having been convicted only once before, several years ago, for common assault. At interview, he was guarded and often requested to see information which referred to him. He could occasionally become hostile if he perceived he was being threatened or unduly controlled. He had systematically written formal complaints about police and probation officers who had alternately supervised him from the same office.

The MAPPP discussion focused on his presentation and interpersonal style. There was a consensus of opinion that this man was dislikeable and antagonistic. This led to assumptions about his lack of remorse and victim empathy, which in turn seemed to justify an agreement on his high risk of reoffending and the imposition of stringent monitoring, including un-announced home visits and child protection measures relating to contact with his teenage children.

The psychologist, referring to her formulation, quoted his static risk as low. The majority of offenders in this risk banding did not reoffend or escalate to contact offences. There was no clear link between personality disorder and the motivation to offend, however there were strong paranoid traits which acted as a maintaining factor for his difficulties, preventing collaboration with professionals and leading to hostile and antagonistic exchanges which hampered progression through his community order. The psychologist communicated his risk level and took time to distinguish his interpersonal style as a responsivity issue rather than a risk factor related to reoffending. The offender was subsequently managed at level 1 and monitoring was relaxed, while the professional approach focused on transparent engagement to minimise his tendency for antagonism and complaints.

Crisis management plan

A crisis management plan, linked to possible future scenarios anticipated from the risk formulation, should be prepared at an early stage of the risk assessment process. This should include the key risk factors to monitor, what likely changes could occur, and the response options available. A list of which agencies are involved, with contact details, increases the speed of response and likelihood of contact during a crisis. The criteria for good decision–making (Table 12.1) help to determine whether a change in risk requires action. Two examples in vignettes 4 and 5 provide alternative experiences.

VIGNETTE 4: A CHANGE IN RISK REQUIRING NO FURTHER ACTION

A 30-year-old male offender with co-morbid borderline and antisocial traits was being seen in a forensic psychological outpatient service for assessment, having been referred by probation following a recent conviction for a public disorder offence. During a discussion about his flatmate, he stated he wanted to 'chop her head off with an axe and watch the blood spurt like a fountain'. This exclamation had followed a comment his flatmate had supposedly made about his treatment of a casual girlfriend, who had recently distanced herself from him after he had verbally abused her in front of her friends.

The psychologist discussed the session with her supervisor the same day. Dramatic expressions of affect were a hallmark of the individual's formulation and the function of the exclamation was understood as a projection of shame feelings, evoked by the humiliating reminder of having acted cruelly to his girlfriend. The severity and imminence of acting on his exclamation were realistic factors, given the content of the stated intention and the opportunity afforded by living with the flatmate. Although the offender had a previous violent history of armed robbery, likelihood was assessed as low as there was no history of ruminative vengeful violence or excessive use of sadistic violence. The key risk factors to monitor via the crisis plan included a relapse into substance misuse, loss of employment and fear of reprisal attacks. None of these risk factors was elevated. Relevant people who could be informed included the flatmate as a potential victim and the probation officer. The likely exacerbating effect of informing the flatmate and the likely response of probation to what might be interpreted as a serious threat of violence was not considered a reasonable method of reducing the risk of what already seemed a slim possibility of acting on the fantasy. The discussion and evaluation was recorded in the notes and no further action was taken.

VIGNETTE 5: A CHANGE IN RISK REQUIRING ACTION

An offender, well known to services, had been managed in the community successfully for some years, and was seen jointly by probation and health in monthly supervision and outpatient appointments, respectively. The individual was assessed as very high risk of harm, with several convictions for actual bodily harm (ABH) and grievous bodily harm (GBH) on file, including attempted murder by strangulation. These offences were mostly related to serious physical assault of long-term ex-partners and partners he had met for casual sex. He was previously managed at MAPPA level 3, one of the critical few, and had been assessed by mental health on numerous occasions, meeting criteria for several personality disorders, including narcissistic, paranoid, borderline, antisocial disorders and psychopathy.

He was a regular attendee of appointments, however over the past two months had missed two without contacting services, was over half an hour late for two other appointments and on presentation was noted to be tearful and suspicious of his new partner's fidelity. He had become more hostile during sessions and his appearance was notably more dishevelled, with an unshaven face, bleary eyes and a whiff of alcohol on his breath at an 11am meeting. At this meeting, he claimed to have locked his partner in their flat, not trusting she would go shopping without attempting to contact her male cousin.

The psychologist, in discussion with her supervisor, evaluated the risk in accordance with the crisis management plan. Key risk factors were raised, including deterioration in a romantic relationship, a suspected increase in use of alcohol and an increase in paranoid thinking related directly to the most common victim group. Potential for violence was rated as imminent, severe and moderately likely. The crisis management plan indicated those who should be informed following a significant increase in risk of violence, initially probation, who would decide whether to recall and/or discuss with police. The potential impact of informing others was considered. The therapeutic alliance had been hard won, however reliance on the offender to take responsibility for reducing risk via a discussion with the therapist seemed unlikely to be effective. On this occasion, the decision to breach confidentiality based on imminent danger to another seemed reasonable. Probation was informed and the offender was recalled to prison.

Risk management plan

Restrictions

For a comprehensive account of restrictions and legislative measures applicable to personality disordered offenders, see Dowsett and Craissati (2008, ch. 5). With the introduction of the offender personality disorder strategy (Department of Health, 2011) and the increase in collaborative risk management between mental health and probation, psychologists consulting to probation should be aware of the available restrictions. A full list of probation community controls can be obtained from the National Offender Management Service (NOMS) (document reference PI 20/2012; see Table 12.2). A psychological view should consider the likely impact of external controls on both short- and long-term risk and the likely response of the offender to the controls – anticipated in line with the formulation. Overly restrictive external controls preventing adequate exposure to situational risk inhibit opportunities for progress and can in the long-term be counterproductive (Department of Health, 2007). Equally, too much emphasis on rehabilitation over public protection has been a criticism in previous inquiries into homicides (NHS South East Coast, 2006). Decisions to impose controls should be taken in consideration of the capacity and motivation for self-management, the impact on responsivity and short- and long-term risk.

TABLE 12.2 An abbreviated list of standard and additional Probation licence conditions

---

- Attendance at supervision
- Travel restrictions
- Approved residence
- Approved work
- Good behaviour condition (incorporating offending and behaviours which might leading to offending)
- Restrictions of activities
- A requirement to maintain contact with specific persons or refrain from contact
- A requirement to engage in a specific activity, obeying curfews, and restrictions on movement

---

Treatment

Treatment aims to enhance the individual's capacity for change in areas related to clinical need, risk, pro-social competencies (e.g. thinking skills, social skills) and protective factors (e.g. education and vocational skills). Treatment for personality disordered offenders is discussed more fully in Chapter 6 in this volume. From the point of view of risk management, the decision to recommend interventions that enhance internal controls should be evaluated against the likely gain from individual work relative to the availability of resources. To what extent will lengthy motivational work with a narcissistic offender, in the hope he will eventually embark on a therapy with limited effectiveness, materially decrease risk in the short and long term? However, a markedly anxious and under-assertive individual, whose offending is directly related to these deficits and is motivated to change distressing aspects of himself, may be considered a more optimistic candidate for treatment. This should not be viewed as therapeutic nihilism, but an allocation of limited resources according to a reasonable evaluation of the likely therapeutic gain.

Environmental planning

Social theories of crime and desistance advocate adapting the environment to reduce the likelihood of triggering problematic traits which initiate challenging behaviour. Several authors have advocated an environmental planning approach to risk management with personality disordered offenders (e.g. Farrall, 2004; Tyrer et al., 2003; Dowsett & Craissati, 2008). These might include aiming to reduce the impact of negative social influences by selective geographical placement, for example by placing an individual away from an antisocial peer group or rejecting a potential hostel known for its easy access to street drugs. Some individuals with significant personality problems have lived for years without offending and decompensate only when their environment has altered. The aim is to anticipate the individual's likely response to the environment in which he is placed, based on the formulation's hypotheses about previous patterns of behaviour. Areas of environmental planning include accommodation, geographical location, proximity to positive and negative social influences, potential access to victims, mentoring schemes to promote social integration and availability of opportunities for meaningful activities (leisure, educational and occupational). A case example involving environmental planning is provided in Vignette 6.

VIGNETTE 6: ENVIRONMENTAL PLANNING

A 50-year-old male offender was being released to the community after having served a two-year prison term for threats to kill. This was his first conviction; however his offence had caused considerable anxiety when he entered a housing office with a mock bomb strapped to his body, threatening to explode it if they did not arrange alternative accommodation immediately. Prior to this, he had lived alone for 30 years, working nights as a security guard for a local building firm. He had lost his job after the company went bust and had not been able to maintain the payments on his flat, resulting in eviction letters which directly preceded the offence.

The formulation suggested he had marked schizoid traits which made unpredictable social interactions highly aversive. He became overwhelmed at the thought of having to deal with multiple agencies and negotiate various levels of bureaucracy to organise benefits, housing and other associated tasks. He was assigned one point of contact in his probation officer, who liaised with other services on his behalf. Stabilising his environment was prioritised above therapeutic endeavours to enhance capacity for social interaction and self-manage anxiety. Housing and benefits were pre-planned before release and he was managed in the community with fortnightly home visits at prearranged times. These were focused on structured discussions about social needs; after four months, they were reduced to monthly visits.

Victim safety planning

A review into homicides by mental health patients named inadequate consideration of risk to victims as a failing of risk management plans (NCIS, 2010). The authors drew attention to risk of spousal assault and safeguarding children in cases where there was a known history of domestic violence. Hart and Logan (2011) include victim safety planning as a core aspect of forensic case management. Statutory duties falling to hospital managers, responsible clinicians and probation services include considering victim representations when deciding the restrictions of community treatment orders and providing information to victims, for example about sentence details or discharge (Department of Health, 2008). Potential victim groups should be identified as part of the risk assessment and steps to minimise harm should be considered in the management plan. The probation victim liaison unit may be able to provide advice and occasionally direct work with victims of certain sexual and violent offenders (London Probation Trust, 2010). Careful evaluation of risks and benefits should precede decisions about disclosing information to potential victims, ideally with the prior knowledge of the offender. Dowsett and Craissati (2008) relate the following *key principles that guide the duty to warn potential victims*, informed by a pivotal American case:

1   Exercising the care and skill of a reasonable professional in identifying those patients who pose a significant risk of physical harm to third parties.
2   Exercising reasonable professional care in protecting third parties from those patients identified as 'dangerous'.
3   Noting and evaluating the intensity and focus of the subject's hostility.
4   Noting threats that have been made and their seriousness and any violent past action.
5   If necessary, obtaining another concurring professional opinion.

The best practice guidance suggests that if a potential victim, who is not a service user, is at risk, the police public protection team or the MAPPP must be consulted for a plan to be activated (Department of Health, 2007). Any disclosure without consent must be clearly documented. A positive risk management approach would seek to enable the offender to make disclosures personally, where it is safe to do so. Service users can increase awareness of their risk, learn how others perceive them and enhance personal responsibility in managing their risk to others by being involved in disclosures to potential victims. Care needs must be balanced against risk needs and when risks are taken this should be based on careful evaluation of the potential harm and benefits (Department of Health, 2007). Where possible, one should incorporate an advance directive into a crisis management plan to agree with the offender how to address the issue of disclosure before future risks occur. An example of disclosure to a potential victim is discussed in Vignette 7.

VIGNETTE 7: DISCLOSURE TO A POTENTIAL VICTIM

At a MAPPP level 2 meeting, an offender who had recently returned to the community after a custodial sentence for rape of an adult female was discussed. The victim was an ex-partner and the offence occurred during an argument in which she informed him she was ending their relationship. The offender had disclosed to his probation officer that he had begun a new relationship with a woman and they had been on two dates together. She was currently away with her parents, but was due to return the following week.

A discussion ensued about the potential harm and benefits of disclosing the offence history to the new girlfriend. The psychologist present had no previous knowledge of the case and remained silent. The Detective Chief Inspector (DCI) chairing the meeting was strongly in favour of disclosing without informing the offender, based on the fact he could have contact with her without professionals knowing. This led to a discussion about how to reach the potential victim before she returned home from her parents and avoid any further unsupervised contact with the offender. There was no discussion to evaluate the risk in terms of severity, imminence or likelihood. In retrospect, severity and likelihood were significant as he was a repeat offender with a history of rape. However, a working formulation that the index offence was triggered by rejection, suggested there was no clear evidence of imminent risk. Given the offender had wilfully disclosed a developing personal relationship, the decision to contact the girlfriend without informing the offender risked disrupting the working relationship and reducing the likelihood of later disclosures, potentially heightening long-term risk. The decision was poorly evaluated resulting in risk-aversive practice.

Interpersonal strategies

Listwan et al. (2007) stress the importance of including personality-related responsivity issues when assessing risk. Higher dropout rates from programmes (Craissati & Beech, 2001) and negative attitudes to authority provide additional reasons to focus on engagement with personality disordered offenders. A consensus opinion on engagement strategies assists with multi-agency work, both to manage anxieties and reduce splitting. One approach to engagement seeks to minimise activation of problematic traits to reduce the chance of oppositional interactions and enhance collaboration. This is different to some treatment approaches which attempt to effect change by activating and challenging problematic traits.

Craissati et al. (2011, appendices) suggest approaches to working with different presentations. The basic premise is informed by a cognitive-behavioural understanding of core interpersonal strategies and adopting a stance that counters the vulnerability. For example for a paranoid personality presentation with a hostile and suspicious interpersonal style, a transparent stance would reduce opportunities for sinister interpretations and lessen hostility. A narcissistic personality's grandiose and superior interpersonal style would be understood as a means of managing anxiety about inferiority and, rather than challenge lofty statements, the stance might be to identify genuine examples of competence and focus on realistic goals. Making recommendations about interpersonal strategies by explicitly describing an approach can improve consistency amongst agencies, enhance collaborative risk management and ultimately reduce risk.

Summary

Mandatory inquiries into homicides have done little to ameliorate anxieties of managing high harm personality disordered offenders in the community. Reports from these tragedies have identified typical shortcomings of risk management and help to focus on areas for improvement. This chapter outlines a positive approach to risk management to build on learning from past failures and combine prominent approaches to increase confidence and assuage anxieties of working with this group. The approach is strongly influenced by a recent focus on joint probation and mental health management of personality disordered offenders, driven by the high harm strategy (Department of Health, 2011). A chief feature of this strategy is to focus resources on the most worrisome cases. The model is elaborated systematically throughout with the intention of demystifying the process. Case studies are used to illustrate ways of applying the model and to highlight examples of typical dilemmas encountered during experiences of piloting the London pathways project (Minoudis et al., 2012). A dynamic and sequential approach to risk management is advocated, involving consideration of the active legislative measures, multi-agency involvement, risk assessment and formulation, leading to a five-point risk management plan, sufficient for defensible practice with this highly anxiety-provoking population.

References

Andrews, D.A. & Bonta, J. (2003) *The Psychology of Criminal Conduct* (3rd edn). Cincinnati, OH: Anderson Publishing.

Bateman, A. & Fonagy, P. (2007) *Mentalization-based Treatment for Borderline Personality Disorder: A Practical Guide*. Oxford: Oxford University Press.

British Psychological Society (BPS) (2011) *Good Practice Guidelines on the Use of Formulation*. Leicester: BPS Division of Clinical Psychology.

Browne, A. & Williams, K.R. (1989) Exploring the effect of resource availability and the likelihood of female-perpetrated homicides. *Law & Society Review*, 23, 75–94.

Cornell, D., Warren, J., Hawk, G., Stafford, E., Oram, G. & Pine, D. (1996) Psychopathy in instrumental and reactive offenders. *Journal of Consulting and Clinical Psychology*, 64, 783–90.

Craissati, J. & Beech, A. (2001) Attrition in a community treatment programme for child sexual abusers. *Journal of Interpersonal Violence*, 16, 205–21.

Craissati, J., Minoudis, P., Shaw, J., Chuan, S.J., Simons, S. & Joseph, N. (2011) *Working with Personality Disordered Offenders: A Practitioner's Guide* [online]. Ministry of Justice publications. http://www.justice.gov.uk/downloads/offenders/mentally-disordered-offenders/working-with-personality-disordered-offenders.pdf.

Crichton, J.H.M. (2011) A review of published independent inquiries in England into psychiatric patient homicide, 1995–2010. *Journal of Forensic Psychiatry & Psychology*, 22(6), 761–89.

Department of Health (2007) *Best Practice in Managing Risk*. National Risk Management Programme. www.dh.gov.uk/publications http://webarchive.nationalarchives.gov.uk/20130107105354/ http://dh.gov.uk/prod_consum_dh/groups/dh_digitalassets/@dh/@en/@ps/documents/digitalasset/dh_133492.pdf (Accessed January 2013).

Department of Health (2008) *Mental Health Act 2007: Guidance on the Extension of Victim's Rights under the Domestic Violence, Crime and Victims Act 2004* [online]. http://www.plymouthcommunityhealthcare.co.uk/images/uploads/content/Policies/M/MAPPA_Appendix_J.pdf (Accessed January 2013).

Department of Health (2011) *Consultation on the Offender Personality Disorder Pathway Implementation Plan* [online]. Department of Health Publications. www.parliament.uk/deposits/depositedpapers/2011/DEP2011–0319.pdf (Accessed 21 July 2011).

Dowsett, J. & Craissati, J. (2008) *Managing Personality Disordered Offenders in the Community: A Psychological Approach*. London: Routledge.

Eastman, N. (1996) Inquiry into homicide by psychiatric patients: systematic audit should replace mandatory inquiries. *British Medical Journal*, 313, 1069–71.

Farrall, S. (2004) *Rethinking What Works with Offenders: Probations, Social Context and Desistance from Crime*. Cullompton: Willan Publishing.

Farrington, D. (1991) Psychological contributions to the explanation of offending. *Proceedings of the First DCLP Annual Conference*. University of Kent at Canterbury, January.

Fonagy, P. (2004) Early-life trauma and the psychogenesis and prevention of violence. *Annals of the New York Academy of Sciences*, 1036, 181–200.

Hamberger, L.K. & Hastings, J.E. (1988) Characteristics of male spouse abusers consistent with personality disorders. *Hospital and Community Psychiatry*, 39, 763–70.

Hamberger, L.K. & Hastings, J.E. (1990) Recidivism following spouse abuse abatement counselling: treatment program implications. *Violence and Victims*, 5, 157–70.

Hanson, K. & Harris, A. (2000) *The Sex Offender Needs Assessment Rating (SONAR): A Method for Measuring Change in Risk Levels*. Ottawa: Department of the Solicitor General.

Hanson, K. & Thornton, D. (1999) *Static 99: Improving Actuarial Risk Assessments for Sex Offenders*. Ottawa: Department of the Solicitor General.

Hare, R.D. (1991) *Manual for the Revised Psychopathy Checklist*. Toronto: Multi-Health Systems.

Hart, S. & Logan, C. (2011) Formulation of violence risk using evidence-based assessments: the structured professional judgment approach. In P. Sturmey and M. McMurran (eds) *Forensic Case Formulation*. Chichester: Wiley.

Hart, S., Sturmey, P., Logan, C. & McMurran, M. (2011) Forensic case formulation. *International Journal of Forensic Mental Health*, 10(2), 118–26.

Hilton, N.Z. & Harris, G.T. (2005) Predicting wife assault: a critical review and implications for policy and practice. *Trauma, Violence and Abuse*, 6, 3–23.

Howard, R.C. (2011) The quest for excitement: a missing link between personality disorder and violence? *Journal of Forensic Psychiatry & Psychology*, 1, 1–14.

Kernberg, O. (1984) *Severe Personality Disorders: Psychotherapeutic Strategies*. New Haven, CT: Yale University Press.

Knight, R.A. & Prentky, R.A. (1990) Classifying sexual offenders: the development and corroboration of taxonomic models. In W.L. Marshall, D.R. Laws & H.E. Barbaree (eds) *Handbook of Sexual Assault: Issues, Theories and Treatment of the Offender* (pp. 257–75). New York: Plenum.

Listwan S.J., Van Voorhis, P. & Ritchey P.N. (2007) Personality, criminal behavior and risk assessment: implications for theory and practice. *Criminal Justice and Behavior*, 34(1), 60–75.

London Probation Trust (2010) *Policy on Work with Victims of Crime* [online]. London Probation Trust general policy document. Website: LPT intranet.

Loranger, A.W., Susman, V.L., Oldham, J.M. et al. (1987) *International Personality Disorder Examination (IPDE)*. White Plains, NY: Cornell Medical Center.

Meloy, J.R. (2001) *Psychology of Stalking: Clinical and Forensic Perspectives*. San Diego, CA: Academic Press.

Millon, T., Millon, C. & Davis, R.O. (1994) *Millon Clinical Multi-Axial Inventory – III*. Minneapolis, MN: National Computer Systems.

Minoudis, P., Shaw, J. & Craissati, J. (2012) The London Pathways Project: Evaluating the effectiveness of a consultation model for personality disordered offenders. *Criminal Behaviour and Mental* Health, 22(3), 218–32.

Moffitt, T. E. (1993) Adolescence-limited and life-course-persistent antisocial behavior: a developmental taxonomy. *Psychological Review*, 100, 674–701.

Morey, L. (1991) *Personality Assessment Inventory – Professional Manual*. Lutz, FL: Psychological Assessment Resources.

Mullen, P.E., Pathe, M. & Purcell, R. (eds) (2000) *Stalking and Their Victims*. Cambridge: Cambridge University Press.

National Confidential Inquiry into Suicide and Homicide by People with Mental Illness (NCIS) (2006) *Avoidable Deaths: Five Year Report of the National Confidential Inquiry into Suicide and Homicide by People with Mental Illness*. www.medicine.manchester.ac.uk/psychiatry/research/suicide/prevention/nci.reports (Accessed January 2013).

National Confidential Inquiry into Suicide and Homicide by People with Mental Illness (NCIS) (2010) *Independent Investigations after Homicide by People Receiving Mental Health Care*. www.medicine.manchester.ac.uk/psychiatry/research/suicide/prevention/nci.reports (Accessed January 2013).

NHS South East Coast (2006) *Report of the Independent Inquiry into the Care and Treatment of Michael Stone*. South East Coast Strategic Health Authority, Kent County Council, Kent Probation Area.

Paris, J. (1996) *Social Factors in the Personality Disorders: A Biopsychosocial Approach to Etiology and Treatment*. Cambridge: Cambridge University Press.

Paris, J. (1998) A biopsychosocial model of psychopathy. In T. Millon, E. Simonsen, M. Birket-Smith & R.D. Davis (eds) *Psychopathy: Antisocial, Criminal and Violent Behaviour.* London: Guilford Press.

Quinsey, V.L., Harris, G., Rice, M. & Cormier, C. (1998) *Violent Offenders: Appraising and Managing Risk.* Washington, DC: American Psychiatric Association.

Rothbart, M.K. & Ahadi, S.A. (1994) Temperament and the development of personality. *Journal of Abnormal Psychology,* 103(1), 55–66.

Shaw, J., Minoudis, P. & Craissati, J. (2012) A comparison of the standardised assessment of personality – abbreviated scale and the offender assessment system personality disorder screen in a probation community sample. *Journal of Forensic Psychiatry & Psychology,* 23(2), 156–67.

Singleton, N., Meltzer, H. & Gatward, R. (1998) *Psychiatric Morbidity among Prisoners in England and Wales.* London: Statistical Office.

Spitzer, R.L., Williams, J.B.W., Gibbon, M. et al. (1987) *Structured Clinical Interview for DSM-IIIR Personality Disorder (SCID-II).* Biometrics Research Department, New York State Psychiatric Institute.

Stone, M.H. (2000) Gradations of antisociality. In J. Gunderson and G.O. Gabbard (eds) *Psychotherapy of Personality Disorders* (pp. 95–130). Washington, DC: American Psychiatric Press.

Stouthamer-Loeber, M., Loeber, R., Wei, E., Farrington, D.P. & Wikstrom, P.H. (2002) Risk and promotive effects in the explanation of persistent serious delinquency in boys. *Journal of Consulting and Clinical Psychology,* 70(1), 111–23.

Sturmey, P. & McMurran, M. (2011) *Forensic Case Formulation.* Chichester: Wiley.

Thornton, D., Mann, R., Webster, S., Blud, L., Travers, R., Friendship, C. et al. (2003) Distinguishing and combining risks for sexual and violent recidivism. *Annals of the New York Academy of Sciences,* 989, 225–35.

Tyrer, P., Sensky, T. & Mitchard, S. (2003) Principles of nidotherapy in the treatment of persistent mental and personality disorders. *Psychotherapy and Psychosomatics,* 72, 350–6.

Tyrer, P., Coombs, N., Ibrahimi, F., Mathilakath, A., Bajaj, P., Ranger, M., Rao, B. & Din, R. (2007) Critical developments in the assessment of personality disorder. *British Journal of Psychiatry,* 190(49), 51–9.

Ward, T. (2002) Towards a comprehensive theory of child sexual abuse: a theory knitting perspective. *Psychology, Crime & Law,* 8, 319–51.

Ward, T. & Stewart, C. (2003) Criminogenic needs and human needs: a theoretical model. *Psychology, Crime & Law,* 9(2), 125–43.

Webster, C.D., Douglas, K.S., Eaves, D. & Hart, S.D. (1997) *HCR-20: Assessing the Risk of Violence* (2nd edn). Vancouver: Mental Health, Law, and Policy Institute, Simon Fraser University.

Weerasekera, P. (1996) *Multiperspective Case Formulation: A Step towards Treatment Integration.* Malabar, FL: Krieger.

Wong, S. & Gordon, A. (2000) *Violence Risk Scale.* Department of Psychology, University of Saskatchewan.

13

DESISTANCE
FROM CRIME

Anthony Bottoms

Most offenders, even persistent offenders, eventually desist from crime; and to a significant extent they do this on their own initiative. To the legendary visitor from Mars, these simple facts – and they are facts – might seem to offer huge hope to earth-bound criminal justice systems. Earthly politicians might therefore be expected constantly to reiterate their truth, while the forensic professions and the probation service might be expected to have forged strong links between 'indigenous' (offender-initiated) desistance and their own rehabilitation programmes and supervision practice. But, of course, in real life none of this has happened, at least until very recently. It is interesting – but beyond the scope of this chapter – to consider how this strange situation arose.

Knowledge of desistance is not exactly new; a character in Shakespeare's *Winter's Tale* commented that between the ages of 10 and 23 (but *only* between those ages) 'there is nothing but getting wenches with child, wronging the ancientry [and] fighting' (Bate and Rasmussen 2007: 733). The modern criminological term for such people (especially if their delinquency starts in the mid-teens) is the *adolescence-limited offender*. This is a phrase coined in a famous paper by Terrie Moffitt (1993), who contrasts this group with the other main group in her 'developmental taxonomy', the *life-course persistent offender*. According to Moffitt, the behavioural difficulties of the life-course persisters begin earlier than those of the adolescence-limited group, and they have more deep-seated neurological and personality deficits; by contrast, the criminality of the 'adolescence-limited' group is more of a situational response to the turbulence of adolescence. Moffitt further suggests that when they reach their twenties, the two groups will 'go different ways' (p. 691). Most 'adolescence-limited' offenders will desist as they confront the fresh situations and life choices presented by young adulthood, recognising that to continue to offend will be damaging to their futures. However, the 'life-course persisters' will mostly continue in crime, given their more intractable psychological difficulties and the greater extent to which they have, by then, become enmeshed in a criminal lifestyle.

This is a neat theory, and it is not without empirical support (see Moffitt 2006). It has two particular strengths: first, it highlights the now well-attested finding that those who start committing crimes at a young age are most at risk of becoming persistent offenders; and second, it draws attention to the assessment of life prospects that many people, including offenders, undertake on the threshold of adulthood. Yet despite these strengths, it is now clear that the concept of the 'dual taxonomy' is too simple, and therefore partially misleading. For one thing, it completely excludes those who are first convicted as adults – some of whom go on to repeat offending (Blokland and Palmen 2012). But, more importantly, those who begin their criminal careers early certainly do not all become 'life-course persisters'; research has shown that there are no predetermined outcomes (see further below).

One of the most significant research studies in the desistance literature is that by John Laub and Robert Sampson (2003). Among other strengths, this research followed up a cohort of registered offenders to age 70, and it therefore contains some important results on the complexity and variety of offending and desistance trajectories over the whole life course. To understand these data fully, the Laub/Sampson research needs to be set in context.

In the mid-twentieth century, a Harvard-based husband-and-wife research team, Sheldon and Eleanor Glueck (1950) published an important volume entitled *Unraveling Juvenile Delinquency*. This was a comparative empirical study of 500 white male institutionalised juvenile delinquents and 500 controls, matched on four key variables; later, the authors followed up these two samples to age 32 (Glueck and Glueck 1968). In the 1980s, after the deaths of both Sheldon and Eleanor Glueck, their data for these research studies were discovered in the basement of Harvard Law Library, and Robert Sampson and John Laub decided to recode, computerise and re-analyse the information: this work was published as *Crime in the Making* (Sampson and Laub 1993). A decade later, the same researchers updated to age 70 the data on the official criminal careers of the originally 'delinquent' sample; and they also traced 52 of these men (both desisters and persisters) and conducted lengthy qualitative interviews with them, looking back over their lives (Laub and Sampson 2003).

Laub and Sampson's 'lifetime trajectory' data, mentioned earlier, were derived from this long-term follow-up of official offending. Recall that all these 500 men were, in adolescence, institutionalised for their delinquency; they were, therefore, mostly persistent juvenile offenders. Tracing their criminality over half a century, six different trajectories were discernible (Laub and Sampson 2003: fig. 5.11, p. 104). Three of these showed patterns of desistance (to a varying extent) that occurred particularly in the twenties (described as the 'classic desisters', the 'moderate desisters' and the 'low-rate chronics'), and together these groups accounted for 70 per cent of the sample. The most criminal group were the 'high-rate chronics', who comprised only 3 per cent of the sample. Even this group, however, were not in the absolute sense 'life-course persisters', because they showed a marked pattern of desistance in their forties.

Despite the strength of Laub and Sampson's research, one must always remember that it is a single study of only 500 males; also, that these subjects became adults half a century ago, when economic and social circumstances were very different from those of today. It is therefore necessary to be cautious in generalising from the study. Given this, it is very helpful that there is now available one other study of official offending trajectories to age 70, based on a large national dataset in the Netherlands; and it is encouraging to note that, as regards trajectories, the findings of this study are 'in many ways . . . similar to Sampson and Laub's' (Blokland et al. 2005: 944).[1] In particular, it is clear from both these studies, as well as from other relevant longitudinal data (e.g. Piquero et al. 2007: fig. 9.3, p. 136), that desistance from relatively persistent offending occurs most frequently in the third decade of life. Given limitations of space, in the remainder of this chapter I shall therefore focus especially on desistance by repeat offenders in this age range.[2] I shall also focus primarily but not exclusively on males, for the simple reason that most of the empirical research in this field has been conducted using male-only samples.[3]

It has been suggested by Maruna (2001: 27–35) that the main explanatory factors so far uncovered in desistance research can be usefully grouped into three broad categories: age and maturity; social bonds; and individual agency. In the following summary of the desistance literature, I shall follow this categorisation, but also add to it a fourth dimension of 'situational desistance'. To conclude the research review, I shall then offer an overview of the process of 'going straight', including a brief discussion of the relevance of socio-structural and cultural contexts for this process. All of these sections are concerned with *descriptive and explanatory questions*: that is, why and how do many repeat offenders desist, and what distinguishes them from those who persist? In the final section of the chapter, however, I shall turn to a more practice-oriented discussion, and consider the implications of desistance research for the work of forensic professionals and probation officers.

Age and maturity

In their retirement, Sheldon and Eleanor Glueck (1974) published a volume in which they offered an 'interpretive panorama' of their life's work, including *Unraveling Juvenile Delinquency* and its follow-up. In this retrospective overview, the authors stated that 'one of the major inferences arrived at during our various follow-up studies is the relation of *belated maturation* to abandonment of criminal activities' (Glueck and Glueck 1974: 169, emphasis in original). 'Maturation' is acknowledged to be a complex process, and is said to embrace 'the development of a stage of physical, intellectual and affective capacity and stability, and a sufficient degree of integration of all major constituents of temperament, personality and intelligence to be adequate to the demands and restrictions of life in organized society' (p. 170). Unfortunately, however, these claims are so general as to leave the authors open to the criticism that their argument might be circular; that is, people cease to offend because they become belatedly mature, while the cessation of offending is at least part of the evidence for their improved maturity (since offending is, for example, clearly not compatible with 'the demands and restrictions of life in organized society'). Learning from this danger, subsequent researchers have been keen to emphasise that a general concept of 'maturity' will not suffice as an explanation of desistance, even though – as we shall see – many of the factors that have now been identified in the literature as contributing to desistance could reasonably be included under the broad heading of 'maturity'.

A very different approach to issues of age and maturity was offered in the more recent, and highly influential, 'General Theory of Crime' proposed by Gottfredson and Hirschi (1990). These authors placed great emphasis on the age–crime curve; that is, the well-known patterning of crime over the life course, peaking in late adolescence and declining thereafter. They further argued that there is an 'invariance of the age [reduction] effect' across different offender populations, widely scattered historically and geographically, although this claim has not been substantiated in the later trajectory studies (see above). More importantly for present purposes, Gottfredson and Hirschi argued that 'individual differences in the likelihood of crime' – based in their view on high or low degrees of 'self-control', established early in life – 'tend to persist across the age-course' (1990: 141). In other words, those with behavioural difficulties at age 10 will also be more criminal at age 20 or age 30, and there is therefore no 'drastic reshuffling of the criminal and noncriminal populations based on unpredictable, situational events' in young adulthood (or beyond). However, since – as the authors acknowledge and indeed stress (see above) – criminality does decline significantly with age, and since this fact needs to be explained, 'we are left with the conclusion that it is due to the inexorable aging of the organism' (p. 141).

As with Moffitt's work, subsequent empirical studies have raised difficulties for these claims. The suggestion that individual differences in crime propensity tend to persist over the life course has been challenged by studies showing that it is not easy to predict adult offending from variables available for the adolescent period (Laub and Sampson 2003: ch.5; Kazemian et al. 2009). Moreover, research from the Pittsburgh longitudinal study (Stouthamer-Loeber et al. 2004) suggests that the factors predicting desistance or otherwise in the twenties are not simply the reverse of adolescent criminogenic factors, but seem to involve the operation of a different set of processes – a hypothesis that has been called 'asymmetric causation' (Uggen and Piliavin 1998). Accordingly, Gottfredson and Hirschi's approach has not provided persuasive evidence of its overall relevance to the explanation of desistance (see also Ezell and Cohen 2005).

Yet before we write off the potential contribution of questions of 'age' and 'maturity' to the study of desistance, two important matters must be mentioned – one general, and one specific. The general point arises from a Dutch study of the effects of the adult life circumstances of offenders, which confirmed the conclusion that such circumstances do affect criminal career patterns, and therefore that what the authors called the 'static position' of Gottfredson and Hirschi is 'untenable'

(Blokland and Nieuwbeerta 2005: 1233). However, this analysis also showed that changes in life circumstances accounted for a relatively small proportion of the overall variance in offending patterns, so the study *concurred with* Gottfredson and Hirschi's conclusion that 'much of the effect age has on crime remains unexplained' (p. 1233). Speculatively, one might suggest that this finding could be connected with Moffitt's insight (in relation to 'adolescence-limited' offenders, but the point might have wider application) that offending reduces in the third decade of life because it no longer seems appropriate to the circumstances in which young adults find themselves. As one young woman put it:

> From the ages of 13 to 19, you're a teenager . . . You're an adult from I'd say about 23 onwards. Then you're going to start experiencing things, then you're going to start thinking for yourself. I'm 23 now, I can't keep going out every weekend robbing people's phones. I'm 23, I've got to look after myself now.
>
> (Barrow Cadbury Trust 2005: 12)

The second and more specific matter relevant to maturation concerns changes in the brain, about which some important new research results have emerged in recent years as a result of rapid advances in brain scanning technology (magnetic resonance imaging, or MRI). To quote a summary by Johnson et al. (2009: 216, emphasis added):

> a growing body of longitudinal neuroimaging research has demonstrated that adolescence is a period of continued brain growth and change, challenging longstanding assumptions that the brain [had] largely finished maturing by puberty. The frontal lobes, home to key components of the neural circuitry underlying 'executive functioning' such as planning, working memory and *impulse control*, are among the last areas of the brain to mature; *they may not be fully developed until halfway through the third decade of life.*

As the same authors point out, some caution is appropriate in drawing conclusions from this emerging research, since 'empirical evidence [specifically] linking neurodevelopmental processes and adolescent real-world behavior remains sparse' (Johnson et al. 2009: 216). Nevertheless, criminologists interested in the relationship of desistance to the concept of 'maturity' will inevitably be very interested in research findings suggesting that, physiologically, individuals' 'impulse control' might not be fully developed until the mid-twenties, mirroring precisely the downslope of the age–crime curve. It is therefore very likely that future years will witness significant attempts to relate this strand of physiological research more closely to criminological concerns, and a helpful initial research review along these lines, specifically linked to the concept of maturity, has recently been provided by David Prior and colleagues (2011).

Social bonds

The 'social bonds' theoretical approach to desistance is especially associated with the work of Sampson and Laub, described above. In their 1993 book, based on a re-analysis of the Gluecks' data to age 32, these authors set out to explain both continuity and change in criminal careers; or, more specifically: (i) the development of childhood and adolescent delinquency; (ii) continuity between adolescent delinquency and adult offending; and (iii) changes in behaviour in the post-adolescent years. To meet these challenges, Sampson and Laub proposed a theory that linked the 'life-course perspective' (Elder 1985) to a developed and modified version of Travis Hirschi's (1969) *control theory*. As Laub et al. (2006: 315) subsequently expressed the matter, the key hypothesis was that:

> delinquency or crime is more likely to occur when an individual's bond to society is attenuated ... Social ties also provide social and psychological resources that individuals may draw on as they move through life transitions. The concept of social bond echoes Toby's (1957) 'stake in conformity', suggesting that the stronger an individual's social bonds, the more that person risks by engaging in criminal behavior.

The postulated social mechanisms underpinning this hypothesis are worth careful attention. The primary mechanism suggested is the influence of *social norms*: if an individual has strong 'bonds to society' (= links through pro-social norms), offending will be lower. However, there is also a claim that social bonds provide 'positive social capital'; that is, social resources upon which the individual can draw, as when family 'know-how' and contacts provide employment opportunities. (See later discussion on social capital.) As a supplementary mechanism, however, strong social bonds provide an *instrumental or prudential incentive* to refrain from offending, because individuals know that such behaviour risks disapproval by valued social groups.

Applying this approach to desistance in young adulthood, Sampson and Laub's research showed that two fresh 'stakes in conformity' arising in that age range had a special capacity to alter the criminal trajectories that had been established during adolescence: these were 'labour force attachment' and 'marital attachment'. Both were found in multivariate analyses to be significant in the explanation of desistance '*independent of* prior [adolescent] individual differences in criminal propensity' (Laub et al. 2006: 315, emphasis added). Accordingly, Sampson and Laub described the successful forging of such attachments as important 'turning points' on the road towards desistance.[4]

Interestingly, however, within a decade Laub and Sampson had modified their theoretical approach to desistance as a result of their second study (as previously discussed). Two main changes were made, both arising out of the qualitative interviews undertaken with 52 of the men: these were the addition of 'structured routine activities' and 'purposeful human agency' to the original key explanatory mechanism of social bonds/social control. The 'routine activities' addition was essentially an empirical modification of the original hypothesis, but it was an important one (to which we shall return):

> Structured routine activities modify the array of behavioral choices available to an individual . . . The modified theory contends that structured routine activities condition the effect of social controls on offending. Persistent offenders are notable in their lack of structured routine activities across the life course. On the other hand, increased structure surrounding routine activities facilitates desistance from crime regardless of prior offending trajectories.
>
> (Laub et al. 2006: 323)

The addition of 'human agency' to the theory was rather more radical, and amounts to nothing less than a modification of some of the ontological assumptions of the original theory. As the authors explained, a key feature of control theories lies in 'their assumption of universal motivation to offend . . . [t]hat is, in the absence of constraints (social controls), individuals will offend' (Laub et al. 2006: 323). However, in the revised theory:

> a less stringent version of control theory is offered, assuming that human nature is malleable across the life course. In addition, the concept of human agency cannot be understood simply as a proxy for motivation. Rather, the concept of agency *has the element of projective or transformative action within structural constraints . . . [which] the modified theory refers to as 'situated choice'.*
>
> (Laub et al. 2006: 323, emphasis added)

Perhaps curiously, however, although the authors introduced human agency into their theory in this way, they ultimately postulated only a limited role for agency in the desistance process (see later section).

Laub and Sampson's 'social bonds' approach is now firmly entrenched as a very important explanatory theory within desistance studies. However, it has received one important challenge. Mark Warr (2002: 101) argued that in advancing their hypothesis about the effects of marriage as a social bond, Laub and Sampson had 'failed to acknowledge or test' a 'highly plausible' alternative explanation of their data, based on the proposition that much youth delinquency stems from association with delinquent peers. Thus:

> If marriage disrupts or dissolves relations with those friends or accomplices, then marriage ought to encourage desistance from crime. The predicted outcome – marriage leads to desistance – is of course the same under either explanation, but the social mechanism that produces the outcome is fundamentally different.
>
> (Warr 2002: 101)

Warr then analysed data from the National Youth Survey in the USA, and found results congruent with his hypothesis. As many observers have subsequently pointed out, this is not necessarily an 'either/or' debate, because in a given case the alternative mechanisms postulated by Laub and Sampson and by Warr might both be in operation. Warr's contribution, however, also has the merit of drawing attention to a point that has importance beyond the specifics of the debate about marriage – namely, that the normative content (and therefore the influence) of social bonds can be either pro-social (as with most marriages) or antisocial (as with groups of delinquent friends).

It is now over 20 years since the first major publication of the 'social bonds' approach to the explanation of desistance (Sampson and Laub 1993), so there has been time for researchers to test empirically whether, in particular, 'marital attachment' and 'labour force attachment' do indeed have the offending-suppressive qualities that Sampson and Laub proposed. The evidence from the considerable number of studies of this kind in relation to young adults has recently been authoritatively summarised by Horney et al. (2012). As they point out, there is always a potential methodological problem with this type of research, namely the so-called 'selection effect'; by way of example, if stable employment seems to be related to subsequent desistance, might this be because those with a lower risk of reoffending are more likely to get and keep jobs in the first place? However, methodological techniques are available to help to minimise this problem, and the review by Horney et al. focuses on studies with appropriate methodological sophistication. On this basis, they conclude that, for males at least,[5] there is 'increasingly strong' evidence for the crime-suppressive effects of marriage (p. 92). There are fewer studies of the effects of cohabitation, but in general the results for this type of relationship are less positive. Since, however, cohabitation can have different cultural connotations in different countries (Savolainen 2009), it is not easy to generalise about the comparative effects of marriage and cohabitation. As regards work, 'most of the research supports the importance of employment in fostering desistance from crime', although the results on this topic 'are somewhat less consistent than the findings on marriage' (Horney et al. 2012: 98–9). Overall, therefore, one can reasonably conclude that the empirical research broadly supports the Laub/Sampson 'social bonds' approach to desistance, although the detailed evidence is quite complex. A clearer picture might emerge as researchers increasingly seek to develop more subtle analyses, focusing on different types of employment and of romantic relationships, and of their meaning to the participants in different cultural contexts.

Situational desistance

Within the field of psychology, it is now well established that actors' behaviour sometimes changes when one or more features of their surrounding environment is altered. A dramatic example of this occurred in Britain in the 1970s when a change in the national gas supply from coal gas (toxic) to North Sea gas (non-toxic) caused a significant drop in the suicide rate (Clarke and Mayhew 1988).

In other words, even people desperate enough to try to end their own lives did not turn to other methods when the gas supply in their homes became non-toxic.

An early reported example of what might be described as 'situational desistance' (desistance as a result of being in altered circumstances) emanated from the celebrated British longitudinal study known as the Cambridge Study in Delinquent Development, which has studied an unselected population of 411 working-class London males from age 8 to age 50 (see Piquero et al. 2007). Osborn (1980) showed that the minority of men in this study who had moved out of London by age 21 had lower offending rates (both official and self-reported) than those who remained, notwithstanding similar background characteristics. However, and despite the similar backgrounds, a selection effect remains a possible interpretation of these data, because it is possible (there is no information on the point) that those who left London did so *because of* a wish to change, and this caused the reduction in offending. Obviously, this kind of possible conflation of variables is not easy to disentangle, but an unexpected by-product of the Hurricane Katrina disaster (2005) has been to provide convincing evidence of a situational desistance effect. A rigorous statistical study by David Kirk (2009) showed that those New Orleans prisoners who, on release after the hurricane, were obliged to relocate to other areas because of the devastation in their home neighbourhoods had lower offending rates than those from other neighbourhoods who were able to return home in the normal way. Of course, this result cannot be attributed to differential motivations in the two groups.

Away from academic debates of this kind, some would-be desisters have long been aware of the possible advantages of a 'geographic cure', as it has been called (Maruna 2001: 153–4): that is, moving to a different area 'to make a fresh start'. Indeed, such 'cures' do not have to involve a change in neighbourhood, but might take the form of deciding to avoid particular 'hotspots' such as nightclubs, and/or spending less time with certain delinquent acquaintances. An offender who adopts such a strategy is admitting to himself that, in certain possible future situations, he might fall prey to (for example) the suggestions of criminal friends; he therefore attempts to control his future actions by imposing on himself in advance certain constraints on his movements or social contacts. This kind of strategy has accordingly been described as 'self-binding' (Elster 2000), or 'diachronic self-control' (Kennett 2001: ch. 5).[6]

Situational self-binding in relation to desistance was recently researched empirically in the Sheffield Desistance Study, co-directed by Joanna Shapland and myself. This is a study of 113 men, mostly persistent offenders, whose mean age at the time of first interview was 20, and who were followed up for 3–4 years, with an intended total of four research interviews during that period (Bottoms and Shapland 2011; Shapland and Bottoms 2011). In a 'qualitative subsample' for whom fully transcribed interview data were available, three-quarters of the men had at some time adopted a tactic of diachronic self-control (Bottoms 2013). Of course, these were not always successful in achieving lasting desistance. However, the large proportion of men who adopted such tactics is of great interest for two reasons:

first, because it provides solid practical evidence that many persistent offenders do indeed wish to desist; and second, because it confirms that would-be desisters often recognise the potential difficulties and temptations involved in trying to 'go straight', and they do not entirely trust themselves to avoid such pitfalls. In response, they therefore put in place tactics of self-binding that, they hope, will prevent them from 'doing something stupid' (as several of them put it).

Agency

Early studies of criminal careers, such as those of the Gluecks or the Cambridge Study in Delinquent Development, paid little attention to what might be described as 'subjective' or 'perceptual' data, in which research subjects are invited to express their own views of their current circumstances and future prospects. The reason for this was that when the fieldwork for these studies was conducted, the dominant perspective within criminology was that research studies should be carried out, so far as possible, in conformity with the established protocols of the natural sciences ('positivism'). However, there are of course alternative paradigms to positivism within the philosophy of the social sciences (see generally Hollis 2002), and in the last decade one of these has become prominent in desistance studies. This alternative paradigm is, like the earlier one, fully willing to accept the causal influence of both individual factors (such as physiological changes in the brain) and social factors (such as the differential criminogenic influences of different neighbourhoods). However, it adds to these factors a concept of *agency*. In this view of the human sciences, therefore, within the constraints of their given situation, the 'players' are able 'to pursue their own ends'; hence, they 'make their own history but they do not do it in conditions entirely of their own choosing' (Hollis 2002: 19). Crucially for present purposes, within such a perspective *the choices and other actions of individual subjects may to a degree shape future outcomes*. Accordingly, the steps that an offender might consciously take to try to desist could in principle be vital in helping to achieve that desired outcome.

How then should the notion of 'agency' be best understood conceptually, and how might it best be utilised within desistance studies? There is a vast literature on the first of these questions, and a growing literature on the second, so it is not possible within the constraints of this chapter to explore this territory in any depth (but for relevant discussions see Bottoms 2006 and Healy 2013). Instead, I shall focus on just a few important topics that have been raised within the agency-related literature on desistance, as it has developed since about the year 2000.[7]

First, as previously mentioned in a quotation from Laub et al. (2006: 323), agency has an important *projective* dimension. In relation to desistance, this future-oriented dimension has been most fully discussed by Paternoster and Bushway (2009), who postulate that at certain points in a criminal career offenders may formulate a notion of a 'desired self' (who they would like to become – for example 'a trusted husband and father') and/or a 'feared self' (who they fear they might become – for example 'spending most of my life in prison'). Contemplating these alternative futures, and considering one's current lifestyle, might then produce a 'crystallization of discontent' which leads to the offender beginning to put in place some attempted moves towards desistance.[8] Qualitative analyses within the Sheffield Desistance Study have confirmed that such thought processes do indeed often occur in the early stages of desistance (see for example Shapland and Bottoms 2011: 262–3 for data on the 'desired self').

But what happens after this initial stage; that is, after an offender has self-acknowledged that s/he is open to change? In an important qualitative study focused primarily on female offenders, Giordano et al. (2002) suggested that the usual next step is to find a 'hook for change'. Such 'hooks', they argue, can be of various kinds: for example finding a partner; the birth of a child or children; employment; religion; or the experience of imprisonment. However, they suggest that the *type* of 'hook' is not in itself particularly important; rather, what matters is whether the hook has 'transformative potential'. That view is taken because, in the explanatory framework of Giordano and her colleagues, successful desistance normally requires a degree of 'cognitive transformation'. It is further suggested that the criteria for judging whether a hook has true transformative potential include: (i) whether it provides a clear pro-social cognitive blueprint; (ii) whether it acts as a gateway to other conforming individuals, who will support the pro-social blueprint; and (iii) whether it offers a broad outline of a 'replacement self' (Giordano et al. 2002: 1029). In the view of these authors, the beginnings of a 'replacement self' (or different self-identity) will hopefully begin to emerge from these 'hook-based' processes; and, as a final stage in the ideal progression, there will be 'a gradual redefinition of deviance as no longer a meaningful, viable component of the actor's behavioral repertoire' (p. 1027).

It is clear from this description that Giordano et al.'s 'hooks for change' are in some ways very similar to Laub and Sampson's 'social bonds'; and indeed both these sets of authors acknowledge a degree of congruence between their respective theories (Giordano et al. 2002: 1056; Laub and Sampson 2003: 299, n. 4). Nevertheless, there is an important difference in emphasis between them. While Giordano et al. prioritise the cognitive transformation process in desistance, Laub and Sampson (2003: 149) claim that such processes are found only among 'some' offenders, and that 'most . . . desist in response to *structurally induced* turning points' (emphasis added). The full meaning of this phrase becomes clearer at a later point, when Laub and Sampson say that:

> The image of '*desistance by default*' best fits the desistance process we found in our data . . . Many men *made a commitment to go straight without even realizing it*. Before they knew it, they had invested so much in a marriage or a job that they did not want to risk losing their investment . . . We agree that the offenders' own perspectives and words need to be brought into the understanding of desistance . . . however, offenders can and do desist without a 'cognitive transformation'.
>
> (Laub and Sampson 2003: 278–9, emphasis added)

Of course, no one doubts that there are some cases of 'desistance by default'; for example an offender might begin a job simply to earn some money, then find that the work is genuinely engaging, and so he begins to re-prioritise his life commitments, move away from his criminal friends, and so on. But whether this is the dominant mode of desistance, as Laub and Sampson explicitly suggest, is more doubtful. Certainly, that conclusion is not compatible with the evidence on the early stages of desistance in the Sheffield study, where there was overwhelming evidence that most of the 20–21-year-old recidivists wished to live a different kind of life (Shapland and Bottoms 2011) and that many of them were already taking active steps to try to achieve this (see above on diachronic self-control) – a very different picture from 'desistance by default'.

What might explain these different results? It seems at least possible that the difference is attributable to contrasting methodologies. Laub and Sampson's interviews with desisters were conducted with men in their mid-sixties, looking back on a process that had, in most instances, occurred many years beforehand. From that time perspective, they might have been particularly likely to identify what seemed retrospectively to be 'turning points', and to see these as pivotal in the desistance process. They might then have forgotten or downplayed any attempts to desist prior to the identified 'turning point' (see also note 4). This suggestion is of course made tentatively; but there is extensive evidence in psychology that distant events are frequently recalled in a faulty manner, and this is therefore a methodological *caveat* to be borne in mind in relation to all retrospective studies of desistance.

As a final key issue in relation to agency, we need to assess the empirical evidence as to whether so-called 'subjective factors' (such as a strongly expressed hope for a better future, or a significant degree of regret for past crimes) do actually help to produce desistance outcomes. (Such evidence will of course be available only from research with a prospective methodology). The best study of this issue to date is perhaps that of Le Bel and colleagues (2008), using data from the Oxford Recidivism Study. Their analysis is complex, and the authors are careful to state the limitations of their study. Nevertheless, they found some evidence supporting both *direct* and *indirect* influences of subjective variables on desistance, and they therefore concluded that the findings:

> provide some support for the importance [for desistance or otherwise] of individual cognitions and meaning systems prior to release from prison . . . [S]ubjective changes may precede life-changing structural events, and, to that extent, individuals can act as agents of their own change . . . [But these things can] work in both positive and negative directions: positive 'mind over matter' helps the individual to triumph over problems and make the best of situations, while a negative frame of mind leads to drift and defeatism in response to the same events.
>
> (Le Bel et al. 2008: 155)

We should not assume, however, that a subject's negative or positive frame of mind is unrelated to external circumstances. In a sobering comment, Giordano et al. (2002: 1026) state that 'under conditions of sufficiently extreme disadvantage', the cognitive transformations and agentic moves that are central to their theory are 'unlikely to be nearly enough' to create successful desistance; and of course in such unfavourable circumstances individuals might find it very hard to generate any positive hope in the first place. Accordingly, 'agency' must always be seen as operating within a given structural and cultural context – an interaction that we must now make more explicit.

The process of 'going straight'

Previous sections have reviewed, under four specific headings, the research literature on the important phenomenon of desistance from crime among persistent young adult offenders. All four sections have reported findings of relevance to the overall explanation of such desistance: these include physiological changes promoting better impulse control; general perceptions of age-related changes in life circumstances; stronger pro-social bonds of both a romantic and an employment-related character; the weakening of social bonds with criminal friends; situational changes, including deliberate situational self-binding; and the exercise of agency through the projection of possible future self-identities, and subsequent processes of choice leading to a degree of cognitive transformation. This is a complex ensemble of factors, which in a given case might interact with one another in many ways. It is also true: (i) that some of the above-listed factors have stronger research support than others; and (ii) that there has to date been very little research on the interaction between the different factors; accordingly, (iii) the overall picture arising from the research remains tentative. Nevertheless, in my judgement this picture has a sufficient degree of research-backed coherence for it to be treated seriously not only by researchers, but also by policy makers and practitioners.

In the current section, I want to add some research-based reflections on the actual *process* of 'going straight', as it unfolds for particular individuals. Three main topics will be briefly discussed: the *gradual* character of most desistance; changes to *routine activities*; and the implications of the fact that those who attempt to desist never do so 'in conditions entirely of their own choosing' (Hollis 2002: 19).

The gradual character of desistance is now well established. Persistent offenders do not usually simply stop offending, but instead gradually reduce their offending levels as they begin to turn to an alternative lifestyle. The reason for this is easy to understand. If one has truly been a *persistent* offender, then offending will have become in effect part of one's daily life, and most of one's friends will also be offenders. In these circumstances, a sudden and complete transformation in lifestyle, while not impossible, is unlikely.

In the Sheffield Desistance Study, which focuses on the early stages of desistance, we have taken this insight a stage further by noting that a would-be desister 'must attempt to negotiate a new way of living, breaking with the habits of the past with the support of whoever is willing to be a significant other' (Bottoms and Shapland 2011: 70). In informal presentations, we have stated this more colloquially: *desistance is a process of learning to live a non-criminal life when one has been living a largely criminal life*. It will be recalled that in the Laub/Sampson study, by the mid-sixties there was a marked difference between 'persisting' and 'desisting' research subjects as regards *routine activities*: the lives of persisters were 'notable in their lack of structured routine activities', while among those who had turned away from crime 'increased structure surrounding routine activities facilitates desistance from crime regardless of prior offending trajectories' (Laub et al. 2006: 323). But this difference does not appear by magic; it has to be worked for. The clear evidence of the Sheffield study is that would-be desisters make many small decisions about daily living – who to mix with, which places to visit, how to respond in particular situations of temptation. They might well encounter obstacles, and there might be setbacks along the way, but if desistance is successfully accomplished, gradually a different pattern of routine activities will take shape. One particularly important issue concerns finance. 'Going straight' after persistent offending frequently entails a loss of income; and since there is research evidence that much property offending by persistent offenders is triggered by a perceived need for immediate cash (Wright and Decker 1994), it is not surprising that most respondents in the Sheffield Desistance Study identified 'lack of money' as a very significant obstacle to their 'going straight' (Bottoms and Shapland 2011: table 2.4, p. 61).[9] How a would-be desister learns to respond to personal financial crises can therefore be vital to his future.

Figure 13.1, reproduced from a publication of the Sheffield Desistance Study, offers a heuristic model of the early stages of desistance. Around the edges of the figure, starting in the top left-hand corner, are a series of stages perceived from the actor's point of view. (These are not dissimilar to the stages in Giordano and colleagues' theory of cognitive transformation.) As has been said in a summary of the Sheffield qualitative study, 'offenders move gradually towards a less offending life: they become more aware of others' views; they try to take more responsibility for themselves and other people; [and] they try to think before they act' (Bottoms 2012: 42). However, an important element in Figure 13.1, which is less explicit in the work of Giordano et al., is the almost ubiquitous experience of 'encountering obstacles' on the road to desistance. When an obstacle is encountered, it might be successfully overcome, but it frequently is not. However, it is important to emphasise that succumbing to an obstacle does not necessarily lead to a complete relapse; it can be simply a partial setback, followed by further efforts to desist.

In the middle of Figure 13.1 are two circles, which are intended to represent the insight that, despite the now demonstrated importance of agency in relation to desistance, agentic struggles always occur within specific contexts. One such context is the past history of the offender, which can be a strong continuing influence. Of course, Sampson and Laub (1993) and others have clearly demon-

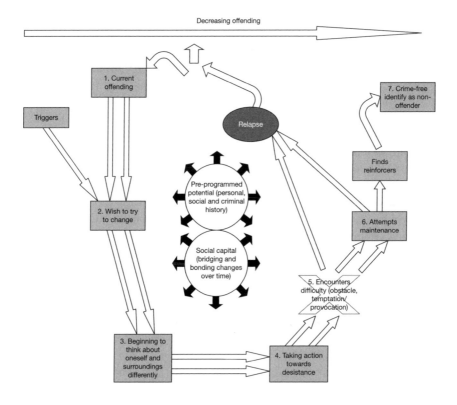

FIGURE 13.1 A model of the early stages of desistance

Source: Bottoms and Shapland (2011: 70). Reproduced with kind permission from Routledge.

strated that offenders can desist in adulthood despite a long record of juvenile crime and highly adverse social circumstances. Nevertheless, it is also true that – as we noted at the beginning of this chapter when discussing the work of Terrie Moffitt – statistically speaking an early start to a criminal career does predict a greater likelihood of persistent offending in adulthood, probably for the reasons outlined by Moffitt (greater neurological and psychological difficulties, and deeper involvement in criminal networks).

The second circle in Figure 13.1 refers to the *social capital* that might or might not be available to the would-be desister, given the social settings in which s/he is placed. This might be either *bonding social capital* (arising out of bonds to family, a partner, etc.), or *bridging social capital* (a concept that refers to wider social resources, such as the availability of work for young adults in the area where the offender lives). (On social capital see generally Halpern 2005.) The concept of bridging social capital of course links the discussion to the wider social–structural context of the particular society, which is an important but somewhat neglected topic within desistance studies (Farrall et al. 2010).

The issue of bonding social capital is probably of more immediate relevance to forensic practitioners and probation staff, and its importance has been very well illustrated in a recent research monograph by Adam Calverley (2013) on paths to desistance among ethnic minority offenders in Britain. In this qualitative study, Calverley found significant differences in 'the experiences and strategies reported by desisting offenders of Indian, Bangladeshi, and Black and dual heritage ethnic origin' (p. 186). For example, the families of origin of Bangladeshi-origin offenders 'played a critical part in prompting, encouraging and maintaining the [desistance] process' and in adopting an attitude of forgiveness which gave the offenders 'hope that a possible life without crime was indeed possible'. Additionally, and in contrast to the other two ethnic groups studied, religion (Islam) 'featured prominently in directing and shaping the decision and motivations of Bangladeshis to desist'; it also provided them with 'places of desistance where their new pro-social identity as "good" Muslims was acknowledged' (p. 187). By contrast, for Black and dual heritage offenders 'the experience [of desistance] was generally a much lonelier journey' because 'they lacked social capital' (p. 187). 'Isolated from strong networks of family and community support', they faced threats to their desistance from 'the "code of the street" . . . and criminally active peers' (p. 188). They responded to their situation by 'investing in themselves', for example by '"pumping iron" in the gym and attending courses or participating in voluntary work in order to improve their CV' (p. 188).

These fascinating contrasts not only illustrate the importance of social capital and cultural context for any given individual's possible road to desistance, they also highlight the markedly different ways in which desistance processes can play out for different people. These matters are of considerable relevance for the shaping of forensic practitioners' handling of desistance issues, as we shall now see.

Desistance and forensic practice

The main argument of this chapter leads naturally to a broad policy conclusion. This has been well expressed by Fergus McNeill (2012: 13), a social work academic with a strong interest in desistance: 'Most people stop offending sometime, with or without interventions, and sometimes even in spite of them . . . [T]he practical challenge is to help them to do so more swiftly and certainly.' This desirable policy goal has been called *assisted desistance*.

What is the relationship between 'assisted desistance' and the more traditional topic of 'offender rehabilitation'? There is obviously some link between them, but the nature of that link has recently been the subject of controversy. In a valuable historical survey, McNeill et al. (2013) pointed out that, for half a century after the work of the Gluecks, there was 'hardly any use of desistance research to inform sentencing and correctional policy and practice'. As a consequence, within the field of rehabilitation there was sometimes 'too much [thinking] about interventions or programmes, and too little about the change processes that they exist to support'

(McNeill and Weaver 2010: 21). This situation began to change in light of empirical studies of desistance, especially those of Maruna (2001) and Farrall (2002). In turn, this led to fresh theoretical constructs – a 'desistance paradigm for offender management' (McNeill 2006) and a wider 'Good Lives Model' for rehabilitation (Ward 2010). These approaches presented themselves as being – to a significant degree, at least – in opposition to the dominant 'risk–needs–responsivity' (RNR) model of rehabilitation, the 'general vision' of which is 'that it is in the best interest for all to provide cognitive behavioural services to offenders' (Bonta and Andrews 2010: 36). Among the main points of contention in these debates were the claims of assisted desistance models that supervisors should: (i) focus on future-oriented desistance goals rather than, as in RNR, on factors and processes that had led to past criminal behaviour; and (ii) develop a so-called 'strengths approach' that would seek to build on offenders' capabilities rather than, as in RNR, to correct weaknesses.[10]

In an important recent paper, the leading rehabilitation scholar Friedrich Lösel (2012: 97–100) has criticised the tendency to present the policy implications of desistance research as a new 'paradigm' for supervision, in opposition to RNR. He argues that:

> [N]either the 'what works' [rehabilitation] research (including the RNR approach) nor the recommended concept of desistance are [true] paradigms.[11] ... They both contain a more-or-less eclectic integration of theories, hypotheses, assessments and intervention measures that can be applied to reducing reoffending. Instead of allowing a paradigm shift to take place, then, it would be more appropriate to use the [Good Lives Model] and the desistance approach to widen perspectives on offender rehabilitation and expand the evidence base.
>
> (Lösel 2012: 99)

More or less simultaneously, Fergus McNeill (2012: 1) suggested the need to 'mov[e] beyond contemporary "paradigm conflicts"'. He also implicitly affirmed his earlier comment (in a jointly authored paper) that publicity about desistance theorisation had perhaps now created an unfortunate 'risk of rejecting or dismissing' the potential role that formal offending behaviour programmes can play in rehabilitation, given the research evidence that such programmes constitute 'a key mechanism for developing offenders' capacities for change by building their human capital' (McNeill and Weaver 2010: 22). There is therefore now a clear recognition from both sides of this debate that it would be helpful to move beyond what McNeill calls 'paradigm conflicts'.

Within this more consensual dialogue, however, McNeill (2012: 13) remains of the view that 'a desistance perspective construes and influences intervention in a way which is subtly different from (but not incompatible with) most forms of rehabilitation theory'. Rehabilitation theories, he claims, 'tend to put intervention itself at the heart of a process of change', whereas 'desistance-based perspectives stress that the process of change exists before, behind and beyond the intervention'. Desistance perspectives therefore 'can and should inform the better development of [rehabilitation] models'. From the perspective of rehabilitation theory, Lösel (2012) is not unsympathetic to such an approach. He points out, for example, that 'desistance concepts are closely related to the field of research on protective factors and resilience in human development' (p. 100),[12] although – curiously – these developmental research results have featured only in a very marginal way in the criminological literature on rehabilitation. In the conclusion to his paper, he also emphasises that 'the "what works" question should not be limited simply to the type of programme, but should take a broader pattern of relevant change factors into account' (p. 103).

Within this fresh framework of dialogue, some leading desistance researchers have helpfully proposed eight 'central themes' that, in their view, seem to emerge when one seeks to interpret the results of desistance research to guide supervision practice (McNeill et al. 2012, 2013). (These authors concede, however, that as yet there is not much empirical research that specifically tests the effects of these suggestions.) The eight 'central themes' are, in paraphrase, as follows:[13]

(i) For persistent offenders, desistance is a complex process, often involving 'lapses and relapses'. Supervisors need to be 'realistic' about this, and therefore find ways to 'manage setbacks and difficulties constructively'.

(ii) Paths to desistance are highly individualised, and often influenced by the offender's particular circumstances and/or cultural background. Supervisors need to be aware of this diversity; 'one-size-fits-all interventions will not work'.

(iii) A key task for supervisors is to develop and maintain motivation and hope among would-be desisters.

(iv) Relationships between 'offenders and those who matter to them' are of great importance for desistance.

(v) Offenders have strengths and resources as well as risks and needs; so 'supporting and developing these capacities can be a useful dimension of criminal justice practice'.

(vi) Since agency is important to desistance, supervisors should 'encourage and respect self-determination'; this will entail 'working *with* offenders, not *on* them'.

(vii) Probation services need to work on developing 'social capital' as well as 'human capital',[14] and also to help desisters to practise their 'newly forming identities (eg "worker" or "father")'.

(viii) The language of supervision practice should 'seek to avoid identifying people with the behaviours we want them to leave behind'.

Hopefully, readers will easily be able to identify the links between these suggestions and the desistance research summarised earlier in this chapter. Thus, it will be no surprise that the present author regards the 'eight central themes' as a very valuable guide for practitioners. But even the best travel guidebooks sometimes have omissions, and in my view the 'central themes' listed above do not sufficiently take into account the research findings showing that successful desisters from persistent crime need to make significant alterations to their daily routine activities. The practice implication of this comment is, perhaps, that supervisors should ideally be able to help offenders to address very practical topics such as handling financial difficulties, disengaging from former delinquent friends, and developing strategies of diachronic self-control. But, as I suggested in an earlier paper, an important implication of this suggestion is that: 'if offenders are to feel that probation supervisors can assist them with such issues, they need to be confident that supervisors really do understand the social worlds they inhabit' (Bottoms 2008: 162).[15]

Conclusion

In the last two decades, there have been very significant advances in our research-based understanding of the processes involved in desistance from crime; and from these advances some potentially important insights for forensic and probation practice can be gleaned. However, desistance research is still developing, and many of the suggestions for practice have yet to be rigorously evaluated. This chapter should therefore be read as a progress report from an exciting and rapidly developing field. The picture presented is well grounded, but it is necessarily subject to modification in light of future developments. Ideally, the practice-based dimensions of these future developments should be the subject of discussions involving not only researchers and practitioners, but also would-be desisters themselves.

Acknowledgements

I would like to express warm thanks to my colleague in the Sheffield Desistance Study, Joanna Shapland, for constant intellectual stimulation as we have tried to understand desistance together, and also for her comments on an earlier draft of this chapter. The Sheffield Desistance Study was funded by the Economic and Social Research Council, and my subsequent work on desistance has been assisted by a Leverhulme Trust Emeritus Research Fellowship.

Notes

1 The main difference between the two studies was that Blokland et al. (2005: 944) identified 'a small group of persistent offenders, making up less than 2 per cent of the sampled population, whose offending trajectory remains relatively flat at about 2 to 2.5 convictions per year from age 30 onward'. Contrary to the prediction by Moffitt (1993), however, these 'life-course persistent' offenders were not disproportionately involved in violent crime; rather they were 'better described as persistent petty thieves for whom incarceration is like "a revolving door"' (p. 945).

2 Research studies on desistance vary in the extent to which they concentrate on persistent offenders. Most researchers agree, however, that to speak about 'desistance' is only meaningful in relation to those who have established something of a pattern of offending; hence 'one-time' offenders are usually excluded from consideration.

3 The most important study of female desistance is that by Giordano et al. (2002). For an interesting British study comparing 20 male and 20 female offenders, see Barry (2006, esp. ch. 6).

4 It is worth noting, however, that the concept of a 'turning point' can only be identified retrospectively. Contemporaneously, neither an outside observer nor the person him/herself can know whether a new attachment will subsequently be identifiable as a 'turning point', as opposed to just another life event.

5 For females, the evidence for marriage effects is 'less clear' (Horney et al. 2012: 88), in part because of the paucity of studies of desistance among women offenders.

6 This conceptualisation of 'self-control' differs from that of Gottfredson and Hirschi (1990), considered earlier, in that it (correctly, in my view) treats self-control as an action in circumstances of temptation or anticipated temptation, rather than a stable bundle of traits. See further, Wikström and Treiber (2007); Bottoms (2013).

7 One agency-relevant topic omitted here is the much-discussed 'redemption script', as described by Shadd Maruna (2001: ch. 5) in his pioneering qualitative research in Liverpool. Such a script, it is said, 'allows the [desisting] person to rewrite a shameful past into a necessary prelude to a productive and worthy life' (p. 87). However, Maruna's findings on this point have not been consistently replicated in later research. Where such 'scripts' are evident, they seem to emerge in the later stages of desistance; by contrast, 'early-stage desisters [are] preoccupied with "becoming normal" and their goals [are] more likely to revolve around finding conventional roles in work and family life' (Healy 2013: 561).

8 There is an obvious link here with the psychological theory of cognitive dissonance (Festinger 1957).

9 The four most frequently identified 'obstacles' in this study were: 'lack of money'; 'opportunity for easy money'; 'need for excitement or to relieve boredom'; and 'lack of work'. A summation of self-identified obstacles was a powerful predictor of subsequent criminality (both official and self-reported): Bottoms and Shapland (2011, tables 2.5 and 2.6).

10 These claims derive their strength from the clear evidence in the desistance literature supporting the existence of 'asymmetric causation' (see earlier section). There is no doubt, however, that – as various critics have pointed out – the claims have sometimes been made in an exaggerated manner.

11 Lösel is here referring to the concept of a scientific paradigm, as discussed in the work of Thomas Kuhn (1962) on the philosophy of science.

12 Lösel (2012: 100) lists ten factors shown by research to have 'a relatively broad and consistent protective function in cases of adversity'. These include: a 'stable and emotional relationship with at least one reference person'; 'adequate social support'; 'social models that encourage constructive coping'; 'cognitive competencies such as realistic future planning'; and gaining 'experience of sense and meaning in life'.

13 All quotations are from McNeill et al. (2012: 8–9). In item (vi), the emphasis is in the original source.

14 'Developing human capital' refers to improving the capabilities of an individual, for example by enhancing his/her work skills; 'developing social capital' refers to enhancing the social context for the activity in question, for example by a probation service improving its capability for helping people find suitable work.

15 That paper also drew attention to two then-recent policies that had seemingly, and unfortunately, 'pulled the probation service away from contact with local communities' (p. 161), namely the closure of many probation area offices and a decline in the practice of probation officers visiting offenders in their homes.

References

Barrow Cadbury Trust (2005) *Lost in Transition: A Report of the Barrow Cadbury Commission on Young Adults and the Criminal Justice System*, London: Barrow Cadbury Trust.

Barry, M. (2006) *Youth Offending in Transition: The Search for Social Recognition*, Abingdon: Routledge.

Bate, J. and Rasmussen, E. (eds) (2007) *William Shakespeare: Complete Works ('The RSC Shakespeare')*, Basingstoke: Macmillan.

Blokland, A. and Nieuwbeerta, P. (2005) 'The effects of life circumstances on individual trajectories of offending', *Criminology*, 43, 1203–40.

Blokland, A. and Palmen, H. (2012) 'Criminal career patterns', in R. Loeber, M. Hoeve, N. W. Slot and P. H. van der Laan (eds) *Persisters and Desisters in Crime from Adolescence into Adulthood*, Farnham: Ashgate.

Blokland, A., Nagin, D. and Nieuwbeerta, P. (2005) 'Life span offending trajectories of a Dutch conviction cohort', *Criminology*, 43, 919–54.

Bonta, J. and Andrews, D. A. (2010) 'Viewing offender assessment and rehabilitation through the lens of the risk–needs–responsivity model', in F. McNeill, P. Raynor and C. Trotter (eds) *Offender Supervision: New Directions in Theory, Research and Practice*, Cullompton: Willan Publishing.

Bottoms, A. E. (2006) 'Desistance, social bonds and human agency: a theoretical exploration', in P.-O. Wikström and R. J. Sampson (eds) *The Explanation of Crime: Context, Mechanisms and Development*, Cambridge: Cambridge University Press.

Bottoms, A. E. (2008) 'The community dimension of community penalties', *Howard Journal of Criminal Justice*, 47, 146–69.

Bottoms, A. E. (2012) 'Active maturation: why crime falls in early adulthood', *Eurovista: Probation and Community Justice*, 2, 39–42.

Bottoms, A. E. (2013) 'Learning from Odysseus: self-applied situational crime prevention as an aid to compliance', in P. Ugwudike and P. Raynor (eds) *What Works in Offender Compliance: International Perspectives and Evidence-Based Practice*, Basingstoke: Palgrave Macmillan.

Bottoms, A. E. and Shapland, J. M. (2011) 'Steps towards desistance among male young adult recidivists', in S. Farrall, M. Hough, S. Maruna and R. Sparks (eds) *Escape Routes: Contemporary Perspectives on Life after Punishment*, London: Routledge.

Calverley, A. (2013) *Cultures of Desistance: Rehabilitation, Reintegration and Ethnic Minorities*, London: Routledge.

Clarke, R. V. and Mayhew, P. (1988) 'The British gas suicide story and its criminological implications', in M. Tonry and N. Morris (eds) *Crime and Justice: A Review of Research*, vol. 10, Chicago, IL: University of Chicago Press.

Elder, G. H. (1985) 'Perspectives on the life-course', in G. H. Elder (ed.) *Life Course Dynamics*, Ithaca, NY: Cornell University Press.

Elster, J. (2000) *Ulysses Unbound*, Cambridge: Cambridge University Press.

Ezell, M. E. and Cohen, L. E. (2005) *Desisting from Crime: Continuity and Change in Long-Term Crime Patterns of Serious Chronic Offenders*, Oxford: Oxford University Press.

Farrall, S. (2002) *Rethinking What Works with Offenders: Probation, Social Context and Desistance from Crime*, Cullompton: Willan Publishing.

Farrall, S., Bottoms, A. E. and Shapland, J. (2010) 'Social structures and desistance from crime', *European Journal of Criminology*, 7, 546–70.

Festinger, L. (1957) *A Theory of Cognitive Dissonance*, Evanston, IL: Row, Peterson.

Giordano, P.C., Cernovitch, S. A. and Rudolph, J. L. (2002) 'Gender, crime and desistance: toward a theory of cognitive transformation', *American Journal of Sociology*, 107, 990–1064.

Glueck, S. and Glueck, E. (1950) *Unraveling Juvenile Delinquency*, Cambridge, MA: Harvard University Press.

Glueck, S. and Glueck, E. (1968) *Delinquents and Nondelinquents in Perspective*, Cambridge, MA: Harvard University Press.

Glueck, S. and Glueck, E. (1974) *Of Delinquency and Crime: A Panorama of Years of Search and Research*, Springfield, IL: Charles C. Thomas.

Gottfredson, M. R. and Hirschi, T. (1990) *A General Theory of Crime*, Stanford, CA: Stanford University Press.

Halpern, D. (2005) *Social Capital*, Cambridge: Polity Press.

Healy, D. (2013) 'Changing fate? Agency and the desistance process', *Theoretical Criminology*, 17, 557–74.

Hirschi, T. (1969) *Causes of Delinquency*, Berkeley: University of California Press.

Hollis, M. (2002) *The Philosophy of Social Science: An Introduction* (revised edn), Cambridge: Cambridge University Press.

Horney, J., Tolan, P. and Weisburd, D. (2012) 'Contextual influences', in R. Loeber and D. P. Farrington (eds) *From Juvenile Delinquency to Adult Crime: Criminal Careers, Justice Policy and Prevention*, New York: Oxford University Press.

Johnson, S. B., Blum, R. W. and Giedd, J. N. (2009) 'Adolescent maturity and the brain: the promise and pitfalls of neuroscience research in adolescent health policy', *Journal of Adolescent Health*, 45, 216–21.

Kazemian, L., Farrington, D. P. and LeBlanc, M. (2009) 'Can we make accurate long-term predictions about patterns of de-escalation in offending behaviour?', *Journal of Youth and Adolescence*, 38, 384–400.

Kirk, D. S. (2009) 'A natural experiment on residential change and recidivism: lessons from Hurricane Katrina', *American Sociological Review*, 74, 484–505.

Kennett, J. (2001) *Agency and Responsibility: A Common-Sense Moral Psychology*, Oxford: Clarendon Press.

Kuhn, T. S. (1962) *The Structure of Scientific Revolutions*, Chicago, IL: University of Chicago Press.

Laub, J. H. and Sampson, R. J. (2003) *Shared Beginnings, Divergent Lives*, Cambridge, MA: Harvard University Press.

Laub, J. H. Sampson, R. J. and Sweeten, G. A. (2006) 'Assessing Sampson and Laub's life-course theory of crime', in F. T. Cullen, J. P. Wright and K. R. Blevins (eds) *Taking Stock: The Status of Criminological Theory*, New Brunswick, NJ: Transaction.

Le Bel, T. P., Burnett, R., Maruna, S. and Bushway, S. (2008) 'The "chicken and egg" of subjective and social factors in desistance from crime', *European Journal of Criminology*, 5, 131–59.

Lösel, F. (2012) 'What works in correctional treatment and rehabilitation for young adults', in F. Lösel, A. E. Bottoms and D. P. Farrington (eds) *Young Adult Offenders: Lost in Transition*, Abingdon: Routledge.

McNeill, F. (2006) 'A desistance paradigm for offender management', *Criminology and Criminal Justice*, 6, 39–62.

McNeill, F. (2012) 'Four forms of "offender" rehabilitation: towards an interdisciplinary perspective', *Legal and Criminological Psychology*, 17, 18–36.

McNeill, F. and Weaver, B. (2010) *Changing Lives? Desistance Research and Offender Management*, Glasgow: Scottish Centre for Crime and Justice Research.

McNeill, F., Farrall, S., Lightowler, C. and Maruna, S. (2012) 'How and why people stop offending: discovering desistance', *Insights: Evidence Summaries to Support Social Services in Scotland, No. 15*, Glasgow: Institute for Research and Innovation in Social Services.

McNeill, F., Farrall, S., Lightowler, C. and Maruna, S. (2013) 'Desistance as a framework for supervision', in G. Bruinsma and D. Weisburd (eds) *The Springer Encyclopedia of Criminology and Criminal Justice*, New York: Springer.

Maruna, S. (2001) *Making Good: How Ex-Convicts Reform and Rebuild their Lives*, Washington, DC: American Psychological Association.

Moffitt, T. E. (1993) 'Adolescence-limited and life-course persistent antisocial behavior: a developmental taxonomy', *Psychological Review*, 100, 674–701.

Moffitt, T. E. (2006) 'A review of research on the taxonomy of life-course persistent versus adolescence-limited antisocial behavior', in F. T. Cullen, J. P. Wright and K. R. Blevins (eds) *Taking Stock: The Status of Criminological Theory*, New Brunswick, NJ: Transaction.

Osborn, S. G. (1980) 'Moving home, leaving London and delinquent trends', *British Journal of Criminology*, 20, 54–61.

Paternoster, R. and Bushway, S. (2009) 'Desistance and the "feared self": toward an identity theory of criminal desistance', *Journal of Criminal Law and Criminology*, 99, 1103–56.

Piquero, A., Farrington, D. P. and Blumstein, A. (2007) *Key Issues in Criminal Career Research: New Analyses of the Cambridge Study in Delinquent Development*, Cambridge: Cambridge University Press.

Prior, D., Farrow, K., Hughes, N., Kelly, G., Manders, G., White, S. and Wilkinson, B. (2011) *Maturity, Young Adults and Criminal Justice*, Birmingham: University of Birmingham Institute of Applied Social Studies.

Sampson, R. J. and Laub, J. H. (1993) *Crime in the Making*, Cambridge, MA: Harvard University Press.

Savolainen, J. (2009) 'Work, family and criminal desistance: adult social bonds in a Nordic welfare state', *British Journal of Criminology*, 49, 285–304.

Shapland, J. M. and Bottoms, A. E. (2011) 'Reflections on social values, offending and desistance among young adult recidivists', *Punishment and Society*, 13, 256–82.

Stouthamer-Loeber, M., Wei, E., Loeber, R. and Master, A. S. (2004) 'Desistance from persistent serious delinquency in the transition to adulthood', *Development and Psychopathology*, 16, 897–918.

Toby, J. (1957) 'Social disorganization and stake in conformity: complementary factors in the predatory behaviour of hoodlums', *Journal of Criminal Law, Criminology and Police Science*, 48, 12–17.

Uggen, C. and Piliavin, I. (1998) 'Asymmetrical causation and criminal desistance', *Journal of Criminal Law and Criminology*, 88, 1399–422.

Ward, T. (2010) 'The Good Lives Model of offender rehabilitation: basic assumptions, aetiological commitments and practice implications', in F. McNeill, P. Raynor and C. Trotter (eds) *Offender Supervision: New Directions in Theory, Research and Practice*, Cullompton: Willan Publishing.

Warr, M. (2002) *Companions in Crime*, Cambridge: Cambridge University Press.

Wikström, P.-O. and Treiber, K. (2007) 'The role of self-control in crime causation: beyond Gottfredson and Hirschi's General Theory of Crime', *European Journal of Criminology*, 4, 237–64.

Wright, R. T. and Decker, S. (1994) *Burglars on the Job: Streetlife and Residential Break-ins*, Boston, MA: Northeastern University Press.

14

FUTURE DIRECTIONS FOR FORENSIC PRACTICE IN THE COMMUNITY

Lord Keith Bradley, John Shine and Rebecca Morland

This chapter is in three sections. The first outlines the context to, and implementation of, the Bradley Report: a review of people with mental health problems or learning disabilities in the criminal justice system. The review was initiated against the background of a large number of people with mental health problems or learning disabilities detained in the British prison system. The Bradley review set out to examine whether prison was always appropriate for them, whilst being mindful of the need to maintain public confidence in the criminal justice system. The second section deals with the specific needs of children and young people with learning disabilities or mental health problems and the importance of good quality assessment and early intervention for these vulnerable groups. The third section summarises the chapters in this volume and links them to some of the key themes in the Bradley review: the emphasis on building up services in the community to prevent young people getting involved in offending behaviour; the importance of good assessment of clinical and forensic needs to guide decision making in the criminal justice system and the need to build partnerships between agencies and organisations to avoid piecemeal thinking and planning. We are excited by the many new ideas set out in this volume and are optimistic that many of them are likely to play a major role in implementation of the Bradley review and set the scene for the development of innovative community-based forensic practice in the future.

Background – The Bradley Report: Lord Bradley's review of people with mental health problems or learning disabilities in the criminal justice system

In December 2007 the Labour government commissioned Lord Bradley to undertake a six-month independent review to determine to what extent offenders with mental health problems or learning disabilities could be diverted from prison to other services and what were the barriers to such diversion. The initial focus of the review was the organisation and effectiveness of court liaison and diversion schemes. However, it was very soon apparent that merely analysing such schemes would be a missed opportunity and a more comprehensive consideration of the 'offender pathway' and the associated mental health service would be more productive. It was agreed, therefore, to extend the review and it subsequently reported to the government in February 2009 and was published in April 2009.

During the review period significant research was undertaken but the key information was gathered by extensive visits to mental health facilities, police stations, courts, prisons and community projects. This was augmented by a series of national, regional and local conferences and meetings, bringing together the key statutory and voluntary organisations, including health and care workers, police officers, magistrates, judges and court officials, prison officials, probation officers, lawyers and the Crown Prosecution Service. Crucially two 'user' groups, one for people with mental health problems and one for people with learning disabilities or difficulties, were established to discuss their experiences of the criminal justice system (CJS) to ensure that the recommendations that were made had a clear relevance to those who had experienced the system.

During the process of conducting the review a number of issues became clear. First, that all too often the organisations were working in silos, whether at a national, regional or local level. As a consequence there was limited information sharing between the staff in these organisations who were dealing with the same individual, resulting in poor continuity of care both within and outside the criminal justice system. Second, there was very poor identification and assessment of people with mental health problems or learning disabilities with no common assessment tool used across the organisations involved. This means that the opportunity to make the appropriate diversion option, normally to health care, does not take place at the earliest opportunity, whether before the person offends or at the first point of contact with the criminal justice system, normally at the police station. Third, there was very poor training of staff in mental health and learning disabilities, even at the most basic awareness level. Further, what training was undertaken would be undertaken in the same silos of the organisation, therefore missing the opportunity to break down the cultural and organisational barriers that exist along the criminal justice pathway. Fourth, it was clear that mental health and learning disabilities were being treated in isolation from other problems that the individual was experiencing, particularly alcohol and drugs issues, therefore missing the opportunity to deal with the wider complex needs of the person.

When the report was published, it made about 80 recommendations, which were accepted by the Labour government and subsequently endorsed by the Coalition government after the 2010 General Election. The overriding objective was to identify and assess people with mental health or learning disabilities as early as possible, ideally before they offend. All too often, particularly with younger people, the opportunity to divert people to appropriate services is missed before they end up in the criminal justice system. For example, better use of community support police officers, appropriately trained, who are the effective 'eyes and ears' of their local communities could identify people at risk of offending and ensure they are properly connected to health or social care services.

However, for those who do offend, the opportunity to identify and assess their health needs must be taken at the first point of contact with the criminal justice system, normally at the police station. To facilitate this, the recommendation to establish Criminal Justice Mental Health Teams, accessible to all custody suites, must be taken. These teams would take responsibility for advising the police on the most appropriate disposal, whether it is to connect or reconnect with health care treatment or to provide information on the health needs of the individual if they travel along the criminal justice pathway to the courts. To implement this and ensure a consistent approach across the country two issues must be addressed. First, a common assessment tool must be developed to properly capture the mental health or learning disabilities of the individual, together with other complex needs including drug and/or alcohol problems. Second, the commissioning of health care in police custody must be transferred to the National Health Service (NHS). In 2006, the commissioning of health care in prisons was transferred to the NHS, with a significant improvement in health care for prisoners. The benefit of a similar transfer for the police would help to ensure that information about the individual would be connected along the CJS pathway and into the health care system outside the criminal justice system. Crucially, this would ensure that more detailed information is available at the first court appearance to enable the judiciary to make the most informed decisions about the disposals available to them at this point. This would reduce the use of remand and the more expensive process of calling for psychiatric reports, whilst the alleged offender is on remand. Also the period spent on remand is often more than the sentence that is subsequently administered, so the person is released without any help or support organised for them and with a likelihood that the person will then reoffend.

Further if the individual progresses from the courts to secure accommodation, whether to prison or health care, this information would be immediately available to the staff. To underpin this process the report recommended better training of all staff both within and between organisations should be developed to ensure a proper understanding of the needs of the individual. An example of the type of good practice in this area is the magistrates' training pack developed by the Prison Reform Trust. This training is aimed at raising awareness of mental health and learning disabilities to ensure that there is a better understanding of the opportunity to use community sentences with a mental health treatment order.

In order to commence the roll-out of such liaison and diversion services across the country, the agreement with the 43 police authorities to transfer the commissioning of their health care to the NHS was reached and the government allocated several million pounds to establish pathway schemes. However, the government also set about structural and organisational changes to the NHS, through the Health and Social Care Act, 2012, which delayed the transition from pathways to national roll-out. These changes mean that the National Commissioning Board (NCB), which is the lead commissioning body for the health needs of offenders, as well as local clinical commissioning groups, health and well-being boards, Directors of Public Health and Police and Crime Commissioners, all have a key role to play in developing liaison and diversion services in their communities. As we now move to the establishment of schemes around the country, it is essential that the national framework, agreed by the NCB, allows for local flexibility and innovation to reflect the particular needs of local communities. It is also important to ensure the schemes are comprehensive enough to address the complex needs of the individual when they are first known to services and seize the opportunity to address offending behaviour.

Specific needs of children and young people

Good quality assessment and early intervention are critical principles to adopt when working with those who commit crime. It is essential to thoroughly understand the issues being faced by those on the edge or within the criminal justice system and address the issues as soon as possible. Once the impairments and difficulties are identified, then the appropriate interventions (adapted as necessary) can begin, referrals can be made to the right services and the family/carers/partners can be successfully supported.

In terms of early intervention, it seems the most important work to be done is with the under 18s. It makes good sense to steer children and young people away from a path of offending and potentially a long career of reoffending, which creates multiple victims. Instead they can be supported to become productive citizens in their communities and become positive parents in the future. For that small proportion of young people that are still with Youth Offending Services as they reach 18, robust, well-planned, individualised transitions need to be in place as they move into the adult world of probation, health, substance misuse services and so on. Unfortunately most young people who go to custody will return, as their contact with antisocial peers increase and positive connections in the community such as education/work are lost.

What do we know about this under 18 population who offend? The cross government document *Healthy Children, Safer Communities* (Department of Health, 2009) sets out the scale of the challenge when intervening with this population of children. Just a sample of the concerning statistics are below and research is revealing more each year:

- Over 75 per cent of those in custody have a history of temporary and permanent school exclusions (Parke, 2009).
- Approximately 60 per cent have significant speech and language difficulties (Bryan et al., 2007).
- Over 50 per cent have problems with peer and family relationships (Harrington et al., 2005).

- Some 25 percent have been identified as having special educational needs, 46 per cent are underachieving at school and 29 per cent have literacy and numeracy difficulties (Youth Justice Board, 2006).
- More than 25 per cent have a learning disability, 23 per cent are assessed with an IQ under 70 (extremely low) and 36 per cent with an IQ between 70 and 79 (Harrington et al., 2005; Hughes et al., 2012).
- A high proportion have experienced loss, bereavement and family breakdown (Childhood Bereavement Network, 2008).
- Many children and young people are exposed to family discord, parental conflict and poor or inconsistent parenting and care, or have one or both parents in prison (Department for Children and Family Services, 2008).
- Over 30 per cent of those using a substance misuse service are from the Youth Justice System (National Treatment Agency, 2009).
- Some 25 per cent to 81 per cent have mental health problems (Hagell, 2002).
- Between two-thirds and three-quarters had suffered a traumatic brain injury (Hughes et al., 2012)
- Children in care, or who have had a care experience, are over-represented, as are children who have or have had child protection plans. These children have also experienced higher levels of abuse (Blades et al., 2011).

Children and young people in the criminal justice system are hugely vulnerable and often have more than one of the difficulties described above. Indeed, it is now well established that high numbers of them have complex support needs, low levels of educational attainment and far more unmet health needs than others of their age (Talbot, 2010). It is stated in *Healthy Children, Safer Communities* (Department of Health, 2009) that the health and well-being needs of children and young people tend to be particularly severe by the time they receive a community sentence and are even more acute for those in custody. Despite the fact that these are children, and children with significant vulnerabilities, they can still be held overnight in police cells with the adults as frequently social care beds are unavailable.

The benefits of early intervention seem difficult to argue against. The interventions will be more effective than waiting until problems and behaviours are entrenched. There are likely to be improved outcomes in terms of education/ employment, improved emotional and physical health and a reduced risk of reoffending/custody in the future. There are great benefits for the child/young person, their family/carers and the wider community, plus the financial savings to various agencies in the short and longer term are also significant.

The concept of early intervention can be further expanded to incorporate 'Diversion'.

> Diversion is a process whereby people are assessed and their needs identified as early as possible in the offender pathway (including prevention and early intervention), thus informing subsequent decisions about where an individual

is best placed to receive treatment, taking into account public safety, safety
of the individual and punishment of an offence.

The Bradley Report (Bradley, 2009, p. 16)

The child or young person must be thoroughly assessed at the earliest opportunity to ensure there is a good understanding of their vulnerabilities. Understanding
these vulnerabilities will allow the police, the Crown Prosecution Service (CPS),
Youth Offending Teams (YOTs) and courts to decide the most appropriate action
to take. The child or young person may then be diverted out of the criminal justice
system completely or diverted within the criminal justice system. The most appropriate services such as children's social care and/or health may alternatively take
the lead in offering the coordinated support and interventions needed.

Liaison and diversion services for both children and adults were a recommendation from Lord Bradley's report, and a selection of pilot projects began in 2009.
In May 2012, the Offender Health Collaborative was selected to support the cross
government Health and Criminal Justice Transition Programme in managing the
development of a national network of liaison and diversion services. The Offender
Health Collaborative is a consortium of six specialist organisations.

In June 2011, the Office of the Children's Commissioner published *I Think I
Must Have Been Born Bad* (Berelowitz, 2011) which reviewed the emotional well-
being and mental health of children and young people in the Youth Justice System.
Sue Berelowitz, the Deputy Children's Commissioner, wrote that there is some
good practice in this area, but there is a lack of consistency in the provision and
a wide variation in the level and quality of services on offer. There was also found
to be a wide variation in the understanding and recognition by staff of young people's
emotional well-being, mental health problems, neurodevelopment disorders and
communication difficulties. Transitions were described as being poor, and these
young people were in the most part defined by their criminality rather than their
needs or vulnerabilities.

In *Seen and Heard* (Talbot, 2010), it was similarly found that in the Youth Justice
System there were inconsistencies in what assessments were being used to measure
vulnerabilities and for many of these vulnerabilities no screening tools were being
used at all. In many cases it was difficult or slow to get information from other
agencies such as education, children's social care and health. There were reported
to be difficulties with poor referral pathways, long waiting lists and difficulties
accessing services for 16 and 17 year olds. The report noted that staff were
generally feeling skilled and confident to identify issues but commented that there
was a greater need for:

• Specialist service provision
• Training and support
• Early and more effective early intervention
• Adapted interventions, appropriate resources and flexibility.

These requests mirror some of the recommendations made by Lord Bradley (2009) with regard to children and young people:

1   Awareness training in mental health and learning disability, so that all staff in schools and primary health care, including GPs, can identify those who need help and refer them to specialist services. A later recommendation also suggests the need for training in these areas for community support officers, police officers, appropriate adults, probation staff, approved premises staff and prison officers.
2   All Youth Offending Teams (YOTs) having a suitably qualified mental health worker with responsibility for making appropriate referrals to other services.
3   Examination of the potential for early intervention and diversion for those children and young people with mental health problems or learning disabilities who have offended or are at risk of offending.

A simple example of diversion can be given for a child with attention deficit hyperactivity disorder (ADHD) who could have a community disposal rather than a custodial sentence, as research shows that nearly half of those in custody have ADHD (Young et al., 2011). If ADHD had been identified early and treated promptly it would likely lead to reduced impulsivity and improved engagement in education and consequently a lower risk of reoffending. It seems, however, there is still far to go as the charity YoungMinds has published a report called *Same Old* . . . (Campbell and Abbott, 2013), which states that very little has changed in the provision of mental health services for young people who offend in the past 20 years. It is reported there are still significant issues with waiting lists, rigid criteria, the gap between child and adult services, medication-led support and a high turnover of staff. The report concludes by calling on politicians, local government, commissioners, Child and Adolescent Mental Health Services, adult mental health services, magistrates, GPs and the children's workforce to ensure children get better mental health interventions as they and society deserves.

Summary of chapters

Against the backdrop of the Bradley review, the contents of this volume are highly relevant as they highlight a range of exciting developments in forensic practice in community settings that are likely to play a significant role in future service development. A number of the key themes contained in the Bradley review pertain directly to areas reviewed and discussed in this volume of work. For example, in the review there was a strong emphasis on building up services in the community to *prevent* young people becoming involved in offending behaviour and the criminal justice system. Chapter 10 by Zoë Ashmore on Multisystemic Therapy (MST) is an example of the type of early intervention approach that can make a real difference in preventing young people at risk of entering care or custody. Many of the principles of MST are based on factors from international research that will be recognisable to readers familiar with the 'What works' literature as being important in the delivery of effective interventions. Examples include the identification of risk factors linked to offending or antisocial activities, the targeting of key problem behaviours and the adoption of present moment, action-based therapeutic approaches, incorporating skill development. Some of the key differences in the MST approach are the much higher levels of intensity in delivering the programme, the delivery of therapy in the home environment rather than a clinic or office setting, the flexibility of the therapeutic model in implementing the principles of MST (whilst maintaining adherence to treatment integrity) and, crucially, the close involvement of members of the individual's family and school as part of a holistic systems approach to learn skills and generalise from the programme to real-life settings. In her chapter, Ashmore illustrates how MST operates in practice through a case example and also summarises the research on MST which suggests that it provides improved outcomes when compared to 'treatment as usual' or traditional methods such as counselling. It will be interesting to see whether the promising findings from the international research on MST can be replicated in the evaluation currently taking place in the UK. MST is more costly than some other community interventions, though cheaper than care/custody or residential schools. But, if it can deliver improved outcomes then the investment will be highly *cost-effective* and is precisely the type of intervention highlighted in the Bradley review as being required to build up services in the area of early intervention.

Early assessment and intervention are also considered critical in the area of substance misuse, as described in Chapter 8 by Matthew Gaskell; this information is then used to allocate access to early intervention and treatment. As Gaskell notes, the evidence from large-scale studies is that treatment, including coerced treatment, for substance misusers does work. Approaches such as motivational interviewing, cognitive behavioural therapy and contingency management have been shown to be effective from randomised control trials, considered to be the strongest form of evidence in evaluating interventions for effectiveness. Gaskell's conclusion that interventions for substance misusers can be best summarised as 'work in progress' is consistent with the Bradley review.

The importance of good assessment is highlighted in several areas of the Bradley review and is a consistent theme in many of the chapters. For many offenders, their first experience of forensic assessment will be via the Probation Service, which, as Andrew Bridges and Kasturi Torchia describe in Chapter 1, has been in the business of providing court reports for over 100 years. These reports have traditionally included a strong emphasis on the assessment of an offender's background, social circumstances, offending history and risk, with the latter area being given increasing emphasis in recent years. Bridges and Torchia describe how the assessment of offenders in the Probation Service has included both an analysis of *why* a person has offended and a plan of *what* needs to be done to reduce the person's risk of reoffending in future. This chapter also outlines how the use of structured assessment tools to assess risk and criminogenic needs such as OASys and ASSET has now been incorporated into modern Probation and Youth Offending Service practice and emphasises the value of these tools in informing Pre-Sentence Reports. Bridges and Torchia go on to highlight the 'assessment conundrum', which is faced by practitioners in real-life settings. Assessment is clearly very important and crucial to informing recommendations for disposal for the court, but can be resource-intensive which can lead to pressures during a climate of budget restraint and drives to improve efficiency. The authors describe how this pressure has led to the production of weighting systems based on the complexity and risk of cases in allocating resources to assessments. The 'assessment conundrum' is that the practitioner often does not know how demanding the case will be until the assessment has concluded. Although Bridges and Torchia base their example from the Probation Service, it is likely that similar 'assessment conundrums' will be faced by all agencies involved in working with offenders during the present economic climate.

Chapter 2 by Joel Harvey provides a detailed exposition of the range of assessments utilised in community forensic settings and the key principles to bear in mind when conducting assessments. Crucial to this process is the need for assessment to be, as far as possible, a *collaborative* process and to be embedded within the wider systems around the person's difficulties. Harvey goes on to outline how the importance of the psychological formulation – a structured approach to conceptualising how an individual's problems originated and the underlying mechanisms through which these problems are maintained – has increased in forensic mental health practice. The growth in formulation-based approaches to assessing risk and needs, alongside the increase in structured risk assessment tools, aids the process of synthesising information about an individual and guiding the approach to treatment.

Many of the chapters in this volume deal with specialist areas, and the use of specific assessments tailored to the particular risk and needs for types of offenders is a growing area of practice in community settings. The management of risk for sex offenders in community settings is an area where good assessment is especially important. In Chapter 5 Derek Perkins outlines some of the most common assessment tools used in this field including the Structured Assessment of Risk and Needs (SARN), the Polygraph and Penile Plethysmograph (PPG). The challenges in assessing sex offenders with learning disabilities are reviewed by Dave Nash in Chapter 7 who concludes that whilst there are many similarities between the assessment and treatment of learning disabled and non-learning disabled offenders the presence of "cultural perceptions, attitudes, biases and assumptions can often blind decision makers to the important differences". Nash illustrates this conclusion through examples from his professional experience and a case study. These examples highlight the dilemmas and tensions within multidisciplinary teams which are sometimes present when working with sex offenders with learning disabilities, who may elicit sympathetic responses from some which can lead to a minimisation of risk; equally, the responses of such offenders to common assessments may be a reflection of their learning disability rather than a valid indication of risk severity. Descriptions of specialist assessments used for personality disorder are provided in Chapter 12 by Phil Minoudis who also highlights the role of psychological formulation based on good assessment and illustrates this with vignettes from probation settings. A particularly detailed and comprehensive overview of the assessment of violent offenders is given in Chapter 6 by Matt Bruce, who, like Joel Harvey in Chapter 2, outlines assessments developed from forensic psychology covering both nomothetic (group-based) and ideographic (individualised) approaches but focuses on violent offenders. Bruce also notes the growing trend to focus on strengths and protective factors in risk assessment.

Building on the strengths and protective factors of offenders to help them lead a crime-free lifestyle is a key part of the growing literature on desistance from crime. Chapter 13 by Anthony Bottoms describes the origins of the desistance approach and outlines its implications for developing forensic practice. On reviewing this chapter, it was noticeable that although the desistance and accredited programmes work from different theoretical perspectives, there is a striking similarity between some of the concepts underlying both the approaches. To take one example, the chapter refers to the idea of 'crystallization of discontent' from the desistance literature as a means of explaining the conflict between an offender's 'desired self' and a 'feared self'. A similar idea is utilised in accredited programmes, for example some sex offender programmes have used exercises based on 'old me/new me' to help offenders develop a plan of their future ideal self and how they could work towards that. This may be a case of 'getting to the same room via different doors' but it opens the possibility of a creative discourse between the dominant risk–needs–responsivity approach and the desistance approach in future. As Bottoms notes, there is recent evidence of a more consensual dialogue between these two approaches as highlighted by some of the leading figures in the rehabilitation literature; it will be interesting to see how this dialogue develops in the future.

Risk assessment is crucial to decisions on whether to divert an offender to community services, as noted in the Bradley review: 'One of the key considerations when deciding whether to prosecute or divert is public protection and a risk assessment based on incomplete information will not be accurate and could lead to tragic consequences' (Bradley, 2009, p. 39). Several of the chapters in this volume describe contemporary practices in risk assessment and identify some of the ethical, practical and empirical issues. A good overview of the approaches to risk assessment, and the role of the statutory and voluntary agencies involved, is given in Chapter 9 by Simone Fox and Richard Latham. They conclude by recommending the use of structured professional judgement tools as standard practice in future community-based risk assessment and extending the use of evidence-based treatment programmes to intervene at an early stage to prevent offending in later life.

In forensic community settings one of the primary functions of assessment is to provide information to guide decision making, in terms of recommendations to courts to inform sentencing decisions or for particular interventions, for example to accredited offender treatment programmes. Chapter 3 by Gerard Drennan, Sara Casado and Louise Minchin is helpful in this respect as it highlights some of the dilemmas involved in forensic risk taking between risk management and the promotion of recovery. Forensic practitioners need opportunities to consider and discuss as a team how such dilemmas can create tensions within teams; the role of reflective practice is critical in providing a protected space for this to occur and it is gratifying to observe how this is emphasised in the chapter, too often the importance of this process is lost. Drennan, Casado and Minchin highlight how reflective practice has shifted away from staff support groups to case-focused team reflection and outline how such forums can be a useful vehicle to assist teams in the process of ethical decision making.

A major theme of the Bradley review was the need to build partnerships between agencies and organisations and to avoid piecemeal thinking and planning: 'One of the most common phrases repeated to me by stakeholders time and again over the course of the last year has been of people and organisations "working in silos".'

This theme is picked up and developed in a number of chapters in this volume, notably the contribution of Richard Shuker and Andrew Bates in Chapter 11 who outline some of the strengths and weaknesses involved in delivering treatment programmes in institutional settings and suggest ways in which the gains from offenders completing treatment programmes may be incorporated into resettlement practice. Examples include better streamlining of programmes and linking post-programme work to post-release supervision strategy. Collaboration and sharing of ideas and policies is extended to the international arena in Chapter 4 by Natalie Woodier, who describes some of the exciting developments that have recently taken place in this field across Europe. Notable examples include the implementation of accredited programmes such as the Aggression Replacement Therapy (ART) programme in Hungary and adaption of the OASys system of offender assessment of risk and needs developed and used in England and Wales for use in Norway and the Czech Republic. The sense that one gets reading this chapter is that these developments are only just beginning and that the future will see a much greater level of international collaboration and sharing of evidence-based practice.

In summary, the chapters in this volume set out an exciting agenda of innovation and creativity that builds on what we have learned from the 'What works' literature and outlines how this can be applied to forensic practice in community settings. But there is an important caveat to these ideas and initiatives: all new developments need leadership in order to become established. This point was made in the Bradley review: "Where we particularly need champions is among the senior leaders of the key partner agencies in order to drive this agenda forward and ensure that services are supported with sufficient resources to make change happen" (Bradley 2009, p. 128). The contributors to this volume are to be congratulated for setting out existing forensic practice in community settings and highlighting exciting and innovative ideas on how this can be developed further. What is needed, in order for these ideas to be translated into practice, are champions in the workplace to take this agenda forward to change organisational cultures to embrace evidence-based community interventions more effectively than has been the case in the past. One hopes that the authors of this volume of work will inspire many others to take on this role in the future.

References

Berelowitz, S. (2011) *I Think I Must Have Been Born Bad*. London: Office of the Children's Commissioner.

Blades, R., Hart, D., Lea, J. and Willmott, N. (2011) *Care – A Stepping Stone into Custody?* London: Prison Reform Trust.

Bradley, Lord K. (2009) *The Bradley Report: Lord Bradley's review of people with mental health problems or learning disabilities in the criminal justice system*. London: Department of Health.

Bryan, K., Freer, J. and Furlong, C. (2007) Language and communication difficulties in juvenile offenders. *International Journal of Language & Communication Disorders*, 42, 505–20.

Campbell, S. and Abbott, S. (2013) *Same Old . . . The Experiences of Young Offenders with Mental Health Needs*. London: YoungMinds.

Childhood Bereavement Network (2008) *Bereavement in the Secure Setting: Delivering Every Child Matters for Bereaved Young People in Custody*. London: National Children's Bureau.

Department of Health, Department for Children, Schools and Families, Ministry of Justice, Home Office (2009) *Healthy Children, Safer Communities*. London: HM Government.

Department for Children and Family Services (2008) *Targeted Youth Support: Integrated Support for Vulnerable Young People. A Guide*. London: HM Government.

Hagell, A. (2002) *The Mental Health of Young Offenders. Bright Futures: Working with Vulnerable Young People*. London: Mental Health Foundation.

Harrington, R. and Bailey, S., et al. (2005) *Mental Health Needs and Effectiveness of Provision for Young Offenders in Custody and in the Community*. London: Youth Justice Board.

Hughes, N., Williams, H., Chitsabesan, P., Davies, R. and Mounce, L. (2012) *Nobody Made the Connection: The Prevalence of Neurodisability in Young People Who Offend*. London: Office of the Children's Commissioner.

National Treatment Agency (2009) *Young People's Specialist Substance Misuse Treatment: Exploring the Evidence*. London: Public Health England.

Parke, S. (2009) *Children and Young People in Custody 2006–2008. An Analysis of the Experiences of 15–18 Year Olds in Prison*. London: HM Inspectorate of Prisons and Youth Justice Board.

Talbot, J. (2010) *Seen and Heard*. London: Prison Reform Trust.

Young, S., Adamou, M., Bolea, B., Gudjonsson, G., Müller, U., Pitts, M., et al. (2011) The identification and management of ADHD offenders within the criminal justice system: a consensus statement from the UK Adult ADHD Network and criminal justice agencies. *BMC Psychiatry*, 11, 32.

Youth Justice Board (2006) *Barriers to Engaging in Education, Training and Employment*. London: Youth Justice Board.

INDEX

Page numbers in *italics* denote a figure/table